HARD CORE

D1207836

HARD CORE

Power, Pleasure, and
the "Frenzy of the Visible"

LINDA WILLIAMS

UNIVERSITY OF CALIFORNIA PRESS
BERKELEY · LOS ANGELES · LONDON

University of California Press
Berkeley and Los Angeles, California

University of California Press, Ltd.
London, England

Expanded Paperback Edition 1999

© 1989 by
The Regents of the University of California

Library of Congress Cataloging-in-Publication Data

Williams, Linda, 1946–
    Hard core : power, pleasure, and the "frenzy of the visible" /
Linda Williams. — Expanded pbk. ed.
        p.   cm.
    Includes bibliographical references and index.
    ISBN 0-520-21943-0 (alk. paper)
    1. Sex in motion pictures.   2. Erotic films—History and
criticism.   3. Pornography.   I. Title.
PN1995.9.S45W5   1999
791.43'6538—dc21   98-38977
                                                         CIP

Printed in the United States of America
1   2   3   4   5   6   7   8   9

The paper used in this publication is both acid-free
and totally chlorine-free (TCF). It meets the minimum
requirements of American Standard for Information
Sciences—Permanence of Paper for Printed Library
Materials, ANSI Z39.48-1984. ∞

For Paul

Contents

Preface to the 1999 Edition

When *Hard Core* was first published in 1989 I braced myself for an onslaught of criticism. I expected colleagues in the academy to oppose my attempt to make pornography the subject of scholarly, textual analysis and I expected anti-pornography feminists to oppose my feminist interest in porn. To my surprise, however, colleagues in the academy seemed quite willing to countenance the academic study of moving-image pornography and anti-porn feminists ignored the book. Instead of having to defend myself, I found I was invited to speak. I spoke at art museums, college campuses, book stores and to community groups throughout the U.S. and Europe. These audiences were frankly interested in the history and analysis of moving-image pornography. No one stormed out of a talk, even when I eventually illustrated them with slides and clips. Reviews of the book were generous to a fault. Even gays and lesbians who had every reason to criticize my failure to include these pornographies in my study, generously chose to welcome my engagement with the genre rather than to criticize its heterosexual limitations. As the first book to deal with the history and textual form of moving-image pornography, *Hard Core* became, in the absence of any competition, a kind of "classic" and I became, sometimes to my pleasure and sometimes to my chagrin, a professor of "porn."

In the decade since the publication of *Hard Core*, a field that might be called pornography studies has emerged. While there had long been an abundance of books and articles about the controversy of pornography, it was finally becoming possible to study pornography without engaging in the fight over its existence. Of course the achievement of a frank, unembarrassed, undefensive investigation of the pornographic field has not always been easy. In a 1993 article I noted how many discussions of pornography have been supercharged with emotions of the critic's own reactions. These included Stephen Marcus writing the whole of *The Other Victorians* while seemingly holding his nose; Susan Sontag, on the contrary, celebrating the avant-garde subversions of the Sade-Bataille tradition; and Andrea Dworkin offering the most meticulous descriptions of pornographic writing or images in tones of monumental outrage yet still complicit with the words and images' power to arouse (Williams 1993, 57).

If these were, as I thought, outmoded and counterproductive attitudes to strike towards the pornographic object of study, then what kind of attitude should be struck towards such a classically "bad object"? I considered my own "solution" in *Hard Core*:

Neutrality of tone seemed the obvious solution to these condemnations or overly defensive appreciations. I therefore resolved to skip the nervous jokes and the easy condemnation of aesthetic or moral shortcomings and to avoid condemnation or defensiveness. I would ask instead what the genre does, how it does it, and I would remove myself from pro or con arguments as much as possible. Yet this objective, distanced stance of the reasoned observer, neither partisan nor condemner, placed me in a position of indifference, as if above the genre. Was it right, or even useful to analysis, to assume to be indifferent to, or unmoved by, these texts? Or, if I was moved, as I was sometimes to either arousal or offense, what was the proper place of this reaction in criticism? While I attempted, ever-so neutrally, to simply describe, wasn't something of my personal reaction already embedded, in a coded way, in the attention I gave to certain texts and subgenres and not others? Donna Haraway once said in passing that one should not "do" cultural studies of objects to which one is not vulnerable. In my case I had begun with what I thought to be an invulnerability, even a disdain for the texts of pornography, but was then surprised to find myself "moved" by some works. What was the place of this vulnerability in writing about the genre? (Williams 1993, 57)

I still don't know the answers to the above questions. However, I increasingly suspect that indifference is fruitless and that some sort of admission of "vulnerability" and interest is preferable. I thus hereby admit, retrospectively, to all prospective readers of this book to a genuinely "prurient interest" in the genre of pornography that is not quite owned up to in the first edition.[1] It is utterly hopeless to be neutral towards so controversial and physically "moving" a topic. Yet to be moved by pornography is not to be uncritical. Thus, despite the fact that this most maligned and scapegoated of cultural forms is often in desperate need of defense, I would not want this prurient interest to become an uncritical enthusiasm. Clearly there are difficult questions of tone and attitude to be navigated in this topic of study.

Given these difficulties of tone and attitude, it is perhaps not surprising that the group of scholars that has most effectively engaged with pornography in the last decade has been the one group that has found itself the least vilified for demonstrating an interest in pornography. "Pro-sex" feminists—by which I mean simply women who are interested in sexuality and who do not see masculine sexuality as the root cause of the oppression of women—have had a distinct advantage over heterosexual men in this regard. These women have emerged from the porn wars as the primary critics and theorists of pornography. This is an extremely diverse and numerous group, comprising heterosexuals, lesbians, and bisexuals, all of whom have found distinct, original, ways to write about explicit sexual images.[2] Gay men constitute another group that has, for often quite different reasons, made enormous strides in engaging the history, theory and practice of erotic and pornographic representations. Unlike the feminists, however, this group has not needed to be defensive about its interest in pornography for the simple reason that since women are not represented in this particular "pornutopia" the usual concerns about the abuse of women fall away. With no anti-porn feminists breathing down their necks, and with a whole culture and history to reclaim, gay historians and critics have engaged

1. I take up this question of the legal term, prurient interest, in this edition's "Epilogue."

2. This list includes Constance Penley, Laura Kipnis, Eithne Johnson, Lynne Segal, Lynda Nead, Anne McClintock, Kelly Dennis, Jane Juffer, Lisa Palac, Chris Straayer, Cindy Patton, Susie Bright, Mary Conway, June Reich, Cherry Smith—not to mention those women who have led the battles for free speech. See the supplementary bibliography at the end of the book.

gaged in a much more celebratory form of criticism and have written about the genre with both eloquence and passion.[3]

The story is very different for heterosexual men, the group that has been the most vilified for its interest in pornography. For all sorts of excellent reasons, heterosexual men have been understandably slower to acknowledge their "vulnerability" to pornography. Consequently they have been slower to acquire a voice, tone, and attitude free of the kind of unproductive *mea culpas* that mark a book like *Men Confront Pornography*. Yet even here there have been remarkable exceptions in the work of men who have managed to "get over" the cultural baggage of their supposedly degrading and harmful interest in the genre to write honestly and well about it.[4] It will be crucial to the development of pornography studies that this group, which still constitutes the majority audience for the consumption of pornography, continue to find ways to express an interest in pornography that is not marked with defensiveness.

With so much good, new work appearing in the last decade, *Hard Core*'s flaws have grown apparent. If I were writing the book today I would no longer duck the study of nonheterosexual forms. Nor would I shrink from illustration.[5] Senator Jesse Helms and the antipornographers should not be the only ones displaying pornographic images. I would also certainly want to explore the class and race dimensions of the form as well as its humor.[6] Writing the book in the mid and late eighties, I did not fully appreciate the dimensions of the electronic revolution. Only the last of these issues is addressed in the Epilogue, "On/Scenities," written for this edition. This new chapter focuses on the increasingly elusive quest to define the "hard core" of obscenity in a decade in which pornographies of all sorts have proliferated in both private and public places. It also investi-

3. This list includes the landmark history of gay eroticism by Tom Waugh and a range of articles and chapters by Richard Dyer, David Pendleton, Kobena Mercer, Richard Fung, Earl Jackson Jr., Scott Tucker, Todd Smith, John Champagne. See supplementary bibliography.
4. This list includes Scott MacDonald, Chuck Kleinhans, Peter Lehman, Robert Eberwein, and Joseph W. Slade.
5. See my cowardly fudging of both these issues on 6–7 and 32–33.
6. Both Constance Penley (1996, 1997) and Peter Lehman (1995) have written on pornography's unmistakable humor; Laura Kipnis (1996) and Penley (1997) have written on class; Richard Fung (1991) and Kobena Mercer (1987, 1991) on race.

gates the nature of pornography's solicitation of the bodies of its viewers. Since this new section is illustrated I also hope it will partially compensate for the first edition's lack of visuals. For the most part, however, the original book has been left to stand, as a testament to one way of looking at the genre of moving-image pornography, and as a catalyst, I hope, to new ways.

Linda Williams
Berkeley, California
August 1998

Foreword

Many years ago I began work on a study that was tentatively entitled *Film Bodies*. It was to be a series of essays on the cinema considered from the point of view of what has most motivated the art forms and the technology: the pleasure in looking at human bodies in movement. I wanted to explore this most basic phenomenon of *the movies*, first in the prehistoric and primitive spectacles of cinematic body movement itself, and then in genres that focus on particular kinds of body movement and body spectacle—musicals, horror films, low comedies, "weepies." My focus was thus on moments of technological innovation that represented moving bodies or genres that were centrally about movement—whether involuntary reflexes of musical rhythm, terror, comedy, or sorrow—and that in turn "moved" the bodies of viewers to similar reflexes. These were also historical moments or genres in which bodies as signifiers of sexual difference figured prominently. Feminist film theory and criticism have argued for many years that this cinematic pleasure in looking is predominantly masculine. My initial thought was simply to see how the male pleasure in looking operated in these other genres as well. As an afterthought, and only because the logic of my approach seemed to dictate it, I determined to examine another genre in which body movement, involuntary physical response, and sexual difference figure prominently: hard-core film pornography.

I put off writing the added chapter on pornography, thinking that this was one chapter, at least, that would require no new thought or research. Here there would be no difficult questions of generic evolution or textual reading. The meanings were self-evident: as every-

one knew, "if you've seen one porn film you've seen them all." Pornography would only demonstrate literal, extreme instances of
everything feminist film critics had already noted about classical cinema: sexual performances designed to gratify male viewers; literal
voyeurism; sadism that punishes women for being as sexual as men
imagine them to be; fetishism of the female body that would provide
a textbook illustration of Freud's famous essay on the subject. I assumed, in short, that film pornography would simply demonstrate
all of the above with the sensationalism endemic to the genre, illustrating a *total* objectification of the female "film body" as object
of male desire.

I was wrong. As soon as I began really to look at a large number
of films across the genre's history rather than to generalize from a
viewing of one or two films, I found that film pornography did not
so neatly illustrate such objectification. I found, in fact, that these
apparently self-evident texts were fraught with contradiction. The
most important of these conflicts was the difficulty hard-core films
have in figuring the visual "knowledge" of women's pleasure. Although the genre as a whole seems to be engaged in a quest for incontrovertible "moving" visual evidence of sexual pleasure in general, and women's pleasure in particular, this is precisely what hard
core could never guarantee.

So the quick-and-easy chapter on pornography that I had envi-
sioned as a small segment of a larger work gradually grew, much to
my initial consternation, into a book of its own. And to my surprise,
in the genre where I expected to see the most unrelieved and unchallenged dominance of the phallus (literally, in the form of the
ubiquitous erect or ejaculating penis), I saw instead a remarkable
uncertainty and instability. I began to see that an understanding of
how power and pleasure function in discourses in which women's
bodies are the object of knowledge could be crucial to any efforts to
alter the dominance of male power and pleasure in the culture at
large, even in this most masculine of film genres.

If the above explanation of my motives for writing this book
sounds defensive, it is because I feel impelled to emphasize how I
found it necessary to study pornography in spite of my "proper"
feminist and womanly predilections against it. I cannot, for example,
say what Alan Soble (1986, iv) says in the preface to his recent book
on pornography—that he walked about in "a daze of scholarly sex-

uality" anticipating the "long-delayed orgasm of publication." For a woman to admit to any such coincidence of scholarly and sexual pleasure undercuts her authority in a way that does not occur with a male scholar. It is not surprising, then, that I should want to protect myself against the perceived contaminations of a "filthy subject"—lest I be condemned along with it. At the same time, however, I feel it is important not to perpetuate the pervasive attitude among feminists that pornography is both the cause and the symptom of all women's problems. For even though I know that the slightest admission that not every image of every film was absolutely disgusting to me may render my insights worthless to many women, I also know that not to admit some enjoyment is to perpetuate an equally invidious double standard that still insists that the nonsexual woman is the credible, "good" woman. Clearly, it is difficult to strike a proper attitude toward pornography.

But proper or not, at this stage in the contemporary proliferation of discourses of sexuality it seems helpful for all of us—men, women, anti-pornography feminists, and anti-censorship feminists—to agree at least that we are moved, whether to anger or to arousal, by these images of hard-core pornography, and to proceed with an analysis of the power and pleasure they hold for us. It is my hope that this study will be of intellectual and political use to those who have a need to get beyond the question of whether pornography should exist to a consideration of what pornography is and what it has offered those viewers—primarily men but, now, women in increasing numbers—who have been "caught looking" at it.

There are four people without whose generous criticisms, suggestions, and encouragement this book would have floundered. To Judith Kegan Gardiner I owe the most. As a friend, neighbor, and colleague she was always there to read the earliest and the least formulated of my thoughts and to say what was salvageable among them. To Carol J. Clover, who saw a later stage of the work, I am indebted for particularly sympathetic and useful suggestions that I hope have made the book more coherent. To my editor Ernest Callenbach, who read everything I wrote immediately and sent back both encouraging and gently prodding comments, I shall be perpetually in debt. And to my husband, Paul Fitzgerald, who read and reread all drafts and who tried never to let me get away with a sloppy idea or a nice-sounding obfuscation, I give thanks for this and all other forms of support.

Tania Modleski, Virginia Wexman, Mary Ann Doane, Andrew Ross, Chuck Kleinhans, Julia Lesage, Dana Polan, Bruce Kawin, Kaja Silverman, Jane Gallop, and Candida Royalle generously read drafts and offered thoughtful advice. Conversations with Lauren Berlant, Mary Beth Rose, Tilde Sankevitch, Marianne Hirsch, Al LaValley, Lucy Fischer, Carol Slingo, Gina Marchetti, and Patricia Erens were similarly helpful, as were discussions with several students, most notably the entire class of English 298. I am grateful also to Mary Janische, Ann Stotts, Abbey Wilkerson, Glynis Kinnan, Deborah Risoya, Karen Hollinger, Kris Hanische, and Jay Lorenz, and to Anne Canright for fine copyediting. Audiences who heard presentations of parts of this work—at Dartmouth College; the University of Pittsburgh; Miami University, Ohio; Northwestern University; the University of Chicago; De Paul University; and the Institute for the Humanities at the University of Illinois, Chicago—helped me to discover what I was trying to say. Finally, I am indebted to the Mary Ingraham Bunting Institute and its community of women scholars, the American Society of Learned Societies, and the Humanities Institute of the University of Illinois, Chicago, for financial support offering the luxury of time to learn.

Chicago, Illinois

1
Speaking Sex
"The Indiscreet Jewels"

Toward the beginning of Denis Diderot's 1748 fable *Les bijoux indiscrets* (The Indiscreet Jewels), the genie Cucufa seeks to gratify the desire of the sultan Mangogul to have the women of his court speak frankly of their sexual adventures. The genie pulls out of his pocket a silver ring:

"You see this ring," he said to the sultan. "Put it on your finger, my son. When you turn the setting of the stone, all the women on whom you turn it will recount their affairs in a loud and clear voice. But do not believe for a moment that it is through their mouths that they speak."

"Through what else then, by God, will they speak?" exclaimed the sultan.

"Through that part which is the most frank in them, and the most knowledgeable about the things you wish to know," said Cucufa; "through their jewels."

(Diderot [1875] 1966, 148–149; my translation)

In marked contrast to the elaborate sexual innuendo of Diderot's fable and its wordplay with jewels and genitals, we might consider an American hard-core pornographic feature film, *The Opening of Misty Beethoven* ("Henry Paris," a.k.a. Radley Metzger, 1975). Near its beginning we meet the female protagonist, Misty Beethoven, in a sleazy Place Pigalle porno movie theater where she gives "hand jobs" to male customers while they watch the film. The film that screens as Misty manipulates a customer to ejaculation is appropriately titled *Le sexe qui parle* (The Speaking Sex). Redundantly, it too shows an ejaculating penis. Like Diderot's elegant fantasy of the silver ring with the power to make "sex" speak, the fantasy of this film—as well as of its film-within-a-film—is also of a speaking sex. But whereas Diderot's naughty literary conceit figures its "sex" as a valuable but unmentionable part of the female anatomy that is compelled to speak the truth of its owner's sexual indiscretions, the pornographic film's sex originates from the male genitals and employs no such euphemism. The "sex" that "speaks" here is typical of the greater indiscretion of the filmic "hard core," of its seemingly more direct graphic display.

It would be futile to argue that Diderot's fable and Metzger's film are both pornography—at least before attempting some definition of this most difficult and politically charged term. Yet both works partake of what the historian Michel Foucault, in his *History of Sexuality*,[1] has called the modern compulsion to speak incessantly about sex. And it is this speaking sex that is probably the most important single thing to be observed about the modern phenomenon of hard core. As Foucault puts it, invoking Diderot's fable as an emblem,

for many years, we have all been living in the realm of Prince Mangogul: under the spell of an immense curiosity about sex, bent on questioning it, with an insatiable desire to hear it speak and be spoken about, quick to invent all sorts of magical rings that might force it to abandon its discretion.

(Foucault 1978, 77)

In this quest for the magic that will make sex speak, the most recent magic has surely been that of motion pictures (and later of video). With this new "magic ring," the modern equivalents of Prince Mangogul seem to be able to satisfy their curiosity about sex directly, to locate themselves as invisible voyeurs positioned to view the sex "act" itself rather than only hearing about it, as Diderot's sultan must, in after-the-fact narration. With this magic it has become pos-

sible to satisfy—but also, Foucault reminds us, to further incite—
the desire not only for pleasure but also for the "knowledge of pleasure," the pleasure of knowing pleasure (Foucault 1978, 177).

This book considers hard-core film and video pornography as one
of the many forms of the "knowledge-pleasure" of sexuality. Its goal
is to trace the changing meaning and function of the genre of pornography in its specific, visual, cinematic form. Foucault's idea that
the pleasures of the body are subject to historically changing social
constructions has been influential, especially the idea that pleasures
of the body do not exist in immutable opposition to a controlling and
repressive power but instead are produced within configurations of
power that put pleasures to particular use.

Foucault thus offers, at least potentially, a way of conceptualizing
power and pleasure within the history of discourses of sexuality. He
argues, for example, that power must be conceptualized positively
for what it constructs in discourse and through knowledge. If we
speak incessantly today about sex in all sorts of modes, including
pornography, to Foucault this only means that a machinery of power
has encroached further on bodies and their pleasures. Through the
osmosis of a pleasure feeding into power and a power feeding into
pleasure, an "implantation of perversions" takes place, with sexualities rigidifying into identities that are then further institutionalized by discourses of medicine, psychiatry, prostitution . . . and
pornography (Foucault 1978, 12).

Important as Foucault's ideas are to a more refined understanding
of sexuality's complex history and of the basic discontinuities in the
cultural construction of sexualities in diverse eras, they are sometimes not as radical as they seem. For women especially, the central
theme of historical discontinuity often seems like the familiar story
of *plus ça change*. For example, Foucault stresses the difference between the *ars erotica* of ancient and non-Western cultures, by
which sexuality is constructed through practice and accumulated experiences that prescribe and teach pleasures as a form of mastery
and self-control, and our modern Western *scientia sexualis*, aimed
at eliciting the confession of the scientific truths of sex. Despite
these differences, in neither the ancient and Eastern construction
of an erotic art nor the Western construction of knowledge-pleasure
have women been the true subjects of sexual art or sexual
knowledge.

Thus, even though pleasure is constructed differently within the *ars erotica* and the *scientia sexualis*, and even though Foucault can argue that "sex" as an entity is radically discontinuous from one culture to the next, the fact remains that the pleasure of women is alien and other to both systems. The erotic arts of ancient and Eastern cultures acknowledged that women are different but did not actively seek detailed knowledge of women's pleasure. Modern Western culture, in contrast, probes the difference of women incessantly, as Diderot's fable—and most modern pornography—shows. Cinema itself, as a narrative form with certain institutionalized pleasures, is, as we shall see in Chapter 2, profoundly related to the sexual pleasures of male viewers through glimpses of the previously hidden, and often sexual, "things" of women.

My point, however, is simply to note that, for women, one constant of the history of sexuality has been a failure to imagine their pleasures outside a dominant male economy. This is to suggest that the disciplinary practices Foucault describes so well have operated more powerfully on the bodies of women than on those of men (Bartky forthcoming); indeed, that even so radical a questioner of the values of humanism and of historical discontinuity can succumb to the phallocentric norms that are at the root of all humanist thought. As Biddy Martin (1982) and others have argued, Foucault has often failed to acknowledge women's situation in the constitution of meaning and power in Western culture, but he still gives us the tools to ask what the articulation of sexual difference involves.[2] Martin (p. 17) puts the question this way: "How are discipline and power constituted at the moment at which woman is made the object of knowledge?"

Modern pornography is perhaps the key genre by which we may begin to answer this question. Yet as Susan Gubar (1987, 731) notes, feminist criticism has been reluctant to "come to terms" with "genres composed by and for men," and especially with pornography. In recent years pornography has been spoken of constantly as the quintessential male genre—as the most extreme example of what women abhor about male power. Listening to men on this topic, one sometimes wonders how the pornography industry survives, since its products are claimed to be so boring and repetitious. Listening to women, one wonders how anything else survives in the face of a pornography that is equated with genocide. The feminist rhetoric of abhorrence has impeded discussion of almost everything but the question of whether pornography deserves to exist at all. Since it does exist, however, we should be asking what it does for viewers; and since it is a genre with basic similarities to other genres, we need to come to terms with it.

Coming to terms with pornography does not mean liking, approving of, or being aroused by it—though these reactions are not precluded either. Rather, it means acknowledging that despite pornography's almost visceral appeal to the body—its ability, as Richard Dyer (1985, 27) puts it, to "move" the body or, in Annette Kuhn's words (1985, 21), to elicit "gut" reactions—it is not the only genre to elicit such "automatic" bodily reactions. Dyer notes that other film genres aimed at moving the body, such as thrillers, weepies, and low comedy, have been almost as slow to be recognized as cultural phenomena. Goose bumps, tears, laughter, and arousal may occur, may seem like reflexes, but they are all culturally mediated. Pornography, even hard-core pornography, we are beginning to realize, can no longer be a matter of Justice Potter Stewart's famous "I don't know what it is, but I know it when I see it" (Stewart 1954, 197).

The middle-class, white male Supreme Court justice who uttered these famous last words was saying, in essence, "It moves me" (whether to arousal or to outrage hardly matters), "and that is all we need to know." To come to terms with pornography in the late 1980s, we need not only to acknowledge the force of but also to get beyond merely reacting to these gut responses. For women this means turning the important methods and insights of feminism on a genre and an ideology that is most transparently about sexual difference as viewed from a male perspective. Because feminist criticism is ideologically committed to disrupting the exclusive prerogatives of this perspective, it is especially well equipped to perform a symptomatic reading of pornography. But to do so it needs a better understanding of power, pleasure, and genre itself than has been offered in the past.

The question I wish to pose regarding early illegal and later massproduced legal film and video pornography is therefore not whether it is misogynistic (much of it is) or whether it is art (much of it is not); rather, I wish to ask just what the genre is and why it has been so popular. The perspective I take in answering this question could best be described as feminist re-visionism in tension with several other approaches: psychoanalytic theories of sexuality and sexual identity; Marxist theories of reification, utopia, and the sexual marketplace; Foucauldian descriptions of power, pleasure, and discourse; and recent work on mass culture, especially mass-produced genres for women—soap opera, romance fiction, and the "woman's film."[3]

My exclusive focus on hard-core, as opposed to soft-core or "erotic," pornography is an attempt to address the genre's only apparent obviousness. For much as we may want to think, along with Potter Stewart, that "we know it when we see it," it is equally true that, as the saying goes, one person's pornography is another person's erotica.[4] The bracketing of hard core only ends up setting the seemingly authentic, acceptable (erotic or soft-core) sex of the self against the inauthentic and unacceptable (pornographic, violent, or obscene) sex of the "other" (Willis 1983, 463).

Most recently, anti-pornography feminists have used this hard/soft distinction to label men's sexuality as pornographic and women's as erotic. But with mass-market romance fiction for women growing sexually more explicit; with hard-core film and video pornography, aimed formerly only at men, now reaching a "couples" and even a new women's market; with women directors like Candida Royalle beginning to make a decidedly different kind of heterosexual hardcore video; and with the emergence of a renegade lesbian pornography celebrating sadomasochistic fantasy, these pat polar oppositions of a soft, tender, nonexplicit women's erotica and a hard, cruel, graphic phallic pornography have begun to break down.[5]

Given the present diversity of pornographies (and sexualities), this study might reasonably have surveyed the spectrum of modes of address to particular spectators—for example, gay, lesbian, heterosexual male, and heterosexual mixed audiences—and so served the important purpose of emphasizing the multiformity of what is usually viewed as a monolithic entity. If I have opted instead for a study of comparatively "mainstream," heterosexual, hard-core pornography in its early stag and later feature-length forms alone, it is for a variety of practical, theoretical, and political reasons.

First, as a heterosexual woman I do not feel that I should be the first one to address questions raised by a body of films not aimed primarily at me. I acknowledge that this did not stop me from presuming, as a woman, to interpret pornographic texts aimed primarily at men; but since heterosexual, predominantly male-oriented sexuality *is* the dominant sexual identity of our culture, such analysis is justifiable. Moreover, ever since the early seventies heterosexual hard-core film and video has been trying—sometimes halfheartedly, sometimes earnestly—to include heterosexual women as viewers. It is thus precisely because heterosexual pornography has begun to address me that I may very well be its ideal reader. Conversely, because lesbian and gay pornography do not address me personally, their initial mapping as genres properly belongs to those who can read them better.

Second, it seems important to begin a generic discussion of film pornography with an analysis of the general stereotype of the genre. According to this stereotype, pornography is deviant and abnormal, but at the same time these qualities are seen as emanating from what has traditionally been defined as typical or "normal" in heterosexual male sexuality: its phallic "hardness" and aggression. It will be enormously important in our generic study of pornographic texts to challenge such contradictory categories of "normal" and "abnormal" on all levels. Minority pornographies should not be bracketed as utterly separate and distinct. While they are different from heterosexual pornography, they nevertheless belong to the overall "speaking sex" phenomenon in modern Western societies. To consider these pornographies as separate and distinct is only to reproduce within the study of pornography the same effect as occurs when pornography is set off from other, more accepted or "normal" forms of speech. Richard Dyer (1984, 1985) and Tom Waugh (1985) have already begun to investigate gay pornography from this perspective, and although I do not know of any extended, text-based analyses of lesbian pornography to date, such studies are sure to emerge soon.

While not a true history, this study is organized along chronological lines. Its goal is to trace the changing meanings and functions of the pornographic genre in its visual, "hard-core," cinematic forms. Beginning in Chapter 2 I focus on a new force in the regulation and incitement of sexuality that occurs with the late-nineteenth-century invention of cinematic "machines of the visible." I see this force as an impetus toward the confession of previously invisible "truths" of bodies and pleasures in an unprecedented "frenzy of the visible."[6] Chapter 3 traces the early stages of the genre proper in an analysis of the primitive stag film. Chapter 4 then discusses the transition from stag film to feature-length narrative, with an excursus into one of the most significant features of the form: the reliance on visible penile ejaculations (money shots) as proof of pleasure.

Analysis of the generic pleasures produced by this new feature-length narrative form continues in Chapters 5 and 6, followed in Chapter 7 by an examination of what many people consider the worst and most typical type of hard-core pornography: sadomasochism, offering the spectacle of masochistic pleasure-in-pain and/or sadistic pleasure-in-power. Chapter 8 then investigates the many ways in which recent hard-core pornography has begun to undergo revision under the scrutiny of women viewers.

I have pursued two courses in my selection of films and videos for discussion. In the area of feature-length narratives produced since the film and videocassette expansion of the seventies, I have tried to focus on titles that are well known and popular and representative of the full range of films now readily available to anyone via video-cassette rental. In the less accessible realm of silent, illegally and anonymously made stag films (Chapter 3), for which no reliable information exists on exhibition history, I have restricted myself to a near-random sampling of films in the large collection at the Kinsey Institute for Research in Sex, Gender, and Reproduction. In this area I make no claim to thoroughness or to an extensive knowledge of all the texts. I simply hope that this initial examination will encourage further discussion about a genre that previously has evoked either so much hostility or so much ridicule as to seem beyond the pale of any analysis.

Before launching this study proper, I will attempt in the remainder of this chapter to acknowledge some of the issues and problems involved in tracing both the history of pornography generally and its hard-core forms more specifically. I have not tried to offer an objective weighing of all sides of the debate that currently rages. In fact, even to try would, I am convinced, mean never to progress beyond the question of whether these texts *should* exist to a discussion of what it means that they *do*. The following sketch of the elusive history of pornography and the questions of power and pleasure variously posed in the pornography debate is not intended to be comprehensive or objective: as will be clear from my summary of the two major feminist positions on pornography, I am squarely on the "anti-censorship" side. My goal, then, is simply to summarize, from this perspective, just what the issue of pornography has become in late-1980s America, now that power has overtaken pleasure as a key term of analysis. It is also to offer an initial, and provisional, answer to the question, What is hard-core pornography?

The Elusive Genre of Pornography

Pornography seems to have a long history. Most studies of the genre gesture toward this presumed history through the *OED*'s etymology: the Greek words *graphos* (writing or description) and *pornei* (prostitutes)—hence "description of the life, manners, etc. of prostitutes or their patrons." But the few actual attempts to write this history convey little sense of a group of texts representing a continuous tradition from antiquity to the present day. H. Montgomery Hyde, for example, begins his 1964 *History of Pornography* with Ovid, then recommences in the Christian world with Boccaccio ("the first work of modern pornography"), devotes a separate chapter to "erotic pornography" of the East, another chapter to "the pornography of perversion" (primarily Sade and Sacher-Masoch), and the remaining three chapters to nineteenth- and twentieth-century questions of law and censorship and the trial of *Fanny Hill*. None of these traditions seems to bear much relation to the others. He concludes (p. 207) with the statement that although much pornography is of little or no literary merit, it is nevertheless of value to "anthropologists and sociologists," whereupon he adds hopefully:

With a rational system of sex hygiene and education . . . the worthless and unaesthetic pornographic product, which can only be productive of a sense of nausea and disgust, must disappear through lack of public demand, leaving only what is well-written and aesthetically satisfying. For, as this book has attempted to show, there is bad pornography, and also good or at least well-written pornography, which with changing social attitudes is gradually winning common acceptance.

By tracing the history of pornography back to antiquity, Hyde suggests the legitimacy of the genre within an illustrious literary tradition; seen in this way, he says, modern pornography will find its true essence and recover its aesthetic goodness.

This (slightly anxious) hope for a more aesthetic modern pornography is an early expression of one thread of the emerging cultural history of pornography in the 1960s and 1970s. In the early flush

of the "sexual revolution," all commentators on the genre agreed
that pornography was now worthy of investigation for increasingly
self-evident "anthropological and sociological"—not to mention
newer psychological and sexological—reasons. As Peter Michelson
put it in *The Aesthetics of Pornography* (1971, 5), pornography is
"for better or for worse the imaginative record of man's sexual will."
Aesthetically minded commentators like Michelson tended to link
pornography to earlier high-art traditions as an argument for its cultural legitimacy. For Hyde this tradition went back to the Greeks
and Romans; for Michelson, who saw pornography as migrating out
of its own genre and into literature at large, the crucial early tradition is decadence; and for Susan Sontag (1969), in her influential
essay "The Pornographic Imagination," it was Sade.

Sontag's essay is in some ways the vindication of Hyde's hope for
a more aesthetic pornography. Analyzing Réage's *The Story of O*,
Bataille's *The Story of the Eye*, and de Berg's *The Image*, Sontag
makes a case for a modern, high-class, exclusively literary pornography that operates at the limits of sensual experience to explore
fantasies that, like the work of Sade, radically transgress social taboos. Like the surrealists who made Sade their patron saint, Sontag
pits an elitist, avant-garde, intellectual, and philosophical pornography of imagination and transgressive fantasy against the mundane,
crass materialism of a dominant mass culture.

Other critics from this period are less concerned to trace an aesthetic tradition of pornography—probably because they were both
less convinced of even the potential value of such texts and less comfortable with the radical claims for the importance of transgression
and excess. To these critics the existence of a modern body of popular pornographic texts with unprecedented mass appeal constituted an acute and historically unique social problem. Steven Marcus (1974) locates this problem in the nineteenth-century attitude
toward sex as a problem revolving around prostitution, sexual hygiene, masturbation, and so forth. The prolific and aesthetically unredeemable pornography of the Victorians was, Marcus maintains,
the natural counterpart of their obsession with all things sexual: like
the Victorian prude, the Victorian pornographer suffered from an
infantile fixation on sex. Although Marcus was not sympathetic to his
subject—he saw both the prudes and the pornographers as fixated
and obsessed—his insight was to see the two groups' dialectical re-

lation: how the repression of sex in one place led to its expression in another. (This purely Freudian explanation, however, left him at a loss to explain the proliferation of pornography in the more sexually "liberated" period in which he himself was writing.) Other critics of pornography were even less sympathetic to these transgressive texts. George Steiner (1974, 228–229), for example, speculated that the "'total freedom' of the uncensored erotic imagination" could easily lead to the "total freedom of the sadist."

Although these and other studies at least vaguely define pornography as visual or written representations depicting sex, none of them—not even those that hoped to lend the dignity of age to their modern exemplars—could actually establish a continuous thread from antiquity. Much more typically Sade figures as the real origin of a relatively modern tradition of pornography, a tradition that is viewed at least as variously as the controversial marquis himself. To Steiner and to the anti-pornography feminists who began to dominate the discourse on pornography in the late seventies, the new prevalence of pornography is a dangerous and harmful unleashing of sadistic power in which aesthetic worth is hardly the issue. Nonetheless, anti-censorship feminist Angela Carter (1978) does see Sade as offering an important opportunity for women to analyze the inscription of power in sexual relations. Unlike Sontag and Michelson, Carter argues for pornography not on aesthetic grounds but on the value of Sade's politicization of sexuality and on his insistence of the right of women "to fuck" as aggressively, tyrannically, and cruelly as men (p. 27).

A recent, nonfeminist contribution to this elusive history of pornography is Walter Kendrick's *The Secret Museum: Pornography in Modern Culture* (1987). Kendrick differs in one important way from all previous attempts to discuss pornography in that he refuses to define pornography—high-class or low, ancient or modern—as a group of texts with *any* common qualities. His point is the fickleness of all definitions: what today is a low-class, mass-consumed form was in the last century the exclusive preserve of elite gentlemen. Building partly on the arguments of Steven Marcus, Kendrick traces the nineteenth-century emergence of a popular pornography as well as the coterminous attempts at censorship. Observing the futility of censorship, since a censored text immediately becomes desirable, Kendrick decides that the only workable definition of pornography is the description of this very process: pornography is simply what-ever representations a particular dominant class or group does not want in the hands of another, less dominant class or group. Those in power construct the definition of pornography through their power to censor it (pp. 92–94).

This approach has the great advantage (and also disadvantage) of simplicity. Kendrick argues, for example, that in the nineteenth century the objectionable texts might be realistic novels, sensational melodramas, reports on prostitution, bawdy limericks, or the famous painting unearthed at Pompeii of a satyr in sexual congress with a goat. The important point is the continuity of social attitudes toward forbidden works. The painting of the satyr and goat had once been on public display at Pompeii; only in the mid-nineteenth century did certain "gentlemen" anthropologists who unearthed these treasures of the ancient world think to lock them up in a "secret museum." Only then, in short, did these texts take on pornographic meaning (p. 66).

Kendrick thus holds—correctly, I think—that the relatively recent emergence of pornography is a problem of modern mass culture. While Steven Marcus implicitly argued the same point by situating his study of pornography in Victorian sexual discourse, Kendrick maintains boldly that pornography as we know it emerges at that moment when the diffusion of new kinds of mass media—novels and magazines in the Victorian era, films and videos today—exacerbates a dominant group's worry about the availability of these media to persons less "responsible" than themselves.

Worry about the effect of pornography on impressionable "young persons" emerged most forcefully in England in 1857 with the passage of the first piece of anti-obscenity legislation: the British Obscene Publications Act. At this time the person most endangered by obscenity was a young, middle-class woman, whose "pornography" consisted of romantic novels. The responsible and powerful "gentleman" desiring to protect her from corruption was a middle- or upper-class man who did not in the least worry about the similar debasing effect of such works on himself.

Kendrick thus dates the most significant emergence of pornography as a problem in modern culture to this 1857 act. His history of pornography, then, is fundamentally the modern story of how those in power react to texts that seem to embody dangerous knowledge when in the hands of the "other," a history that extends from the building of the "secret museum" at Pompeii, through the establishment of a legal category of obscenity and the famous book trials of the late nineteenth and early twentieth centuries, right up to the recent redefinition of pornography by the Meese Commission and Women Against Pornography as sexual violence and dehumanization.

In his section on recent events, however, we begin to see the limitations of Kendrick's definition of pornography as a construction simply of the power of the censor. He claims, for example, that this later stage is really the same as all earlier stages, only with the sexes reversed; that is, now it is Women Against Pornography who define the genre as abusive violence, the old power of the "gentleman" having simply changed sides. Similarly, today's impressionable "young person" is now a lustful, illiterate male who, instead of reading novels, looks at films and videotapes that lead him to commit crimes against women (pp. 332–338).

By concluding that the modern-day feminist anti-pornography campaign simply repeats the past history of censorship, Kendrick reveals the basic problem with his approach: an inability to measure the real changes in the idea of pornography through the eyes of its beholders. Certainly one crucial dissimilarity between now and then lies in the power differential and the varying historical situations of the male and female "gentlemen" so determined to censor pornography. And Kendrick's polemical lesson that the history of pornography teaches the futility of censorship, while perhaps true, never addresses the very different reasons why other groups might *want* to pursue such a course. In fact, his concluding statement (p. 239) that "pornography is not eternal, nor are its dangers self evident," seems not so much a conclusion as the dialectical point of origin for a polemic against the Women Against Pornography position that pornography *is* eternal (though, contradictorily, growing worse all the time) and its dangers decidedly self-evident.

The lengths to which Kendrick is willing to go to attack censoring feminists suggest both the influence of the anti-pornography position and just how polarized recent discussions of pornography have become. In his analysis we also see the difficulty—rampant in studies of pornography—of talking about a genre without first defining its form. Though often clever, Kendrick's ironic history never comes to grips with what most bothers anti-pornography feminists about pornography: the nature of the sexual representations themselves.

Curiously, however, the two sides of this dialectic are similar. Kendrick's argument is that we must learn from history the futility of censorship. The anti-pornography feminist lesson (discussed at length below) is that since history is the same old story of an abusive male power, the only recourse is to censor the representations created by that power. Both positions assert, though very differently, that the history of pornography is a history of power: for Kendrick it is an elitist power on the side of the censors, whereas for anti-pornography feminists it is, more simply, a misogynist power in which the text dominates its women victims.

We can observe in this dialectic how the issue of censorship has overwhelmed all other discussion. Thus all histories of pornography, such as they are, have turned into histories of the legal battles fought in the wake of relatively recent laws against obscenity. Kendrick's insight—and his limitation—is to have claimed that the various attempts to censor pornography, whatever it is, *are* its history. The argument that the history of modern pornography consists only in what has offended the fickle "gentlemen" is too facile. Certainly modern pornography is intimately tied up with legal and moral attempts at censorship, but like all productions of culture it has its own "relative autonomy" as well.[7]

The history of pornography as a definitive cultural form has not yet been written. The very marginality of pornography within culture has led us to argue only about whether pornography, like sex, should be liberated or repressed. And the fact that, as with sex, we simultaneously take for granted its "obvious" definition—assuming, for example, that it is either a liberating pleasure or an abusive power—has only confused matters.

This dilemma is, precisely, our "sexual fix," as critic Stephen Heath (1982, 3) puts it. In the spirit of Foucault's criticism of the once-vaunted sexual liberation, on grounds that the idea of liberation through increased knowledge or freedom is an illusion, Heath argues that such knowledge inevitably leads to more complete control, conformity, and regulation, producing no "pure" pleasure but only an increasingly intensified, commodified form of sexuality: a "sexual fix." Caught in this fix, we cannot see that the two main sides in the debates about pornography—the one that sees sexuality as

the source of all our problems, and the one that sees sexual liberation as the beginning of a solution—are just as much part of the
compulsion to talk about an essential, self-evident sexual "truth" as
is pornography itself.

Depending on the (sexual) politics of the perceiver, the "truth"
of pornographic power or pleasure is viewed either as deserving to
speak or as so "unspeakable" as to require suppression. Among feminists, only the anti-censorship groups seem willing to discuss the
meaning of these truths and not to take them as self-evident. As the
editors of the 1983 anthology *Powers of Desire* put it, the constant
speaking about sex does not necessarily advance the cause of sexual
freedom; yet at the same time, feminists can't *not* speak about sex
for the simple reason that, until quite recently, almost all sexual discourse—from the writings of Denis Diderot to hard-core film—has
been spoken by men to other men (Snitow, Stansell, and Thompson
1983, 9–10).

Even though the definition and history of pornography are elusive, then, there is remarkable consensus concerning the need to
include "power" as the significant new term in their formulation. We
see the term in Angela Carter's feminist-liberationist reading of
Sade's sexual politics as well as in the diametrically opposed
feminist–anti-pornographic reading of Sade as inciting aggression
against women victims. We see it in a different way in Susanne Kappeler's (1986) location of pornographic power in the very form of
representation, in Kendrick's idea that pornography is created by
those with the power to censor, and in Alan Soble's (1986) notion
that in a future communist society pornography would be free of the
contamination of power altogether. Only one thing seems clear: the
force of this newly introduced term has rendered the older arguments of the sixties and seventies obsolete—whether, like Sontag's
and Michelson's, based on elitist aesthetics or, like Marcus's and
Steiner's, concerned only with pornography's effect on the morality
of the masses.

Nowhere has the impact of this new concept of pornography-as-
power been more forcefully invoked or more massively diffused than
in the 1986 *Final Report* of the Attorney General's Commission on
Pornography. This document, overseen by Attorney General Edwin
Meese, is a curious hybrid of empirical and moral arguments against
pornography culled from social scientists, new-right "moral major-

ity," and anti-pornography feminists.[8] Even though each of these groups has a very different interpretation of the meaning and importance of sexuality and pornography, their alliance has definitively shifted the debate about pornography from a discussion of aesthetics and morals by academic literary critics and intellectuals in consultation with the judiciary, to another, equally unresolved, discussion about abusive forms of power and the threatened civil rights of women. The claims of this document and its problematic relation to feminism therefore warrant careful examination.

The Meese Commission and Women Against Pornography

As early as page seventy-eight of the commission's two-volume, 1,960-page report, it becomes apparent how thoroughly the feminist anti-pornography position had, by the mid-1980s, altered the terms of the public debate on pornography. Commissioner James Dobson writes:

Pornography is degrading to women. . . . It is provided primarily for the lustful pleasure of men and boys who use it to generate excitation. And it is my belief, though evidence is not easily obtained, that a small but dangerous minority will then choose to act aggressively against the nearest available females. Pornography is the theory; rape is the practice.

(Attorney General's Commission on
Pornography 1986, 1:78)

The absence of quotation marks around this almost verbatim quotation of Robin Morgan's famous anti-pornography slogan, "Pornography is the theory, and rape the practice" (1980, 139), indicates the extent to which an emotionally felt, if causally unproven, link between the imaginative fantasy of pornography and the reality of abusive practices is now assumed.

In 1970, an earlier Presidential Commission on Pornography had concluded that, unlike explicit depictions of violence, pornography had no measurable adverse social effects; Richard Nixon rejected this liberal commission's recommendations. The 1986 commission, in contrast, appointed by Ronald Reagan and dominated by moral majority conservatives, came to the overwhelming conclusion that hard-core pornography *is* violence, and that this violence hurts women most of all. Although the commission never defined pornography (indeed, it even endorsed Justice Potter Stewart's admission that although he couldn't define it, he knew it when he saw it),[9] its alphabetical listings of magazines, paperback books, films, and videotape cassettes culled from sixteen "Adults Only" pornographic outlets make clear that the pornography the commission was attacking was not the avant-garde, literary pornography discussed by Sontag. The commission (1986, 1:320–330) therefore encouraged prosecution of the two most reprehensible—and, it was implied, most representative—pornographic categories that it identified: Class I (violent) and Class II (not violent, but "degrading"). Violent pornography in which images of pain and coercion are central was thus taken for granted as the most objectionable essence of pornography, and against it all other categories were measured.

The commission gave the clear impression (though no evidence, beyond statistics on the proliferation of hard core in general) that this violent category was increasing exponentially,[10] with pornography that depicts rape constituting a prime example of such violence—a consequence, perhaps, of the success of the feminist movement in seeing rape categorized as sexual violence against women rather than as a pleasure for which all women secretly long. Yet a problem arises when we consider the difference between actual abusive sexual practices and their representation in pornographic fantasy. Robin Morgan's slogan obscures this distinction by stressing the connection between a male supremacist ideology—viewed as the content of pornography—and specific abusive practices—viewed as its effects.

To anti-pornography feminists like Morgan, Andrea Dworkin, Susan Griffin, Catherine MacKinnon, and Susanne Kappeler, violence is inherent in the male role in "normal" heterosexual relations.[11] This violence finds its most extreme expression in the weaponlike use of the penis in rape. These feminists view women who find pleasure in rape fantasies as guilty victims of false consciousness. Andrea Dworkin takes this argument the furthest in her recent book *Intercourse*, where she points to heterosexual intercourse—defined as the penetration-invasion of one passive (female) object by an active (male) subject—as the root cause of sexual violence. Women who enjoy violent fantasies or sexual practices (a group in

which Dworkin seems to include any woman who enjoys heterosexual relations that include intercourse) are collaborators with the
phallic enemy (see Dworkin 1987, 122–142). Or, as Susanne Kappeler puts it in her book *The Pornography of Representation* (1986,
214), "with lovers like men, who needs torturers?"

Following these arguments, women who read the "soft-core" descriptions of rape in romance novels are collaborating with their torturers as well. The anti-pornography critique of male violence, in
short, makes no distinction between the rapes authored and consumed by women in sexual fantasy or romance fiction and the rapes
of hard-core pornography authored and consumed by men. As a result, the political value of denouncing rape in real life leads to a blanket condemnation of the representation of rape in sexual fantasy—
a condemnation that begins to seem a little like dictating the proper
content of dreams. The trouble is that existing power relations between the sexes are inextricably tied both to our fantasies and to the
expressions and enactments of sexual pleasures (though not necessarily in directly reflective ways)—a situation that explains, for example, how a powerful man may find pleasure in masochistic sexual
fantasy.

Sadomasochistic scenarios present an even more difficult problem in the Meese Commission's assessment of violence in sexual
representation, for here the violence is depicted not as actual coercion but as a highly ritualized game in which the participants consent to play predetermined roles of dominance and submission.
Discussion thus often ignores the fact that in these scenarios women
can just as well be—and often are—the dominators.[12]

The commission's creation of a prime category of violent pornography nevertheless taps into a genuine concern about the excess
of violence, especially violence against women, in contemporary
culture. Yet this critique can only be activated by emphasizing the
sexual nature of violence in a genre that is already vulnerable to censorship because of its explicit sexual representations. For example,
the commission notes at least twice (1:329, 361) that although other
genres mixing nonexplicit sexual themes with violence, such as teen
"slasher" films, are more likely than pornography proper to produce
antisocial effects in viewers, since nonexplicit sexual representations
are not vulnerable to existing obscenity laws such films cannot be
prosecuted. The commission then contradictorily continues to in-

dict pornography as if it were the ultimate harm, thus displacing legitimate concern for runaway violence and violent sexual crimes onto the legally vulnerable scapegoat of pornography.

As the (noncommensurate) example of sexual violence in slasher films and pornography suggests, and as the adoption of social scientific and feminist language only thinly disguises, the not-so-hidden agenda of the Meese Commission report is to condemn those unorthodox sexualities that can be construed as perverse. Commissioner Park Elliott Dietz states his abhorrence of such unorthodoxy clearly:

A person who learned about human sexuality in the . . . pornography outlets of America would be a person who had never conceived of a man and woman marrying or even falling in love before having intercourse . . . who had never conceived of vaginal intercourse with ejaculation during intromission, and who had never conceived of procreation as a purpose of sexual union.

(1:43)

"Normal" sexuality, the commission implies, is never violent, not even in the imagination. The attack on violence, together with the rhetoric of harm borrowed from radical feminism—replacing an older and less effective conservative rhetoric opposed simply to immorality, "smut," or just plain bad art—allows this arm of the "moral majority" to assert sexual norms under the guise of protecting pornography's victims.

It seems likely that the radical feminists and the commissioners struck an implicit bargain to facilitate a combined attack on pornography as abusive power. While the commissioners accepted elements of the radical feminist critique of phallic pleasure as violent and reprehensible assertions of male power, in return they curbed their disapproval of the sexual unorthodoxies of gay or lesbian pornography (or sexual practices), even though these obviously defy the above-mentioned norms of "vaginal intercourse" and "procreation as a purpose of sexual union." The rhetoric of violence cannot be mobilized against these modes, since they do not present women as victims of phallic power.

Each party to this bargain has both gained and lost something. The Meese Commission members gained new leverage against some forms of obscenity; anti-pornography feminists got to assert the abnormality of a graphically depicted phallic power that was once considered a natural aspect of sexual pleasure. But license to outright condemn was granted to neither the Meese Commission, in the case of all unorthodox sexualities—unless these could be construed as violent—nor the radical feminists, in the case of all patriarchal phallocentrism—except as it constituted sexual violence. So although the two sides had very different notions of what the norms of sexual behavior should be, in the end they struck an uneasy bargain on what the norms should *not* be. The unfortunate result—and a result that I do not believe to be in the best interests of any kind of feminism—is a strengthening of the idea of sexual norms altogether.

If phallic sexuality is contaminated by power, this tactic seems to say, if it is *essentially* violent and perverse, then female sexuality shall be defined as its opposite: as not-violent and not-perverse—a pure and natural pleasure uncontaminated by power. In Andrea Dworkin's *Pornography: Men Possessing Women* (1979), women are viewed as colonized victims of male aggression, victims of the "brutality of male history" (p. 68) who are nevertheless acted on by this history. Women who have had no choice but to live in this history, women who have learned to find pleasure in relative powerlessness, are treated as phallic sympathizers for not recognizing their victimization. They become, as Ellen Willis (1983, 465) has pointed out, a new form of the "bad girl," recast in deviant terms.

This analysis of phallic power has two serious flaws. The first is the assumption that women are natural beings and that their sexuality, if somehow left alone in a state of nature, outside of history, could be free of power. The implications of Dworkin's argument—and of the anti-pornography feminist position in general—is that men are carnal, perverse, powerful, violent beings who "love murder" (Dworkin in Lederer 1980, 148), while women are asexual or gently sexual and even inherently lesbian beings. This argument suggests, erroneously I believe, that if female sexuality were ever to get free of its patriarchal contaminations it would express no violence, would have no relations of power, and would produce no transgressive sexual fantasies.

A second flaw is perhaps more telling: having stated to the Meese Commission that the problem is women's role as victims of male sexual abuse, anti-pornography feminists did not cease to play the role

of victim but instead played it to the hilt. Dworkin's testimony before the commission is a prime example. She alludes, on the one
hand, to a series of photographs published in *Penthouse* magazine
of Asian women bound and hung from trees and, on the other, to a
New York Times article about the rape and murder of an eight-year-
old Chinese girl in North Carolina whose body was left hanging from
a tree. Dworkin assumes a causal connection between the magazine
photos and the crime, even though no evidence apart from the circumstances exists. At the end of an exhortation against such "concentration camp" pornography, Dworkin returns to these images of
Asian women, only by now the focus is no longer the *Penthouse* photos or the *Times* image of the Asian girl, but a condensation of both
into a general female victim who transcends any specific historical
situation but embodies all the political victims of all the ages.

I am asking you to help the exploited, not the exploiters. You have a tre-
mendous opportunity here. I am asking you as individuals to have the courage, because I think it's what you will need to actually be willing yourselves
to go and cut that woman down and untie her hands and take the gag out
of her mouth and to do something for her freedom.

> (Attorney General's Commission on
> Pornography 1986, 1:772)

Commissioner Park Elliott Dietz, speaking for several of the other
commissioners as well, tells us his reaction to this challenge: "I
cried. And I still cry at that image, even as I write, because if we do
not act with compassion and conviction and courage for the hostages
and victims of the pornographers, we do not deserve the freedoms
that our founding fathers bequeathed us" (p. 52).

It is in the rhetoric of Dworkin's challenge-cum-appeal and Commissioner Dietz's manly-yet-compassionate response that we can
best measure the success and failure of this feminist alliance with
the patriarchs. For only by casting her archetypal "suffering woman"
in the role of the absolute victim of history can Dworkin utter her
appeal to the compassionate man who will rescue her; only by giving
up both the power of action herself and the contaminated pleasure
of an abnormal, masochistic—"concentration camp"—orgasm can
she get her woman victim cut down from that tree.

The *frisson* of melodrama in this exchange offers a telling commentary on the perpetuation of traditional male and female roles.

It is significant, for example, that Dworkin's bound and gagged heroine can appeal to our pity only passively, while Dietz and his colleagues play the role of the quixotic heroes who perform the action that ultimately saves her. Together these traditional male and female figures are tilting against the windmills of a pornographic fantasy whose eradication seems to offer freedom to exploiter and exploited alike. In fact, though, it is only Dworkin's rhetoric that makes all the real abuses of history seem to converge in a single pornographic image. The women in the *Penthouse* photo are posed in a sadomasochistic fantasy that is unquestionably informed by the ideology of patriarchal power. But is cutting these imaginary women down any way to keep other, real, victims from being raped and killed? The real question is, what *will* keep another victim from getting strung up? As long as we emphasize woman's role as the absolute victim of male sadism, we only perpetuate the supposedly essential nature of woman's powerlessness.

Thus, while I would agree with anti-pornography feminists that pornography—especially the heterosexual film pornography examined in this book—offers exemplary symbolic representations of patriarchal power in heterosexual pleasure, and while I believe that a feminist critique of this power is crucial, I side with the anti-censorship feminists who hold that censorship of these pleasures offers no real solution to patriarchal violence and abuse.

The model of representation employed by both Dworkin and even more sophisticated anti-pornography feminists like Susanne Kappeler is too simple. The fact that pornography is not a love story, to borrow the title of an influential anti-pornography documentary, is hardly surprising. Nor would a "love story" necessarily preclude relations of power. Just as westerns for so long offered myths and fantasies of America's agrarian past as told exclusively from the viewpoint of the white male settlers who exploited and overpowered the native American inhabitants, so has pornography long been a myth of sexual pleasure told from the point of view of men with the power to exploit and objectify the sexuality of women. Indeed, only recently has it become possible for pornography, as a genre, to introduce the alternative perspective of women's power and pleasure.

Given the many possible viewpoints on sexuality, we need to beware of arguments that state that pornography is inadequate to the whole truth of sexuality. Here the implication is that a whole truth of sexuality actually exists, outside of language, discourse, and power. This idea, I argue, is the central fallacy of all the anti-porn feminist positions: that a single, whole sexuality exists opposed to the supposed deviations and abnormalities of somebody else's fragmentation.

A better feminist position on pornography and sexuality must work against such notions of a whole and natural sexuality that stands outside history and free of power. Although the idea of the natural may seem to offer the utopian promise of change, of liberation from power, actually it impedes resistance to existing forms of power by reducing power to a matter of personal agency, with (gendered) individuals controlling other (gendered) individuals. As long as a long-suffering, victimized, and repressed natural female sexuality is viewed as the antithesis to a falsely ideological, constructed, sadistic male sexuality (or any other kind of "perversion"), practical resistance to what many women do find inimical in that sexuality is limited to the condemnation of unorthodoxies measured against an orthodox norm.

The Anti-Censorship Feminists

The above emphasis on the social and historical construction of diverse sexualities characterizes what has been called, for lack of a better name, the "anti-censorship" feminists.[13] The label is misleading to the extent that this "group" does not organize its position around pornography as a central issue and certainly does not defend pornography in all its forms. These women are interested, however, in defending the expression of sexual differences and in opposing the hierarchization of some sexualities as better, or more normal, than others (see Rubin 1984).

One difficulty with the labels of both the anti-pornography and the anti-censorship feminists is their similar identification as being *against* something—porn on the one side, the censorship of porn on the other. Obviously both groups are *for* something as well; it is simply a measure of the confusion and defensiveness engendered by the issue of sexuality that each side poses the conflict between them reactively as anti-anti. A better name for the second group would probably be the "social construction" feminists, given their emphasis on social and historical factors in the construction of sexuality and their work to defend the expression of diverse sexualities and to oppose the notion of any kind of "politically correct," ideal sexuality. Typical of the greater diversity of this "position" is the fact that no single representative voice or theory speaks for it and that its ideas are scattered throughout numerous books and journals.

The 1985 anthology *Women Against Censorship* (Burstyn 1985) addresses pornography directly and the type of censorship that anti-pornography feminists propose. Most of these essays question the choice of pornography as the central issue of feminist politics and pose a symptomatic, rather than causal, relation between pornography's instrumental use of bodies and pleasure. In one essay, Carole Vance, Lisa Duggan, and Nan Hunter examine the underlying assumptions of the MacKinnan/Dworkin-authored city ordinances (subsequently ruled unconstitutional) that attempted to define pornography as the "sexually explicit subordination of women" and thus as a violation of women's civil rights. A key problem of this definition, they argue, is the meaning of the term *subordination*: "To some, *any* graphic sexual act violates women's dignity and therefore subordinates them"; to others, it is the absence of the "boundaries of procreation and marriage" that seem subordinating (Burstyn 1985, 140)—as the Meese Commission was very soon to demonstrate.

The authors cite an amicus brief filed in support of the Indianapolis ordinance by Catherine MacKinnon on behalf of Linda Marchiano (a.k.a. Linda Lovelace, of *Deep Throat* fame). The brief is aimed at suppressing the film in which Marchiano appears and which represents the kind of pornography that would be covered by the law. The anti-censorship arguments against this brief are worth examining here, for in demonstrating the ambiguity of the term *subordination* the authors focus on a film that will be important to the present study. MacKinnon argues that the film "subordinates women by using women . . . sexually, specifically as eager servicing receptacles for male genitalia and ejaculate" in "postures of sexual submission and/or servility." The City of Indianapolis agreed, saying that the film shows a woman as being "ever eager for oral penetration . . . often on her hands and knees" (Burstyn 1985, 138).

But as is argued in the essay, "the notion that the female character is 'used' by men suggests that it is improbable that a woman would engage in fellatio of her own accord" (ibid.). In other words, MacKinnon invokes a norm—in this case a feminist norm regarding the inherently submissive nature of fellatio for women—to condemn the representation and performance of a politically incorrect sexual practice. This is not to say that *Deep Throat* is free of sexism; but as the authors note, the sexist subordination and objectification of women that it portrays are common to the culture at large. It seems clear that MacKinnon is using normative attitudes about sexual practices (along with unproven extratextual allegations by Linda Marchiano that she was coerced into performing the acts depicted in the film) to argue for censorship of the representation of certain sexual acts. Are feminists to declare themselves against representations of fellatio, against being on their knees during sex, against anything other than absolutely egalitarian forms of mutual love and affection? Indeed, what forms of sex *are* egalitarian?

Before we can adequately read the significance for women—let alone men—of the representation of nonnormative sexual acts in pornography, we will need to think more about how such acts are represented, for whom they are represented, and how they function in narrative context. *Deep Throat*, for example, was one of the first hard-core features to be seen by large numbers of women in theaters. It was also one of the first pornographic films to concentrate on the problem of a woman's pleasure and to suggest that some sexual acts were less than earthshaking. While none of this makes *Deep Throat* a progressive or feminist work, it does suggest, as I will elaborate in Chapter 4, the complexity involved in reading sexual acts in hard-core films.

In general, anti-censorship feminists agree that pornographic representations are often sexist, but they do not necessarily agree on which representations are sexist or why; nor are they about to settle on explicit representations of sexual acts as the key to sexist oppression. For the moment they prefer to open up a Pandora's box of plaguing and difficult questions about sexuality. Moreover, they suggest that the very reason these sexual questions are proving so insistent now is precisely because feminists closed the lid so tightly on them in the seventies. Certainly there are risks involved in asking these questions; but not to ask them would be to close down rather than to open up the discussion of sexuality as an important—though not all-determining—force in women's lives. The questions that Ann Snitow asks in this same volume are worth quoting for their honest address of the deeper issues of pornography:

What is the actual content of porn and how is porn related to the broader questions of arousal? . . . What makes something sexy, and what part does power play in the sexualization of a person or situation? Is it a feminist belief that without gender inequality all issues of power will wither away, or do we have a model for the future that will handle inequalities differently? Are there kinds of arousal we know and experience that are entirely absent in porn? How expressive is it of our full sexual range? How representative? How conventional and subject to its own aesthetic laws?

(Burstyn 1985, 119)

These are precisely the questions that can put the study of pornography on the right track.

It is easy to see why the anti-pornography position has been so popular: it provides answers, albeit simplistic ones, whereas anti-censorship feminists mostly ask questions. Carole Vance's introduction to the anthology *Pleasure and Danger* (the proceedings of the controversial 1982 Barnard conference "Toward a Politics of Sexuality") comprises a long string of questions about the construction of sexuality and its meaning—in terms of sexual pleasure and sexual danger—to women. The one thing Vance knows for sure is that sexuality is not only the "oppression of male violence, brutality and coercion"; there is also oppression in the forced repression of female desire (Vance 1984, 23). To Vance, "to speak only of sexual violence and oppression ignores women's experience with sexual agency and choice and unwittingly increases the sexual terror and despair in which women live" (p. 1).

Thus one important point of agreement, in this volume and in the equally rich *Powers of Desire* (Snitow, Stansell, and Thompson 1983) is that feminism must not retrench around notions of some "politically correct" sexuality. The radical, utopian dreams of achieving a better, more egalitarian set of sexual arrangements too easily slips into what Alice Echols (1984) calls a new "feminist biological determinism" and what Carole Vance (1984, 21) calls "setting norms." Among lesbians and heterosexual women both, this overzealous application of the "personal is political" idea sometimes leads to a repressive "policing of desire" (Watney 1987). As Ruby Rich (1986) notes in an excellent review article of feminist writing from the "sex wars" of the 1980s, this repression of the fact of sexual power imbalances has led to an even more dramatic "return of the repressed," in the emergence of sadomasochistic sexualities in a variety of genres. Following Ann Snitow's (1983) early work on mass-market romance, Rich suggests that the repression haunting us in both straight and lesbian mass-market genres is the specter of being "in thrall"—for heterosexual women, to a man; for lesbians, to a woman. In either case thralldom has been condemned, Rich suggests (1986, 536), even though in a variety of erotic fiction and fantasy it has been shown to raise complex questions about what turns women on.

One thing is clear: many very different things, very imperfectly understood, turn both women and men on, including being dominated and dominating. Since at least the seventies women have been partaking of both kinds of pleasure as they have increasingly joined the sexual marketplace as consumers themselves, and not just as objects of consumption. Barbara Ehrenreich, Elizabeth Hess, and Gloria Jacobs, in their book *Re-Making Love* (1986), see this as a sign that the sexual revolution has not been for men only and that the "feminization of sex" continues to be an important agenda item.

A recent anthology about pornography dramatically poses the possibilities of this "feminization." *Caught Looking* is a porn magazine for women that juxtaposes hard- and soft-core photos, drawings, and graphics with a variety of essays on "feminism, pornography, and censorship" composed by members of FACT—the Feminist Anti-Censorship Taskforce.[14] The written texts include diverse juxtapositions, such as Barbara O'Dair and Abby Tallmer's wildly contradictory list of seventy-three "Sex Premises." The anthology's visual message is that if we think we know what pornographic imagery is, we should look again and reconsider the "pleasures of looking and imagining" (K. Ellis et al. 1986, 5). What we see may seem fantastic, delicately sensuous, crudely humorous, cruel, or beautiful. A single image can convey several of these qualities at once, and the same image may seem very different to different people. Some images are turn-of-the-century and quaint, some very recent. Many bear the mark of conventions, traditions, and fashions of sexuality that, as Foucault would put it, have become "stuck to an age" (1978, 48). All that these images share is an apparent intent to arouse someone somewhere, the fact that they are in black-and-white, and the fact that now female eyes have been "caught looking" at them.

The total effect of the magazine is of a collage of sexual images and ideas removed from their initial, arousing contexts. Gay porn, lesbian porn, S/M heterosexual porn, images of hermaphrodites, typical girlie magazine photos, artistic erotic poses of men and women, and images that defy classification are all mixed together. We are struck by the difference and variety; we wonder who likes what, and we wonder at what we like. At the same time, we are distanced by the presence of both scholarly and nonscholarly texts and by the academic nature of the question, What turns you on? *Hustler* this is not. And yet by looking at this magazine one can begin to imagine trying to understand—not just deploring or becoming aroused by—the images in *Hustler* or other porn magazines.

I find the *Caught Looking* anthology particularly helpful as a starting point for the feminist analysis of graphic pornography. Although none of the writers attempt to read any of the diverse images represented, or even to describe the genre, the very fact that hardcore pornographic images have been placed side by side with articles aimed at opening up a discussion of pornography as an issue represents a startling breakthrough. Up until this anthology feminists tended to deploy pornographic images in an entirely sensationalist way, as in the documentary film *Not a Love Story* or in horror slide shows of Women Against Pornography, which quote only the most misogynistic or "kinky" of images wildly out of context. Even the images reproduced in the anti-censorship *Heresies* "sex issue" or Samois's *Coming to Power* (1982) count on sensationalism: "Love me—and my sexual identity—or leave me alone," they seem to say. The images in *Caught Looking* are obviously sensational and quoted out of context as well, but since they do not advocate or celebrate a particular sexual identity—or condemn any either—they seem to cry out for further reflection and analysis. We want more than to be aroused or offended by these images; we want the further historical and generic contextualization that would allow us to interpret them.

Yet precisely here lies the enormous difficulty in the study of all visual pornographies. Because most of these images, until very recently, have circulated only underground and have been incriminating to their owners and producers, we know almost nothing of their production and use. Thus, the *Caught Looking* anthology dramatizes a dilemma that I face in the early portion of my study of hard-core film as well: how to say anything about texts whose history has not even begun to be written; how to talk about a tradition much of which has been lost, burned, or allowed to disintegrate from neglect, whose authors and dates are unknown, and whose visual content is perceived by many publishers as too controversial to be reproduced for analysis.

It is no wonder that so much has been written about the issue of pornography and so little about its actual texts. This lack of knowledge about texts that are nevertheless quite numerous feeds into the anti-pornography feminist stance that sets pornography off from the rest of cultural production, showcasing it as the extreme case of patriarchal power. Anti-censorship feminists, in response, have argued eloquently against isolating pornography as a special case; instead they focus on a continuous pornographic tradition that runs throughout dominant culture. This is the strategy, for example, of Mariana Valverde in her chapters on pornography in *Sex, Power, and Pleasure* (1985) and of Annette Kuhn in her discussion of film pornography in *Women's Pictures* (1982) and in a chapter of her later book *The Power of the Image* (1985).

While I appreciate the political importance of this wider focus, at a certain point such an approach becomes self-defeating, for how can we adequately discuss the pornogra*hic* without making some stab at a description of specific pornogra*hy?*[15] Annette Kuhn's (1985, 109–128) excellent analysis of the questions that pornography poses for women and of the economic, legal, and patriarchal structures in which pornography occurs is a case in point: when Kuhn finally gets down to an examination of texts in a section called "Cinema and Pornography," what she actually delivers, for reasons that I understand all too well, is yet another discussion of the pornogra*hic*—instanced here by the nonexplicit sexual violence of Brian de Palma's *Dressed to Kill*. I agree that de Palma's film exhibits sexual violence, but the particular brand portrayed clearly belongs to a genre of (horror/slasher) film that differs significantly from pornography.[16] To swerve away from pornography before examining any examples, into a discussion of the (related) horror-film genre is to allow an assumed a priori notion of violence presumably shared by both genres to stand in for the hard-core essence of pornography.[17]

Pornography may not be special, but it does have a specificity distinct from other genres. It is this specificity that I wish to address. A first step will be to define film pornography minimally, and as neutrally as possible, as the visual (and sometimes aural) representation of living, moving bodies engaged in explicit, usually unfaked, sexual acts with a primary intent of arousing viewers.[18] What distinguishes film and video pornography from written pornography—or even, to a lesser degree, from still photography—is the element of performance contained in the term *sexual act*. Annette Kuhn (1985, 24) has usefully suggested a further constant: that pornography in general produces meanings "pivoting on gender difference." To this we could add Beverley Brown's (1981, 10) notion that pornography reveals current regimes of sexual relationships as "a coincidence of sexual phantasy, genre and culture in an erotic organization of visibility."

The task of this book is to see what the organization of these regimes and these "phantasies" has been at different historical moments. It is also to ask why and how the regimes and phantasies have changed. We need to keep in mind, however, that an erotic organization of visibility is different for cinema than it is for written, or even photographic, pornography. Since the very impetus for the invention of cinema was precisely that it seemed able to register the previously invisible hard-core "truth" of bodies and pleasures in a direct and unmediated fashion, Chapter 2 will take a close look at this key moment in cinematic history.

Let us return, momentarily, to the questions with which this chapter began: to Diderot's literary fable of jewel-genitals that claim to reveal the truth of women's sexual indiscretions and the relation of this "speaking sex" hard-core film pornography. Perhaps the most important aspect of this comparison is the continuity that both texts show with the modern age's compulsion to make sex speak. If we first accept the pervasive force of this compulsion, then we can go on to distinguish among its different forms.

Both Diderot's story and contemporary hard-core film pornography exhibit misogynistic regimes of sexual relationships, and both are narrative vehicles for the spectacular, involuntary presentation of the knowledge of pleasure as confessions of socially disruptive "sexual truths." In eighteenth-century "pornographic" works as diverse as *Les bijoux indiscrets*, Sade's *Philosophy in the Bedroom*, and Cleland's *Fanny Hill*, confessions of sexual pleasure are described with varying degrees of explicitness, but in every case the confession of the *woman's* pleasure carries a special, socially satiric or socially subversive, charge.

By the late nineteenth century, however, this confession of pleasure has changed in both meaning and form. One of the most striking features of the 1888 *My Secret Life* is its male protagonist's incessant desire to investigate the genitals of his numerous female sexual conquests—not just to feel his own pleasure and to witness the social disruption caused when a woman's pleasure diverges from communal expectations of female modesty, but to have a precise knowledge of the details of her pleasure. In this work, and in Frank Harris's later *My Life and Loves* (1925–1929), the shift to more and more precise attempts to know, name, and measure the different pleasures of the different sexes seems to find its perfect tool in the contemporaneous photographic "machines of the visible."

Whether we choose to call all these works pornography and to differentiate among them on the level of form and function, or whether for us pornography is only those works that offer explicit descriptions or performances of sexual acts, the crucial issue is that we acknowledge not only the continuity of a tradition that seeks knowledge of the pleasures of sex, but also the variations within it. Both Diderot's fable and the hard-core film *The Opening of Misty Beethoven*, for example, share the goal of figuring and measuring the "truth" of sex with the particular magic at their disposal; yet to each this truth is a very different thing.

Diderot conjures a magical silver ring with the power to make the female sex speak. The confessional "truth" that is spoken in the presence of the invisible prince provides evidence that the elegant women of his court are not the figures of propriety that they seem. This lesson is certainly a feature of any pornography: the body is recalcitrant; it has desires and appetites that do not necessarily conform to social expectations. Over two hundred years later, "Henry Paris" 's film continues many aspects of this pornographic tradition. Now, however, although bodily desires and appetites are still socially disruptive, the mere fact of their existence is not enough to sustain a story, and the joke of their confession is elaborated into a narrative that must distinguish between different qualities and kinds of sex acts.

Where Diderot's genie conjures up the magic silver ring that renders the prince invisible and forces the women to confess their pleasures unaware of his presence, the wizardry of cinematic representation provides its spectators with a seemingly perfected form of invisibility. Each viewer is transported, by the magic of camera close-ups and editing, to the ideal position for witnessing bodies' confessions of pleasure. And just as Diderot's literary magic makes the prince an auditory voyeur to an involuntary narration, so does cinematic magic allow spectators to see and hear everything without being seen or heard themselves. But seeing everything—especially seeing the truth of sex—proves a more difficult project than one might think, especially in the case of women's bodies, whose truths are most at stake. For whereas the women in Diderot's fable could satisfy male curiosity by recounting their adventures in a "loud and clear voice" through their genital-jewels, the visual terms of the cinema do not allow the female protagonists of hard-core films to authenticate their pleasure. This may be one reason why the confessing jewels in the filmic case are male, rather than female, genitals.

In the chapters that follow we will see that this seemingly perfected magic of cinema—this transition from the magic silver ring that elicits the confession of sex to the silver halide of celluloid emulsion that registers the "truth" of body movements on film—is actually no more truthful than Diderot's fable. Motion pictures take over from the magic of Mangogul's silver ring to offer the illusion of a more truthful, hard-core, confession. I hope to show that although this filmic pornography is different in form and function from the literary pornography that precedes it, it is no less rhetorical in operation than the fanciful figure of so many "indiscreet jewels."

With this goal of illustrating rhetorical function, the perceptive reader might ask, why are no images offered for detailed analysis as is generally the custom in books about film? The answer might seem obvious: the images could offend, they might be "read" the wrong way, hard-core illustrations have no place in a scholarly book, academic publishers should not be in the business of selling sex. Obviously, though, these are cowardly answers, for even with only verbal descriptions of films, the publisher and I still unavoidably participate in selling sex. Moreover, such arguments smell of the very censorship I oppose in these pages.

If my point is that the apparent hard-core literal meaning of these images always means something other or more than what they seem to say, why not show them? The problem is that there is no getting around the ability of such images, especially if quoted out of context, to leap off the page to move viewers and thus to prove too facilely whatever "truths" of sex seem most immediately apparent. Rather than run the risk of having a few quoted images stand out too boldly against the ground of my attempts to read whole texts and the context of a genre, and rather than offer up images that could be read either as or against pornography, I forgo the luxury of illustration. I note, however, that nearly all the feature-length hard-core films, and some compilations of stag films, are readily available for rental in the adult sections of many video outlets.

2

Prehistory

The "Frenzy of the Visible"

1878: the Muybridge equine series
Studying the horse, we understand
how hard-core followed the invention
of photography. There's a dark compelling
muscle framed by the flanks. There's
a question, an academic question, of at
which point in a leap the female breast
is highest? In the early stopwatched studies,
light sloped down the breasts like a scree. There's
a question of time, there's a sepia
exactitude. The powder erupts:
in the foreground—two lovers/a basket/red wine.
In the back, a clocked thoroughbred sudses.
Is there ever a moment when all four feet leave the
                                                    ground?
And so we invent pornography.

Albert Goldbarth,
"The Origin of Porno," in *Comings Back*

Scientia Sexualis and The Origin of Porno

In *The History of Sexuality* Michel Foucault (1985, 91–92) distinguishes between two primary ways of organizing the knowledge of sexuality. Where ancient and non-Western cultures had organized the knowledge of sex around an erotic art, or *ars erotica*, aimed at passing general knowledge from the experienced to the initiate without specifying or classifying the details of this knowledge, modern Western cultures have increasingly constructed a *scientia sexualis*—a hermeneutics of desire aimed at ever more detailed explorations of the scientific truths of sexuality (Foucault 1978, 51–73). The *scientia sexualis*, Foucault argues, constructs modern sexualities according to a conjunction of power and knowledge that probes the measurable, confessable "truths" of a sexuality that governs bodies and their pleasures.

It is no longer a question of saying what was done—the sexual act—and how it was done; but of reconstructing, in and around the act, the thoughts that recapitulated it, the obsessions that accompanied it, the images, desires, modulations, and quality of the pleasure that animated it. For the first time, no doubt, a society has taken upon itself to solicit and hear the imparting of individual pleasures.

(Foucault 1978, 63)

Since Foucault did not live to complete his projected six-volume history of sexuality, we cannot know the details of his analysis of the different power/knowledge conjunctions operating in the modern age. Yet we do know, especially from the first-volume introduction to this history, that confession plays a central role in the production of this modern sexuality: it is the technique for exercising power over the pleasures that we seem to be so "free" to confess, the means of producing a "knowledge of pleasure: a pleasure that comes of knowing pleasure" (Foucault 1978, 77), and it operates in many discourses—in medicine, law, psychoanalysis, and pornography (p. 48).

According to Foucault, then, the proliferating medical, psychological, juridical, and pornographic discourses of sexuality have functioned as transfer points of knowledge, power, and pleasure. They are places where sexualities could be specified and solidified. Foucault defines the twofold effect of this process: on the one hand, the power that took charge of sexuality itself became sensualized ("it wrapped the sexual body in its embrace"), and on the other, the pleasure thus discovered "fed back into the power that encircled it" (pp. 44–45). Through this osmosis of a pleasure feeding power and a power feeding pleasure, the "implantation of perversions" gradually took place, and "scattered sexualities rigidified, became stuck to an age, a place, a type of practice" (p. 12).

In the optical inventions of the late nineteenth century—cameras, magic lanterns, zoetropes, Kinetographs, Kinetoscopes, and the early precursors of movies as we know them today—we can see a powerful manifestation of both the surveillance mechanisms described by Foucault and this *scientia sexualis*.[1] Discourses of sexuality elaborated in the modern age reach a kind of crescendo in what film historian Jean-Louis Comolli has called "machines of the visible."[2] In what follows I would like to isolate a particular moment in the modern Western construction of the *scientia sexualis*, lying in the photographic motion studies that were the immediate pre-cursors to the invention of cinema. One of my goals is to show that a cinematic hard core emerges more from this *scientia sexualis* and its construction of new forms of body knowledge than from ancient traditions of erotic art. Another goal is to emphasize the specific cin-ematic nature of this emerging *scientia sexualis* and to show how it becomes, as Foucault notes, a "transfer point" of knowledge, power, and pleasure; thus we can begin to recognize how the desire to see and know more of the human body—in this case, to answer "aca-demic questions" of the mechanics of body movement—underlies the very invention of cinema.

Goldbarth's poem quoted in the chapter epigraph eloquently sug-gests that it is but a short leap from the "academic question" of body movement mechanics to the "pornographic answer," wherein the elusive and prurient "truth" is located in increasingly more detailed investigations of the bodies of women. Although I recognize that such historical quests for origins can never reach their goals, I would like nevertheless to take the perhaps mythical "invention" of cinema as the first key moment in the history of the filmic hard core. During this protracted moment of invention, photographic machines par-ticipated in an intensification of what Comolli (1980, 122) calls the "field of the visible," as the direct human vision of events, places, and bodies began to be mediated by an optical apparatus that sees in place of the "naked eye" (p. 123).

Borrowing from Comolli, I call the visual, hard-core knowledge-pleasure produced by the *scientia sexualis* a "frenzy of the visible." Even though it sounds extreme, this frenzy is neither an aberration nor an excess; rather, it is a logical outcome of a variety of discourses of sexuality that converge in, and help further to produce, tech-nologies of the visible. Goldbarth's poem emphasizes the way in which hard-core, pornographic answers proceed from new "aca-demic questions" that can be asked in this intensified field of the vis-ible. As we shall see, the reverse can also be true: the very invention of cinema develops, to a certain extent, from the desire to place the clocked and measured bodies produced by the first machines into narratives that naturalize their movements: "two lovers/a basket/red wine." Thus, cinematic "implantation of perversions" in ever more visible filmic bodies and in the enhanced vision of spectators goes hand in hand with the developing pleasures of the medium.[3]

At issue here is not yet the appearance of the first hard-core films but instead an earlier moment when scientists first subjected the body's own movement to the mechanical eye of a camera that saw better than the human eye.[4] The most dramatic instance of the machine's greater accuracy of vision is that to which Goldbarth's poem refers, the famous question posed by Leland Stanford about the horse's motion during a fast trot: "Is there ever a moment when all four feet leave the ground?"

This story, now familiar in the annals of film history, has always seemed to illustrate a peculiarly American mixture of applied science, sportsmanship, and pleasure.[5] Leland Stanford, former governor of California, aficionado of popular science, and well-known horse breeder, had a hunch—one that ran contrary to all conventional artistic and scientific representations of trotting horses up to that time—that at a certain moment in the fast trot all four feet do leave the ground. In 1873, therefore, Stanford hired Eadweard Muybridge to photograph his prize trotter, Occident, in motion. A wager was supposedly made, and the newspapers made much of the entire undertaking.[6] Prior to this experiment so-called instantaneous photography (photography of brief instants of motion) had only managed exposures of one-tenth of a second, and then only of relatively slow movements. Not many details of Muybridge's first results are known except that he did manage to produce a single photograph—probably no more than a blurry silhouette—that proved, at least to Stanford's satisfaction, that all four feet *do* leave the ground.

By 1877 Muybridge and Stanford had succeeded in producing a series of photos that were clear enough to be published on the cover of *Scientific American* (Muybridge 1979, 1:xvii). The American public, which had first doubted the truth of Stanford's hunch, now had no choice but to believe the visual evidence thus presented. To further convince and educate, Muybridge began in that same year to give public lectures accompanied by projected slides of his motion sequences (Haas 1976, 116–120).

Audiences often laughed at the awkwardness of the now visible, intermediate stages of movement revealed by Muybridge's growing batteries of stop-action cameras. Intent on convincing audiences of the veracity of these movements even further, Muybridge next built a machine that could synthesize these photographic fragments back into an illusion of the motions from which they were originally taken. This apparatus, the zoopraxiscope, was nothing more than a magic lantern of zoetropic projection applied to sequences of instantaneous photographs taken at relatively close intervals. As such it was not a particularly novel invention, but the use of photographs of many intermediate positions of movement (rather than the succession of static drawings or photographic poses typical of other zoetropes) made all the difference in creating lifelike movement. Motion could now be stopped or slowed for analysis, reconstituted to prove its veracity, and endlessly repeated to the satisfaction of an amazed and delighted public.

By 1881 Muybridge was delighting and amazing popular and scientific audiences alike with lecture demonstrations of his remarkable prototype of the motion picture projector. The high point of his "show" was the moment when, after presenting various still slides of horses for purposes of analysis, he hand-cranked his zoopraxiscope to project short, larger-than-life motion sequences. As one reporter commented, "So perfect was the synthesis that a dog in the lecture room barked and endeavored to chase the phantom horses as they galloped across the screen" (Muybridge 1883, app. A).

These phantom horses were soon followed by phantom humans, who ran and turned somersaults to even greater admiration. The "frenzy of the visible" made possible by the proliferation of optical machines like Muybridge's zoopraxiscope had thus taken a quantum leap forward. But the crucial point is not so much that the new machine captured life—as its name implies—but rather, as Comolli notes, that the same principles of mechanical repetition that made possible industrial production had now made movement more visible. Movement itself had become a "visible mechanics" (Comolli 1980, 123).

We can isolate four factors that operated in this protocinematic will-to-knowledge of the body in movement: first, an increasing tendency to think of the body itself as a mechanism, as, for example, in physiologist Etienne Jules Marey's 1874 study of movement, *La machine animale* (Animal Mechanism); second, an accompanying doubt as to the ability of the human eye to observe accurately the mechanics of the body; third, the construction of better machines of observation to measure and record bodies now conceived themselves as machines; and fourth, an unanticipated pleasure attached to the visual spectacle of lifelike moving bodies. In other words, the specific and unprecedented cinematic pleasure of the illusion of bodily motion emerged partly as a by-product of the quest for the initially unseeable "truths" of this motion. At the origin of its invention, then, cinema is caught up in a technology that produces this body in its own image—as an infinitely repeatable mechanism.

So if Muybridge's first audiences came simply to learn the new truths of bodily motion, they stayed to see more because this new knowledge was also infused with an unsuspected visual pleasure. The appeal of seeing first horses and then humans trotting obligingly across the walls of his lecture hall was thus never purely scientific. In Muybridge's longer and more sustained examples of naked and nearly naked male and female bodies, we begin to see an illustration of Foucault's point that the power exerted over bodies *in* technology is rendered pleasurable *through* technology.

Muybridge's eleven-volume opus, *Animal Locomotion*, published in 1887 (reprint 1979 in 3 vols.), offers the most striking illustration of this osmosis of knowledge and pleasure. These volumes are a giant pictorial study of men, women, children, and animals performing, in a series of usually twelve to twenty-four instantaneous photographs, short tasks designed to elicit a wide range of movements. Naked and semi-naked men, for example, walk, run, jump, throw, catch, box, wrestle, and perform simple trades such as carpentry. While naked and semi-naked women perform many of these same tasks, in their activities and gestures we see how the greater sexuality already culturally encoded in the woman's body feeds into a new cinematic power exerted over her whole physical being. We see, in other words, how an unprecedented conjunction of pleasure and power "implants" a cinematic perversion of fetishism in the prototypical cinema's first halting steps toward narrative.

When the women perform the same activities as the men, these activities are often accompanied by some superfluous detail, such as the inexplicable raising of a hand to the mouth, which lends a mark of difference to the woman's motion as compared to the man's. If a woman runs, her run is marked by a similarly gratuitous gesture of grasping her breast. While the men go about their business rather like Occident, Stanford's trotter, simply performing the functions they do best, the physical business of the women is less clearly defined, and their self-consciousness in its performance is much greater; they blow kisses, narcissistically twirl about, endlessly flirt fans, and wear transparent drapery that emphasizes the nudity underneath.

Moreover, when the male movements require props, these props are always simple, such as a saw and some wood for carpentry. But when the women require props or tools, these are not only more numerous but often do not even serve the activity being illustrated. For example, when a woman lies down in a sequence that parallels a male series entitled "Lying Down," she does not just lie down: she lies down to read a newspaper, or she lies down to go to bed in a bed equipped with pillow, sheets, and blankets.

Again and again the woman's body appears to be embedded in a mise-en-scène that places her in a more specific imaginary place and time. This trait is especially apparent in the motion sequences showing two women together. The parallel here is to the male sequences of combat sports, but it would have been absurd to expect women of this period to engage in male sports. Muybridge therefore had to invent physically interactive activities for women; like the other female motion series, these inventions offer an additional visual element—in many cases by conjuring up an even greater sense of the scene of the interaction.

In one such scene, a woman pours a bucket of water over a woman seated in a basin. In another, a woman pours water from a large jug into the mouth of a second woman. In a third, most enigmatic scene, a woman leans against the chair of another woman who is smoking a cigarette. In this last instance Muybridge has abandoned movement altogether for the highly charged emotional tone of what could only be called longing.

Women's bodies are quite simply fetishized in these motion studies. There is nothing very startling in this observation, since women's bodies are fetishized in social existence as well. In this sense, Muybridge could simply be regarded as the faithful recorder of what John Berger has called the different "social presence" of men and women—the fact, as Berger (1977, 47) succinctly puts it, that *"men act* and *women appear.*" The transparent draperies, flirting fans, superfluous props, and narcissistic gestures of Muybridge's women could simply be viewed as part of Western art's long tradition of representing the nude woman.

If so, however, it is nevertheless striking how this ostensibly scientific discourse on the human body immediately elicits surplus aestheticism in the fetishization of its women subjects. There is something incongruous about the application of Muybridge's chronographic apparatus, with its batteries of cameras and measurement grids, to the increasingly fantastic scenes conjured up in the women's section of *Animal Locomotion*. This incongruity arises in part from the very impossibility of measuring the female body with apparati and grids that are more appropriate to the throwing of a baseball than to the "flirting" of a fan, to traditionally masculine, aggressive movements of propulsion than to traditionally feminine movements of twirling and self-touching. It is as if Muybridge could only represent the female body against the standards used to measure male movement and gesture. As a result, what began as the scientific impulse to record the "truth" of the body quickly became a powerful fantasy that drove cinema's first rudimentary achievements of narrative diegesis and mise-en-scène.

Muybridge's prehistoric cinema can thus allow us to observe that moment in the emergence of the cinematic apparatus when the unprecedented illusion of the filmic body acutely posed the problem of sexual difference to the male image maker and viewer. Psychoanalytic theory views fetishization of the female body as one kind of "perverse" solution to the problem of sexual difference. Although I will have more to say about perversions in general, and fetishization in particular, in later chapters, let me for the present propose a working psychoanalytic definition of the term that has considerable currency in film theory and criticism.

To Freud, fetishism is the process whereby a male viewer of female sexual difference "masters" the threat of castration posed by this difference through a compensatory investment in the fetish. Because the naked female body, when first seen by the little boy, seemed to "lack" a penis, the unconscious desire of the male who has recourse to fetishism is to disavow this "lack" by putting a fetish in its place. In Freud's formulation, the fetish (whatever it may be— a shoe, an undergarment, the woman herself) becomes the substitute for the phallus "which the little boy once believed in" and in which he still wants to believe (Freud [1927] 1963, 214).

In her influential article "Visual Pleasure and Narrative Cinema," feminist filmmaker and theorist Laura Mulvey (1975, 13) has argued that the sight of the female body, "displayed for the gaze and

enjoyment of men . . . always threatens to evoke the anxiety it originally signified." Cinema, to Mulvey, offers a dramatic re-posing of
this original threat to male visual pleasure. One typical cinematic
avenue of escape from the anxiety of castration is to disavow castration through the "substitution of a fetish object or turning the represented figure itself into a fetish so that it becomes reassuring
rather than dangerous (hence over-valuation, the cult of the female
star)" (pp. 13–14).

If we want to follow Mulvey (I will later suggest ways in which we
might want to diverge as well),[7] we could say that in Muybridge's
prototypical cinema, images of naked and transparently draped
women insist on their nakedness even as they disavow it. That is, if
Muybridge always gives us more of women to see—more of their
bodies, more of their gestures, and more objects to decorate or situate them in specific times and places—then this "more" could arise
from the male fear that their bodies are really less: that they pose the
terrifying threat of "lack." We could say, then, that the obsessive
gaze of Muybridge's apparatus on the naked female body attempts
to reassure itself in the very sight of this "lack" by the fetish-
substitutes that endow the woman with a surplus of erotic meaning.
By denying the woman-in-movement any existence apart from these
marks of difference, Muybridge himself could be said to have begun
the cinematic tradition of fetishization that exerts mastery over
difference.[8]

One problem with the above application of Mulvey's theory of fetishism to cinematic history is that it views the work of fetishization
as always the same: the icon of woman "*always* threatens to evoke
the anxiety it originally signified" (p. 13); cinema simply restages an
original oedipal scenario of castration. Yet even if we accept fetishization as one explanation for how this machine constructs the woman's body, it is immediately apparent that there are enormous differences between the fetishization of Freud's scenario of the little
boy's encounter with sexual difference in the body of his mother, of
Muybridge's protocinema, of the later classical narrative cinema discussed by Mulvey, and, as we shall see, of the cinematic hard core.

The example that Mulvey gives from classical cinema is the extremely fetishized body of Marlene Dietrich in the films of Josef
von Sternberg. Mulvey's claim is that fetishization works the same
for the fetishist as it does in the whole of narrative cinema: to place

the woman outside the (narrative) flow of action and event, flatten
the verisimilitude of the representation of woman, and turn her into
an icon (p. 12).

Quite the opposite is true of the fetishized female body in Muybridge. Here it is precisely verisimilitude of diegesis and incipient
narrative that are produced, as if as by-products of the woman's fetishization. Men's naked bodies appear natural in action: they act
and do; women's must be explained and situated: they act and appear in mini-dramas that perpetually circle about the question of
their femininity. In other words, in Muybridge's case fetishization
seems to *call* for narrative, not to retard it. What are we to make of
such a discrepancy and, by extension, of the explanatory power of
this perversion in general?

In Mulvey's oedipally driven scenario, the power of the woman is
already lost before the game of cinematic representation begins.
Her body exists only as a reminder of a power that once evoked the
threat of castration. In this sense, the fetishization helps to explain
why women have become icons who seem to stand outside cinema's
dominant narrative form. Mulvey's analysis thus assumes these perversions to be eternal even as it implies a historically new imple-
mentation of them by the cinema. In this formulation, male
pleasure-in-looking struggles against the displeasure of the threat of
castration in a static realm of iconicity that always constructs the image of the woman as an ultimately reassuring mirror of the man. Patriarchal power invariably wins; the struggle is over before it begins.
Power in this analysis is understood only as the narrative power of
action, of propulsive movements, a realm that already excludes the
woman. In both cases we observe the negative operation of a repressive and prohibitory power, but not the positive operation of a
power that feeds off of and constructs further pleasures.

Muybridge's motion studies may only appear to contradict Mulvey's notion that fetishization of the female body retards narrative:
if there is not yet a narrative, then the female body may act to promote it. The important point is that fetishization of the woman pro-
vokes a disturbance in the text—whether (as in Muybridge) to create
a narrative or (as in classical narrative) to retard it. Thus, while phallic concerns about the threat of castration could be at work in Muybridge, they are at work in a historically different and quite specific
way. The sexual difference of the female body frozen in movement

on the pages of *Animal Locomotion* and the screens of Muybridge's lecture halls offered a new kind of visual pleasure based in the photographic illusion of reality, a brand new "implantation of perversions."

What was new in the visual pleasure of looking at the fetishized female body was what Christian Metz (1977) refers to as the cinema's paradoxical combination of the illusion of reality with the radical physical absence of the object represented: its "imaginary signifier." Theorists like Metz in *The Imaginary Signifier* and Jean-Louis Baudry in his essay "The Apparatus" (1986a) have argued that the cinema's famous "impression of reality" derives not from some pure resemblance to reality but instead from the paradoxical absence in the image of a materially real object and the greater activation of sensual perception to see that which is not really there. Like dreams and hallucinations, cinema facilitates a temporary regression on the part of the viewing subject to a psychically earlier, pre-oedipal mode of merger in which the separation between body and world is not well defined and in which "representations"—whether of the unconscious or of the film—"are taken as perception" (Baudry 1986a, 314).

According to these psychoanalytic theories of cinema, the subject-effect of the apparatus tends toward a "hallucinatory psychosis of desire," in which archaic desires for an illusory unity and coherence are satisfied through the activation of what Metz (1977, 58) calls "the passion for perceiving." Metz thus describes the pleasures of cinema—again, apart from the specific signifieds represented in it—as marked particularly by higher degrees of voyeurism (unauthorized spying, the ability to be everywhere and to see all that is forbidden, hidden) and fetishism (defined here in a more structural sense as the conflict between undeniable perceptual knowledge and the belief that attempts to disavow that knowledge).

The problem with the descriptions by Metz and Baudry of the cinematic apparatus is the same noted already with regard to Mulvey. All three theorists assume that the desire for these visual pleasures is already inscribed in the subject. Baudry even goes so far as to trace the desire for cinema back to Plato's allegory of the cave. He suggests that even though Plato abhors the deception of the simulacrum, his remarkable anticipation of the apparatus represents a repressed desire for it. All these theorists assume the effect of the cinematic apparatus to be simply an enhancement of perverse desires that already exist in the subject.

But the example of Muybridge and the lesson of Foucault's "implantation of perversions" may suggest something quite different. The fetishization enacted in this originally scientific exploration of movement is historically quite new and inseparable from the unprecedented hallucinatory impression of reality encoded in the image of bodies produced by the machines. In this case the cinematic magnification and projection of human bodies would not simply restage the original scenario of castration (and the male "solutions" or escapes of fetishization and voyeurism) at the sight of female difference. Rather, it would produce a new kind of body, which viewers experience through this optical machine. The new, larger-than-life, projected film body is ideally visible; although on display for the viewer, it goes about its business as if unaware of being watched. The little scenarios providing opportunities for movement produce, in the case of the woman's body, a first step in the direction of narratives that will facilitate seeing her previously hidden further truths. At the origin of cinema, then, we have not only a psychic apparatus with a "passion for perceiving" and a technological apparatus that makes this perception possible; we have, as Comolli stresses, a social apparatus as well. And this social apparatus is ultimately what constructs women as the objects rather than the subjects of vision, for it is what places women in front of the camera and what determines the repertoire of activities in which they will engage.

At the moment of cinematic origin with which we are concerned, then, all three of these apparatuses—social, psychic, and technological—are working together to channel the scientific discovery of bodily motion into new forms of knowledge and pleasure. What I wish to stress in this origin, therefore, is not the eternal nature of the perverse pleasures of the apparatus, but their specific historical and social construction. If Muybridge's prototypical cinema became rather quickly, for the female bodies represented in it, a kind of pornographic girlie show that belied its more serious scientific pretensions, it is not because men are naturally voyeurs and fetishists and that these perverse pleasures overwhelmed science. Rather, science and perversion interpenetrated in the construction of cinematic discourse—and they could do so partly because within the social formation there were no women among the early audience of sportsmen-scientists in a position to say, "That's not the truth of my movement, that's an artist's model acting out his fantasy," or "Show me a man touching himself, I want to know more about him and his world." These alternatives may seem fanciful, but they are important to remember when we invoke psychoanalytic concepts to explain pleasures that seem built into the medium.

With the invention of cinema, in other words, fetishism and voyeurism gained new importance and normality through their link to the positivist quest for the truth of visible phenomena. No longer were they relatively rare sexual perversions practiced by certain men to overcome difficulties in sexual performance. Cinema implanted these perversions more firmly, normalizing them in technological and social "ways of seeing." As a result, viewers gradually came to expect that seeing human bodies in motion in the better way afforded by cinema would include these perverse pleasures as a matter of course.

All of which is to say that psychoanalysis itself should not be regarded as the key to understanding the cinematic apparatus; instead, like the cinema itself, it should be seen simply as another late-nineteenth-century discourse of sexuality, another apparatus for aligning socially produced sexual desires with oedipal and familial norms. Considered in this light, cinema and psychoanalysis are both historically determined—and determining—mechanisms of power and pleasure. The parallels and coincidences of the invention of both cinema and psychoanalysis are thus of interest as mutually reinforcing discourses of sexuality producing particular forms of knowledge and pleasure. Freud's theory of the fetish develops out of a particular way of seeing women as "lacking" that cinema participates in as well. Neither institution actually reflects the confessional truths they purport to record; rather, they *produce* these truths in their new forms of power and pleasure.

We have seen something of how this process works with respect to fetishization and the female filmic body. But perhaps an even more pertinent example lies in the relatively direct connection between early studies of hysteria—which formed the very basis of psychoanalysis—and the cinematic hard core. Foucault (1978) cites Charcot's pre-Freudian investigations into hysteria as evidence that psychoanalysis did not suddenly *discover* the unconscious sexual motives of human behavior; instead, he argues, these sexual motives were gradually *constructed* in a variety of scientific discourses that preceded and set the stage for Freud.

Charcot's medical-neurological study of hysteria is of special interest to Foucault. He calls Charcot's clinic, the Salpêtrière, an "enormous apparatus for observation, with its examinations, interrogations, and experiments"; but, he adds, it was also at the same time "a machinery for incitement," complete with public presentations and carefully staged theaters of ritual crises (p. 55). To Foucault, Charcot's staging and observation of the hysterical attack was important as a matter not only of sensation and pleasure but also "of truth and falsehood." Already for Charcot, and even though he would not directly speak its name, sex was a "problem of truth" (p. 56). A new construction of sex had begun.

Of special interest for our purposes is the photographic record that accompanied these stagings of sexual truth. The dates (1878–1881) of the *Iconographie photographique de la Salpêtrière* coincide with Muybridge's second series of horse photographs and the emergence into popular consciousness of the new truths of animal locomotion. Like *Animal Locomotion*, the *Iconographie* is a multivolume collection of "instantaneous" photographs of bodies in motion, mostly of women in the grips of convulsive attacks of hysteria. The very photographic techniques, in fact, are those developed by Muybridge.[9]

The influence worked both ways, however. In 1891 Muybridge included in *Animal Locomotion* a rather curious group of photographs of male and female subjects whose motions are abnormal owing to physical disabilities. Most striking among these photos is a motion sequence of an attractive naked woman with no visible disability who writhes on the floor in the throes of convulsion. Although we know from information provided in the introduction to the Dover reprint of this work that this woman was not a hysteric but a professional artist's model who had been asked to hold a position known to induce in her hysterialike convulsions (Muybridge 1979, 1:xxxii), the sequence is remarkable for its similarity to the convulsive gestures already produced at the Salpêtrière.

It would seem that Muybridge, whose equine studies technologically influenced Charcot's "iconographic" record of hysterics, was in turn influenced by Charcot's subject matter. In Muybridge's more detailed and extended protocinematic representation of a woman's involuntary convulsions, then, we begin to see the extent to which the filmic representation of bodies feeds and is fed by other technologies for producing (not simply recording) the "confessions" of a female body—a body that is increasingly regarded as saturated with sexuality. Thus, with this ability to induce and photograph a bodily confession of involuntary spasm, Muybridge's prototypical cinema arrives at the condition of possibility for cinematic hard core.

Hard Core

"Studying the horse, we understand / how hard-core followed the invention / of photography"—and studying Foucault, we begin to understand how a (cinematic) invention of photography is more than simply a technology for recording; it is part of the very will-to-knowledge/power of the *scientia sexualis*. We begin to see, for example, how this sexual science gives form to the "truths" that are confessed. For although the cinematic hard core will present itself as the unfaked, unstaged mechanics of sexual action, the representation of this movement is shaped—like Charcot's mise-en-scène of involuntary hysterical convulsion, like Freud's involuntary slips of the tongue and verbal associations, and like Muybridge's staging of a hysterical attack—by techniques of confession that are applied first and foremost to female bodies.

What, then, are the specific cinematic means of the drive for knowledge through confession in the prehistory of hard-core film? The German feminist art and film critic Gertrud Koch (forthcoming) suggests that all film pornography is a "drive for knowledge" that takes place through a voyeurism structured as a cognitive urge. Invoking Foucault, Koch argues that film pornography can be viewed as an important mechanism in the wholesale restructuring of the experience of sexuality into a visual form. According to Koch, for example, it is no accident that visual pornography has seen itself as contributing to sex research, sex education, and practical self-help guides, nor that the genre has consistently maintained certain clinical-documentary qualities at the expense of other forms of realism or artistry that might actually be more arousing. We might call this latter feature the principle of *maximum visibility*.

In the hard core proper, this principle has operated in different ways at different stages of the genre's history: to privilege close-ups of body parts over other shots; to overlight easily obscured genitals; to select sexual positions that show the most of bodies and organs; and, later, to create generic conventions, such as the variety of sexual "numbers" or the externally ejaculating penis—so important to the 1970s feature-length manifestations of the genre. The principle of maximum visibility operates in the hard-core film as though Muybridge's measurement grids were still in place, trying to gauge with increasing exactitude the genital equivalent of "at / which point in a leap the female breast / is highest."

The narrative cinema that eventually grows, via a prolonged stage of "primitivism," out of Muybridge's fetishization of the female body, then, channels and displaces an original male will-to-knowledge—the "academic question"—into so many games of peekaboo around this body. In contrast to both mainstream fictional narrative and soft-core indirection, hard core tries *not* to play peekaboo with either its male or its female bodies. It obsessively seeks knowledge, through a voyeuristic record of confessional, involuntary paroxysm, of the "thing" itself.

The irony, however, is that, while it is possible, in a certain limited and reductive way, to "represent" the physical pleasure of the male by showing erection and ejaculation, this maximum visibility proves elusive in the parallel confession of female sexual pleasure. Anatomically, female orgasm takes place, as both Dennis Giles (1977) and Yanne Lardeau (1978) have noted, in an "invisible place" that cannot be easily seen. As Koch (forthcoming) puts it, "the place where a woman is supposed to have a phallus and orgasm, is just as invisible as the phantom penis men search for. Naturalistic porn film's lack of expressiveness reaches of necessity, its limit literally 'ante portas,' before achieving its goal of viewing the secret place of a woman's pleasure."

The history of hard-core film could thus be summarized in part as the history of the various strategies devised to overcome this problem of invisibility within a regime that is, as Beverley Brown (1981, 10) has noted, an "erotic organization of visibility." For while a significant aspect of cinema's development as a narrative form accepts and even cultivates, in the "masquerade of femininity," a range of fetish substitutes for the visible truth of women's sexual difference, hard core is the one film genre that always tries to strip this

mask away and see the visible "truth" of sexual pleasure itself. Since
the genre must keep close to the documentary evidence of this
truth, it has habitually resisted narrative elaboration, complex plots,
character development, and so forth. Even in its more recent
feature-length, narrative incarnation, hard core has remained, as we
shall see, a relatively episodic form.

Thus, whereas in classical narrative cinema fetishization of the
woman's body may solve the problem of sexual difference for the
male, in hard core this same masquerade remains a serious imped-
iment to the goal of making visible the involuntary confession of
bodily pleasure. The self-conscious control and surveillance normally exercised by the "properly" socialized woman over her appearance, and so evident in the soft-core "turn on," is precisely what
the hard core wants to circumvent. Hard core desires assurance that
it is witnessing not the voluntary performance of feminine pleasure,
but its involuntary confession. The woman's ability to fake the orgasm that the man can never fake (at least according to certain standards of evidence) seems to be at the root of all the genre's attempts
to solicit what it can never be sure of: the out-of-control confession
of pleasure, a hard-core "frenzy of the visible."

The animating male fantasy of hard-core cinema might therefore
be described as the (impossible) attempt to capture visually this
frenzy of the visible in a female body whose orgasmic excitement
can never be objectively measured. It is not surprising, then, that
so much early hard-core fantasy revolves around situations in which
the woman's sexual pleasure is elicited involuntarily, often against
her will, in scenarios of rape or ravishment. In these scenarios the
unwilling victim's eventual manifestations of pleasure are offered as
the genre's proof of a sincerity that under other conditions might
seem less sure.

Hence, the many devices employed to elicit the involuntary
confession of female pleasure may in fact be nothing but attempts
to argue, as fetishistic disavowal also argues, for the fundamental
sameness of male and female pleasure. In Charcot's mise-en-scène
of female bodies in the grips of hysteria, male-derived patterns of
pleasure were imposed on female bodies. As Stephen Heath (1982,
37) has noted, Charcot's running commentary on the "passionate attitudes" recorded in the photographic record of the hysterical attack
is arranged in narrative succession: "'threat,' 'appeal,' 'amorous sup-

plication,' 'eroticism,' 'ecstasy.' " The very terms suggest nothing so much as the standard, hard-core depiction of the progression to climax ending in male orgasm. As in most pornography, the woman's body is solicited, questioned, and probed for secrets that are best revealed when she herself is not in control.

In Charcot we can see to what extent the scientific will-to-knowledge of the female body is already intersected by the solicitation of a pleasurable and prurient show. But we should not forget that the reverse is also true: the emerging visual pleasures of the late-nineteenth-century frenzy of the visible remain wedded to the scientific will-to-knowledge. The next step in American cinematic prehistory extends from motion study to the point at which the motion picture camera (Kinetograph) and projection machine (the peephole viewing Kinetoscope) are in place and ready to give viewers pleasure for the money they drop in the slot. Here, in this more fully "invented" form of cinema, we see a new mix of scientific will-to-knowledge and prurient show.

Fred Ott's Sneeze is an Edison Laboratory test film from 1893–1894, manufactured for, but never actually projected in, the Kinetoscope. This short film of a sneeze has been much discussed by cinema historians for its long list of putative firsts: Edison's first film; the first film to use an actor; and the first cinematic close-up. Gordon Hendricks (1972, 90–95), however, has shown that the film strip is actually none of these things, though it remains important for its position midway between Muybridgean prehistoric motion study and the primitive cinema's more overt goal of mass-producing short segments of visual pleasure.

Fred Ott's Sneeze was made just when Edison had lost his initial enthusiasm for the kinetograph, when he learned that the technical limits of short strips of film and imperfect sound synchronization rendered his dream of recording opera and full-length plays unfeasible. With these grandiose plans shattered, Edison was temporarily at a loss for what to record with his new invention. Early tests of the Kinetograph involved such dull subjects as inventor W. K. L. Dickson removing his hat and bowing (1891), or the crude physical antics of lab employees (the so-called Monkeyshines of 1890). The *Sneeze* was produced between these early tests and the later (1894 and after) films produced for actual distribution to Kinetoscope parlors (typically novelty acts of female dancers, Sandow the Strongman, restaged prize fights, famous moments from well-known plays, American Indian dances, and the like).

The story goes that the *Sneeze* was made at the request of Barnet Phillips, an enterprising reporter for *Harper's Weekly* who had visited Edison's West Orange laboratory to see the newly invented Kinetoscope. Unimpressed by the dull subjects filmed previously, Phillips wrote to Edison proposing something more exciting. "Might I then ask if you would not kindly have some nice looking young person perform a sneeze for the Kinetograph?" In a subsequent letter Phillips stated more clearly that he wanted to see a woman "in the act of sneezing" (Hendricks 1972, 91).

Edison could not refuse a journalist so willing to help promote the about-to-be-manufactured Kinetoscope in the pages of a popular magazine. The sneeze was duly made at a total length of eighty-one frames—far too short to have actually been projected in a Kinetoscope. Nevertheless, it was sent to *Harper's* not as a strip of film but mounted side-by-side on paper, much the way Muybridge's photos were printed in *Animal Locomotion*.

Phillips's article "Record of a Sneeze" accompanies the photos. In it Phillips falsely represents the film as an actual kinetoscopic projection, as though he had in fact seen it through such a machine. He then offers a semicomic explanation of the physiology of sneezing, followed by tidbits of sneeze lore, a plug for the new Kinetoscope ("The illusion is so perfect that you involuntarily say, Bless You!"), and a breakdown and analysis of the "minutiae" of the ten stages of "this curious gamut of grimace"—stages that before this invention had remained in what Phillips calls the realm of the "partially unseen" (Hendricks 1972, 92, 93).

If we recall that Phillips's original choice for this experiment was not the mustachioed Fred Ott, the Edison lab assistant chosen out of mere convenience, but a pretty young woman who would have lent prurient interest to the involuntary comic action of a sneeze, then we begin to see the importance of this single-shot, close-up "film." In short, the *Sneeze* stands as a marker in the trajectory between the prehistoric scientific motion studies of Muybridge and the sensationalist later spectacles that were to mark the more advanced stages of the primitive cinema and the primitive hard core. From the *Sneeze* and *The Kiss* (Edison, 1896)—the famous close-up of the John Rice–May Irwin smooch borrowed from a much longer stage play[10]—all the way to such relatively complex multiple-shot films as *The Gay Shoe Clerk* (Porter, 1903), with its illicit shot of the female customer's foot and ankle, one intractable direction of cinematic narrative evolution follows the pleasure of seeing previously hidden parts, or motions, of the woman's body.

Yet, as suggested above, it may be more important to recognize how thoroughly scientism and prurience interpenetrate. There is remarkably little difference, for example, between the scientific analysis of the "gamut of grimace" in the sneeze into such elements as "nascent sensation" and "expectancy," culminating in "beatitude . . . oblivion . . . explosion," and the breakdown by Heath of Charcot's hysterics into a list of emotions that ends in "ecstasy." In both, science and spectacle impel each other according to the principle of maximum visibility. The ability to see and name each stage of processes that were previously "partially unseen" fuels the reformulation of this knowledge as pleasure, and of this pleasure as knowledge. From Charcot to Muybridge, from Freud to Edison, and from these theorists and technicians of pleasure to the hard core itself, each new formulation of a *scientia sexualis* proceeds by soliciting further confessions of the hidden secrets of female pleasure.

In each case, however, the confession of pleasure is organized according to male norms that fail to recognize—or perhaps to imagine—difference. The more the male investigator probes the mysteries of female sexuality to capture the single moment revealing the secret of her mechanism (as he once tried to capture the moment of truth in a horse's fast trot), the more he succeeds only in reproducing the woman's pleasure based on the model, and measured against the standard, of his own.

This much is constant in male discourses of sexuality, ranging from Hesiod's story of the argument between Zeus and Hera over who derives the greatest pleasure from sex[11] to "Les bijoux indiscrets," *My Secret Life, Fanny Hill*, Masters and Johnson, and *Deep Throat*. There is thus a paradoxical sense in which all of these confessions, and especially those caught up in the modern frenzy of the visible, have been blind to the very difference they so assiduously investigate.

In *Speculum of the Other Woman*, in an essay eloquently called "Blind Spot of an Old Dream of Symmetry," French feminist psychoanalyst Luce Irigaray refers to Freud's particular manifestation

of this phallic blindness. In Freud, and especially in his theory of the
fetish, woman's sexual difference is derived from an a priori assumption of her sameness to man: man has the phallus, woman is
defined conversely as absence or lack; man is clearly representable,
woman is the "dark continent," a "nothing to see" (Irigaray 1986,
46–49). In view of the present discussion of late-nineteenth-
century discourses of sexuality, we might borrow Irigaray's terms to
say that each of these discourses provides the man with a "speculum" that only confirms the "truth" of his own sexual identity. All
the man sees is a difference of degree (female sexual pleasure as
measured against the standard of the phallus and the single male
orgasm) rather than kind (female sexual pleasure as its own standard). As the word *speculum* itself suggests, the scientific instrument with which the man's analytic eye tries to penetrate the woman's body—"to see," as Irigaray notes, "with speculative intent"—
defeats this investigation, for inevitably it mirrors only the man himself. "Woman, having been misinterpreted, forgotten, variously frozen in show cases, rolled up in metaphors, buried beneath carefully
stylized figures, raised up in different idealities, would now become
the 'object' to be investigated." As we have seen with respect to hard
core, the cinematic speculum that tracks down what can be *seen* of
female sexuality encounters an optical failure in the "hole," or
"lack," of the female genitalia, which are so hidden that they seem
like "nothing to see." In the end, in Irigaray's utopian formulation,
"the transcendental keeps its secret" and the phallus is left staring
at its own reflection (pp. 144–145).

Although Irigaray intends her discussion of the speculum metaphorically, as the "blind spot" of Western metaphysics and its phallic visual economy, her metaphor has near-literal application to the
camera of prehistoric, primitive, and hard-core pornography. Like
the scientific, gynecological speculum, this camera probes the hidden secrets of the female body and female pleasure; and like the
mirror-speculum, it ends up staring at its own reflection, frustrated
in the "nothing to see" of woman. Irigaray's major point, of course,
is that Western metaphysics has always been blind to the "other" of
woman. She too, like Foucault and Baudry, goes back to the
Greeks—in this case to Plato's allegory of the cave, which Baudry
saw as so similar to the cinematic and hallucinatory "impression of
reality." But where Foucault stresses the discontinuity between the

Greek use of pleasure and our own—between an *ars erotica* and a *scientia sexualis*—Irigaray, like Baudry, stresses continuity. Arguing that a specular, visual organization of reality has existed in Western culture from its very beginnings with the Greeks, she thus aligns Freud and Plato much as Baudry does—though in her case the reason is to emphasize the blindness of both discourses to the difference of women.

If Baudry's ahistoricism allows us to see the Western metaphysical dream of a return to hallucinatory "representations taken as perception," Irigaray's ahistoricism allows us to see that Western metaphysics is founded on a blindness to woman's difference. Yet it is important to note that her notion of the speculum encompasses not only the idea of a masculine instrument of knowledge that probes woman's "truth," but also the utopian projection of an *other* truth that reflects female difference in a positive way. Though blatantly essentialist and grounded in the determinations of a different female biology, such ideas are important, notwithstanding, as a starting place for the articulation of female differences that are *not* based on male norms.

Moreover, if Irigaray shows us the blindness of Western metaphysics to difference, Foucault allows us to see the historical variations that nevertheless obtain within the diverse stages of this metaphysics. Thus, both the essentialist and the anti-essentialist perspectives prove useful. Irigaray, for example, can remind us that Baudry's interpretation of Plato's dream of the cinema excludes women as the dreamers, and that Foucault's emphasis on historical discontinuity and difference fundamentally elides sexual difference itself. But Foucault, in turn, can remind us that since we are all, men and women both, constructed within these proliferating discourses of sexuality, we should pay close attention to how they have constructed us in order that we may deconstruct them.

To return to the question of origins with which this chapter began, we can perhaps conclude in two ways. On the one hand, we can say with Irigaray, and possibly with some members of the feminist anti-pornography movement as well, that as long as women find it necessary to argue about power or pleasure entirely on male (phallogocentric) terms, they will lose; whatever is distinctive and "authentic" in their own power and pleasure will be interpreted negatively and to their disadvantage. In this sense there is not much difference between literary confessions (written by men but often focused on women) of female pleasure *for women* and the more direct and graphic confession of pleasure by women's bodies in hard core.[12] Both are examples of men speaking about women's sex to other men; both want to know more about the pleasure of women; both see this pleasure as excessive; both see it as opposed to power.

On the other hand, we can say with Foucault, and with most anti-censorship feminists, that there are important differences to be noted in the uses of pleasure from one society to another and one technology to another. Indeed, the particular interpenetration of power and pleasure can be extremely important in the local attempt to resist or counter the oppressive effects of each. Just as power exists as a multiplicity of force relations rather than a single force, state, or individual, so resistance to power is a "multiplicity of points of resistance" (Foucault 1978, 95).

The value of this plural conceptualization of power, pleasure, and resistance lies in its potential to prevent the feminist critique of patriarchy from succumbing to the same imposition of a unitary norm as the phallogocentrism being criticized. It also suggests that resistance can begin anywhere, wherever this power is felt to be oppressive. There is a danger, however, in thus reconceptualizing a previously unitary and static concept of sexual identity: namely, the decentering involved could cause women to lose the gender identification that most effectively recognizes our experience of oppression and provides the most dramatic impetus to resist.[13] Women's resistance must therefore continue to rely on the fiction of the unity "woman" insofar as oppression continues to make that unity felt. But women must also be flexible enough to locate their own empowering points of resistance within discursive practices that are no longer taken as essential truths. This is the lesson of the "origins" of cinema and of porno. These origins are not inevitable; all they show is that seeing from the single perspective of the phallus and the male orgasm is not to see woman at all but to see only, as Irigaray tells us, the one and the same of man against the more or the less of woman.

In this chapter we have seen how the intensification and "frenzy" of the visible begins, in the late-nineteenth-century invention of "machines of the visible," to create even more peculiar forms of blindness. At the same time, we have found that this very blindness, this inability to make the invisible pleasure of woman manifestly visible and quantifiable, is the hard-core text's most vulnerable point of contradiction and the place where feminists who would resist a monolithic, masculine, hard-core discourse of sexuality can seek the power of resistance. It is in the spirit of this resistance that I undertake the following examination of the various manifestations of the genre.

3

The Stag Film

Genital Show and Genital Event

The stag film or dirty movie was, and is, the cinéma
vérité *of the forbidden, an invaluable record of the
images openly unacknowledged feelings about sex
assume. In a time when verbal and visual images of
sex were suppressed, when open art could only
euphemize, the stags documented those isolated and
unmentionable private experiences which were
nonetheless in some form universal. By sharing the
mysteries of sexual data through collective rituals of
masculine emergence, American and European males
(primarily the former) received through the stags a
non-credit course in sex education. The films proved
that a world of sexuality existed outside one's limited
individual experiences. Here were real people and
real sexual activity made all the more real because
their esthetic embodiment was so weak, the
"performers" so clearly not "actors."*

Al Di Lauro and Gerald Rabkin,
Dirty Movies

In their amply illustrated history of the stag film, *Dirty Movies*, Al
Di Lauro and Gerald Rabkin (1976) offer a nostalgic appreciation of
a now mostly defunct form of hard-core film. Writing in the mid-
seventies, when the feature-length, legitimate, X-rated "porno"
had dramatically supplanted the silent, one-reel, illegally made and
exhibited stag, Di Lauro and Rabkin wished to pay homage to a
body of films that were part of a ritual folk tradition of the American
male. Concerned that the newer, more sophisticated feature-length
porno, equipped with sound, color, and name "stars," could not contribute as the stag film had to the social bonding and camaraderie of
a once exclusively male audience, they contrasted the silent ab-
sorption of today's spectators to the raucous, collective sexual banter
and bravado characteristic of stag "smoker" audiences of yesteryear
(p. 25).

To the aesthetic judgment that there was too little art in such films Di Lauro and Rabkin answer that the very crudeness, the raw "reality" of the form—the absence, for example, of sound or professional actors—was a crucial value to audiences whose primary concern was to be instructed about the hidden mechanisms of sexual functioning. Titles such as *Wonders of the Unseen World* (1927) aptly express this graphic revelation of the roles of bodies and organs that were often difficult to see in the backseat of a car (p. 55). To the feminist criticism that the values of such films are the same exclusively male ones that have contributed to the historical degradation and subjugation of women Di Lauro and Rabkin answer that the male performers in these films are objectified too, indeed, that "they are even less 'humanized' than the women, who are, after all, the focus of attention" (p. 26). These men, they say,

exist only as surrogates for the male audience. They are the means whereby the individual fantasist possesses his lust's desire, an image idealized as often as it is demeaned. To say that both men and women are degraded equally because of the specialization of their performance seems as sensible as claiming that clowns, acrobats, or ball players are degraded because as performers they are not visible in their full humanity.

(pp. 26–27)

This defense of pornography sounds familiar. Like most such defenses, it ignores the larger power structure in which the presumably equalized dehumanization and objectification occur. In particular, it ignores the power implied in the films' predominant address to men. The male performers in these films may be surrogates for the male viewers (we will examine this notion more closely below), but if they are, it is because male subjectivity is dominant. The female "wonders of the unseen world" may be celebrated and exalted in some stag films, but they are always viewed, as Luce Irigaray would put it, from the point of view of the phallus.

In arguing that women are not unduly objectified in stag films because they are the films' real subjects, Di Lauro and Rabkin play fast and loose with a crucial difference between subject matter and subjectivity. As art critic John Berger (1977, 54) has said of the long tradition in European art of oil paintings of nudes, the principal protagonist (the real subject) of these paintings never even appears on the canvas: "He is the spectator in front of the picture and he is pre-

sumed to be a man. . . . It is for him that the figures have assumed
their nudity." Berger's point applies even more emphatically to the
"nudes" of the stag film and to the private screenings from which
women viewers were rigorously excluded.

My goal in this chapter is thus to begin where Di Lauro and Rabkin begin, with descriptions of the primitive nature of these texts,
with observations about the ritual, group character of their reception, and, finally, with comments on the nature and meaning of the
pleasures represented. But I do so in a different spirit and with a
different aim: not to reminisce nostalgically about a lost golden age
of simpler pleasures and closer male bonds, but to explore the
deeper questions of subject and subjectivity that these earlier critics
so blithely dismiss.

The films I describe were all viewed at the Kinsey Institute for
Sex Research in Sex, Gender, and Reproduction on either 16 or 8
mm film. Although I did look at some of the "classics" of the genre
(that is, films that have been anthologized in histories of the genre
or written about in the few existing critical studies of the genre),[1] I
also viewed titles at random. Many of the films I wanted to see
proved to be in a state of such decay that they could not be projected. What I saw represents only the smallest fraction of a collection of twelve hundred classic stag films; they have been assigned
approximate dates by the Kinsey Institute, many of which are
merely guesses, since these illegally made and distributed films
have no copyright or real credits.

Primitivism

Stag films are, in a word, primitive. To a film scholar they can be fascinating for their preservation of primitive styles and modes of address that departed from the legitimate cinema long before the arrival of sound. The most obvious primitive qualities of stag films are
short length, usually filling a single reel (a thousand feet, up to fifteen minutes) or less; silence and lack of color; and frequent lack of
narrative coherence, thus resembling films of the actual primitive
era (roughly 1896–1911). Stag films remained primitive in these
ways long after the legitimate primitive films had developed into
feature-length sound narratives. Contrary to what would be ex-

pected, moreover, the earliest stag films are often technically and narratively more accomplished than the later ones.

Let me give an initial sense of this primitivism by describing three of the earliest films in the Kinsey collection. *Am Abend* (Germany, ca. 1910) is a ten-minute film that begins with a man looking through a keyhole. The next shot shows a woman masturbating alone in a bedroom, framed by the keyhole. In the next shot the man enters the room and removes his clothes. The man and woman then join in a number of discontinuous sexual positions: "straight sex" (penetration with the man on top), fellatio, more masturbation by the woman, penetration from the rear. The hard-core action is viewed alternately in a full master shot of the couple on the bed and in inserted close-ups for detail. Some shots succeed more than others at clearly showing the genital action, which consists, except for fellatio, entirely of penetration.

Another early film, *El satario* (Argentina, ca. 1907–1912), offers a more elaborate, outdoor setting and several different scenes. Several women go bathing in a river at the edge of a jungle. They frolic in the water in long shot and stroke one another a little. Back on the bank they hold hands and dance in a circle. A devil with horns, tail, and false whiskers emerges from the foliage and chases the women until he captures one of them and abducts her to a meadow. An abrupt cut seems to place the "couple" in a darker setting and in a tighter frame. First we see the woman fellate the devil and climb onto him in the 69 position. Then, in a longer shot, the devil is on top. Each new shot is of a different position, some showing close views of genitals, some whole body shots. At the end the woman climbs off the devil and a wad of ejaculate drips out of her. They sleep in the meadow until awakened by the other women; the devil runs away, and the other women crowd around the one who was abducted.

A third film, the earliest American stag film in the Kinsey collection, is narratively more complex than the others. Entitled *A Free Ride* (also known as *A Grass Sandwich*), it employs credits, title cards with dialogue or commentary on the action, outdoor scenes, and fairly elaborate editing. Yet it, too, is primitive. Although the Kinsey Institute dates it circa 1917–1919, Di Lauro and Rabkin (1976, 47) and filmmaker Alex de Renzy, in his anthology film *A His-*

tory of the Blue Movie (1970), date it at 1915. Both these sources refer to it as the earliest extant American stag, but this seems doubtful.

After the title card the credits appear, employing crude humor that is typical of American stags from this and later eras: "Directed by A. WISE GUY / Photographed by WILL B. HARD / Titles by WILL SHE." A man in a sporty convertible picks up two women for a drive in the country. He stops in the woods to urinate. The women follow to sneak a look at him. A close-up shows his hand and penis. The two women begin to fondle themselves, and a title card has one of them say, "Oh, isn't he wonderful!" When the man returns, the women go to relieve themselves as well. As they squat we see the man spying on them and fondling himself. A title card interjects his comment, "Oh, Baby," whereupon another comments on the ensuing action: "When youth meets youth, a party is on." The "party" shows the still-dressed threesome fondling one another and the two women vying for the man's attention. The first woman pulls out the man's still-limp penis, the man pulls up her dress. The second woman says, "Please give me a little," and then gets on her knees and presents her naked buttocks to the man.

At this point the print I viewed shows a naked woman performing fellatio on a naked man in an indeterminate setting. The man plays with the woman's breast while mugging directly at the camera. Suddenly a foot (whose?) strokes a penis (whose?) in close-up; a hand taps the penis, and it ejaculates onto the foot. A woman rubs the ejaculate on her breasts. Then, in an indoor setting, a woman performs fellatio in close-up on a bed, then sits on the penis with her back to the man. The woman moves up and down, and we see the shaft of the penis repeatedly appear and disappear. Another close-up of penetration shows the woman's buttocks elevated by a pillow as the penis goes slowly in and out. An intertitle informs us that "a little cold cream does a lot of good sometimes," and the woman applies some. A final scene shows the couple copulating while standing and gyrating in a circle. The rhythms of the gyration grow slower, and finally stop.

Up until the actions described in the last paragraph, the film proceeds along a continuous, though crude, narrative line. At the point of the hard-core action itself, however, something strange occurs: the events that begin with the close-up of fellatio and end with the standing gyration are borrowed from the ending of a much later (1924) stag film, *The Casting Couch*. How the end of a 1924 film came to replace that of a film produced in the teens I cannot say. Nor can I say where the other hard-core sequences come from. While it is usual for later stag films to borrow footage from earlier ones, the reverse remains an anomaly—though one perhaps suggestive of the chaos that reigns in a genre with no copyright, no dates, and no acknowledged authorship. Most likely this quirk is limited to the particular print I viewed, since Di Lauro and Rabkin, who discuss *The Casting Couch*, make no mention of it.

Nevertheless, the haphazard stringing together of explicit hard-core scenes in this print can stand as an extreme example of the radical narrative discontinuity that often occurs in the sex sequences of stag films. Indeed, it suggests a need to clarify Di Lauro and Rabkin's observation that stag films are technically indistinguishable from other silent one-reelers. For even if the print had ended more typically, with hard-core genital action occurring between the original partners in a time and space narratively consistent with earlier events—as occurs, for example, in *The Casting Couch* itself, and perhaps even in other prints of *A Free Ride*—there would still be no mistaking the shift in the hard-core sequences to more primitive modes of cinematic representation.

The rule seems to be this: narratives that are already rudimentary become truly primitive during their hard-core sequences. Primitive cinema is usually characterized as ranging from the earliest films made, in which a fascination with cinematic movement for movement's sake was paramount, to the more ambitious but often only "minimally intelligible" attempts at narrative (Bordwell, Staiger, and Thompson 1985, 174) that continued into the early teens. Though actually belonging to cinematic prehistory, *Fred Ott's Sneeze* (Edison, 1894; see Chapter 2) is typical of the early stage of primitivism: films that are intelligible but not narrative, showing such things as dancing women, flexing strongmen, restaged boxing matches, the electrocution of an elephant, travelogues, natural disasters, and street scenes. An oft-cited example of primitivism's minimal narrative intelligibility is *Tom, Tom, the Piper's Son* (American Mutoscope and Biograph Company, 1905) in which a series of single-shot tableaux are combined into a sequence concerning the theft of a pig and the ensuing chase of the thief. The film's primitiveness consists in its inability to incorporate the close-ups of which cinema was technically capable (cf. *Fred Ott's Sneeze*) into the cause-effect structure of the pig theft. Thus the theft itself and many of the events of the ensuing chase are incomprehensible to today's viewers. The films offers a flurry of movement for movement's sake that neither focuses or centers its events nor resolves in a cinematically structured climax and denouement.

All three of the stag films described above take a step beyond the primitivism of the *Sneeze* and *Tom, Tom*. Especially in their preliminary sequences, before the hard-core action begins, each demonstrates a mastery of the art of rudimentary narration. In Kristin Thompson's terms, this means the narrative is told implicitly through the systematic combination of film devices building one on another (Bordwell, Staiger, and Thompson 1985, 174). In *Am Abend* and *A Free Ride* (and to a lesser extent in *El satario*, which does not actually show spyer and spied-upon separately), voyeur-characters within the narrative catch glimpses of normally hidden body parts of the opposite sex. Then the film viewer sees what the voyeur sees: the woman through the keyhole masturbating; the man urinating. As this vision leads to the looking character's arousal, the hard-core action ensues in turn. Thompson quotes a 1913 scenario guidebook offering advice to filmmakers on how to achieve cinematic unity, the elements of which comprehend, "first, 'cause' or beginning; secondly, development; third, crisis; fourth, climax or effect; fifth, denouement or sequence." By the early teens, she notes, the cinema had replaced crowded and confusing primitive frenzies of movement for movement's sake with a compressed set of linear causes and effects of this type (Bordwell, Staiger, and Thompson 1985, 175).

All three of the films would seem to have mastered the narrative progression through cause and effect up until they arrive at the quite literal "crisis" and "climax" of their hard-core sequences. Yet since crisis and climax and frenzies of movement are what the hard-core film is fundamentally about, and since the hard-core sequences occupy most of the typically ten to fifteen minutes of screen time, we would do well to examine the primitive nature of these sequences more carefully.

As we have seen, in the hard-core parts of these early stags a crude but relatively linear focused narrative gives way to the minimal legibility of primitivism. But this primitivism is not unfocused in the manner of *Tom, Tom, the Piper's Son*. Not only does it center and fix the genital details of the sexual couplings that constitute its primary action, but it does so obsessively and repetitively—though without also providing temporal continuity. It is as if, having mastered the limited degree of narrative technique necessary to bring the hard-core genital action into focus for the spectator, the stag film was then content to offer up these details as so many discontinuous spectacles, each separate shot being, we are to infer, a good enough show in itself.[2]

In his pamphlet *Correction Please—or How We Got into Pictures* (n.d.), Noël Burch emphasizes that filmic primitivism is not simply an absence of narrative but the presence of many forms of visual pleasure that preexisted the relatively focused and delimited narrative pleasure of more recent film.[3] Burch (p. 8) emphasizes the multitude of ways in which spectators "got into" the spatial and temporal fictions of film narrative by identifying with the closer, penetrating look of the camera and the logic that pieces together isolated fragments of space and time into narrative sequence and diegetic unity. This logic was not just a matter of centering the narrative images; the spectator, too, had to be metaphorically centered within the illusory world created out of an assemblage of shots. The illusion of a single space-time continuum and of the spectator as a unified subject of vision who moves from one vantage point to another within that continuum is created by the many converging codes of representation: linear perspective, camera ubiquity, camera movement, eyeline matching, continuity editing, and so on (Burch n.d., 3, 10).

Burch cites Edwin S. Porter's *The Gay Shoe Clerk* (Edison, 1903) as an example of a primitive film that has learned how to bring the spectator into its diegesis at the crucial moment of action. This film is composed of a static long shot taken from the hypothetical front row of the theater (as if through the missing fourth wall of a shoe store). A clerk is tidying up, when two women enter. The younger woman seats herself before the clerk as the older woman's attention wanders. When the clerk begins to try a shoe on the young woman, the master long shot is replaced by an "insert" close-up of her foot and ankle showing the clerk's hands fondling the foot. As the shot continues the woman's full-length skirt rises, and the audience gets a good view of her stockinged calf. Returning to the original long shot, we see the rest of the action: the clerk, apparently aroused by the sight and touch of her calf, kisses the young woman; the older woman finally notices and begins beating him on the head with her umbrella.

The Gay Shoe Clerk represents an advanced form of primitivism; not only does it bring the spectator into the story at the critical moment, but it also allows the spectator to "cop a glance," just as the clerk "cops a feel," of the previously hidden part of the woman's body. Nonetheless, this relatively advanced structuring of the camera's look at narrative events does not fully permit the viewer's penetration of scenic space that so characterizes the more seamless web of classical narrative cinema. As Burch (p. 8) points out, the "originating frontality" of the long shot of the stage set "leaves its mark on this system." Because the inserted close-up of the woman's leg and foot maintains the "originating frontality" of the master shot, it necessarily fails to show what the shoe clerk sees from his own, above-the-foot point of view; instead it constitutes an inset of the master shot, preserving the viewpoint only of the theater audience.[4]

The Gay Shoe Clerk is a fairly accomplished example of a category of "voyeur" films that flourished during the primitive period. Many of the earliest such films employed some sort of optical device to motivate what amounted to the first truly narrative use of close-ups in the cinema. Barry Salt (1978, 150) notes, for example, three early films that used this technique to dissect their scenes—that is, to break down the single master shot into fragments of space. *Grandma's Reading Glass* (1900), *As Seen Through a Telescope* (1900), and *Scenes on Every Floor* (1902), all by G. A. Smith, employed a reading glass, a telescope, and a keyhole, respectively, to motivate close-ups through the specific points of view of the films' rudimentary "characters"—the only instances of scene dissection occurring in this early period.

In these early primitive films, the force behind the shift to close-up is often, as in the *The Gay Shoe Clerk*, the desire to see more of the female body in detail. For instance, *One Way of Taking a Girl's Picture* (a.k.a. *The Picture the Photographer Took*, AM&B, 1904) begins with a single camera setup of a photographer taking pictures of a partly disrobed model in his studio; the film's final shot, however, consists of a close-up of the model that is meant to be seen as the photographer's own still photo. Another similar film is interesting for its representation of the female object's resistance to the optical device. In *A Subject for the Rogues Gallery* (a.k.a. *Photographing a Female Crook*, AM&B, 1904), a woman is brought into a station house to have her mug shot taken. As the still camera takes her picture, the motion picture camera dollies in for a close-up; at this point the woman begins to grimace wildly, making her face quite unrecognizable and thus resisting the camera's penetration of her space.[5]

Although the voyeur films were among the first to permit spectators to penetrate the image, or as Burch puts it, to "get into" the picture, primitive modes of representation still put limits on that penetration. Endings were particularly problematic, often consisting of the simple continuation of either the look at the body or, as in *The Gay Shoe Clerk*, the punishment for having obtained the look—until the camera ran out of film. In *A Subject for the Rogues Gallery*, some prints include a remarkable moment in which the grimacing and then crying woman, apparently thinking that her role in the film is over, resumes a more normal, relaxed expression and then smiles; more typical is the case in the otherwise advanced *Gay Shoe Clerk*, in which the prolonged final punishment of the clerk has no real closure. As Burch (n.d., 14) writes, using language particularly suggestive of the issues of primitivism as they relate to the stag film,

It took over ten years to develop the science of the "true" ending as we know it, that "rounding off" which produces for us the impression of natural completion rather than brutal, arbitrary interruption, which allows the spectator to *withdraw satisfied*, with the sense that there is no more left to see, that the film and its world have done with him and he with it.

The stag films described above can thus be said to be primitive not in the strict sense of *Tom, Tom, the Piper's Son*, but in the more advanced sense of *The Gay Shoe Clerk* or the scenically "dissected" voyeur films. They offer a limited mastery of devices that allow a closer look at previously hidden details, but they do not yet permit the male spectator's gaze to enter fully the diegetic space of the narrative, from which, having vicariously experienced all the stages of cause and effect, it can then "withdraw satisfied." In its hard-core sequences especially, the stag film seems to want to remind viewers of their position in the theater or at the smoker, on the edges of a frame that cannot be fully "penetrated," witnessing a spectacle that still has aspects of what could be called a (genital) *show* rather than identifying with the actions of a temporally sequenced (genital) *event*.

Am Abend and *A Free Ride* are typical of many stag films in incorporating voyeurism into their narratives as strategies both for arousing their characters and for matching the character's "look" with that of the spectator in their beginning sequences. They are also typical in failing to sustain a voyeuristic penetration of the scene in their hard-core sequences—despite the fact that what these scenes depict is itself genital penetration.

It would be logical to attribute these two films' primitivism to their early dates (ca. 1910 and 1915); and *El satario*, which may be even earlier (ca. 1907–1912), could be regarded as more primitive still, given the single shot/single scene structure of its early narrative sequence. But such logic is quickly dispelled if we look at two U.S. examples from the twenties—the period that some critics consider to be the stag film's golden age (Di Lauro and Rabkin 1976, 59). The first, *The Casting Couch* (1924), represents the primitive limits of stag film narrative; the second, *The Virgin with the Hot Pants* (ca. 1923–1925), represents a radically more discontinuous form that makes no attempt at narrative coherence. Considered together, they represent the two poles of (limited) narrative continuity and (primitive) discontinuity in the stag film.

Discussed by Di Lauro and Rabkin and anthologized in *A History of the Blue Movie*, *The Casting Couch*, like *A Free Ride*, is considered a classic of the genre. (It is also the film whose ending was spliced onto the Kinsey Institute's print of *A Free Ride*.) This conventional story of an aspiring starlet who learns, in the words of the film's final intertitle, that "the only way to become a star is to get under a good director and work your way up," begins when the would-be star arrives for an interview with a casting director. He insists that she model in a bathing suit, so she goes into another room and removes her clothes. The casting director peers through the keyhole as she changes and then abruptly enters to seduce her. The woman is outraged and throws him out. While he is gone, however, she reads a manual, *How to Become a Movie Star*, that advises actresses to comply with the casting director. She calls him back.

The hard-core sequences occupy the remaining half of this

roughly ten-minute film. The woman takes down the man's pants. He asks her to "breathe" on his penis, which she does in close-up. He demands more, and she begins to fellate him. A separate close-up shows the blissful reaction on his face. They move to the next room, containing the eponymous couch, and disrobe. The woman tells the man that he will have to wear a "fish skin." He puts on a condom and penetrates her. Subsequent close-ups of the penis reveal that the condom is no longer there. Another gap in continuity occurs as the woman begins to fellate the now supine man in a now much darker room. In both cases of genital engagement, full body shots alternate with extreme close-ups. Next the woman sits on the man's penis with her back to him. This and what follows are the portion of the film that has been added to *A Free Ride*: she puts on cold cream; they stand while copulating front to front and gyrate in ever slower rhythms until the woman's body goes limp.

The hard-core sequences of *The Casting Couch* are marked by a much greater degree of temporal discontinuity than the scenes that lead up to them. Abrupt changes of position and lighting, the unexplained loss of the "fish skin," the confused duration of the sexual event—all are in marked contrast with the cause-effect linearity and temporal continuity of the film's opening. This opening, like *Am Abend* and, in part, *A Free Ride*, consists of a voyeuristic prelude that encourages spectator identification with the male who looks at the female's body within the unfolding narrative. In contrast, the four major sections of the hard-core sequence (fellatio with the man standing, penetration with both partners lying down, fellatio with both lying down, and penetration with both standing) do not necessarily follow one another; rather, they are arranged as so many disparate fragments of sexual show. Even if we consider such discontinuities as evidence of technical ineptitude, we must nevertheless acknowledge that discontinuity is accepted practice only within hard-core sequences.

Comparing *The Casting Couch* to *The Gay Shoe Clerk*, we might say that the imperfectly integrated single shot of the shoe clerk "copping a feel" has been expanded into an entire sequence of such shots. Similarly, the film's ending is marked more by the seemingly arbitrary cessation of this genital show than by what Burch calls the narrative "rounding off" that would allow the spectator to "withdraw satisfied" from the vicarious experience of a genital sexual event.

Even a highly professional, competently shot, edited, and acted stag classic fully in command of such techniques as shot/reverse shot and eye-line matches can be seen to resist the full identification of the spectator with the spatially and temporally "suturing" look of the camera in its hard-core sequences.[6] In these sequences, the stag film typically reverts to a primitivism that consists of direct address to the camera (as in the early body show films), the linear cause-effect of its earlier narrative portion all but forgotten.

Let us use *The Casting Couch* to represent the (still primitive) heights that stag film narrative can attain. And let us use another film, *The Virgin with the Hot Pants*, to represent the primitive depths of crude body show. Defined by the Kinsey Institute as a "potpourri," *The Virgin with the Hot Pants* belongs to a class of stags that make no attempt at narrative but simply string together various disparate sexual activities onto a single reel. It is a form of the stag film rarely discussed in histories or anthologies of the genre. Perhaps its lack of narrative makes it difficult to remember; perhaps also its more profound misogyny renders it less susceptible to nostalgia.[7]

The film begins with an animated sequence that is a string of visual dirty jokes. A cartoon woman is chased around a room by a cartoon penis-and-testicles, which finally catches and penetrates her while she hangs from a chandelier. Next a cartoon mouse with a giant penis penetrates a cat. "Live" action sequences then portray a series of "lesbian" activities as two or three naked women dance, kiss, and play with a dildo. A title card addresses a member of the audience directly: "You there in the front row, spread those lips apart for us." We see a close-up of a man's hands spreading apart the labia of one of the women. "Turn over honey so we can see how it looks from behind." The woman obliges and displays her genitals from the rear, as if for an inspecting eye. Another intertitle makes a further request: "How about you two getting into your favorite dish?" The responding shot is a close-up of a man performing cunnilingus on one of the women. Again a title card: "Just a minute girls, this is an art picture!" In another close-up a beer bottle is inserted into a vagina.

In a later section a man and woman take off their clothes but without revealing their faces. The man sits, and the woman sits on his penis facing him. A shot from above, aimed down their bodies toward the point of genital contact, barely catches occasional glimpses of the penis as it goes in and out. This final close-up—we might call it an "insert of an insert"—constitutes the film's climax. A last title card punningly writes "The End" over a still photo of a woman's buttocks.

The Virgin in the Hot Pants is primitivism with a vengeance. Composed only of disconnected hard-core sequences, the film makes no attempt either to stage an integrated narrative event of copulation or to live up to the narrative and characterological promise of its title. Rather, it breaks down what might have been constructed as narrative events into relatively unrelated—in some cases nearly frozen—close-up moments of genital show. The spread labia, the view of "how it looks from behind," the bottle in the vagina— all are close-up "inserts" performed in direct address to a camera explicitly aligned with the perspective of the male spectator in the "first row."

Most of these close-ups preserve the same primitive frontality as the single insert of the shoe in *The Gay Shoe Clerk*. Occasionally, however, the film tries to represent copulation and climax according to the rules of temporal sequence; but when it does, it encounters a problem. Here, the device of point of view that was so crucial to the organization of early voyeur narratives cannot function to motivate the viewer's closer look at the sexual act. For when the bodies within the film frame come so close that their means of relation is no longer looking but touching, the film reverts to a close-up version of theatrical frontality, as if the genital show were being performed directly to a front-row camera. It is, in short, as if the spectacle of the naked or nearly naked body, male or female, retards any possible forward narrative drive. It seems in effect to be saying, "Let's just feast our eyes and arrest our gaze on the hidden things that ordinary vision, and certainly ordinary filmic vision, cannot see: a penis, a breast, a vulva, looking right at us; who needs more?"

Not all stag films present such a genuinely primitive genital show or make such a point of addressing their spectators directly. Nor are they all as overtly misogynist as this one. But most stag films do, in their hard-core sequences, use some form of address to a camera whose point of view is aligned more with the front-row (male) spectator brought momentarily closer for a better look than with the free-floating, shifting points of internal identification that operate in the linear cause-effect of cinematic narration.

I argued in Chapter 2 that hard core in general is that which promises to present visual evidence of the "thing" itself. Ideally this "thing" consists of an involuntary convulsion, a confession of the body in the grips of pleasure. We need now to specify what constitutes this pleasure in the stag film and to see how it differs from later instances of the hard-core genre. A crude but effective way of summarizing the different forms of bodily confession offered first by the stag and later by the feature-length narrative pornographic film is to focus on the "sense of an ending" offered by each.

From "Meat" to "Money"

The feature-length pornographic film differs from the stag film in many ways. Most relevant to our discussion here is the greater narrative coherence of both the feature film as a whole and each of its sexual "numbers." In feature-length "pornos," these numbers tend to be complete dramas of arousal, excitement, climax, and (usually) satisfaction that permit both the (male) characters *in* the film and the (usually male) viewers *of* the film to "withdraw satisfied" after getting first into and then back out of the picture. In the primitive stag film, by contrast, the ending is typically abrupt, usually following a close-up "insert of an insert." Although apt, in this case, in denoting not only the form of the shot but also its content, "insert" is an archaic film-editing term that connotes a theatrically conceived scenic space, or master shot, into which a close-up detail has been inserted. Classical narrative cinema has abandoned this theatrical conception of scenic space, articulating its seamless illusion of a space-time continuum instead by "weaving a narrative" out of a multitude of spatial and temporal fragments.[8]

In current hard-core narrative film, the specialized term for the "insert of an insert" that I have been describing is the "meat shot" (Ziplow 1977, 34). This is the quintessential stag film shot: a close-up of penetration that shows that hard-core sexual activity is taking place. Although most current feature-length pornos would not be complete without a great many meat shots in any given sex sequence, these films do not usually end their numbers, as the stag film typically does, with this visual evidence of penetration. The later form of the genre has a "higher" narrative goal: to prove that not only penetration but *also* satisfaction has taken place. This satisfaction might be signaled in a variety of ways. For example, the addition of sound permits performers to communicate their pleasure in groans, moans, and sighs, as well as in actual verbal articulations, an ability that immediately enhances the sense of the sex as an event occurring between the performers rather than a show (as in the more stylized silent-film acting) put on for the camera.

Probably the most striking way that the feature-length hard-core film signals the narrative conclusion of sexual action, however, is through the new convention of external penile ejaculation—or, to use the jargon of the industry, the "money shot."[9] Although the stag film occasionally offers the spectacle of visible ejaculation (sometimes inadvertently: we see one example in the mysterious ending of *A Free Ride*, another in the glob of apparent ejaculate that drips from the woman at the end of *El satario*), it is not until very late in the stag's development that such shots are seen with any regularity, and it is not until the rise of the feature-length porno that they function to signal the climax of the hard-core action.

I shall have more to say later about the significance of "meat" and "money" as the culminating points of visual pleasure in these two instances of the genre; for the present, however, let me just stress that both offer distinct types of spectator pleasure for their predominantly male audiences. In the primitive stag film, the primary pleasure seems to involve forming a gender-based bond with other male spectators. Di Lauro and Rabkin (1976, 26) see this bonding as a ritual initiation into manhood, a means of dispelling many of the anxieties of the inexperienced male. Certainly much of what we have observed in the primitive stag film—its clinical, objectifying scrutiny of the female body ("spread those lips"), its inscription of and address to a specifically male viewer ("you there in the first row"), its puerile reactions to the visual evidence of sexual difference itself ("turn over honey so we can see how it looks from behind")—seems to bear this out.

But as in the above examples, this ritual bonding of audience members works against Di Lauro and Rabkin's idea that the male characters in the film act as surrogates for the male spectators. For if what we have observed about the primitivism of these films has credibility, identification with a male performer who gets physically into and out of the woman, much as the spectator gets imaginatively into and out of the filmic diegesis, is more typical of the feature-length porno than it is of the stag film. After all, it is the feature-length narrative with its multiple dramas of arousal and climax that permits the male performer and spectator to "withdraw satisfied." The stag film does not seem to want to "satisfy" in this sense at all; its role seems rather to arouse and then precisely *not* to satisfy a spectator, who must subsequently seek satisfaction outside the purely visual terms of the film—whether in masturbation, in actual sexual relations, or by channeling sexual arousal into communal wisecracking or verbal ejaculation of the "homosocial" variety.[10]

The two primary ways in which stag films were—and to some extent still are—exhibited substantiate this point. In Europe, as Gertrud Koch has observed, stag films were associated mainly with brothels, their major function being economic: to arouse the viewer to the point of purchasing the services of the women of the house.[11] A fully satisfied viewer would not need to make such expenditures. A French film, *Le télégraphiste* (ca. 1921–1926), illustrates this assumption of the stag film's function quite well. The narrative involves a telegraph boy who, in the process of delivering his message, becomes sexually entangled first with the family maid, then with her mistress, and finally with both the mistress and her husband.[12] At the film's end the husband reads the telegram, which turns out to be a message to the audience: "After seeing this picture, rush over to some nice girl and get taken care of."

This film aptly illustrates Koch's point that the illegally exhibited stag films aimed primarily at engaging spectators in sexual preliminaries, or foreplay. The American "smoker," hosted by some exclusively male club (the Elks or a college fraternity, for example) and attended by invited female "guests," was only a slightly less public and commercial parallel to the European brothel screenings in this regard. The important characteristic of both, however, was not so much whether male spectators could actually obtain the services of a woman upon arousal, but rather the assumption, confirmed by the film's mode of address, that its function was primarily *to arouse*. This emphasis on arousal contrasts markedly with publicly exhibited, feature-length pornographic films, which have no connection to houses of prostitution and whose aim, I submit, is to offer satisfaction on more exclusively narrative terms.

Modes of Reception

It is worth noting that in many respects the primitive structure and explicit function of the stag film have persisted into the present, although in a much altered mode of reception. Many of the adult arcades that sell magazines, tapes, and sexual paraphernalia have several solitary cubicles where Super 8mm films, spliced together in loops, are projected onto the wall. Every half-minute or so the film stops, at no particular demarcation in the events depicted, and more coins, or tokens purchased at the desk, must be fed into the machine. Viewers begin watching randomly, depending on where the last viewer left off. The films themselves are very much like the stags described above: they are short, silent, rigorously amateurish, and their film language tends toward the primitive; the only major difference is that they are usually in color. Some of the loops actually are recycled stags. What sets them apart from early stag films, of course, is how they are seen—not by the social group at the Elks Club but by solitary men shopping for a booth with loops to suit them, who deposit coins not until the film ends but until they achieve satisfaction.

Scott MacDonald (1983, 12) has written perceptively, and honestly, of this particular viewing experience with regard to primitive arcade films, describing it as one of "shared embarrassment" and avoided eye contact and the masturbation in the booth as the "climax" of the visit. "In my experience," he writes, "the masturbation itself seems less important as an experience than as a way of releasing the excitement created by the imagery." MacDonald also briefly describes the more public experience of the porno theater proper: the public place where, in the 1970s, feature-length hardcore narratives were consumed until supplanted by the videocassette. There, in contrast to the private booths, viewers rarely masturbated.

MacDonald's experience suggests the importance of the social use of these films. The loops shown in adult arcades are very much the stag films of the present era. Like the stags, their primary function is to arouse; but unlike them, the social context in which they are consumed means that arousal is no longer channeled into other social rituals of male bonding or sexual consumption. Now the solitary viewer in the arcade just quietly gets off.

Yet as a complement to this more private and furtive way of experiencing hard core, we find the relatively public and open mode of viewing for the new feature-length narrative pornos as well. It is thus not simply that men have become more covert in consuming hard-core film. Since the increased legalization of hard core in general, they have gone in both directions at once: they have grown private and furtive in their consumption of hard core in the arcades that cater mostly to men *and* more open and public in their consumption of feature-length hard-core films, watching not only with other men but also, and increasingly throughout the 1970s, in the company of women. In these theatrical feature films, moreover, they enjoyed increasingly vicarious forms of arousal and satisfaction.

In neither case, however, is precisely the old "stag" form of male bonding possible. Although it might seem that this situation would change now that videocassettes allow men to duplicate in their own homes the earlier private stag party, the very legality of such screenings, together with the fact that these cassettes are available for viewing by women—and in many cases were produced for theatrical audiences that specifically included women—has made such duplication impossible. Thus, even though some stag films are currently available, whether on videocassette or as loops in arcades, the mode of reception that bonded men around primitive genital shows is now a thing of the past.

The Subject of Stags

A male film spectator who is encouraged to talk to, and even to reach his hands into, the screen; a female film body who spreads her legs (and labia) for the eye and hand behind the camera—these are the most distinctively primitive qualities of the stag film. Compared to the more fully developed narratives of later feature-length pornos, where sexual relations are no longer addressed to the camera but, as in other kinds of narrative, "seem to recount themselves,"[13] we can see that the stag film retains many of the theatrical elements of the striptease—without, however, the striptease's most basic element: the coincidence of stripper and audience in the same theatrical space and time. It seems useful, therefore, to locate the stag film within a historical continuum of performative sexual display in order to say more precisely just what kinds of pleasures, and what kind of viewing subject, the films construct.

In an excellent but unpublished article on pornography and its precursor forms of sexual spectacle, David James (n.d.) argues that the striptease consists of a continual oscillation between exposure and concealment—the satisfaction of seeing all and the frustration of having that sight cut off in a "premature climax." James also suggests that in the striptease the art of dancing is played off against the non-art of the sexual act that the dance suggests. The artistry of performance comes to compensate for what is missing in discursive exchange between performer and audience.

The idea of compensation invoked here is interesting. Borrowing from James, we can say that each historically successive form of the representation of sexual acts using living, moving bodies must compensate its viewers for the formal limits of the medium. This compensation is measured against the ideal of the viewer's actual sexual relation with a partner. Because the striptease is live, it offers a very direct relation between stripper and audience. The spectator is cast as the hypothetical partner; the stripper addresses him verbally, looks him in the eye, and throws her discarded clothes at him. The show tantalizes by seeming to risk turning into a live sexual exchange. But since such an exchange would privilege one member of the audience over all others, it cannot occur. Hence, the sexual show offered takes on a highly ritualized, theatrical quality in which actual touching and, in classic striptease, showing of genitals is excluded. From the very beginning, then, this show is a spectacle that stands in compensatory substitution for sexual relations themselves, the bump and grind a spectacular mime of sexual relations that takes the audience member as imaginary partner.

In contrast to the professional stage stripper, the female stag actress seems crude, awkward, and amateurish, both as she displays her wares to the camera and as she performs sexual acts with male and female partners. These qualities are not inadvertent aesthetic defects, however, but a crucial aspect of the very different visual pleasures that the stag film constructs. The performer's self-consciousness, the smiles and giggles that would be out of place either in a professional stripper's act or in the next stage of this continuum, a feature-length hard-core narrative, become here a form of reassurance that *this* show is no act.[14] As if in proof, the stag film then shows more of the act.

Amateurism—marking performances *in* the film as well as the technical performance *of* the film—is thus an important feature of the stag form, offering compensation for the spectator's physical and temporal separation from the sexual performance he observes. It is as if the spectator's ability to get into the act, through identification with the male performer who "gets into" the woman, partially offsets the loss of his own direct exchange with the performing body of the woman. The hard-core sequences of the stag film are thus like a magnified and amateurized striptease in which the spectator sees more of the real sexual act as compensation for the loss of his own direct sexual relation to the performing body.

A stag film entitled *A Country Stud Horse* (USA, ca. 1920) is of interest for its illustration of these compensatory trade-offs.[15] The film begins with a man peering into a mutoscope (a hand-cranked version of the motor-driven Kinetoscope—individual viewing machines that preceded screen projectors). The next shot shows what he sees in the machine: a scantily clad woman performing a dance for the camera much as Little Egypt and Fatima did in the early Edison films. In this case, however, the dance continues into a striptease. As this occurs, we see the male viewer beginning to masturbate through his clothes as he continues to crank the machine.

The striptease in this film-within-a-film continues past the conventional end of the stage stripper's act to complete nudity. Close-up inserts reveal isolated portions of her anatomy—her pelvis and breasts—as she continues to gyrate. Meanwhile, in a long shot, we see the man still cranking and peeping; but now his penis is out and erect. Again we see what he sees in the machine: the woman smoking in an armchair, looking directly at the camera and displaying her vulva—seen in close-up. The man continues to masturbate and crank. The woman holds open her labia, again in close-up.

This close-up ends the film-within-the-film. Thus far the film has recapitulated and gone beyond the exhibitionist body performance of the early Kinetoscopes of Fatima or Little Egypt, or of the stage stripper, reaching the limits of theatrical body performance when the woman takes off all her clothes and proffers her labia for visual inspection. This hard-core film striptease thus begins where the stage striptease ends: at the point where most of the woman's clothes have already been removed. And it continues past the point of what David James calls its "premature climax," in nakedness or near-nakedness, to a new climax specific to the photographic medium: the close-up of the vulva. Although this close-up shows more of the exhibitionist female body than can be seen in the stage show, the spectator must pay with temporal and spatial disconnection from that body. This isolation is perfectly represented in this film by the image of the male spectator masturbating with one hand while cranking a peephole viewing machine with the other. Hands that might once have been available for touch, even if only to catch the garment thrown by the stripper, are now occupied maintaining the compensatory fetish-regime of the primitive apparatus itself—just as today in the arcades these hands must feed the machines their tokens and still maintain autoerotic arousal.

But *A Country Stud Horse* does not end here. In the film's further narrative we can see how the primitive stag film compensates its viewer. A title card introduces a new phase of the action: "Mary picks up some business." A new character, "Mary," approaches the man who is still cranking the mutoscope and proposes that they "go to a room." Inside the room, another striptease begins, but unlike the stripper in the machine, Mary disrobes in short order. A meat shot of vaginal penetration occurs even before the man's clothes have been removed. The usual discontinuity of hard-core stag action follows (a discontinuity marked here particularly by shots of a limp penis followed immediately by a hard one). Variations of the meat shot follow, from the side and from between the legs of the woman astride the man—a position that offers an optimum view of the penis as it penetrates the vagina. The film finally "ends" with typical primitive abruptness when someone (the director?) tosses a towel onto the bed and "Mary" begins to wipe up.

This ending, which one is tempted to see as a metaphoric as well as literal enactment of all primitive cinema's "throwing in of the towel," is a fitting reminder of the narrative limits of the early stag film. For although as a narrative *A Country Stud Horse* is relatively complex, and self-reflexive at that, its abrupt climax in a discontinuous succession of meat shots leading to no definitive closure is much the same as the climaxes offered in *A Free Ride*, *The Virgin with the Hot Pants*, *The Casting Couch*, and countless other stag films. Although the meat shots that end these films depict the sexual act of penetration, they only partly accomplish the viewer's own imaginary penetration into a narrative of these acts.

The visual pleasure of the stag film might thus be characterized as a prolonged oscillation between two poles of pleasure. The first is inherited from, but more extensive than, the striptease: it is the pleasure of the collective male group expressing its heterosexual desire for the bodies of women on display. In this pleasure the woman's body mediates the achievement of masculine identity. The second pole of pleasure consists in moving toward, but never fully achieving, identification with a male protagonist who performs sexual acts with the female body that shows itself to the viewer. In the mode of reception characteristic of stag film, this full-fledged identification with sexual actors is impeded by apparently more pressing needs to identify with the other men in the audience, who prefer knowledge of the "wonders of the unseen world"—including not only what women's bodies look like but also, as Scott MacDonald (1983, 13) has noted, what men's bodies look like when erect and when "cocks" thrust into "cunts"—to vicarious identification with their surrogate sexual actors. The visual pleasure of the stag film thus seems perpetually to hesitate between these two forms of pleasure: on the one hand, a pleasure still clinging to remnants of the stage striptease but now performed for a camera that sees more—exemplified in *A Country Stud Horse* by the shot of the spread labia that ends the striptease sequence—and on the other, a pleasure anticipating, but not quite achieving, the further organization of these elements into narrative events—exemplified here by the discontinuous succession of meat shots and the "throwing in of the towel."

To summarize: the stag film oscillates between the impossible direct relation between a spectator and the exhibitionist object he watches in close-up and the ideal voyeurism of a spectator who observes a sexual event in which a surrogate male acts for him. Two shots typify this oscillation: the close-up "split beaver" (genitals visible, legs ajar) addressed directly to the film spectator, which shows more of the female body as object of pleasure than any previous theatrical or photographic form of institutionalized sexual show; and the meat shot, which shows more of the "genital event" than ever before seen by a mass audience (but which is still not the full narrative event that we will encounter in hard-core features).

Here we might pause to consider the identificatory process of the stag spectator who moves between this "direct" contemplation and voyeuristic penetration. In a pioneering study of the contemporary hard-core pornographic film, Dennis Giles (1977) noted of the hard-core feature what Di Lauro and Rabkin note of the stag film: that the male character is not the true hero of the film; that compared to the female character he is relatively devoid of personality, even less individualized than the woman. But where Di Lauro and Rabkin use this observation to argue that women are the films' "primary subjects," Giles (pp. 55–57) offers a more sophisticated psychoanalytic interpretation: the male spectator identifies with the man not so much as a character but as "bearer of the phallus," and so vicariously "possesses" the woman through this other man; hence the woman can never really be the subject.

But to possess the woman through the man involves looking at the man's penis. MacDonald (1983, 14) has suggested that there is both pleasure and curiosity in this look:

To a considerable extent theater and arcade porn films are about erections. The standard anti-porn response to this is to see the porn film phallus as a combined battering ram/totem which encapsulates the male drive for power. . . . And yet, for me the pervasiveness of erect penises in porn has at least as much to do with simple curiosity. The darkness of porn houses and the privacy of arcade booths allow one to see erections close-up. The presence of women has its own power, but in this particular context one of the primary functions of the female presence is to serve as a sign—to others and to oneself—that looking at erections, even finding them sexy, does not mean that the viewer defines himself as a homosexual.

Both Giles and MacDonald suggest that seeing and satisfying curiosity about the erect penis is at least as important as seeing the female "wonders of the unseen world." It is important to note, however, that while the display of female genitals in a heterosexual stag film can be sufficiently fascinating to constitute an end in itself, the similar display of male genitals cannot. In other words, simple curiosity, as MacDonald puts it, may not be quite so simple as it seems. For as MacDonald himself suggests, to enjoy looking at penises would be for the male to risk the specter of homosexual desire. To defend against this desire, the viewer proves his masculinity either by bonding with the other male spectators in the scrutiny of female difference or by penetrating the female "wonders" vicariously.

But does this mean that the male viewer identifies only with the

phallus and so objectifies the vulva? I can merely suggest that this
formulation, too, seems a bit too simple. As we saw in the discussion
of fetishism in Chapter 2, Freudian psychoanalysis insists that there
is something traumatic for the male in the sight of the woman's genitals that necessitates the creation of fantasies disavowing female difference. This trauma is traced to the male child's first discovery of
the female "lack" of a penis and his presumed disavowal of that lack
in the fetishization of the woman's body, body part, or garment.
Hence, the "simple curiosity" about body parts and functions that
MacDonald speaks of is quite definitely not so simple at all, since
the knowledge gained, according to this theory, is immediately invested with a fantasy of disavowal that says, in effect, "This body is
not really so different from mine; it is not castrated; here is the fetish
that proves it."

We have already seen the influence of the psychoanalytic theory
of fetishization in explaining the dominance of male subjectivity and
the relegation of woman to fetishized object in narrative films that
themselves never stage an actual confrontation with anatomical sexual difference. But since hard-core film focuses obsessively on this
very discovery and examination of female sexual difference, the process by which, in this context, the disavowal of castration could occur
seems unclear. In other words, in neither stag nor hard-core feature
film does it seem plausible that the male curiosity and delight taken
in the view of the vulva is compensating for castration anxiety.[16]

Dennis Giles has made an important attempt to explain these
matters with regard to hard-core features. In his view, the male
viewer's scrutiny of the vulva is an occasion for (unconscious) identification with the woman herself. The viewer projects and expels
qualities, feelings, and wishes that he himself possesses but refuses
to recognize. Through this "projective identification," the male
viewer does not merge with the female on the screen, as in more
typical primary identification; rather, he projects his own feminine
traits of passivity and sexual urges onto the body of the woman as
"other." Only then is the spectator free to desire the very qualities
he himself has expelled; he is now in a position to identify with both
active and passive roles simultaneously. To Giles, then, narcissistic
self-possession of the (male) self as (female) "other" seems the best
way of describing the identificatory process embodied in heterosexual hard-core films. It reduces, as Giles argues, to a Lacanian

presence/absence dichotomy of man as phallus and woman as hole, and to the male subject's quest to fill the hole-gap-absence in his own being (Giles 1977, 56–57, 64).

While I do think that this interpretation may begin to describe and explain the greater bisexuality and complexity of the identificatory process for the male spectator of many stag films, I would not extend it to the whole of hard-core pornography. For one thing, the more elaborate narratives of feature-length hard core offer other points of secondary, fictional identification beyond those merely of phallus or hole. For another, even the films we have examined (*A Free Ride*, for instance) have moments when female characters are the voyeurs who look at the male sign of difference. Although exceptional, and difficult to imagine as points of entrance for the desires of females who were not in the audience anyway, such moments warn us—as indeed Giles's description of the male subject's desire to possess projected/rejected aspects of his own femininity warns us—that easy dichotomizations of masculine subjects as active-voyeuristic and of feminine subjects as passive-exhibitionistic need careful scrutiny.

Finally, it is important to realize that the desires that animate these processes of identification are subject to change through the mediation of the very forms of their representation. At any given point in its history, we find the hard-core film's "solution" to the problems of desire, sexual difference, and visual representation to be highly unstable. Take, for example, the obsessively repeated meat shot as one such moment of solution; we can see that it oscillates restlessly between genital show and genital event, sometimes signifying climax, culmination, possession, other times signifying the undeniable fact that the "scopic regime" of cinema cannot depict such climax, culmination, possession, simply because the event of climactic pleasure cannot be shown. Thus we begin to see as well the dynamic of change that the cinematic process of compensation/disavowal involves: since he cannot touch the woman, the spectator gets to see more of her; but seeing more means confronting the hidden "wonders" of sexual difference, which in turn may create the further need to prove masculinity by watching someone else going *inside*.

This vicarious journey to the "wonders of the unseen world" eventually generates a new, substitute object of vision in the money shot of feature-length hard core (see Chapter 4), which represents a new stage in the genre's desire to see more of the hidden wonders of sexual pleasure. Thus Giles is not quite right when he says (1977, 59) that the pornographic film "accepts that visually 'knowing' the act in the sexual interior is impossible" and that it therefore displaces this visual knowledge onto the narrative event of masculine orgasm. As the stag films discussed here suggest, it took a long time for the pornographic film genre to "accept" this impossibility; the pleasures of the stag film, in short, were not yet fully wedded to the representation of sexual pleasure as a narrative event viewed by a spectator-voyeur. At the same time, though, the relation of the stag film to its precursor and subsequent forms indicates that some kind of visual compensation occurs each time the cinematic ability to see more and better replaces "real" physical connection to a performing body.

We saw in Chapter 2 that feminist film theory has been quick to relate the abusive powers of patriarchy to the institutionalized voyeurism and fetishism of narrative cinema. In the stag film, however, a relatively primitive, nonnarrative visual pleasure in which fetishism and voyeurism function very differently has reigned supreme for over half a century. One lesson of the stag form would therefore seem to be that the cinematic visual pleasure of narrative is not quite so monolithic as we sometimes like to think. Pleasure, as Foucault teaches, has a history—and even though that history has usually functioned to oppress women, it has not always done so in the same way.

An important question still to be asked, however, is, Why did these particular pleasures of the stag film persist as long as they did? Why did this primitive, single-reel, silent form of filmmaking continue when the rest of cinema quickly developed into the institutional mode of narrative? One ready answer is that these illegal, anonymously made texts, offering a view of genital sexuality never before glimpsed in any other form of visual representation, persisted simply because they were cut off from more public discourses of sexuality. Under these conditions of official invisibility, in the absence of open discussion about any aspect of their form or content, stag films had little reason to change: they needed only to go on providing the hard-core "frenzy" of sexual actions that could not be found elsewhere.

The answer to the logical next question—how this static genre finally did come to change—is more difficult. To answer it fully we would need to examine the whole history of twentieth-century discourses of sexuality, particularly the legal decisions leading, in the many book trials of the late fifties and early sixties, to what Charles Rembar (1969) has called the "end of obscenity" and, more complexly, to what Richard Ellis (1988, 27) has called the ideological "repositioning of pornography within the social formation." Briefly, then, let us examine a few key moments from the American scene of this early history.

American Decensorship

In the United States, the stag film's heyday occurred in the teens and twenties, at the end of Anthony Comstock's crusades against smut. Comstock worked as an avid "special agent" for the Post Office prosecuting an 1873 congressional law (dubbed the "Comstock Law"). This law provided

that no obscene, lewd, or lascivious book, pamphlet, picture, paper, print, or other publication of an indecent character, or any article or thing designed or intended for the prevention of conception or procuring of abortion, nor any article or thing intended or adapted for any indecent or immoral use or nature . . . shall be carried in the mail.

(Quoted in Kendrick 1987, 134)

From the law's enactment to 1915, Comstock energetically seized and burned all such materials that were sent through the mails. In this crusade, however, the works most vulnerable to seizure were not the illegally produced and shown stag films, which purveyors would have been too careful to send by mail in any case, but rather those works belonging to the "gray areas" of sexual discourse: works of art that spoke too brazenly about sex, such as Shaw's *Man and Superman* (1905), and scientific works containing explicit clinical information, such as Margaret Sanger's birth control pamphlet *What Every Girl Should Know* (1913).

While we can look back at these crusades and their targets as ludicrous "Comstockery" and gross misconstructions of the idea of obscenity, it may be more pertinent to recognize, as Walter Kendrick (1987) does, that legal tests such as these were what caused more contemporary definitions of obscenity to be formulated in the first place—that only through "smut trials" did the notion of "hard core" begin to emerge at all. Kendrick's history of modern pornographic censorship shows that the really significant factor in Comstock's crusades was that they were just as instrumental in making the discussion of sexuality public as were figures like Sanger, Shaw, or even the purveyors of "dirty" postcards. All of these voices participated in a total increase of speaking about sex (whether for or against). The dirty postcards distributor was one voice in opposition to Comstock, but so was Shaw's voice against marriage and Sanger's voice for sex and for women's greater control over their own bodies in sex.

We have here the flip side of Foucault's lesson about the role of power in discourse: power pervades discourse, but "where there is power, there is resistance" (Foucault 1978, 95). The proliferation of warring discourses of sexuality, creating sexuality as an object not only of pleasure but of knowledge as well, increases the ways in which power controls the life of the body and of the species. But at the same time that power itself emerges, so does resistance to that power, and this too occurs in discourse. Only in the context of the growing discussion of sexual hygiene, for example—from Lord Acton's 1857 *Functions and Disorders of the Reproductive Organs* to the many Victorian treatises on the problem of prostitution, Charcot's investigations into hysteria, Freud's determination that sex is the primary motive in human life, and Havelock Ellis's turn-of-the-century work on sexual inversion—could Margaret Sanger's work on birth control have emerged.

Stag films offering explicit, hard-core representations of sexual acts were for a long time outside the arena of these other public discussions of sex. They escaped Comstock's opprobrium because they were the private preserve of private individuals. Unlike the misogynist, phallocentric sexual discourses of Freudian psychology, which as early as the 1920s elicited the protest of a Karen Horney, this early form of film pornography was unavailable to women; they therefore exercised no power of resistance in this area. Stag movies, and most other forms of what we would today call hard-core pornography, thus continued as a relatively insular and unresisted genre compared to the modern novel, mainstream cinema, psychoanalysis, and early sexological investigations.

Today the public debate over the stag movie's modern successor is at the center of a field of warring discourses of sexuality; and in this debate, women's voices are the loudest. Although anti-pornography feminists might not like to acknowledge it, these voices of resistance have increasingly been heard even within the genre itself. The new, legal cinematic pornography is more responsive to the public war over sexuality than were the insular and illegal stags. This is not to say that this cinema is not still misogynist and phallocentric; but certainly the emergence of hard core as a genre more like other film genres, one not entirely cut off from public criticism, generic self-reflection, and the particular criticism of women, has significantly modified, and in some cases supplanted, the rampant misogyny of stags.

How, then, did this new form of the genre come into existence? How did hard core become legal and thereby subject to the broader influence of other sexual discourses? How have power and pleasure as self-conscious (and increasingly gender-conscious) elements of the genre been introduced? The answer, ironically, appears to lie in the very process by which the supposedly unacceptable "hard core" of obscenity was isolated out of the many books, pamphlets, pictures, papers, prints, and other publications described in the 1873 Comstock Law.

In that law, obscenity was vaguely defined as socially unacceptable representations or discussions of sex—those that were lustful, impure, indecent, and lewd. The difficulty in prosecuting such vague definitions was, of course, their subjectivity: indecent and lewd to whom? Comstock failed, for example, in his attempts to prosecute both Shaw and Sanger, though he was more successful against the dirty postcards. In 1930 the definition of obscenity was further qualified in Judge Woolsey's famous ruling that James Joyce's *Ulysses* (1914–1921; first U.S. edition 1933) could not be called obscene because its sometimes lewd descriptions were not, as the judge put it, "dirt for dirt's sake" (Kendrick 1987, 158–187). By 1930 in America, in marked contrast to Comstock's age, it was acceptable to talk about sex, provided such talk was not conducted for the sole "sake" of sex; when that happened, the talk was presumed to be unredeemable obscenity. Through such reasoning both Joyce's *Ulysses* and the marriage manual *Married Love* (1918) were admitted to public view by Judge Woolsey as socially valuable discourses of sexuality.[17]

With this apparent clarification, and with the narrowing of the definition of obscenity, pornography came into a new existence as a category of social and aesthetic worthlessness; in this sense it was quite different from the more socially and aesthetically ambiguous works that mid-nineteenth-century "gentlemen" had once housed in such places as the "secret museum" of Pompeii. As Kendrick (p. 196) puts it, "No clear statement has ever been enunciated, but over a period of decades [roughly 1930–1960] the omnium gatherum called 'obscenity' was steadily pared down, like some fleshy fruit with an indigestible stone at its heart, to lay bare what came to be known as the 'hard core.'"

The term *hard core* entered legal discourse in the landmark *United States v. Roth* decision of 1957, in which Supreme Court Justice William Brennan determined once and for all—or so it then seemed—that the "indigestible" pit of hard-core pornography was "utterly without redeeming social importance" (Kendrick 1987, 201). Roth had been convicted of mailing a magazine containing nude pictures and erotic stories, *American Aphrodite*. The Supreme Court, accustomed to making rulings in the gray areas of modern art and literature and scientific sexological treatises, had never been presented with such a clear-cut case of aesthetically "unredeemable" material (p. 196). Solicitor General Rankin argued that "'hard-core' pornography"—described as photographs, movies, and books representing men and women engaged in "every conceivable kind of normal and abnormal sexual relations"—contained only one "idea": "there is pleasure in sexual gratification." To Rankin the "social value" of such an idea was obviously nil (p. 197). Justice Brennan agreed and went on to rule that hard-core obscenity was "not within the area of constitutionally protected speech or press." He clarified that it was not the portrayal of sex that was "utterly without redeeming social importance," but only material "which deals with sex in a manner appealing to prurient interest" (pp. 201, 206). In fact, sex was given an unprecedented degree of importance in his ruling: "Sex, a great and mysterious motive force in human life, has indisputably been a subject of absorbing interest to mankind through the ages; it is one of the vital problems of human interest and public concern" (p. 201).

Most commentators, including Kendrick, have focused on the unforeseen effects of those fateful words "utterly without redeeming social importance." With them, Justice Brennan appeared to have closed the matter: all the average person had to do was apply "contemporary community standards" to see if a work had social importance; if not, it was mere prurience. But the ironic effect of Brennan's clarification was that subsequent to this ruling all sorts of surprising works were discovered to be not without some "nugget" of social, historical, or even aesthetic worth. The *Roth* decision, then, marked "the opening of the floodgates" to U.S. publication of all the long-suppressed classics—*My Secret Life* (1888) and D. H. Lawrence's *Lady Chatterley's Lover* (1929) in 1959, John Cleland's *Fanny Hill* in 1966—as well as newer works such as Pauline Réage's *The Story of O* and Henry Miller's *The Tropic of Cancer* (Kendrick 1987, 202–204).

More important than the "without redeeming social importance" loophole, however, was the new status given to sex as a "motive force" and "vital problem," language that indicates just how thoroughly the many debates over sexuality had permeated judicial discourse, as well as how politicized representations of sexuality had become. This politicization is of enormous significance. The usual way of understanding the gradual legal acceptance in this period of works depicting sex is as a reflection of larger processes in which social attitudes toward sex as a whole were being liberalized—as, for example, Charles Rembar argues in *The End of Obscenity* (1969, 87). More recently, however, Richard Ellis has argued that moral standards have in fact not become more liberal over time, indeed, that to explain the "decensorship" of pornography by "changing social values" is to place the debate within the censors' own terms and to subscribe to the very division between worthless pornography and works of redeeming social value that changing standards had succeeded in "liberating" (R. Ellis 1988, 38). A more apt approach, Ellis suggests, involves replacing the misleading concept of liberation with that of politicization. To Ellis, the publishers who so successfully launched anti-censorship campaigns in the early and mid-sixties did not liberate the erotic according to more relaxed community standards; rather, they achieved a more pervasive "'politicisation' of the erotic/pornographic," which has been continuing ever since (p. 40). In the legal battles fought and won by such publishers as Grove Press, the "erotic text," no longer "shrouded by the laws of obscenity," became more "plainly available as a representational discourse, a deployment of signifiers within contemporary culture in an age of mechanical reproduction. . . . Notions of hard versus soft pornography are quite beside the point" (p. 41).

Thus, paradoxically, while decisions like Justice Brennan's attempted to narrow the definition of obscenity to a "hard core" that was unmistakable in its prurient intent, that very narrowing was undermined by the construction of sex as a political and social problem belonging to society as a whole. Once so constructed by juridical discourse, any sex, even that which is "for sex's sake," was automatically important and of interest. So even while the idea of obscenity was being "pared down" (Kendrick's term) to apply to works that, in the nineteenth century, no one would have dared think of bringing into the public eye, the idea of sex was growing so important that there was less and less reason to suppress its expression. This new political importance of sex would, in turn, become an internal influence on the transformation of hard core into a new genre about the many different problems of sex.

Hence, it is not just that the "without redeeming social value" definition "opened the floodgates" to already-existent material, but rather that a process of constituting the new importance of sex as a problem of knowledge and pleasure was taking place everywhere: at the Kinsey Institute in the late fifties, and with Masters and Johnson and all the sexology and "orgasm" research begun in the late sixties and popularized in dozens of sex manuals; in the legal battles aimed at decensoring the "auratic authenticity" of once-shrouded obscene texts (R. Ellis 1988, 41), in that heterogeneous event called the "sexual revolution," and in the second wave of feminism, which arose to resist and challenge many of the male-oriented assumptions of that revolution. Even obscenity and pornography proper—defined legally in the mid-1960s as near-worthless forms of explicit sexual representation—had themselves become, as they have continued to be, increasingly respectable objects of study, as long as they were bracketed as social and political problems rather than cultural forms. Given the larger context of the discursive formation of sex as a problem, it is not surprising that the films, and later videos, that emerged in the wake of this new legal definition began, as the stag film had not, to portray sex itself as a problem. As we shall see in the following chapters, this new problematization of sex is ultimately the most significant difference between the illegal stag film and the modern feature-length hard-core narrative. The problematization of sex is what elicits, for example, the new, extended narrative treatments of the stag film's earlier, primitive oscillation between simple genital show and genital event.

Conclusion

These pages on the primitive stag film, along with Chapter 2's discussion of the hard core in cinematic prehistory, have tentatively sketched the first stages in the history of pornography at a time when sex was relatively unpoliticized and unproblematic. For example, the question of the woman's or man's sexual satisfaction almost never came up in these films: to insert a penis into any orifice was automatically presumed to be satisfying to both man and woman. In these early, primitive forms of hard core, sex is more simply (that is, less problematically) represented according to certain basic principles of maximum visibility—whether that visibility constructs a narrative event or not.

In Chapter 2 we saw that as new optical machines saw more of women's bodies, they gratuitously fetishized the representation of these bodies in protonarratives that channeled the anxieties elicited by unprecedented lifelike visual representation. In the stag film, in contrast, primitive sexual show seems stuck in a prolonged oscillation between genital show and genital event.

If we invoke a historical model of perverse compensation to understand the changes that occur in the hard-core film genre, we could say that with the improved ability at each stage of development to see the female body "more and better," a new form of resistance to a hegemonic yet always vulnerable male pleasure is also introduced. In other words, at each new stage of visual intensification the previous institution of pleasure is questioned. Perversions, after all, are themselves temporary and often unstable substitute solutions to what can never be grasped in sexual relations—the infinitely receding lost object as the source of all desire—and so are inherently contradictory. To say that a proliferation of perversions occurs with the new machines of the visible is thus to say that a proliferation of sexual contradictions occurs as well. I will argue in the next chapter that the money shot is one of the biggest of these contradictions and that its exclusive narcissistic focus on the male organ in many ways exposes, to new female viewers, the real concerns of the genre up to that point.

Di Lauro and Rabkin would have us believe that the stag film's primitivism is to be valued for the comparative innocence and naïveté of spectators who wanted only to see more of the "wonders of the unseen world." Yet this nostalgia for an adolescent curiosity that is content to gape at what the cinematic medium makes visible—the magnified close-up of female bodily difference—misses the point. In its own time, and in relation to its own precinematic precursors, this primitive hard core defined its own "implantation of perversions," located somewhere between the old pleasure of watching a stage striptease and the new pleasure of voyeuristically identifying with the performance of sexual acts. If the stag's primitivism is to be found in its more directly discursive "I-you" relation to the image—rather than in complete narrative identification with, and penetration of, narrative diegesis—then the very fact that a discursive relation is established to an *image*, rather than with the flesh-and-blood body of a performer, is what seems most significant.

The stag film is neither a porno feature manqué nor a naive and innocent type of primitivism. Di Lauro and Rabkin's nostalgia for the simplicity of this form conflates primitive cinematic technique with innocuous adolescent content and so emphasizes the tradition of *A Free Ride* over the more primitive and more misogynist tradition of *The Virgin with the Hot Pants.* Even without dredging up some of the more egregious examples of this misogyny,[18] we can see that any nostalgia for these films must also partake of a nostalgia for an age when male spectators of pornography could take their pleasure in investigating the woman without having to worry much about *her* pleasure. Perhaps we can do without nostalgia like that. For, as we shall see next, this lack of concern for the woman's pleasure is precisely what the contemporary hard-core narrative feature can no longer exhibit.

4

Fetishism and Hard Core

Marx, Freud, and the "Money Shot"

*There are those who believe that the come shot, or, as
some refer to it, "the money shot," is the most
important element in the movie and that everything
else (if necessary) should be sacrificed at its expense.
Of course, this depends on the outlook of the
producer, but one thing is for sure: if you don't have
the come shots, you don't have a porno picture. Plan
on at least ten separate come shots.*

Stephen Ziplow,
The Film Maker's Guide to Pornography

Stephen Ziplow's manual of advice for the frugal pornographer asserts what had by 1977 become the sine qua non of the hard-core
feature-length narrative: the necessity of showing external ejaculation of the penis as the ultimate climax—the sense of an ending—
for each heterosexual sex act represented. Where the earlier short,
silent stag films occasionally included spectacles of external ejaculation (in some cases inadvertently), it was not until the early seventies, with the rise of the hard-core feature, that the money shot
assumed the narrative function of signaling the climax of a genital
event. Previously, hard-core sequences tended to be organized as
discontinuous, relatively nonlinear moments of genital show in meat
shots offering visual evidence of penetration.

Each shot—"meat" or "money"—is emblematic of the different

"climax" of its generic form. Each shot seeks maximum visibility in its representation but encounters the limits of visibility of its particular form. The stag film, seeking to learn more about the "wonders of the unseen world," encounters its limits of visibility, as Gertrud Koch (forthcoming) notes, *ante portas* in penetration: for the male performer to penetrate the wonders is to make it nearly impossible for the viewer to see what is penetrated.

The money shot, however, succeeds in extending visibility to the next stage of representation of the heterosexual sex act: to the point of seeing climax. But this new visibility extends only to a knowledge of the hydraulics of male ejaculation, which, though certainly of interest, is a poor substitute for the knowledge of female wonders that the genre as a whole still seeks. The gynecological sense of the speculum that penetrates the female interior here really does give way to that of a self-reflecting mirror. While undeniably spectacular, the money shot is also hopelessly specular; it can only reflect back to the male gaze that purports to want knowledge of the woman's pleasure the man's own climax. This climax is now rendered in glorious Eastmancolor, sometimes even on a wide screen with optical or slow-motion effects, and accompanied by all the moans, groans, and cries, synchronized or post-synched, appropriate to such activity.

With all these changes, and especially with this late arrival of sound as a key element in the heightened explicitness of the genre, it is tempting to conclude that the feature-length pornographic film arrives at a truly realistic "hard core." In these films we seem to see not the representation of sex acts as such but, as the Meese Commission and others have put it, "sex itself," in living color and breathing sound. Yet we have only to read Ziplow's advice to porn producers and to observe with what regularity money shots are dispersed through hard-core films made in the decade after 1972 to realize the futility of assimilating hard core to a simple case of escalating verisimilitude. For obviously nothing could be more conventional than a money shot: like Diderot's speaking jewels, it is a rhetorical figure that permits the genre to speak in a certain way about sex.

The ultimate goal of the rest of this book is to determine how feature-length hard core "speaks" of sex. The present chapter will limit this discussion to the polysemic money shot alone and to the film by which that shot became best known, Gerard Damiano's *Deep*

Throat. The goal here is to determine how best to understand both the form and the content of this most prevalent device of the new hard-core film's attempt to capture an involuntary confession of pleasure.

As a substitute for what cannot be seen, the money shot can be viewed as yet another form of cinematic perversion—as a fetish substitute for less visible but more "direct" instances of genital connection. As a shot whose name derives from mainstream film industry slang for the film image that costs the most money to produce (porn producers pay their male performers extra for it), the money shot can also be viewed as an ideal instance of commodity fetishism. Finally, as the most blatantly phallic of all hard-core film representations, the money shot can be viewed as the most representative instance of phallic power and pleasure. All three of these possible meanings—Marxian, Freudian, and feminist—will be explored below.

First, though, we need to backtrack in history and ask: through what process did stag films and their primitive successors in the adult arcades evolve into feature-length pornos? How did these films come to be exhibited in public theaters and then become even more widely available through over-the-counter purchase or rental to every VCR owner in the country?

In the last chapter we saw how, partly as a result of legal battles over pornography, sexuality grew in social importance as a "vital problem" and "motive force" (Justice Brennan, quoted in Kendrick 1987, 201) of human existence while at the same time definitions of obscenity were (apparently) clarified and applied to specific texts. Paradoxically, however, as sexuality was increasingly politicized, simultaneous legal efforts to isolate and eradicate socially indigestible "cores" of obscenity proved difficult. The more a wide variety of medical, sexological, psychological, photographic, and juridical discourses constructed sex as a problem, the harder it was for any of them to isolate that part of sex which was an obscene "sex for sex's sake." In fact, as we saw in Chapter 3, precisely because isolation of a pure, prurient pleasure proved difficult, a new definition of obscenity as abusive power began to emerge.

Try as one might to identify a pornography without "redeeming social importance," it was becoming increasingly clear that all sex was socially important. For although sex was biological and "natural," the gender system in which it resided was entirely social. As this recognition of social forces in the construction of sexuality began to be admitted, the proverbial "floodgates" of pornography opened. By the early 1970s a wide variety of sexual acts could be read about or viewed in illustrated sex manuals, in the various studies of Masters and Johnson, in contemporary fiction, in new and reissued pornographic "classics," and, finally, in legal, hard-core film.

Hard-core film's route to (relatively) mainstream legitimacy progressed via three stages, each of which extended the previous limits of legal exhibition. First, in the late 1950s and 1960s, came the so-called exploitation picture. Though not hard-core, these films capitalized on spectacles of sex or violence in quickly and cheaply made feature-length narratives publicly exhibited in legitimate, but often not very respectable, movie houses. On the sex side, exploitation pictures tended to be "nudie cuties." An early example was Russ Meyer's *The Immoral Mr. Teas* (1959), a film shot in four days for $24,000. The story concerns a peripatetic delivery man who, after a visit to a dentist, develops the ability—shared by the audience— to see normally dressed women in the nude. A well-known later example was the Swedish import *I Am Curious—Yellow* (1968). As Kenneth Turan and Stephen F. Zito (1974, 11) write in their account of the American pornographic movie industry, these exploitation films could turn a large profit on cheaply made productions simply by showing more "tits and ass" than mainstream film. In the aftermath of several late-sixties Supreme Court decisions, the theaters showing such films became the testing ground and, ultimately, the outlet for hard-core material once exclusive to the illegal stags.

But before hard-core stag-film elements were incorporated into feature-length exploitation films in the early 1970s, a second stage in the formation of the new genre was reached, exemplified by the so-called beaver film. A subgenre of the illegal stag, these very short loops showing women stripping to display their naked pubis were shown in peep-show arcades and sold through private mail order. Turan and Zito (pp. 85–86) report that sometime in 1967 a San Francisco exploitation theater exhibitor showed beaver films along with his regular fare and got away with it. The next step toward hard core was to show "split beaver" films—variations of the above adding the spreading of legs or labia to facilitate a better view—followed by the "action beaver," with "action" restricted to the woman herself or another woman fondling the genital area and sometimes simulating cunnilingus.

Action beavers pushed the outer limits of what constituted legality in public exhibition at that time. They showed no hard-core action, where "action" is significantly defined as penetration of any sort, even by finger or tongue. Though much less explicit than stag films available under-the-counter or in peep-show arcades, what was new in these movies, aside from their occasional color and sound, was the simple fact of their exhibition on large, legal, public screens. Exhibitors were sometimes prosecuted, but fines were minimal and the market for the product was growing. We might note here the genesis of a number that was to become a staple of many feature-length hard-core films: the so-called lesbian or girl/girl number. "Lesbian" activities were of course common in stag films, but at this transitional moment the action beavers showing lesbian "play" had the combined ability to display the female body to maximum advantage and to defeat the censors as well. With the appearance of these films, hard core was further delimited to the display of the erect penis and penetration alone.

But before stag, beaver, and exploitation film merged into the new feature-length hard-core porno complete with sound, color, and an hour-long narrative, yet another cinematic form made its contribution. The first films to show hard-core material (now definitionally pared down) in public exploitation theaters were neither stag films nor expanded action beavers, but two documentaries about Denmark and its then-recent legalization of mass-produced visual pornography: *Sexual Freedom in Denmark* (John Lamb, 1970) and *Censorship in Denmark: A New Approach* (Alex de Renzy, 1970). Both films took immediate and clever advantage of the "redeeming social importance" clause of the 1966 Supreme Court rulings. Purporting to be (and in a sense they actually were) investigative documents of the new Danish permissiveness, the films reported on that country's pornography industry.

Censorship in Denmark, for example, begins as a travelogue of Copenhagen during a major sex-trade show, interviewing people on the streets, touring sex shops, and, in a gesture that incorporates action beaver conventions, documenting a live nightclub "lesbian" sex act entitled "Olga and Her Sex Circus." A hard-core porno actress is interviewed while naked, and we see scenes from one of her films, photographed off an actual theater screen. We also see the filming of a Danish hard-core film. In both films-within-the-film the long-withheld erect penis finally appears (the documentary may even suggest one reason for its belated arrival on the legitimate screen: the male actor on the set has difficulty sustaining his erection and must be helped by a woman with a vibrator). Although we see what the audience of both the live sex act and the screened film see, the film that we are watching fulfills its documentary (as opposed to "purely" prurient) function by showing us the socially significant content as well: the simple fact that Danish audiences can watch what Americans could not yet watch—though the exhibition of this "document" proved that we were quickly catching up.

Audiences who might never have gone to see a lesbian act on the stage, and who still could not legally see a hard-core pornographic film in a theater, could, if they wanted, justify seeing this film as part of a quest for knowledge about the sexual mores of a different culture. The new wave of visual pornography of the late sixties and early seventies was thus never intended simply to celebrate a sexual permissiveness "liberated" by the American sexual revolution; it was at least partly linked, as this revolution was itself linked, to a quest for greater knowledge about sexuality.

It is easy to make light of the sincerity of this quest. Certainly the early films spawned by this confluence of forces—films such as *Case Histories from Krafft-Ebing* (Dakota Bros., 1971); compilation films like Alex de Renzy's *History of the Blue Movie* (1970), which turned a studious eye on the stag film; massage parlor "exposés" such as *Rabin's Revenge* (Mitchell Bros., 1971); or behind-the-scenes "reports" on exploitation film directors like *The Casting Call* (Gentlemen II Prod., 1970)—could hardly be taken seriously as advancing scientific knowledge of sexual practices. Yet as these early titles suggest, there is in fact no separating "sex for sex's sake" from the quest for knowledge of sex being undertaken by investigators into the *scientia sexualis* (Foucault 1978, 57–58).

In the transition from illicit stag films to the legal, fictional narratives that burst on the public consciousness in 1972 with *Deep Throat*, then, a scientific "discourse of sexuality" purporting to elicit a confession of further "truths" of sex once again played a major role. By 1972 hard-core pornography had become a household word, growing even more familiar through shortening to "porn" and "porno." For the first time cinematic works containing hard-core action were reviewed by the entertainment media and viewed by a wide spectrum of the population, including, most significantly, women. Performers and directors were named and became "known." Although *Deep Throat* was undoubtedly the best-known title, other films of 1972, such as *Behind the Green Door* (Mitchell Bros.) and *The Devil in Miss Jones* (Damiano), were also well known. As for *Deep Throat*, "not to have seen it," said Nora Ephron, writing for *Esquire*, "seemed somehow . . . derelict" (quoted in Smith 1973, 721).

Deep Throat opened in the summer of 1972 in a typical exploitation theater, the New Mature World Theater in Times Square. Richard Smith (1973, 8–9) describes the theater as a typical "grind house" of the neighborhood, catering to what came to be called the "raincoat brigade"—furtive, middle-aged men who went to see the exploitation fare, the beaver films, and whatever else was becoming legal on the big screen in the late sixties and early seventies, and so named for their presumed masturbatory activity under raincoats. Had *Deep Throat* attracted the attention of only this relatively small, but loyal, audience, no one would have remembered it, even despite, I would suggest, its "deep throat" gimmick.

What was memorable in *Deep Throat* was precisely what most people disparaged about it: its "threadbare," "poor excuse" for a plot. Yet in concentrating on this defect vis-à-vis other forms of narrative, critics missed the more important fact that the film had a plot at all, and a coherent one to boot, with the actions of characters more or less plausibly motivated. For the first time in hard-core cinematic pornography a feature-length film—not a documentary or a pseudodocumentary, not a single-reel, silent stag film or the genital show of beaver films—managed to integrate a variety of sexual numbers (even more than the ten Ziplow advises) into a narrative that was shown in a legitimate theater.

Or almost legitimate, for *Deep Throat*'s theater owner was arrested twice for promoting obscenity. Cleaning Times Square of the likes of such films became a major issue in New York's mayoral election of that year. The publicity, of course, only helped business. Like most of the previous book trials, the trial of *Deep Throat* enhanced the public's desire to see what censors would withhold: the latest revelations about sex. So even though the New Mature World Theater was ordered closed in March 1973, the film had already been seen in New York alone by over a quarter of a million people and had grossed over a million dollars.

The audience was clearly no longer the much-maligned "raincoat brigade," nor was attendance furtive. What brought the crowds was not what the critics said about the film—most panned it both as a film and as "eroticism"; rather, what counted was the mere fact that critics were talking about it at all. Among reviewers only Al Goldstein of *Screw* magazine gave the film a rave, calling it the "very best porno ever made" (quoted in Smith 1973, 31). Goldstein was perhaps one of the few critics positioned to look at the film in relation to its generic tradition. He saw what the legitimate critics, too shell-shocked by a first public encounter with phallic hard core, could not see: an unprecedented merger of extended narration and hard-core sex. He also saw deep-throat fellatio followed by a money shot, which seemed to him an affirmation of an organ that had been kept under wraps for far too long.

The Money Shot

Up and down, up and down, to the very depths of cosmic truth I saw that two-inches-short-of-a-foot-long cock engulfed like some soft vacuum cleaner taking vengeance on man for eons of past suckfuls. Then the climactic moment I was poised and ready for appeared! Hot white cum shot out and *Our Lady of the Lips* lapped it up. I was never so moved by any theatrical performance since stuttering through my own bar mitz-vah. "Stupendous!" was all I could shout as I stood up and spent my applause on the glory that mine eyes had just seen.

(Al Goldstein, quoted in
Smith 1973, 32)

For the first time in the history of the American cinema, a penis central to the action of a story appeared "in action" on the big screen of a legitimate theater.[1] Goldstein seems fully identified with the penis that achieves this "climactic moment" for which he was poised: climax is the end of the story, the signal that it is time to "spend" his applause. Thus with the money shot we appear to arrive at what the cinematic will-to-knowledge had relentlessly pursued ever since photographer Eadweard Muybridge first threw the image of naked moving bodies on the screen of his lecture hall and ever since Thomas Edison ordered his technicians to photograph a sneeze: the visual evidence of the mechanical "truth" of bodily pleasure caught in involuntary spasm; the ultimate and uncontrollable—ultimate *because* uncontrollable—confession of sexual pleasure in the climax of orgasm.

At the same time, however, this confirming close-up of what is after all only *male* orgasm, this ultimate confessional moment of "truth," can also be seen as the very limit of the visual representation of sexual pleasure. For to show the quantifiable, material "truth" of his pleasure, the male pornographic film performer must withdraw from any tactile connection with the genitals or mouth of the woman so that the "spending" of his ejaculate is visible. With this convention, viewers are asked to believe that the sexual performers within the film *want* to shift from a tactile to a visual pleasure at the crucial moment of the male's orgasm. It is a common conceit of much early-seventies hard-core pornography that the woman prefers the sight of the ejaculating penis or the external touch of the semen to the thrust of the penis inside her. She will frequently call for the money shot in the familiar "dirty talk" of the newly voiced genre, saying, for example, that she wants the man to "come all over her face," to see it come out of his "big hard cock," or to feel the hot substance spurt on some specific part of her body. Nevertheless, it is always quite evident that this spectacle is not really for her eyes. She may even close her eyes if the man comes on her face; and, try as she might, she cannot possibly see the ejaculate when he comes, as frequently he does, on her buttocks or the small of her back.

The man, in contrast, almost always sees himself ejaculate; the act seems much more clearly intended for his eyes and those of the viewer. The money shot is thus an obvious perversion—in the literal sense of the term, as a swerving away from more "direct" forms of genital engagement—of the tactile sexual connection. It substitutes for the relation between the actors the more solitary (and literally disconnected) visual pleasure of the male performer and the male viewer. Perhaps even more perverse—at least to female viewers, who can now, if they wish, see these films—is the genre's frequent insistence that this visual confession of a solitary male "truth" coincides with the orgasmic bliss of the female. Such is, of course, the conceit of *Deep Throat*: the placement of clitoris in the female protagonist's throat is a repositioning that aligns visible male orgasm with the face's power of expression.

I use the term *perversion* here in a neutral sense, as a swerving away from more direct forms of pleasure in general. It is fundamentally a way of describing the substitutive nature of the money shot. But it would be naive to expect such a loaded term to remain truly neutral. The money shot could be derided all too easily as a perversion of more "natural" heterosexual or even lesbian couplings. Feminists must thus be particularly careful when invoking *perversion* in this way, since the embrace of sexual technologies or practices that patriarchal interests have defined as perversions— such as abortion, contraception, lesbianism, and the sexology of the clitoris—have all had potential liberatory value for some women.

Gayatri Spivak (1981) has written in this regard that male orgasmic pleasure "normally" entails an element of the male reproductive function: it produces sperm. Female orgasmic pleasure, in contrast, does not necessarily entail any component of the female reproductive cycle—ovulation, fertilization, conception, gestation, or birth. Thus "the clitoris escapes reproductive framing."

In legally defining woman as object of exchange in terms of reproduction, it is not only the womb that is literally appropriated, it is the clitoris as the signifier of the sexed subject that is effaced. All investigation into the definition of woman as legal object falls into varieties of the effacement of the clitoris.

(Spivak 1981, 181)

While celebration of the clitoris thus might constitute one way to begin to challenge the power of a phallic economy of pleasure, it could do so only if the goal were not to set up an alternative organ of fetishistic worship but rather to dismantle the hierarchy of norm and deviation and so create a plurality of pleasures accepting of difference.

Deep Throat's peculiar fetish, then, poses a special problem to feminists who want to challenge phallic power and pleasure without condemning it as perverse and without re-fetishizing woman's own organs in its place. Caught, as it were, between the devil of buying into (even if also reversing the terms of) a normative phallic sexuality, on the one hand, and the deep blue sea of embracing (potentially) liberating "perversions" on the other, we need to scrutinize carefully the structure of perversions that currently reign in feature-length pornography, as well as the theories that help explain them. What system of references do we invoke when we call the money shot a fetish? When we employ these references, are we thereby playing into a dichotomy of norm/deviation? What alternatives are available to us?

The Marxian and Freudian Fetish

In a famous passage from *Capital*, Marx defines the commodity as a "mysterious thing" in which the "social character of men's labour" appears to be "stamped" on the very products of that labor. Through an extended analogy to vision that is especially appropriate to visual representation, Marx explains that just as "the light from an object is perceived by us not as the subjective excitation of our optic nerve, but as the objective form of something outside the eye itself," so we see the commodity as objectively possessing certain qualities. But whereas in the act of seeing there is "an actual passage of light from one thing to another," in the subjective perception of commodities, all is illusion. For in those commodities, the "social relation between men" assumes "the fantastic form of a relation between things." Marx finally finds his proper analogy in the "mist-enveloped regions of the religious world," where fetish objects of worship are "endowed with life" by the "productions of the human brain": "So it is in the world of commodities with the products of men's hands. This I call the Fetishism which attaches itself to the products of labour, so soon as they are produced as commodities, and which is therefore inseparable from the production of commodities" (Marx [1867] 1906, 83). To Marx, then, the fetish is a form of delusion whereby the workers who produce a commodity fail to recognize the product of their own labor.

In an equally famous passage written a half-century later (one that we have already had occasion to examine), Sigmund Freud, too, defines the fetish as a delusion: it is a substitute phallus created in the unconscious of a little boy who does not want to surrender the belief that his mother has a penis.

He retains this belief but he also gives it up; during the conflict between the deadweight of the unwelcome perception and the force of the opposite wish, a compromise is constructed such as is only possible in the realm of unconscious modes of thought. . . . In the world of psychical reality the woman still has a penis in spite of all, but this penis is no longer the same as it once was. Something else . . . now absorbs all the interest which formerly belonged to the penis. But this interest undergoes yet another very strong reinforcement, because the horror of castration sets up a sort of permanent memorial to itself by creating this substitute. Aversion from the real female genitals, which is never lacking in any fetishist, also remains as an indelible stigma of the repression that has taken place. One can now see what the fetish achieves and how it is enabled to persist. It remains a token of triumph over the threat of castration and a safeguard against it.

(Freud [1927] 1963, 153)

Although Marx and Freud define their fetishes very differently, they both share a common will to expose the processes by which individuals fall victim to an illusory belief in the exalted value of certain (fetish) objects. Thus both writers pose the illusion of the fetish object's intrinsic value against their own greater knowledge of the social-economic or psychic conditions that construct that illusion. For Marx in 1867, and for Freud in 1927, the term *fetish* already carried a conventional opprobrium inherited from eighteenth-century studies of primitive religion.[2]

The savages whom travelers in the 1700s saw bowing before crude, and often phallic, "stocks and stones" were not only, in their worship of graven images, disobeying one of the most important tenets of Protestantism, but they were also so blinded by the sensuous materiality of their fetishes that they forgot that it was they themselves who had invested these objects with value. In its original, religious definition, then, fetishism was understood as a delusion whereby the fetish makers worshiped their own constructions not simply as conventional human-produced *symbols* of supernatural power, but as the literal embodiment of that power. They gave up, in other words, their own productive powers.

In transposing earlier studies of religion, Marx and Freud share the insight that worshipers delude themselves into thinking that the fetish object has intrinsic value: the Marxian and Freudian fetishist locates illusory and compensatory pleasure and power in the gleam of gold or the lacy frill of an undergarment. In a sense, then, both theorists offer an economic application of what in the eighteenth century had originally been a critique of religion, Marx in the direct economic terms of the investment of labor, and Freud in the more indirect sense of psychic investment in a libidinal economy. For both, fetishization involves the construction of a substitute object to evade the complex realities of social or psychic relations.

Fetishes are thus short-term, short-sighted solutions to more fundamental problems of power and pleasure in social relations. For Freud, however, the illusory and compensatory belief in the fetish is a relatively minor perversion. He accepts as perceptual truth the "horror" and the "threat" of a castration objectively located in the "real female genitals," thus tending to sympathize with the fetishist's delusion. He does not, like Marx, condemn the delusion as savagery; rather, he universalizes it as part of the primary process of unconscious and infantile thought.

Where Freud normalizes the perversion, Marx rhetorically presses the point of a modern commodity-fetishistic savagery. For Marx the horror lies in the perversity of an exchange in which persons begin relating to each other as things, and things take on the social relations of persons (Marx [1867] 1906, 73; Mitchell 1986, 190). Marx is thus the theorist most inclined to employ *fetishism* as a term of old-fashioned, moralizing abuse. He forthrightly accuses all under the commodity's spell of being like the savages who have given up their very humanity to a thing.

Freud is more sympathetic. As the explorer of the human rationale behind the perversions, instead of the revolutionary who would overthrow them, he seems to accept the visual truth of what the fetishist sees when he looks at the woman's body. Freud thus shares some of the fetishist's belief in the "horror of castration" embodied in the female genitalia, unable himself to see beyond appearances to recognize how social relations of power have constructed him to so perceive women's genitals. Since Freud's scenario of vision asserts a self-evident perceptual "truth" of female lack, his very explanation originates in a fetishistic misrecognition of a sensuous, perceptual thing, followed by the creation of a compensatory substitute, the fetish. It is as if Freud trusts the fetishist's vision in initially judging women's sexual difference as lack but mistrusts the ability of the fetish to solve the problem of the "truth" it confronts. Hence, only in the second part of his analysis—when he disavows what he already knows to be true—does Freud not fall victim to the very process he is attempting to analyze.

Marx's explanation of commodity fetishism is, in contrast, more suspicious of sight from the outset. He looks critically at the physics of sight and at how we assume that sight originates in the object of vision when actually it is a "subjective excitation" of the optic nerve. Marx is then quick to point out that even this analogy is flawed, for while the act of seeing at least involves a relation, an actual passage of light from the object to the eye, no real relation obtains between the physical properties of commodities and the values that accrue to them. In looking at commodities we can never see the things themselves but only the value that has been stamped on them: the money they are worth rather than the social relations that have given them their value. We project the value of our own human labor onto the products of that labor.

Marx, then, sees a "horror" that lies not in the object of vision but in the subjective process of fetishization—in what happens to the idolater who fails to see his connection to other human producers and who therefore loses his own humanity as he invests inanimate objects with human attributes. Freud, too, sees an idolater who invests in an inanimate object, but this idolater retains his own humanity by turning the woman into an object even *before* he invests his desire in the substitute for her missing phallus. Thus for Freud there is an original moment of "true" vision that is horrified by the radical otherness of what it sees. For Marx, however, the reality of social and economic relations involves a dialectical process that does not lend itself to a single view. It is for this reason that a Marxian, political analysis of the prior *social* fact of the devaluation of women must always be factored into a discussion of the Freudian fetish.

The Money Shot and *Deep Throat*

This comparison of the Marxian and Freudian fetish can help us to understand how commodity culture, sexual pleasure, and phallic subjectivity interpenetrate in the hard-core porno's money shot. As the industry's slang term for the moment the hard-core film "delivers the goods" of sexual pleasure, the money shot seems the perfect embodiment of the illusory and insubstantial "one-dimensional" "society of the spectacle" of advanced capitalism—that is, a society that consumes images even more avidly than it consumes objects (Marcuse 1964; Debord 1967).

But of course, it is in its connection to both ejaculate and money proper (that ultimate obscenity) that the money shot is most obviously a fetish. In combining money and sexual pleasure—those simultaneously valuable and dirty things—the money shot most perfectly embodies the profound alienation of contemporary consumer society. Marx's insight into the analogy between commodities and money on the one hand and the "stocks and stones" of religious fetishes on the other is that although both may conveniently represent human labor in a fixed and stable form, ultimately labor produces commodities that are the very means of relations of exchange and hence cannot be so fixed. When it *is* so fixed, then this very stability and representability operate to dissolve all sense of human connection and process. Thus money comes to be seen, as W. T. J. Mitchell (1986, 191–192) notes, not as "an 'imaginary' symbol of exchange-value, but as 'the direct incarnation of all human labor,' the 'embodiment' of value."

Once money takes on the function of representing the exchange value of an object, the process of commodity exchange splits, as F. W. Haug (1986, 32) observes, into the two isolated and antithetical components of sale and purchase. The consumer uses money to obtain use value, while the seller uses use value to extract exchange value in the form of money. The contradictory aims of consumer and producer very quickly create a situation in which it no longer matters what the actual use value of a commodity is so long as the commodity *appears* useful to the consumer. Thus very early in the development of capitalism, aesthetic illusion became an independent function of selling. Packaging and desirability, as opposed to proven usefulness, began to substitute for the tangible product.

What is most characteristic of late-capitalist fetishistic consumption, then, is that increasingly nothing tangible is purchased. We might compare the pleasure of viewing a contemporary porno film to the more straightforward exchange between prostitute and john, where the consumer does, at least momentarily, possess the "goods" (or, for that matter, to the early stag film, where the "goods" actually address the spectator as consumer and put on a show). The advantage (to capital) of this vicarious image-satisfaction is that the very insubstantiality of the use value purchased feeds back into the structure of needs, renewing the consumer's willingness to pay for that which will never be owned (Haug 1986, 55).

As Haug (p. 19) puts it, adapting Marx, "commodities borrow

their aesthetic language from human courtship" and cast flirtatious glances at their buyers. The effect of such commodity courtship mediated by money is that "people are conditioned to enjoy that which betrays them," even when, like the fetishist, they know that their enjoyment is founded on an illusion (p. 53). In a postindustrial society, spending (it is said) is the key to a healthy, though inflated, economy. Perhaps in the money shot's repeatedly inflated, "spending" penis we can see condensed all the principles of late capitalism's pleasure-oriented consumer society: pleasure figured as an orgasm of spending; the fetish not simply as commodity but as the surplus value of orgasm.

But before we ourselves buy too far into the seductive attractions of this economic analogy, we should explore some of the sexual assumptions that lie beneath its surface—for there is something almost *too* phallic about this money shot. In the predominantly male-oriented economy of contemporary sexual pleasure, typically the *woman's* body has functioned as the fetish commodity, the surplus value, of pleasure. Steven Marcus was one of the first critics of pornography to note this fact when, in *The Other Victorians* (1974, viii–xiv), he wrote of the "exquisite" correspondence of the "unlimited female orgasmic capacity" and contemporary consumer society. The crucial link between "unlimited female orgasmic capacity"— the familiar image of the insatiable pornographic woman—and contemporary consumerism may thus seem more apt than the money shot as an emblem of mass-produced sexual fantasies, especially if this woman is masturbating, as Marcus tells us she probably would be, "with the aid of a mechanical-electrical instrument" (p. xiv)— yet another commodity fetish.

The passage just quoted occurs in an updated introduction to Marcus's 1966 study of nineteenth-century Victorian pornography and represents the author's attempt to acknowledge the prevalence of the new (film) pornography that seems almost too perfectly to realize the genre's goals of sexual abundance. Although Marcus is no fan of pornography in general, he recognizes its function of fantasy wish-fulfillment in nineteenth-century pornography, with its emphasis on male pleasure. In this single allusion to modern film pornography, however, Marcus implies that the twentieth-century image of a masturbating woman can be interpreted as the very symbol of alienated consumer culture: a glut of the senses. He thus abandons in this instance his theory of pornography as Freudian wish-fulfillment acting out abundance where really there is scarcity, in favor of a (more Marxist) reading of the pornographic body as directly *reflecting* the alienated conditions of its economic base.

In nineteenth-century pornography the fantasy is the reverse of reality: "all men are infinitely rich in substance, all men are limitlessly endowed with that universal fluid currency which can be spent without loss" (Marcus 1974, 22). In the twentieth century the fantasy, for Marcus, has become the horrible truth of a newly discovered female orgasmic potential. Marcus may be right in observing that a fundamental shift occurs in the representation of sexual pleasure from the nineteenth to the twentieth century. He may also be right in suggesting that this shift is related to changes in the dominant economic modes of production and consumption in these periods, and to the male and female models of sexuality that attach to these modes.

Marcus invokes a curious double standard, however, when he offers a utopian model of nineteenth-century (male-economic) pornography, or "pornotopia," and a realistically reflective, dystopian model of twentieth-century (female-economic) pornography. Here we can glimpse some of the past pitfalls of invoking Marx and Freud in the pornographic critique. This characterization of a nineteenth-century, male-oriented pornography as active utopian longing and a twentieth-century, female-oriented pornography as a passive glut of the senses reflective of an insatiable society of consumption dramatizes the difficulty of bringing economics and psychoanalysis to bear on the history of sexual representations. Like Freud, and like the pornography he discusses, Marcus offers a dramatic illustration of the inability of a phallic visual economy to imagine female pleasure as anything but either insufficiency or excess.

Nonetheless, Marcus's attempt to characterize the change in pornography—from literary to film, from male pleasure to female pleasure—remains instructive. The image of the masturbatory female haunts a great deal of pornography; but the masturbatory female using an electrical-mechanical instrument and in no dire need of a man to satisfy her is new. This woman is simultaneously insatiable *and* satisfied, capable both of continuing her pleasure indefinitely and of satisfying herself through her own efforts at clitoral stimulation. Writing in the wake of Masters and Johnson and *Deep Throat*, and just before Shere Hite's 1976 report documenting the masturbatory experiences of women, Marcus seems to resist the new concern with the quantitative and qualitative difference of female sexuality.

This difference is, indeed, what the story of *Deep Throat* is all about. For all its silliness and obvious misogyny, this movie attempts to perceive the different "truth" of women's pleasure in ways unparalleled in previous film pornography. The movie's numerous money shots are posed as the answer to the female protagonist's dissatisfaction with her previous experiments of sex. The story is this: a young "swinging single" named Linda (played by Linda Lovelace) confesses to a more experienced woman friend that she finds sex pleasant—"a lot of little tingles"—but not earthshakingly orgasmic—no "bells ringing, dams bursting, or bombs going off." "Experiments" with numerous men in a variety of numbers confirm this fact. The emphasis in these experiments, it should be noted, is primarily on "meat" rather than "money."

We can already note an important difference between this scenario and that of the stag film. Whereas the one-reel stag gets down to its sexual business very quickly, assuming that the act (or show) of sex is significant or fulfilling in its own right, *Deep Throat* is typical of the new wave of post-1972 narrative hard core in that it problematizes satisfaction itself. For the difficulty that Linda confesses at the film's beginning is not the peccadillo of transgressive sexual adventure, as in *Les bijoux indiscrets*, but a much more shameful crime: the failure to find absolute fulfillment in these adventures.

The film thus begins with a premise that is quite rare in the stag film—the idea that sexual pleasure is not the same for everyone or, as Linda's older and wiser female friend puts it, the need for "diff'rent strokes for diff'rent folks." This well-known seventies cliché is an apt description of the new ethic of hard-core film, which sees itself as welcoming and encouraging a greater variety of sexual practice than could ever be represented in the short stag film. In the film's narrative the discovery of Linda's anatomical difference seems to stand symbolically for a male perception of the different sexual pleasure of women in general. This difference then becomes the motive for further experimentation.

Experimentation takes place under the auspices of therapy—yet another seventies cliché. In a clinical examination that involves a telescope in place of a speculum, Linda's sexologist doctor (the ubiquitous Harry Reems) informs her that she is different: she doesn't "have one." In a phallogocentric misunderstanding that Luce Irigaray would appreciate, Linda responds: "I'm a woman, I'm not supposed to have one." What is at stake in this film, however—and, I would argue, in much feature-length pornography of this period— is precisely the extent to which Irigaray's notion of the phallic "one" can be used to figure and then fix the "two" (or more) of feminine difference.

When the doctor finally locates Linda's clitoris in her throat, he reassures her that having "one" there is better than having "none at all." Her concern is with the freak status this lends her—"What if your balls were in your ears!" (His answer, "Then I could hear myself coming," is in keeping with the male obsession with measurable evidence of pleasure.) Physiotherapy soon comes to the rescue and, with much practice, beginning on the doctor himself, Linda learns the "deep throat" technique that leads to a climactic money shot —narratively presented as simultaneous with Linda's own long- awaited climax—that is enhanced by intercutting with fireworks, ringing bells, bursting bombs, and firing missiles.

The deep throat gimmick thus works to naturalize what in the stag film had always been the most photogenic of all sexual practices: fellatio. Fellatio—culminating in a money shot in which ejaculation occurs on the woman's face and mouth—becomes, in the wake of *Deep Throat*'s enormous popularity, the privileged figure for the expression of climax and satisfaction (reaching, in fact, a kind of apotheosis in *Behind the Green Door*, made later that same year).

Satisfied for the first time in her life, Linda wants only to marry her doctor and be, as she says, his "slave." But the doctor has a more modern idea: she will become a physiotherapist. What follows is an extended parody of Masters and Johnson–style sex therapy in which Linda administers to various mildly kinky men while still undergoing "therapy" herself with the doctor. He soon lands in bed with a bandage around his exhausted penis, unable to meet her demands for more sex. Though comically treated, the specter of the insatiable woman has been shown to take its toll on more limited men. The final "gag" that ends the film "solves" this problem by introducing a bigger and better penis. In her work as a physiotherapist Linda encounters Wilbur, who likes to play the role of a sadistic burglar caught in the act of spying on her. Beneath this superficial kink, however, he is sweet and gentle, the man of her dreams. When he proposes to Linda, she insists that the man she marries must have a "nine-inch cock" to satisfy the demands of her "deep throat." Wilbur instantly calls the doctor, saying he is only four inches away from happiness. The doctor reassures him, and Wilbur turns to Linda with the news that his thirteen-inch penis can be cut down to any size she wants. Little Wilbur is thus her ideal man.

In just about every sense, *Deep Throat* can be said—for all its talk about the clitoris—visually to fetishize the penis. Yet as we have seen, the question of how to read this fetishization cannot be answered without recognizing the new importance of the clitoris. An oversimplistic feminist reading of this film might miss the sense in which the newly prominent clitoris has called for the money shot. It would only see the money shot as depriving women of "natural," organic pleasure by imposing on them the perversion not merely of fellatio, but of this particular degrading, gagging, "deep throat" variety (see Chapter 1). Gloria Steinem (1986b, 275), for example, writes that Damiano, the film's director, invented a gimmick that was "second only to Freud's complete elimination of the clitoris as a proper source of female pleasure. . . . Though his physiological fiction about *one* woman was far less ambitious than Freud's fiction about *all* women, his porn movie had a whammo audiovisual impact; a teaching device that Freudian theory had lacked." Thus the "millions of women" whose boyfriends, husbands, or pimps took them to the film were taught how to please a man by the example of this humiliating obeisance to the fetish.

In Steinem's interpretation, the woman is cast as Marx's savage fetishist who bows down and surrenders her own "proper source of female pleasure" to the power and pleasure of the phallus. The repeated ejaculations onto her face could thus be read as visual proof of her objectification and humiliation. Although there is a smile on that face, we read in Linda Lovelace (Marchiano's) autobiography that this smile was a lie masking terror and pain, that she was a sex slave to the man who was her pimp and manager, and that her entire life at this time was, like the title of this autobiography, an ordeal (Lovelace and McGrady 1980).

While I am inclined to believe Marchiano's allegations that she was coerced off screen to perform inauthentic pleasures on screen, and while I do not question the importance for feminists to reject as inauthentic the pleasures of women portrayed in such films, I do question the notion, strongly implied in Steinem's argument, that the film and, indeed, all pornography repress a "proper" female pleasure. I would argue instead that even though *Deep Throat* elides the visual representation of Linda Lovelace's clitoris, and even though its money shot fetish operates, in Gayatri Spivak's words, to "efface" that organ, its narrative is constantly soliciting and trying to find a visual equivalent for the invisible moments of clitoral orgasm. So if on the one hand the film tries to efface sexual difference through a gimmick that renders the practice of fellatio more "natural," on the other hand this very effacement could be said to allegorize the problem of difference by actually giving it Linda Lovelace's face.

All of the film's solicitous concern for the location of the clitoris thus needs to be seen in the context of the relatively new prominence this organ has received in other forms of the *scientia sexualis*. This new knowledge views the clitoris precisely not as a diminished or absent version of the penis—as in Freud's account of the phallic economy of the one—but as a new economy not reducible to that one: an economy of the *many*, of "diff'rent strokes for diff'rent folks." Even though the film's fetishization of the phallus attempts to disavow difference at the moment of orgasm and to model that orgasm on a decidedly phallic model of "bursting bombs," and even though the woman is portrayed as dependent for her pleasure on the "one" of the man, a contradictory subtext of plurality and difference is also registered. The very fact that the expanded narrative of the new feature-length hard-core film parodically joins with the scientific, Masters and Johnson–style quest for the "truth" of woman's difference indicates how fully the woman's invisible and unquantifiable pleasure has now been brought into frame, onto the scene of the obscene.

The paradox of contemporary feature-length pornography and its fetish of the money shot might therefore be described as follows: it is the obsessive attempt of a phallic visual economy to represent and "fix" the exact moment of the sexual act's involuntary convulsion of pleasure. The money shot utterly fails to represent the satisfaction of desire as involving a desire for, or of, the other; it can only figure satisfaction as failing to do what masculine sexual ideology frequently claims that the man does to the woman: to occupy, penetrate, possess her. Thus the solipsistic withdrawal from the other to the self paradoxically constructs another "memorial to lack" right where we might most expect to see presence and fullness. It would be wrong, however, to repeat Freud's misrecognition and to call this lack "castration." We might more properly call it a lack of relation to the other, a lack of ability to imagine a relation to the other in anything but the phallic terms of self.

Even though the money shot offers perhaps the clearest example of the phallic economy's failure to recognize difference, we must realize that it has been posed as a solution precisely because that economy is more aware of sexual difference and varying pleasures than it was in previous pornography. So rather than compare the phallic economy invoked by *Deep Throat* with that of Freud, as Steinem does, we might do better to contrast them. In Freud, fetishization is an obvious way for the male subject to maintain the phallic economy of the one. As we saw earlier, the Freudian fetishist attempts to preserve his own humanity at the expense of stressing the freakish inhumanity—the "horror"—of the female other. *Deep Throat* does not simply repeat this objectification of the female other; or, rather, if it does repeat it, it so blatantly puts the reigning "phallocracy" on display that we can glimpse, in the univocal limitations of its economy of the one, possible elaborations of economies of the many.

Foucault (1978, 48) writes that along with the incitement to sexuality contained in the modern age's proliferating discourses on the subject comes an increasing tendency to identify and address many different specialized sexual practices and in that process to "implant" these perversions. However absurd it may seem, I think one might say that the perverse implantation of the clitoris in *Deep Throat* represents something more than simple horror at the freakishness of female sexual "lack." It represents a phallic economy's highly ambivalent and contradictory attempt to count beyond the number one, to recognize, as the proliferating discourses of sexuality take hold, that there can no longer be any such thing as a fixed sexuality—male, female, or otherwise—that now there are proliferating sexual*ities*. For if the "implantation of perversions" is, as Foucault says, an instrument *and* an effect of power, then as discourses of sexuality name, identify, and ultimately produce a bewildering array of pleasures and perversions, the very multiplicity of these pleasures and perversions inevitably works against the older idea of a single norm—an economy of the one—against which all else is measured.

Fetishism

A fetish is indeed, as Marx said, "a mysterious thing." The lesson that feminism can draw from both Marx's and Freud's understanding of this mystery is to not fall back on the simple religious condemnation of fetishism as an illusory fraud perpetrated on the credulous. In an essay entitled "Women on the Market," Luce Irigaray offers an extended analysis of the analogy between the Marxian definition of value as predicated on exchange and the valuation of women's bodies created in the exchange of women by men. Even though women, like commodities, do have an intrinsic use value related to their reproductive function, she argues, it is in the process of placing two women in a quantifiable relation to a third term—whether gold or a phallus—that women lose their own bodily specificity and become, like the commodity, an abstract and undifferentiated "product of man's labor." Thus desire, in the context of exchange, "perverts" need, "but that perversion will be attributed to commodities (*marchandises*) and to their alleged relations." In fact, though, since these commodities have "no relationships except from the perspective of speculating third parties," woman-as-commodity exists both as a natural body with a *use value* and as a body with a socially constructed *exchange value* that mirrors masculine desire (Irigaray 1985, 177). As Gayle Rubin (1979, 176) has similarly noted in a classic essay that examines the Marxian and the Lévi-Straussian aspects of the exchange of women by men, this seemingly natural system, on which economics and kinship are both based, in the end keeps women from engaging in use and exchange among themselves.[3]

Irigaray's and Rubin's adaptations of Marxian economics help to explain why the contemporary pornographic film's fascination with female pleasure has such difficulty representing what this pleasure means to women. Without defining positively what woman's sexuality is, Irigaray suggests that it might be possible to recognize the existence of a nonunitary, plural economy of female pleasures. But to do so we would have to abandon the sort of either/or opposition posed by Freud, which speaks solely of the one and only phallic pleasure. The question is not one of a choice, as Freud insists, between an active, clitoral pleasure and a passive, vaginal one; rather, it concerns the additive combination of a "multiplicity of erogenous zones"—the clitoris *and* the vagina, the lips *and* the vulva, and so forth. Such lists enumerating the many locations of female pleasure help to break down the either/or, active/passive dichotomies that underlie phallic sexual economies.

In both the Marxian economic and the Freudian libidinal senses, then, the fetish of the hard-core money shot compensates for scarcity and loss. But in its Freudian sense this fetish is peculiarly literal: in place of the psychic compromise that invests pleasure in a relatively indifferent signifier (Freud's example is the young man for whom a certain "shine on the nose" of a woman was necessary to his sexual pleasure), the money shot offers a real penis substituting for the mythic phallus Freud's little boy fears to have lost. Indeed, these close-ups of remarkably long, perpetually hard, ejaculating penises might seem to be literal embodiments of this idealized fantasy phallus which Freud says we all—men and women—desire. The ejaculating penis of the money shot could, in this sense, be said to disavow castration by avoiding visual association with the woman's genitalia. This, after all, is the genius of *Deep Throat*'s gimmick. By placing the clitoris in Linda Lovelace's throat, the film constructs its narrative on the importance of this organ while at the same time never having to look at it. It is as if the male fetishistic imagination, at this point in the history of the genre's attempts to capture the hard-core "truth" of pleasure, could not countenance any vision of female difference when representing the orgasmic heights of its own pleasure.

In her perceptive essay "Blind Spot of an Old Dream of Symmetry," Irigaray argues that the male-signifying economy has an overcathexis of vision, a "rule" of visibility and "specularization," that can only theorize woman as absence, lack, nothingness. If men think women are castrated versions of themselves, she argues, it is because of a fundamental castration—"a hole"—in their own limited signifying economy that can envision woman's desire only as the desire for, and of, the penis (Irigaray 1986, 49).

The value of such an analysis is that it locates castration fear and fetishization where they really belong: in the self-perceived inadequacies of the body and mind of the male consumer of pornography. From the perspective of female empowerment, Irigaray's most hopeful pronouncement (p. 51) is that the phobia about the uncanny strangeness of the "nothing to be seen" of woman is actually the fear that she does not possess the envy the man presumes her to possess. The fear, in other words, is that she has desires different from his own.

Irigaray's main point is that men are *blind* to women: to their different and multiple sex organs. We might therefore say in response to the money shot that the solution to this blindness is not to celebrate or (in turn) fix a single visual emblem of woman's difference (as, for example, the clitoris), for this too would be to fetishize, to isolate organs from the dynamic relation of exchange within which they operate. The money shot could thus finally be viewed as that moment when the phallic male libidinal and material economy most falters, most reverts to an absolute and unitary standard of value. But the import of this statement should not be that pornography is hopelessly and monolithically phallic; instead it should be that pornography is insistently phallic *in this particular way, at this particular time,* because of pressures within its own discourse to represent the visual truth of female pleasures about which it knows very little. This phallicism, then, has risen at least partly in response to the clitoris that it cannot easily fix and frame.

Today, Stephen Ziplow's 1977 formulation of the generic law "if you don't have the come shots, you don't have a porno picture" (p. 34) has been placed in doubt; not all films, as we shall see in the following chapters, observe it. One day this law may be looked back on, like the convention in westerns of good guys in white hats and bad guys in black, as an archaism no longer viable in the representation of sexual pleasures. It is probably no mere coincidence that this partial waning of the money shot has occurred as more women have gotten involved in hard-core pornography, as both makers and viewers.[4] Irigaray (1985, 203) hopefully suggests, "Perhaps if the phallocracy that reigns everywhere is put unblushingly on display, a different sexual economy may become possible." Perhaps there is strategic value to a feminist scrutiny of pornography that seeks the seeds of a different sexual economy in the limitations and inadequacies of the reigning one. Perhaps also if women can begin to ask these questions of existing pornography we will be on a path that leads to the representation of sexual pleasures becoming grounded in an economy of abundance rather than scarcity, of many rather than one.

It is this dismantling of the very idea of the norm that I find most helpful for a feminist reading of, and defense against, contemporary film pornography. For if there is no such thing as a "natural" pleasure independent of its production in social discourse, then one effective strategy for women concerned with the abusive intersection of power and pleasure in pornography may be to begin to understand the contradictions within the genre's production of pleasure. Similarly, if power, as Foucault (1978, 92) says, is to be located in discourse, and if resistance to power is "a multiple field of force relations" rather than a single revolutionary point of opposition, then clearly reestablishment of an essential truth against which the illusion of the fetish will be measured would seem an ineffective way to resist the fetish's power, since to do so would only be to establish new, potentially repressive, norms—hardly a solution to the already repressive norm of the phallus.

The Marxian fetish of commodity capital, the Freudian fetish of castration disavowal, and their convergence in the money shot can be characterized as forms of repressive power. But we need to understand that this power is not instituted from on high. Thus the Marxian tradition of iconoclasm might not serve us in resisting this fetishization either, for if we become too iconoclastic, if our only goal is to smash the abnormal and perverse idols of mammon in order to destroy the false consciousness they engender, then we may fail to grasp, and effectively to combat, the real appeal of capitalist and patriarchal power and pleasure. At the same time, if we, like Freud, lend too much legitimacy to the supposedly universal causes that have created the need for the (phallic) fetish, then we are in danger of becoming rational fetishists ourselves—of normalizing and justifying the fetish function in the name of universal processes of desire that elide the existence of the female subject.

We must come back, therefore, to the question of the most effective feminist use of the notion of perversion. For since there can be no authentic, true, or normal position from which to resist the repression of the feminine as currently enacted in visual pornography, but only the hope of breaking out of the economy of the one, it seems to me that the most effective strategy is to embrace the liberatory potential contained in the very idea of an "implantation of perversions."

The example of *Deep Throat* can thus afford the following tentative conclusions. On the one hand, it is undeniable that the film attempts, through the visual domination of the money shot, to represent the climax of a heterosexual act in entirely phallic terms: the inflated, powerful penis producing evidence of its pleasure. On the other hand, the very fact that the film seems to require this escalated visual evidence of pleasure suggests an uneasiness, a lack of belief in the previous standard for representation of pleasure. In the stag film, female genital show, male erection, and penetration sufficed. Now, under the new challenge of a different clitoral pleasure and a new narrative elaboration of pleasure, a more detailed sequence is called for: erection, penetration, climax. But since greater detail only calls attention to the impossibility of representing the climax as experienced in the "wonders of the unseen world," the climax that is represented becomes a new figure of lack.

I have tried to show that the "lack" disavowed by the fetish is not a true lack but only a perception based on the prior social and economic devaluation of women. The fetish of the money shot typifies one solution offered by hard-core film to the perennial male problem of understanding woman's difference. Another lesson, though, is that such solutions are fraught with contradictions that may open up possible routes to the resistance of hegemonic sexual pleasures. As we shall see in the next chapter, the new feature-length narrative porno will use these contradictions to locate more moments of climax in ever wider ranges of sexual numbers.

5

Generic Pleasures

Number and Narrative

In becoming legal, feature length, and narrative, hard-core film joined the entertainment mainstream. No matter how much it might still be regarded as a pariah, the new "porno" was now more a genre among other genres than it was a special case. As if to insist on this fact, hard-core narratives went about imitating other Hollywood genres with a vengeance, inflecting well-known titles and genres with an X-rated difference. Films with titles such as *Sexorcist Devil* (1974), *Beach Blanket Bango* (1975), *Flesh Gordon* (1978), *Dracula Sucks* (1979), *Downstairs Upstairs* (1980), and *Urban Cowgirls* (1981) were now exhibited in movie theaters that looked—almost—like other movie theaters. Stories, too, were almost like other film stories. Audiences, though still disproportionately male, were also becoming more like other film audiences. By the early eighties, this normalization of hard core would be further dramatized in the many videocassette rental outlets that offered X-rated adult videos on the same shelves as or adjacent to the latest horror film or teen comedy.

The present chapter examines this "genre-among-genres" quality of feature-length hard core. The goal here is not to celebrate a hardcore coming of age or the achievements of the genre's emerging *auteurs*; rather, it is to explore the significance of hard core's now-mainstream popularity. This new popularity with and appeal to more general audiences, it seems clear, represents an unprecedented mass commercialization of sex as visual pleasure and spectator sport. But the particular form that this commercialization has taken has not been adequately appreciated, owing to the embattled nature of the pornography debates. We must begin, then, with a basic question: of what, apart from the essential ingredient of the money shot, and its placement within some kind of narrative, does the genre consist?

On its face, the answer is easy: hard core consists of sexual action in, and as, narrative. This action is now rendered in color and sound in films and, increasingly, videotapes that run at least sixty minutes. Since hard-core action cannot be filmed or taped without the performance of sexual acts, it might be tempting to say that hard core is synonymous with sex itself, for we now see the sex act as event more than we see the sexual show of the stag film. But if we have learned anything from the previous chapter's lengthy analysis of the money shot, it is that although the physical act of sex obviously must take place in order to be filmed, the visual spectacle of external penile ejaculation is a tacit acknowledgment that such real-live sex acts can be communicated to viewers only through certain visual and aural conventions of representation. What, besides the money shot, are these conventions, and how do they function? Most of this chapter will be taken up with exploring the iconography of the various sexual numbers and their relation to narrative. Before turning to this subject, however, we need to examine the conventions arising from the genre's most striking new source of realist effect: its belated integration of sound technology.

The Sounds of Pleasure

The previous examination of the hard-core quest for an involuntary, self-evident "frenzy of the visible" has revealed that what passes for a confessional frenzy is really just another way of speaking about and constructing the apparent "truths" of sex. The metaphor of speech—of discourses of sexuality as ways of talking about sex—has been crucial to this construction. And yet real speech has been remarkably absent thanks to the genre's unusually prolonged silence. Thirty years after the rest of cinema had been wired for sound, the stag film still relied on the power of its images alone, persisting in the "exquisite embarrassment" of silence.

It is worth asking, then, just what difference sound made when it did become a necessary ingredient in the genre. To a certain extent, sound functions in hard core the way it functions in mainstream narrative cinema: to situate and give realistic effect to the more important image. Rick Altman (1980, 69) has noted that the single most important difference between silent and sound film is the latter's increased proportion of scenes of people talking to one another. In showing the source of sound, then, narrative cinema employs sound as an anchor to the image.

All sound, whether music, sound effects, or speech, thus functions to bolster the diegetic illusion of an imaginary space-time and of the human body's place within it. Extradiegetic music brought in from outside the depicted scene may enhance the mood and establish rhythms that complement the movements of bodies and smooth over the temporal-spatial gaps created by editing. Sound effects give solidity and spatial dimension to the depiction of the diegetic world. And synchronous speech ties the body to the voice.

Theorists of cinema sound such as Pascal Bonitzer (1976), Rick Altman (1980), Alan Williams (1980), Mary Ann Doane (1980), and Kaja Silverman (1988a) have emphasized the way these uses of sound create the illusion of the viewing subject's unity.[1] Silverman in *The Acoustic Mirror*, for example, stresses the different organization of male and female voice in mainstream cinema and the importance of nonsynchronization of female body and voice in avant-garde practices that deconstruct the dominance of the image, especially the patriarchal, fetishized image of women.

In hard-core film and video, however, the relation of sound to image differs from that in dominant cinema, though without having the function of avant-garde deconstruction. In these films, when characters talk their lips often fail to match the sounds spoken, and in the sexual numbers a dubbed-over "disembodied" female voice (saying "oooh" and "aaah") may stand as the most prominent signifier of female pleasure in the absence of other, more visual assurances. Sounds of pleasure, in this latter instance, seem almost to flout the realist function of anchoring body to image, halfway becoming aural fetishes of the female pleasures we cannot see.[2]

The articulate and inarticulate sounds of pleasure that dominate in aural hard core are primarily the cries of women. Though male moans and cries are heard as well, they are never as loud or dramatic. Other sounds of pleasure include the smack of a kiss or a slap, the slurp of fellatio and cunnilingus, the whoosh of penetration-engulfment, not to mention the sounds of bedsprings; they can also be actual words spoken by the performers during sex, from the clichés of "fuck me harder" and "I'm going to come" to less usual communiqués such as "I love you" or phrases like "ripe mango take two" (which only make sense in the particular narrative context—see below).

As in mainstream cinema, these sounds of pleasure augment the realist effect of what in cinema is the hierarchically more important visual register, lending an extra level of sensory perception to the pleasures depicted. But because of increasingly common post-dubbing, these sounds are not invoked with the same realism as sound in the mainstream feature. Many sexual numbers, especially of early hard-core sound features, were, and still are—like the musical numbers of musicals—shot "*mit* out sound." Sound is recorded elsewhere and added later in the "mix." (Ziplow [1977, 76], for example, tells his frugal would-be pornographer to order silence on the set to record some "room tone," and then to have his "sound man pick up some extra moaning and groaning" in "extra-curricular vocal work" from the performers.) In all cases, however, the effect of non-synchronous sound is to detract from the spatial realism of synchronous sound. Prerecorded (or postrecorded) sound is achieved, unlike sound recording done on the set, by placing microphones close to the body. As Alan Williams (1981, 150–151) notes of sound in movie musicals, the purpose of this closeness, of this extra sonic presence of the body, is greater clarity in the music and sung lyrics—and for this reason, movie musicals do not record sound live.

In this respect hard-core films are more like musicals than like other kinds of narrative. While hard-core sound does not seek clarity of music and lyrics, it does seek an effect of closeness and intimacy, rather than of spatial reality. In hearing the sounds of pleasure with greater clarity and from closer up, auditors of hard core sacrifice the ability to gauge the distances between bodies and their situation in space for a sense of connectedness with the sounds they hear. Williams (p. 151) refers to this effect as one of spacelessness: "To imagine this effect outside of the musical, the reader has only to think of any badly dubbed foreign film. . . . The voices seem 'too close' and whatever implied spatial environment they do possess does not change."

This, indeed, is often the (surreal) effect of a great many post-dubbed sex scenes, as well as of the dialogue sequences of the more cheaply made hard-core features. When the lip movements of the performer do not match the sounds that come from those lips, the hard-won illusions of suture are rendered null and void. It is worth asking, then, why this convention has been so popular in a genre apparently engaged in an interminable quest for realism. Certainly various practical reasons can be cited: it is both easier and cheaper to shoot sexual numbers without sound; camera operators can move close in without worrying about the sound they make; and since music, like voice and sound effects, is typically added later anyway, "live" sound hardly seems worth the added effort. But because many relatively big-budget hard-core films, which in their nonperforming, dialogue sequences do use synchronous sound, revert to nonsynchronous sound in the "numbers," this technique would seem to be an important *formal* feature of the genre's representation of sex. It is also a feature that places the hard-core film in close aural connection to the movie musical. To a great extent, in fact, the hard-core feature film *is* a kind of musical, with sexual number taking the place of musical number. The generic implications of this analogy will be explored below; for the moment, however, it is worth noting the similar rhythmic and melodic features of the sounds of pleasure on the one hand and the "sounds of music" on the other.

One observation to be drawn from this analogy is that visual and aural closeness are not commensurate. Although the movie musical and the hard-core porno prefer sounds to be "taken" from close up, there is no such thing as a close-up of sound, as there is of image. Alan Williams (1980, 53) has argued, in fact, that there is no such thing as sound in itself, and that sound recording is in no way parallel to image recording. In one sense, we could say that the close-up sound of pleasure attempts to offer the "spectacular" aural equivalent of the close-ups of "meat" and "money." Nevertheless, the aural "ejaculation" of pleasure, especially in post-synchronized sound, gives none of the same guarantee of truth that the visual ejaculation does.

A 1981 feature by Alan Vydra entitled *The Sounds of Love* illustrates this point well. In a narrative that is as (ineptly) based on the false analogy of audio overhearing to visual voyeurism as Brian de Palma's *Blow Out* is to Antonioni's *Blow-Up*, a musician is determined to record and replay for his own apocalyptic pleasure the most perfect and expressive sound of female orgasm. He hires a young stud-detective to tap the phones and wire the bedrooms of numerous women in his quest for the most powerful, natural, and spontaneous of orgasms. Echoing *Deep Throat*'s fetishization of the invisible place of female pleasure, he says: "I must be able to hear the approaching orgasm from her throat." The film, however, does not quite trust this fetishization of sound over image; all it offers (in Dolby to home viewers with the appropriate stereo equipment) are some very loud and often deep growly sounds emanating from women's throats.

The film is of interest for its failure to acknowledge the difference between the sounds and the images of pleasure. It proceeds as if the musician's quest was for a discrete single sound—a single note almost—that could do for the audiophile what the meat or money shot is presumed to do for the image fetishist. In the end the musician hears this sound in a live sequence of eavesdropping in which his own wife is brought to orgasm by the stud-detective. The musician's response is to blow them all—himself included—to kingdom come, whether out of jealousy or *jouissance* we do not know. But the film's feeble apocalyptic climax (in which sounds of an explosion accompany images of the same) merely underscores the fact that visual and aural voyeurism are very different things. The attempt to "foreground" the sounds of pleasure fails. As Mary Ann Doane points out in "The Voice in the Cinema" (1980, 39), sound cannot be "framed" as the image can, for sound is all over the theater, it "*envelops* the spectator." It is this nondiscrete, enveloping quality that, when added to the close-miked, nonsynchronous sounds of pleasure, seems particularly important in the hard-core auditor-viewer's pleasure in sound.

Although aspects of sound are measurable—in decibels, in pitch, in tone—diffuse, enveloping sound differs importantly from the discrete and framable image of the body. The allure of the sounds of pleasure resides at least partly in the fact that they come from inside the body and are often not articulate signs (meaningful combinations of sound and sense) but, rather, inarticulate sounds that speak, almost preverbally, of primitive pleasures. Although they seem to arise spontaneously, they are not involuntary as the "frenzy of the visible" of male orgasm is.

This apparent spontaneity is particularly important in the pornographic quest to represent the female desires and pleasures that come from "deep inside." *Deep Throat* is but one of many films and tapes to pose this problem, in which "depth" becomes a metaphor for getting underneath deceptive appearances. Thus depth of sound does not lend itself to the same illusion of involuntary frenzy as that offered by the visible. Nevertheless, although there can be no such thing as hard-core sound, there remains the potential, developed in some films to be discussed in the next chapter, for performers to converse with one another, in articulate or inarticulate vocables, about their pleasure.

Sexual Numbers

Let us return to the more central, visible iconography of the new hard-core feature. As we have seen, the money shot is crucial: "If you don't have the come shots you don't have a porno picture." But this shot cannot exist in isolation; it must be worked into a variety of narratives and a variety of sexual numbers. Perhaps the second most important feature of the genre, then, is that a little something is offered to satisfy a diverse, but not all-inclusive, range of sexual tastes. Stephen Ziplow, in his *Film Maker's Guide to Pornography* (1977), provides a checklist of the various sexual acts that should be included in a porno, along with the best way to film them. This extremely functional guide to the would-be pornographer is useful because it also goes to the heart of the genre's conventionality. The list includes

1. "Masturbation": with or without paraphernalia, but always including well-lit close-ups of genitalia. Although Ziplow does not

specify the sex of the masturbator, it is clear from his description that he assumes the act will be performed by a female
("It's always a lot of fun to watch a pretty lady getting off on her
own body," p. 31). Compared to the stag film, in fact, hard-
core feature-length pornography has very few scenes of male
masturbation.

2. "Straight sex": defined as male-female, penis-to-vagina penetration in a variety of positions, which Ziplow enumerates as man
   on top, woman on top, side to side, and "doggie" (p. 31).

3. "Lesbianism": here Ziplow is terse; all he says is that it is "a major
   turn-on to a larger portion of your heterosexual audience" (p.
   31).

4. "Oral sex": defined as both cunnilingus and fellatio. Ziplow notes
   that "cunnilingus presents technical difficulties" of visibility,
   since the man's head obscures the "action," whereas "blow jobs,"
   which present no such difficulty and have the further advantage
   of facilitating the money shot, are "always a hit with the porno
   crowd." His advice in both cases is to block out the action well
   in advance (p. 31).

5. "Ménage à trois": a threesome with male or female as the third
   party (p. 32). (It seems to go without saying that while two female
   members of such a configuration may involve themselves with
   each other, it is taboo for two men to do so in heterosexual hard
   core.)

6. "Orgies": "a lot of people making it together." Ziplow warns that
   these can be expensive (p. 32).

7. "Anal sex." Ziplow presumes the person receiving anal sex to be
   female (p. 32).

These are the sexual acts that Ziplow deems essential to a hard-core
feature circa 1977. But even a cursory look at a random sample of
films from 1972 on suggests that to this list could be added at least
one more "optional component," which I shall also define, in the jargon of the industry, as

8. "Sadie-max": a scene depicting sadomasochistic relations such as
   whipping, spanking, or bondage, performed with or without
   paraphernalia.

This list of sexual numbers, although quite varied—and many pornographic features do their best systematically to work in as many of these numbers as possible—is still far from inclusive. In heterosexual porno, for example, no male-to-male relations of any kind occur, nor is there any bestiality or "kiddie porn."

Iconography

The visual content of the acts listed above, including the way they are lit and photographed, constitutes the conventional iconography of the genre. Iconography is simply the pattern of visual imagery one expects to see in a given genre. Just as we expect to see monsters in horror films, guns, suits, and hats in gangster films, and horses and cowboys in westerns, so in a porno do we expect to see naked bodies engaging in sexual numbers. Yet as Stephen Neale (1980, 13) notes in a useful pamphlet on film genres, lists of visual content are only the first step to understanding genre; though helpful as descriptions of the elements of generic structure, such lists do not begin to address the dynamics of structuration. Thus, although iconography attempts to define the visual specificity of a genre—that which makes it distinct from other genres—it cannot explain *why* such visuals are employed, except as reflections of reality.

In the case of the western, for example, it is not sufficient to say that the genre simply reflects the historical reality of the American West; such a notion is tantamount to saying that the very aesthetic form of the genre itself is determined by the events of America's agrarian past (Neale 1980, 15). We have only to apply this reflective formula to pornography to see its limitation: does feature-length hard-core pornography simply reflect the sexual activities performed in American bedrooms in the wake of the sexual revolution? Is the money shot a realistic reflection of these activities?

A more fruitful approach sees genre to be less a reflection of some determinant reality than a form of modern mythmaking—a way of doing something to the world, of acting symbolically upon it. Here iconography and narrative work together to intensify oppositions and contradictions that exist within a culture, in order to seek imaginary forms of resolution. To critics Leo Braudy and Thomas Schatz, for example, a film genre's success—its ability to continue to offer something to audiences—depends on the significance of the conflicts it addresses and its flexibility in adjusting to audience and film-makers' changing attitudes toward these conflicts (Braudy 1977, 109, 179; Schatz 1981, 38).

A particularly sophisticated example of the way genres address so-cial problems is offered by Fredric Jameson in *The Political Uncon-scious* (1981). Jameson (pp. 118–119) argues that originally the genre of medieval romance was devised to solve the problem, not important in earlier epic narratives, of how an enemy from one's own class could be thought of as an evil "other" who must be destroyed. The narrative form that, typically, tells the story of an unknown and hostile knight who will not say his name or show his face stages a struggle between same-class enemies in which the hostile knight is perceived as the malevolent other, much as in earlier epic forms pa-gans were. Once defeated, however, this knight asks for mercy, lifts his visor, and tells his name, at which point he is reinserted into the unity of the social class to which he belongs; he loses his sinister oth-erness. Jameson argues that this new genre—the story of the un-known knight who first seems evil and alien, then later seems similar, offers a formal, narrative solution to the problem of an evil that can no longer be permanently assigned to whole categories of "others."

Jameson's analysis is useful because it does not see generic form as simply reflecting important aspects of history. The battles of me-dieval romance do not mirror knightly combat as it actually occurred any more than the stylized gunfights of westerns reflect how cow-boys really fought. Both scenes represent crucial moments in nar-ratives that have reworked the reality of combat in ways that permit the resolution of deeper problems, not necessarily manifest on the texts' surface. Both medieval romance and westerns rework some aspect of the past into a form for the present. Each is "talking to it-self," as Colin McArthur (1972) puts it in regard to the gangster genre, about problems that have urgency and currency in the pres-ent moment. The repetitive forms of each seem to insist on the pos-sibility of solutions, as long as the problems persist. These solutions themselves then become part of the social fabric and, in turn, im-portant in the formation of new sociohistorical realities (Neale 1980, 16).

We can therefore ask of the current hard-core genre, What prob-lems does it seek to solve? What is it "talking to itself" about? Ob-viously it is talking to itself about sex—specifically, about masturbatory, straight, "lesbian," oral, ménage à trois, anal, orgiastic, and sadomasochistic sex. By the same token, it is *not* talking to itself, except as a structuring absence, about male homosexual sex. We can also ask, What problems does the deployment of this iconography seek to solve? To answer this question, we need to understand more about how sexual iconography works with narrative.

Narrative and Number

Any of the sexual practices in the above list could be found somewhere in a stag film, as could some that are not listed. What is different about the hard-core feature, however, is the assumption, implicit in Ziplow's guide, that as many of these practices as possible will be worked into, or called forth by, the newly expanded narrative. Ziplow himself offers no description of narrative in the genre, but he is clear that it should exist; specifically, it should occupy approximately 40 percent of the screen time and should serve as a vehicle to the sexual numbers represented in the remaining 60 percent.

Although Ziplow does not explain why, narrative is assumed to be necessary to number. Now it is a commonplace for critics and viewers to ridicule narrative genres that seem to be only flimsy excuses for something else—musicals and pornography in particular are often singled out as being *really* about song and dance or sex. But as much recent work on the movie musical has demonstrated, the episodic narratives typical of the genre are not simply frivolous pretexts for the display of song and dance;[3] rather, narrative often permits the staging of song and dance spectacles as events themselves within the larger structure afforded by the story line. Narrative informs number, and number, in turn, informs narrative. Part of the pleasure of the movie musical resides in the tension between these different discursive registers, each seeking to establish its own equilibrium.

Steve Neale (1980), for example, notes the seemingly obvious but nevertheless important fact that all mainstream narrative cinema moves from relative equilibrium to disequilibrium and back. Certain genres achieve this equilibratory disruption and restoration in specific ways. In the western, the gangster, and the detective film, for example, disequilibrium is figured as physical violence: through violence, equilibrium is reestablished (pp. 20–21). Violence exists in other genres, too, such as the horror film. But here the specificity of the genre lies not so much *in* violence as in the conjunction of violence with images and definitions of the monstrous. In this genre, order and disorder are articulated across categories (and images) of "the human" versus "the monstrous" (p. 22). In the case of the musical and the melodrama, however—generic structures that bring us somewhat closer to feature-length pornography—narrative is set in motion neither by violence nor by the monstrous, but by the "eruption of (hetero)sexual desire into an already established social order" (p. 22). In these genres, disequilibrium is specified as the process of desire itself and the various blockages to its fulfillment.

The advantage of Neale's formulation over more traditional descriptions of iconography and narrative form is its location of elements of generic specificity that may exist in different combinations in other genres. For instance, whereas heterosexual desire is found in a great many genres, the role it plays in the musical and melodrama is quite specific and central. What is unique in the musical is the specific inscription of music itself, especially of song and dance, into the narrative movement from equilibrium through disequilibrium and back; performance numbers woven into narrative thus become the key to particularly intense statements, and sometimes resolutions, of narrative conflicts. In the justly famous "Dancing in the Dark" number from the movie musical *The Band Wagon* (Vincente Minnelli, 1953), for example, Fred Astaire and Cyd Charisse's "spontaneous" discovery of their ability to dance together off stage in a park resolves their inability to dance on stage in a show, and so ultimately assures the success of that show. The number also resolves their earlier hostility toward each other and Astaire's loneliness. Although not all musical numbers are so integrated into their narratives, all musicals do have numbers that either restate or resolve the problems posed by the narrative in other numbers (Mueller 1984, 33–35).

One can also examine how some numbers relate to other numbers in a narrative. In *Easter Parade* (Charles Walters, 1948), the story concerns Fred Astaire's attempt to prove to the former dancing partner who has jilted him that he can take any woman and make her into a star simply by dancing with her. The fact that the former partner is Ann Miller, known primarily for her dancing, and the new partner

Judy Garland, known primarily for her singing, complicates the nature of the numbers that will allow Astaire to succeed. Nor does he succeed until he significantly revises his original sense of what it means to dance—that is, to perform a number—with a woman.

The resolution of these problems comes about not through the narrative, or through any one number, but through the relation of number to narrative and number to number. Astaire at first tries to fit Garland into the sophisticated ballroom-dancer mold of Miller. The result is a comic fiasco of sabotaged elegance as the feathers on Garland's overplumed gown fly and she dances wildly out of control, foiling all of Astaire's valiant attempts to recover their equilibrium. But if Garland can't dance like Miller, she can sing like no one else. And it is when she *sings* what had been Astaire and Miller's dancing theme song, "It Only Happens When I Dance with You," that Astaire finally falls for her and learns to appreciate her unique qualities. Professional success follows as they learn to sing and dance together in a more comic vein. The climax of this success occurs with the famous "Couple of Swells" number, in which each portrays a male tramp singing and dancing in a comic imitation of elegance.

But professional success does not automatically solve the problem of the mutually shared song-dance performance that expresses romantic love. And so, even in their triumph—and even though the *narrative* asserts that Astaire and Garland love each other—when Astaire is manipulated into performing one more time with Miller, a jealous Garland walks out. The real solution must be sought on the level of the number; the film must find the Garland-Astaire love song-and-dance that will better the Miller-Astaire performance. That number is the title song inflected by role reversal: Garland sends Astaire an Easter bonnet, and she takes *him* to the Fifth Avenue Easter Parade, where the number's grand finale is performed. Astaire may have succeeded in transforming her into a star, but in so doing he has had to adapt his own performance to the talents and desires of this particular woman.

These examples of the function of musical numbers in a movie musical can help us to understand the similar function of sexual numbers in the pornographic feature. To begin with, there is the obvious sense of the musical number, especially the romantic song-dance duet, as a sublimated expression of heterosexual desire and satisfaction. Beyond that there is the fact that the hard-core feature—unlike the silent stag—is quite literally a musical: original music and even songs with lyrics (as, for example, the execrable *Deep Throat* theme song) frequently accompany numbers, especially the "big production" numbers. Finally, there is the obvious sense in which the sexual acts listed above constitute a virtual typology of numbers in the pornographic feature. Masturbation, for example, can be seen as a solo song or dance of self-love and enjoyment—à la the "Singin' in the Rain" number in the musical of that name; straight sex is like a classic heterosexual duet—as in "You Were Meant for Me," also from *Singin' in the Rain*—with oral sex as a variation of this same theme; "lesbian" sex is like the narcissistic "I Feel Pretty" number from *West Side Story*; ménage à trois is a trio—"Good Mornin'" from *Singin'* or the beginning of the "Hungry Eyes" number from *Dirty Dancing*;[4] "sadie-max" is a particularly violent and fetishistic dramatization of dominance and submission—à la the Cyd Charisse–Gene Kelly number in the "Broadway Melody" section of *Singin' in the Rain*; and orgies are like choral love songs celebrating the sexual union of an entire community—"Broadway Rhythm" in *Singin'* or the "everybody-out-on-the-dance-floor" number of communal integration that ends *Dirty Dancing* ("The Time of My Life").

A major difference between the genres, however, is the fact that many more of the numbers in hard core are, in a sense, "love" songs expressing the desire for or act of union. Although movie musicals certainly emphasize the love song or dance, many solos, duets, trios, and so forth have nothing to do with desire or longing. Nevertheless, feature-length hard-core films still closely resemble musicals structurally in their tendency to give one particular number the conflict-resolving function or expression of ultimate satisfaction of the musical's love song (like "Dancing in the Dark," "You Are My Lucky Star," or "The Time of My Life"). In *Deep Throat*, for example, oral sex—specifically fellatio—has this status. The problem that the fellatio number eventually solves is introduced in another number: the uninspiring "straight sex" that Linda Lovelace engages in at the beginning of the film.

In this last respect, however, the hard-core genre is not entirely parallel to the musical. For in the musical, the always-sublimated expression of desire in the love song or dance is a priori pleasurable, whereas in feature-length pornography unsublimated sex, especially that occurring early in the film, is often not pleasurable at all to at least one of its participants. In *The Resurrection of Eve* (Mitchell Bros., 1973), *Angel on Fire* (Roberta Findlay, 1979), and *Taboo* (Kirdy Stevens, 1980), for instance, the initial numbers range from simply listless to overtly distasteful to one or more of the characters involved. A most peculiar quality of this narrative form of the genre, then, would seem to be this paradox: although built on the premise that the pleasure of sex is self-evident, the underlying and motivating anxiety is that sometimes it is not. Out of this contradiction comes the need for a combined solution of narrative and number.

In hard-core narrative we might say that sex numbers can function in the following ways: (1) as regular moments of pleasure that may be gratifying either to viewers or to the characters performing the acts; (2) as statements of sexual conflicts that are manifest in the number (in *Taboo*, for example, the film begins with a fellatio number between a husband and wife; the husband insists on leaving the light on; the wife resists and does not enjoy their encounter; the performance continues to the point of his orgasm, but her dissatisfaction is apparent); (3) as statements, or restatements, of conflicts that are manifest in the narrative; or (4) as resolutions of conflicts stated either in the narrative or in the other numbers. In other words, as in the movie musical, the episodic structure of the hard-core narrative is something more than a flimsy excuse for sexual numbers: it is part and parcel of the way the genre goes about resolving the often contradictory desires of its characters.

Male and Female Centers of Power

In his impressive book *The American Film Musical*, Rick Altman (1987, 16–27) writes that the distinctive episodic structure of the genre is basic to the way it goes about resolving the contradictory desires and needs of its characters. Noting that number does not simply interrupt narrative but rather that the two function in carefully orchestrated parallel scenes involving both the male and the female protagonist, Altman suggests that the dynamic principle motivating narrative in the musical must be the fundamental difference between male and female.

To express this most basic opposition, the narrative structure of the musical diverges from the classical Hollywood norm of chronological, linear progression and causal sequence. The MGM operetta *New Moon*, for example, proceeds via parallels in narrative and number between the male and female protagonists, played by (none other than) Nelson Eddy and Jeanette MacDonald. MacDonald plays a wealthy French aristocrat on board a ship carrying her to New Orleans in 1789. She is asked to sing for the other nobles on the deck. Her song is drowned out by another song that comes from below deck—a group of poor Frenchmen about to be sold into slavery sing to forget their troubles. They are led by a young nobleman in disguise, Nelson Eddy (Altman 1987, 17–19).

Altman argues that the sequence is less a causal relation between two events than a setting forth of paired oppositions: "*She* sings on deck, *he* sings in the hold; *she* sings to entertain a bevy of society women, *he* sings to relieve the misery of a group of penniless men" (p. 17). The film thus develops two centers of opposed power (male and female), each provided with a set of secondary characteristics that are also opposed: "*the female*—rich, cultured, beautiful, easily offended; *the male*—poor, practical, energetic, tenacious. Yet they share one essential attribute: they both sing" (p. 19).

This dual focus of the musical, constructed on parallel stars of opposite sex and divergent values, is a defining feature of the genre and can help us to pin down Neale's general observation about the centrality of heterosexual desire in some genres. If male and female are the primary oppositions of the musical genre, their basic resolution occurs through the mediation of secondary oppositions. In *New Moon*, for example, both narrative and number operate to resolve the secondary oppositions (rich/poor) as each protagonist adopts characteristics of the other: Eddy learns some of MacDonald's restraint, and MacDonald takes on some of Eddy's energy (pp. 19–20).

Altman's point is that although most movie musicals divide the world into male and female in order to bring the two sexes together in some sort of implicitly monogamous happily-ever-after, in the end it is the *secondary* oppositions that this union actually mediates. From *The Gold Diggers* to *Gentlemen Prefer Blondes* to *Gigi*, the most common opposition has been that between female beauty (the most prevalent female "center of power") and male riches (the most prevalent form of male power). (Here Altman [p. 25] quotes Marilyn Monroe's famous line from *Gentlemen Prefer Blondes*: "Don't you know that a man being rich is like a girl being pretty?" Recent musicals often reverse these terms—with rich "girl" and pretty "man.") Sexual union performs the merger of the primary gender oppositions, but only with the help of secondary oppositions.

We can begin to see how this mediation occurs in hard-core film by looking at *The Opening of Misty Beethoven* ("Henry Paris," a.k.a. Radley Metzger, 1975). Since this movie is itself a loose re-working of George Bernard Shaw's *Pygmalion*, familiar to many in its musical incarnation as *My Fair Lady*, some of the parallels to musical-genre structure will be a little too neat. But since these parallels are only more consistent in this film than in others I will use them to get to the heart of the structures that to some degree are found in most hard-core narrative.

Like a classic musical, *Misty Beethoven* is about heterosexual desire. To use Altman's terminology, it is narratively structured on a fundamental male/female opposition accompanied by opposed secondary characteristics. *He* is Dr. Seymour Love (Jamie Gillis), a wealthy, sophisticated sexologist. *She* is Misty Beethoven (Constance Money), a poor, unsophisticated whore who makes her living giving "hand jobs" to old men in a porno theater in Pigalle and working in an adjacent brothel.

They meet in the theater, where Seymour is doing research and where Misty has left her chewing gum on a seat back. (Earlier we saw Misty give a hand job to an old man named Napoleon who ejaculates—in a typical money shot—in unison with the screen performer. The title of the film they watch is *Le sexe qui parle*.) Seymour hires Misty to study her. They go to a private room where a vulgarly made up, gum-chewing Misty, wearing a T-shirt with AMERICAN EXPRESS and MASTER CARD emblazoned on the front, recites her repertoire: "I do a straight fuck, I don't take it in the mouth, I don't take it in the ass," and even "I don't take it in the bed"—presumably she prefers the movie theater. But Seymour, the cold scientist, is only interested in interviewing her: he finds her vulgarity fascinating; she is the "perfect specimen" of a "sexual civil service worker."

Seymour arrogantly boasts that he could transform even this unlikely material into the most desired sexual performer of the international jet set: the "Golden Rod Girl." What Henry Higgins did with Eliza Doolittle and vowels, what Fred Astaire did with Judy Garland and a few dance steps, Seymour proposese to do with Misty and sexual technique. As in these musicals, too, the fundamental issue underlying linguistic, musical, or sexual performance is power—for what all these men have in common are those most typical characteristics of the male center of power: money, class, and knowledge (the last typically being, in hard core, knowledge of sex). And what Eliza, Judy, and Misty have in common is the raw material of the most typical characteristics of female power: beauty and talent. In a Foucauldian sense, then, the knowledge of sexual technique that Misty stands to gain is offered by Seymour as a potential form of power. But in typical male-chauvinist style, he sees this power as the gift that only he, sophisticated author and sexologist, has the knowledge to give.

In his New York mansion–cum–training school—where the constant sexual activity in the background creates an atmosphere similar to the rehearsals of a Busby Berkeley backstage musical or the workouts in a boxing film—Misty begins training. Dressed in a jogging suit, she practices manual and oral sexual techniques on plaster cast penises and ubiquitous live male "models" who double as servants. With Seymour's coaching, Misty is supposedly learning to convert a "mundane routine, a daily act, into something stimulating."

But there is something in the rote repetition of the training itself—and especially its mechanical use of fellatio—that belies this goal. In fact, the initial emphasis on fellatio tends to posit this particular sexual act much as "straight sex" is posited in *Deep Throat*— as ordinary, run-of-the-mill sexual performance, against which more inspired and interesting performances will eventually shine. At first, however, Seymour's emphasis on high-class techniques for sucking and licking a penis stands in direct opposition to Misty's crude pleasure-giving method: the no-frills hand job that we saw her give the old man.

Like Nelson Eddy and Jeanette MacDonald, Seymour and Misty not only possess opposing secondary characteristics, but these characteristics are also restated, mediated, and ultimately resolved in the sexual numbers. Misty's no-frills approach to both life and sex is contrasted to Seymour's connoisseurship. At first the contrast is posed as a simple professional difference over which technique does the job best. But soon it is linked to a more fundamental and familiar opposition expressed as the antagonism between the sexes. Misty and Seymour state this antagonism succinctly early in the film: "I think men stink," she says in response to Seymour's arrogant coaching. "They think you stink," he replies; "it's one of the most perfectly balanced equations in nature."

Actually, the "equation" is not perfectly balanced at all, either "in nature" or in Misty's relation to the men she must learn to please. Her unequal position as sexual trainee in the one-sided giving of pleasure to men is quite typical of women's position within a phallogocentric symbolic system. It forces her to accommodate her sexuality and her desire to that of the male. Not all hard-core narratives state this opposition so baldly, but as in the movie musical, some form of this classic, and unequal, battle between the sexes seems to animate the conflicts that both genres seek in their own ways to resolve. (In *Deep Throat*, for example, the opposition is posed as pure anatomical difference, with the resolution coming through the right number with the "right" man, though in fact the fellatio "solution" really works *for the male*. In the 1987 *Careful, He May Be Watching* (Henry Pachinko) the solution is more complex: a married woman (Seka) is, unbeknownst to her airline pilot husband, a porno star. He loves his wife but wants to spice up their relationship, introducing another woman into their bed. The wife is reluctant. Resolution occurs when, in her double life as porno star, the wife tries a "lesbian" girl-girl number and likes it. When her husband brings home an airline stewardess, she is ready for further experimentation. The finale of the film is a ménage à trois that is satisfying to all and "solves" the minor skirmish between husband and wife. Resolution occurs, but again, its terms are ultimately the man's.)

Like the female protagonists of musicals, Misty knows that the larger power structure in which she operates constructs the woman in the image of male desire. The only power she stands to gain will come from following the advice of her Pygmalion and giving the man what he wants. A reluctant Galatea, she does her maker's bidding and achieves her first triumph seducing an Italian nobleman in the toilet of the Rome Opera. The seduction scene itself is intercut with Seymour's verbal representation of what, in his careful orchestration of the event, should be happening at each moment. As he narrates and we see the events happening according to his plan, we also see Seymour being simultaneously and mechanically "serviced" by one of the many female servant-trainers who inhabit his sexological empire.

Misty's second challenge is more difficult: she must seduce an art dealer in Geneva whom Seymour initially describes as "impotent" but whose appearance is visually coded as gay. The training for this seduction-performance involves more elaborate rehearsals, leading, for the first time in the film, to a number that exhibits something more than mere professional technique. Seymour has enlisted two experienced women friends, Geraldine and Tania, to aid in his training of Misty. Through elaborate cross-gender role playing—with Tania playing Misty and Geraldine playing the role of the man Misty will seduce—he has them rehearse Misty's next seduction before a movie camera. He also has Tania talk through each stage so that Misty later can listen in to the record of this rehearsal (through an earphone) and let the audio cues trigger visual memories. Misty watches this rehearsal on the set as Seymour, all the while being fellated by another one of his anonymous female trainers, directs the "action."

This elaborate cinematic rehearsal for Misty's next seduction offers an image of sexual relations as complicated sexual role playing aimed at, and directed by, a male voyeur-viewer who "gets off" at the performance. Although the scene employs two female participants in what looks like a standard "lesbian" scene, the fact that one of these woman is acting the part of the male seducee calls attention to a quality inherent in many of the seemingly "obligatory lesbian" scenes of 1970s narrative hard core: the women in them are not enacting their own desires but are going through motions aimed more at pleasing male viewers than one another. Seymour's presence as aroused director-viewer calling the shots and telling the women what to do while having one of them "play" the male herself is a remarkably self-reflexive commentary on the male control exercised in such scenes.

Yet the role of seducer that Misty is learning to play will eventually emphasize her "masculine" control of the scene. (The number will end, for example, with Misty on top.) Seymour tells Tania, who is playing Misty's seducer's role, to say to Geraldine, who is playing the gay male seducee: "I'm going to lick your cock like it's the inside of a ripe mango." A mango's "inside" is not a particularly apt simile for an erect penis, in spite of the presence at its center of what in Spanish, at least, is called the "bone." But it is precisely this sexual ambivalence—between hard bone and soft flesh whose "inside" is licked—that this entire rehearsal seems designed to express. It could be that this particular director simply takes a special delight in confounding sexual role playing (as other films by Radley Metzger seem to confirm). But it could also be that scenes like this, as well as the much simpler "lesbian" girl-girl numbers of most hard-core films, show how readily cross-gender identification takes place.

This question of cross-gender identification raises the further question of whether the "lesbian" number is a sexual event in its own right. In many stag films and hard-core pornos the "lesbian" number is presented, as it is here, as a warm-up or rehearsal for a "better," more satisfying, number that will follow. (The "lesbian" scene above, for example, is followed immediately by Seymour's getting into the act himself.) It would indeed be strange for heterosexual hard-core films aimed primarily at male audiences to posit the "lesbian" number as the "big production" key to satisfaction. Yet as this complex number in *Misty Beethoven* suggests, to dismiss the girl-girl number would be to define hard core as consisting totally of the action of the phallus and to explain the so-called obligatory "lesbian" number only as a setup for girl-boy numbers.

If a "lesbian" number is constructed so that one woman gives pleasure to the other, then the woman giving the pleasure typically shows, and often also speaks, her knowledge of what pleases the other. Putting aside for the moment the question of how women might identify with and take pleasure in such action, it certainly seems possible that male viewers can identify with the active woman, with her superior knowledge of how the more passive woman feels. But perhaps we should not rule out less active forms of identification—that is, identification with the passive woman who is given pleasure and abandons herself to the control of the other. Spectatorial pleasure in such scenes may very well involve the ability to identify both ways.

In *Misty Beethoven* the cross-gender identifications are written into the film in defiance of the participants' genders: Geraldine, a woman, plays the role of the passive male who will be seduced by Misty; after this "lesbian" rehearsal, Tania, the seducer playing

Misty, asks to do the "sequel" right away, this time with Seymour as the seducee. The "big production" number that follows thus shows an apparently aroused and envious Misty (wearing a perhaps symbolic green dress) watching her own stand-in perform a sexual number with Seymour. This number contrasts strongly with all the film's previous numbers. Considerably longer, it develops in several major sections, each with a distinct mood, and creates a sense of spontaneous and sustained passion—like a sexual jam session where some members of the combo put down their instruments to watch and listen as the others perform. Although this number's sexual content consists only of a highly conventional progression from oral sex to straight sex to money shot, much of the number is in a straight sex dorsal-ventral position that is most favorable to visibility of the full frontal female body while simultaneously showing the insertion of penis in vagina.

In this section of the number, Tania, the more active seducer, proceeds from fellatio to sitting on Seymour's penis as he lies nearly supine and she leans back. Thus both sexual position and the elaborate movements of an overhead, circling camera privilege this number as more special, and more spectacular, than anything previously shown. The number takes on significance in relation not only to the narrative—as a contrast to the businesslike professionalism espoused by Misty and Seymour—but also to other numbers. For example, its length, relative spontaneity, and passion are contrasted positively and in ascending order to Misty's crude hand job, to the many previous, overrehearsed fellatio training sessions, and to the "lesbian" rehearsal. Even its "end" offers something more: Seymour and Tania continue to embrace and laugh together after the money shot, exhilarated and delighted by their own performance.

Misty, however, in her new position as audience to a rehearsal that, like so many of those magical rehearsals of backstage movie musicals, is already a showstopper, doubts her ability to emulate such a spectacular performance. The question of her own sexual desire in all this is worth pondering, given her marked presence as on-scene spectator to both the "lesbian" and the heterosexual rehearsals for her own upcoming performance. What does Misty want? And with whom might she identify in these two numbers? Does she identify with the passive enjoyment of the man (first played by a woman) who is seduced, or with her own female stand-in? Or with both? Her momentary displacement from performer to spectator poses, but does not answer, these questions. Moreover, these are precisely the questions that need to be asked of the female spectator of pornography in general. *Misty Beethoven's* way of posing the question seems to suggest that a purely passive identification with the woman performer is not the whole story.

Significantly, Misty at this moment begins to question the entire enterprise. She tries to back out of the seduction, saying that she won't be able to fool anyone, that she would be crazy to "try to sell phony merchandise. . . . On the street it's simpler; everybody does their own number, but nobody fools anybody." Misty's "number," we must remember, is the no-frills hand job. To attempt a more elaborate number—ultimately, one that would pretend not even to be a number—is, in her mind, simply "phony." Seymour's counter to this challenge is contradictory. On the one hand, he tells her that she isn't a phony, since her talent has aroused his own interest— here he holds out to her a vague promise of getting to know her better when the project is over. On the other hand, he provides her with the listening device that feeds her the verbal directions from the rehearsal number. Not only does the device cue her on what to say and do in the actual seduction scene, which takes place on the floor of an art gallery, but it also allows her memory to see what the film audience sees: black-and-white images of the rehearsal film. In other words, Seymour's goal of passing off his Galatea as the most desired woman of sophisticated sexual circles is thoroughly saturated with the calculated values of engineering in opposition to real spontaneity. The work of the film, however, will be to resolve this contradiction by foiling his too perfect sexual creation.

Seymour's apparent goal is to transform Misty from an "honest whore" who gets direct payment for services into a pleasure-giving automaton whose indirect payment is access to a higher social class. In the process, however, he forces Misty to rely increasingly on complex technological aids, which in turn become fetishized as necessary to the pleasure. In the seduction scene, for example, Misty parrots the "mango" line from the rehearsal film, to which she is simultaneously listening, and then unwittingly repeats Tania's ad lib indicating her desire to continue the rehearsal: "ripe mango take two." Taking the line as part of Misty's own kinky fantasy, the seducee replies, "Roll it," and leans back to enjoy Misty's performance on his sexual organ.

But even though Misty's performance is a "success"—measured in the art dealer's ejaculation in a money shot—and even though she gains proficiency in ever more complicated numbers, each of these numbers stands in contrast to the spontaneity and emotion of Tania and Seymour's prolonged duet. Her final triumph, for example, is the seduction of Larry Layman, a vain Hugh Hefner–style editor of a famous men's magazine and the unofficial power behind the election of the "Golden Rod Girl." In this number Misty takes charge, even improvising on Seymour's plan of attack as she takes on not only Layman but his woman friend Barbara as well. In a ménage à trois with paraphernalia—which climaxes (for Layman at least) in a daisy chain that has Layman penetrating Barbara frontally while being penetrated from the rear by Misty, who wears a dildo—complexity defeats both spontaneity and involvement.

In this number Misty's control is absolute. Like Seymour during the rehearsal, she wields the phallus *and* she calls the shots. But although she functions successfully as the unmistakable catalyst to Layman and Barbara's pleasure, she is just as unmistakably an accessory to it. It is Layman and Barbara who connect. Misty enhances that connection, but, as the dildo demonstrates, she is not quite connected herself. As in her final training session, where Misty makes three male models ejaculate simultaneously—the equivalent of the "By George, She's Got It!" number in *My Fair Lady*—her proficiency is a tour de force of mere technique. She herself is no more involved than when she jerked off Napoleon while watching the money shot in the porno film.

After her "triumph" with Layman, Misty encounters Seymour at the same party. He is casually engaged in his own two-woman ménage à trois while dressed (or half-undressed) as Julius Caesar and telling misogynistic stories about how to handle women. Disappointed and angry because she had taken his earlier promise of a date seriously, Misty turns to leave. Seymour arrogantly orders her to stay with the inducement, "You can have Caesar." "Why? I already have Napoleon," she says.

With Misty gone, the cocky Seymour deflates. He looks for her back in the porno theater in Pigalle, endures the humiliation of gossip that suggests that his Galatea has gone to live with Layman, mopes about his mansion watching the old training films of Misty as he is listlessly fellated by one female servant after another. While he is engaged in this activity, Misty returns and takes over fellatio during a change of shifts that Seymour doesn't even notice because he is so absorbed in watching Misty on screen.

Soon, though, he becomes aware of her touch. Delighted but pretending not to be, he complains of the screen Misty that "she never did get it right. She was too stupid, unexciting—a sexual civil service worker." In answer, the real Misty bites his penis. A verbal argument ensues. Seymour talks fast. Misty gives him back one of his own lines: "People have sexual problems because they talk too damn much." In answer, he kisses her. The straight sex number that ensues is the film's duet finale—the equivalent of MacDonald and Eddy's reprise of "Lover Come Back to Me" in *New Moon*, Astaire and Rogers's "Cheek to Cheek" number in *Top Hat*, the "Easter Parade" number in *Easter Parade*, and "The Time of My Life" in *Dirty Dancing*. Significantly, this number contains no fellatio, no anal penetration, no sexual paraphernalia, and only the briefest of money shots.

Misty and Seymour make love all over the room in a variety of positions and moods, but the emphasis throughout is on romantic and spontaneous involvement rather than complex gymnastics. At the end, a close-up of penis and vagina, apart but still drawn to each other, confirms the impression of this number as the fulfilled expression of romantic heterosexual desire enacted primarily through male and female genitals. In a coda, we find Seymour's sexual training school flourishes, but now with Misty as head instructor and with Seymour as a docile student in dog collar and chain.

To return to our musical analogy, we can see that Altman's notion of the musical as structured by the dynamic opposition between male and female centers of power operates forcefully in *Misty Beethoven*. "Men stink/women stink" seems to be its plainest expression. Also as in the musical, secondary oppositions function to resolve the contradictory desires and needs of the primary opposition between male and female characters. As male and female, Misty and Seymour constitute opposing (and, we should never forget, unequal) centers of power. But these primary oppositions are then mediated through the merger of secondary oppositions—his sophisticated connoisseurship and technique, her directness and honesty.

As we have seen, this mediation occurs not in any one moment of the narrative or in any one sexual number but through meanings created by the structured oppositions of both narrative and numbers. Misty's honesty is asserted in the narrative in her speech about what numbers she does and does not do and in her sustained criticism of phoniness; Seymour's connoisseurship is asserted in his constant exploitation of cinematic and sexual technique and encouragement of complex, even kinky, sexual expressions. Over the course of the film, Misty becomes more sophisticated and kinky, while Seymour becomes attached (literally, in the dog collar at the end) to Misty alone.

Thus the original source of their differences lies both in sex itself—their obvious and original male and female sexual differences—and in their different attitudes toward the performance of sex. And it is in these *secondary* oppositions concerning sexual performance that mediation occurs. The numbers are structured initially to contrast Misty's no-frills hand job with Seymour's insistence that she cultivate technique and learn to "take it in the mouth." As rehearsals and performance proceed in alternation, Seymour's method of complexity and sophistication gains; Misty's no-frills directness wanes. But the real mediation leading to the final duet in which Misty fulfills all of her initial conditions ("I do a straight fuck, I don't take it in the mouth, I don't take it in the ass . . . I don't take it in the bed") yet merges them with Seymour's greater connoisseurship comes from the film's discovery of something more, something that has been lacking all along in both their approaches.

This lack is spontaneity: an involvement in the number that transcends its performative aspect, turning it into something more than a number, more than a performance of sex—into a utopia of desire and fulfillment. These spontaneous, unstaged, and unrehearsed events occur as if of their own accord out of the merged desires of the sexual performers. The first introduction of spontaneity, of course, occurs midway through the film in the impromptu "sequel" to the overchoreographed rehearsal. In this number Tania and Seymour "jam" together while Misty watches. This freewheeling quality—expressed in neither Misty's nor Seymour's original sexual credos—emerges to undermine and transform the original opposition between "plain" and "fancy" sex into a merger of both through spontaneous involvement.

The final number between Misty and Seymour effects this merger. It is "fancy" compared to Misty's original no-frills approach, but it is "plain" compared to the highly choreographed rehearsals or to the final performance with Layman, in which Misty is smooth-functioning accessory to Layman's pleasure. In short, this final number—like the "Dancing in the Dark" number in *The Band Wagon*—takes on significance through the dramatized opposition between it and the increasingly complex, but alienated, rehearsal and performance numbers. In both cases the successful performance—of sex or of song and dance—depends on the number's seeming not to *be* a performance but to arise naturally and spontaneously from the sexual desires of the performing couple.

In her fine book *The Hollywood Musical*, film critic Jane Feuer has shown that the musical as a genre is founded on a contradiction between highly engineered, choreographed, and rehearsed numbers (which all filmed song and dance numbers necessarily are) and the desire to make these numbers seem unrehearsed, as if they arose naturally and spontaneously out of the rhythms and harmonies of song and dance itself. This contradiction, Feuer (1982, 1–23) argues, animates the musical's extreme valuation of certain myths—of spontaneity, of performers' communion with audience, of community integration through song and dance—myths that in turn work to overcome the "original sin" of cinema itself: the fact that, as a mass art of canned performance, cinema can never really bring audience and performer together; that it must always be elaborately rehearsed and choreographed for camera and lighting to be right and for lips to synchronize to prerecorded sound. In an age of mechanical reproduction, postmodern simulacra, and heightened voyeurism, the rhetoric of the genre must work overtime, so to speak, to compensate for what has been lost. Even the most elaborate production numbers, which historically have been the most highly engineered and rehearsed of all the Hollywood product, rhetorically attempt to "cancel" or "erase" this engineering through the appearance of what Feuer (pp. 3–4), borrowing from Lévi-Strauss, calls "bricolage": making it up as you go along out of whatever materials are at hand.

Thus the most complexly engineered of the famous songs and dances by the great movie performers have been the numbers that most gave the illusion of being created spontaneously out of the materials at hand: an umbrella, a puddle, a lamppost. This erasure of rehearsal and professional performance by a supposedly natural, unstudied bricolage operates both within numbers—as in "Singin' in the Rain"—and between numbers—as in the contrast between Kelly's "natural" song and dance ability and the engineered phoniness of this film's nonsinging, nondancing villainess.

As we have seen, similar contradictions seem to animate the myths of the pornographic feature as well, at least in the (vast majority of) films that work toward what I have been calling the solution to the problem of sex through the performance of sex. In such films, sex as a spontaneous *event* enacted for its own sake stands in perpetual opposition to sex as an elaborately engineered and choreographed *show* enacted by professional performers for a camera. And just as the filmed musical number must rhetorically do everything in its power to deny its engineered, choreographed professionalism, so the hard-core sexual number must as well. Indeed, it must do even more, for it is in this most directly sexual context that the sense of the word *number* rejoins that of the prostitute's performed and choreographed "trick" and thus mirrors the entire problematic of hard core's utopian project of offering visual proof of authentic and involuntary spasms of pleasure.

From this perspective we can see that in *The Opening of Misty Beethoven* the isolation of, and solution to, the problem of "phoniness"—of insincere sexual performance—is absolutely central to what the feature-length hard-core genre is all about. Just as *Deep Throat* posed and then "resolved" the problem of the authenticity of Linda Lovelace's pleasure, so in a more complex way—a way that might be said to constitute both a classical statement and a more meditative self-reflexive formulation of what the pornographic feature-length narrative is "talking to itself" about—*Misty Beethoven* poses and then solves the problem of sexual performance as "trick" or show played for the camera versus spontaneously pleasurable real event.

The comparison between the two movies is instructive. Both feature male sexologists, who occupy the position once held in literary pornography by the traditional figure of the libertine. The sexologist's professional-scientific interest in sex can thus be viewed as a thin disguise for traditional libertine pleasures. But it is also something more. Whether presented as the comic professor who invents an aphrodisiac (as in *Blondes Have More Fun* [John Seeman, 1975]), a serious psychiatrist who tries to effect a cure (as in the takeoff on *10, 11* [Harry Lewis, 1981], in which an apparently unarousable male client undergoes therapy to learn to fantasize the woman of his dreams), or the disembodied voice of therapeutic authority (as in *Carnal Haven* [Sharon Thorpe, 1976], in which the unhappy sex lives of four married couples and their stay in a sex-therapy clinic are commented on), these figures are not simply pleasure seekers. Their expert discourse also functions to define the very terms of the quest for the knowledge of pleasure. And it is this scientific knowledge of the pleasure of sexuality (often, but not always, posed as male knowledge of female pleasure) that leads in many of these films to the great variety of sexual numbers that characterizes the form.

In *Deep Throat* this quest for scientific knowledge culminates in a gimmick that "solves" the problem by locating pleasure fancifully in deep-throat fellatio. As if in self-conscious response to this well-known hard-core solution, *Misty Beethoven* poses fellatio as one of the more "mundane" of its panoply of sexual numbers, building instead a complex set of oppositions between professional gimmicks and tricks and the spontaneous, mutual pleasure located in rigorously heterosexual, but not unimaginative, straight sex. In both movies, however, sexual performance poses a problem, and the exploration of a range of different sexual acts ultimately leads to the "solution."

Even without the presence of the sexologist-hero we can see how this quest for the knowledge of sexual pleasure operates within the parameters of a "diff'rent strokes for diff'rent folks" sexological framework. In the first installment of the popular *Taboo* series of hard-core family melodrama, the woman who was described above as objecting to having the light on while engaged in fellatio with her husband is left by him for his young secretary. On her own now, the woman tries the world of swinging singles but is embarrassed by the public orgies in which she is invited to participate. At home later, she masturbates in the dark to the visual fantasy of sexual coupling with a not quite discernible mate. Disturbed by a noise, she wanders into the bedroom of her college-aged son who is having a bad dream. Spontaneously aroused by this son, she begins to make love in the dark room to his still-sleeping body; meanwhile, the fleeting images of her masturbatory fantasy are staying on the screen longer, eventually to merge with the present number. The son awakens to find his mother fellating him; with an amazed "Jesus Christ" he joins in, moving to a straight sex position with the mother on top reaching her orgasm and saying "I'm coming" as the son continues to thrust. The money shot occurs later as he places his penis between her breasts and comes onto her face.

Taboo offers a particularly interesting—and popular[5]—opposition between spontaneous, exciting (good) sex and unexciting, unspontaneous, phony or contrived (bad) sex. In this film, spontaneity is located in the taboo incestuous coupling of mother and son in a dim room hidden from the rest of the world. This dark, secret sex functions in opposition to the brightly lit sex of the opening and to the communal, public scene of the orgy, neither of which turns the mother on. Remarkably few repercussions attend the breaking of what is often taken to be the most fundamental of sexual taboos. The mother offers only weak resistance to subsequent encounters. (In a sequel, *Taboo IV*, the mother will undergo therapy to rid herself of this nagging desire.) In this first film, when the mother confesses her problem to a female friend, instead of shock or disapproval the friend's only reaction is to masturbate in vicarious excitement. In the end the mother establishes a relationship with an employer who proposes marriage; although she refuses marriage, she does agree to keep him as her lover. The implication is that he will offer a good cover to her ongoing secret relationship with her son.

"Good" sex, in other words, might be located almost anywhere—in fellatio (as in *Deep Throat*), in anal sex (as in *Loose Ends* [Bruce Seven, 1984]), in straight sex (as in *Misty Beethoven*), or even in incest (as in *Taboo*). "Diff'rent strokes for diff'rent folks" is, after all, the guiding ethic. Yet despite the apparent inclusiveness, some "strokes" remain genuinely taboo within the heterosexual limits of the genre: father-son incest, for example, is unthinkable. What counts is not so much the intrinsic content of the sexual numbers, but how they are played (that is, performed, lit, shot, edited) and how the film constructs the knowledge of the "truth" of that sex. Here we depart from our model of the musical. In the musical, one type of number, the romantic duet, is generally privileged over all others in the reconciliation of opposites that is the means to heterosexual union. In feature-length pornography, however, any one of the possible numbers listed by Ziplow could perform the reconciliation of opposites if set up properly with respect to narrative and other numbers. In the musical, the romantic dance duet and love song are the most appropriate vehicles for communicating het-

erosexual desire; in the hard-core feature, while all the numbers potentially communicate sexual desire and pleasure, some numbers do
so more than others.

Fellatio is the most common number used to express maximum
spontaneous pleasure in the films of the seventies. We have already
noted in Chapter 4, on the money shot, how displacement of female
genital pleasure onto oral satisfaction offers only a provisional, and
ultimately unstable, solution to the problem of fixing visual pleasure. It is a solution that is already gently parodied in *Misty Beethoven*. Seymour, for example, tries to teach Misty to look with
pride on an erection achieved through fellatio, to say to herself, "I
made that." But as we have seen, the film as a whole views fellatio
as the overused gimmick that by the late seventies it had indeed become, and thus as the antithesis to spontaneous sex. To a certain extent the money shot's original value as a solution to the problem of
sex depended on a novelty that by the eighties had begun to wear
thin. Of course, in the context of an older literary pornographic tradition the representation of fellatio is really not very novel at all.
There was novelty, though, in its cinematic reproduction in a non-
literary, mass-entertainment form consumed by both men and
women. For this more general audience fellatio, and its less familiar,
less visible counterpart, cunnilingus, stood momentarily for the
very idea of sexual exploration exposed by the then-expanding
"sexual revolution." Precisely because oral sex had once seemed an
exotic, even forbidden, practice, one not mentioned in the traditional prerevolutionary "marriage manuals," it could function as the
sexual act most apt to generate spontaneous desires. That it could
just as easily become the rote number that *Misty Beethoven* paro-
dies in 1975 attests to the importance in this genre of always seeking
the "new" and spontaneous sexual solution to the problem of sex.

In other films the solution could be an orgy, as in *Behind the
Green Door* (1972) and *The Resurrection of Eve* (1973) by the
Mitchell Brothers; a ménage à trois, as in *Insatiable II* (Godfrey
Daniels, 1984) and *Careful, He May Be Watching* (Richard Pa-
chinko, 1987); a dramatically privileged form of straight sex, as in
Throat—Twelve Years After (Gerard Damiano, 1984); or sadie-max,
as in *New Wave Hookers* (Dark Bros., 1975) and *Insatiable* (Godfrey
Daniels, 1980). And in many films a voyeuristic twist is added to the

above acts to provide a mediatory solution to the problem of sex. In the bizarre *Café Flesh* (F. X. Pope, 1982), for example, we find the pure voyeurism of postapocalyptic "sex negatives" who can only watch the sexual performances of "sex positives." In the more conventional *I Like to Watch* (Paul G. Vatelli, 1983), voyeurism is the device that gets everyone to join in. And in *Talk Dirty to Me One More Time* (Anthony Spinelli, 1985), it is a voyeuristic husband's view of his wife that finally cures him of impotence.

In all, however, at least until the early eighties, one rarely sees the dramatic climax of pleasure figured without the ubiquitous money shot. Nor do practices like cunnilingus—especially "lesbian" cunnilingus, in which a penis performs no important role—although frequently depicted, receive the same climactic emphasis as mediator of opposites that the above numbers do. This situation will, however, begin to change when more women take on the task of directing hard-core films in the mid-eighties, as we shall see.

Conclusion

One conclusion to be drawn from this chapter's comparison of feature-length pornography and Hollywood musicals is that in hard core a wider variety of numbers can be used to mediate the oppositions that structure the narrative, though certain numbers do remain genuinely taboo, most significantly male-to-male sex. A corollary, and more important, difference between hard core and the movie musical is that narrative equilibrium does not necessarily lie in the permanent union of the couple. Although *Misty Beethoven* does imitate the musical model by celebrating, with its straight sex emphasis, a heterosexual union, the other examples we have considered suggest that within the genre as a whole numerous sexual pleasures with diverse partners can, if properly placed in the narrative and in relation to other numbers, succeed in solving problems in the realm of sex. The formation of a couple, Susan Sontag (1969, 66) has noted, is not primarily what pornography is about.

As we have seen, what this new cinematic form of pornography *is* about is not only the multiplication of depictions of graphic sexual acts but also the conventionalized deployment of these acts within narratives that aim, as Foucault (1978, 63) puts it, not just at "confessing" sex, but at "reconstructing, in and around the act . . . the images, desires, modulations, and quality of the pleasure that animated it."

In this intensification of pleasure in the very *knowledge* of pleasure, the hard-core narrative film resembles more "legitimate" recent deployments of sexuality, whether medical, sexological, or psychiatric. As in these other discourses, sexuality is constructed as a problem that a greater knowledge of sexuality will "solve." Also as in these other discourses, the problem of differences between the sexes, or of the different pleasures derived from various sexual practices, becomes increasingly paramount. Of these discourses, pornography and sexology are the most alike, in both purpose and narrative form.

That the "solutions" to the problems of sex are most often constructed from the dominant power knowledge of male subjectivity should come as no surprise. Classic movie musicals, as we have seen, do much the same thing. What may surprise, however, especially in contrast to the earlier stag film, is the extent to which sexual difference itself, together with its corollary of (unequal) male and female centers of power and pleasure, has moved to the foreground of hard-core generic expectation. In place of the musical's utopian solution of a couple united through the harmony and rhythm of song and dance, hard-core narrative offers a materialism of different varieties, quantities, and qualities of sexual pleasure as the utopian solution to all sexual ills, including that most fundamental ill: the lack of sexual accommodation between men and women.

6

Hard-Core Utopias
Problems and Solutions

They say that Teiresias saw two snakes mating on
Cithaeron and that, when he killed the female, he was
changed into a woman, and again, when he killed the
male, took again his own nature. This same Teiresias
was chosen by Zeus and Hera to decide the question
whether the male or the female has most pleasure in
intercourse. And he said:
"Of ten parts a man enjoys one only; but a woman's
sense enjoys all ten in full."
For this Hera was angry and blinded him, but Zeus
gave him the seer's power.

Hesiod,
The Homeric Hymns and Homerica

"I want more, more, more. . . ."

Marilyn Chambers, in *Insatiable*

When Teiresias reveals the quantitative secret of female sexual pleasure, he puts Hera in a position of weakness vis-à-vis the power of
Zeus. To the Greeks, sexual pleasure was constructed in opposition
to the ideal of self-mastery and control; so when Hera is portrayed
as having the whole of the pleasure of sex, the apparent moral is that
she is an out-of-control female. In contrast, Zeus's mere one-tenth
of pleasure demonstrates the moderation and self-mastery that earn
him the right of patriarchal authority over others, including his wife.
We can probably also assume that Teiresias's revelation further
causes Hera to lose in her well-known domestic quarrel over Zeus's
philandering. Any way we look at this early report from the front in
the war between the sexes, the female loses the game of power if she
wins that of pleasure. It is as if women, who had no part in Greek

political or public life, were granted the greater part of pleasure both as a consolation for their lack of power and as proof that they were incapable of exercising power in the first place. Thus in the end pleasure, although desirable, was damning.

The question that motivates this chapter on utopian problem solving in hard-core film narrative is whether the pornographic confession/celebration of female sexual pleasure is still as damning as it was for Hera. Does the level of scrutiny apparent in modern pornography's "frenzy of the visible" necessarily objectify, demean, and disempower the female body that exhibits its pleasure? What does it mean when in *Insatiable* (Godfrey Daniels, 1980) Marilyn Chambers's multiply orgasmic heroine cries out for "more, more, more," even though she has apparently had an enormous amount of sexual pleasure already? Is Chambers a modern-day Hera damning herself once again by letting out the quantitative secret of her ability to keep on enjoying? To answer these questions, we need to comprehend better the ways in which the word *utopia* can be applied to hard-core features.

We might first recall, however, that this image of Chambers calling out for more in the masturbatory scene that ends *Insatiable* is almost the embodiment of the graphic and explicit visual pornography that Steven Marcus sees as the ironic achievement of an excess of pleasure: the multiply orgasmic female "masturbating with the aid of a mechanical-electrical instrument." As we saw in Chapter 4, to Marcus such an image is decidedly not utopian; rather, it reflects perfectly the ugly reality of an alienated consumer society. But as we also saw, Marcus seems to invoke a double standard when he calls the representation of female pleasure dystopian.

A better approach than Marcus's, one that we began to explore in Chapter 5, is to take seriously the utopian problem-solving intent of the genre as a whole and then to distinguish among the ways it occurs. Because hard-core fantasy offers symbolic solutions to problems that viewers perceive as real, in order to "solve" these problems contemporary pornography has had to "talk to itself" about sexual relations, to acknowledge that sex is more of a problem than we have ever before admitted.

In cinematic hard core we encounter a profoundly "escapist" genre that distracts audiences from the deeper social or political causes of the disturbed relations between the sexes; and yet paradoxically, if it is to distract effectively, a popular genre must address some of the real experiences and needs of its audience. Writing of the utopian function of mass entertainment in general and the movie musical in particular, Richard Dyer (1981, 177) argues that although mass entertainment offers an image of something better to escape into, it does not necessarily fashion an entire model of utopian society. Instead it is content merely to suggest what utopia would "feel like."

Dyer (pp. 180–185) goes on to construct several categories of the movie musical's utopian sensibility, each of which offers a solution to various real inadequacies in the social realities it addresses. *Energy*, for example, is the solution to exhaustion, *abundance* to scarcity, *intensity* to dreariness, *transparency* to manipulation, and *community* to fragmentation. In Dyer's view, entertainment does not simply give people what they want; it also partly *defines* wants through its orientation of problems. Abundance, for example, is often interpreted narratively as mere consumerism, energy as personal freedom. In order to be satisfactorily resolved, the real social problems that these categories of the utopian sensibility point to must first be aroused. Dyer calls this arousal "playing with fire." His point is that utopian entertainment only plays with those fires that the dominant power structure—capitalism (and patriarchy)—can put out. And so the problems that mass entertainment tends to avoid are usually those most stubborn and fundamental problems of class, sex, and race.

Again, the contrast between movie musical and pornography is instructive. Initially the utopian sensibility of contemporary film pornography seems quite similar to the sensibility outlined in Dyer's categories, at least with regard to (sexual) energy, abundance, intensity, and transparency, if not community. But cinematic hard core raises more directly than any other form of mass entertainment one problem that Dyer claims the musical normally evades: that of sexual difference. In this sense pornography might be said to "play with fire" more recklessly than most forms of mass entertainment. (It is also one of the few genres to place the problem of sexual difference in relation to other issues of race and class.) So even though feature-length pornography will avoid treating the social and political *sources* of the power inequity between men and women, and even though its solutions are typically sought facilely in the greater energy, abundance, intensity, or transparency of sexual performance, the form itself nevertheless brings questions of power relations between the sexes into view.

An examination of several popular films of 1972–1987, focused in the career of Marilyn Chambers, one of the most prolific and durable of the post-seventies "porn queens," may help us to understand the extent to which the genre has—and has not—addressed questions of sexual power and pleasure. It will also aid us in assessing some of the major changes that have occurred in the genre during this period.

Marilyn Chambers and the Utopian Energy of Sex

Originally known as the 100-percent-pure Ivory Snow Girl who scandalized the advertising industry by associating herself with "dirty movies" in the 1972 *Behind the Green Door* (Mitchell Bros.), Chambers was Linda Lovelace's main competitor. When Lovelace quit the industry and freed herself from her allegedly brutal and tyrannical manager, Chuck Traynor, Chambers succeeded her, turning into the consummate sexual performer (others would say alienated automaton) that Lovelace finally resisted becoming. Chambers also became Traynor's new "protégée" and has apparently remained so over the intervening years, starring in dozens of films, including the enormously popular *Insatiable* series.

Chambers, in *Behind the Green Door*, and Lovelace, in *Deep Throat*, were the first hard-core female stars to reach a mixed-sex mass audience in the new wave of pornographic features that started in 1972. In some ways these two films were similar: both had central gimmicks designed to privilege the money shot as the movie's central showpiece. In *Deep Throat* the gimmick was the biological fantasy of the clitoris in the throat; in *Green Door* it was the cinematic pyrotechnics of optically printed, multicolored, slow-motion close-ups of a great many money shots during the "show-stopping" climax of an orgy.

In other ways, though, the films are remarkably different. *Deep Throat*'s utopian problem solving is achieved in a variety of "deep throat" numbers interspersed throughout the narrative at regular intervals. These numbers function much as the numbers in an "integrated" musical do: they cue the transition to song and dance through narrative. *Green Door*'s format, in contrast, is more like that of the "separated" backstage movie musical, in which numbers are clustered around actual performances of the show and narrative exposition is set completely apart. In the rigorously separated Busby Berkeley movie musicals, for example, Berkeley directed only the musical-number sequences; other directors did the narratives.

Since this separated structure represents what I shall argue is one important—though also particularly regressive and misogynist—strain of contemporary feature-length hard core, it is worth describing in detail for *Behind the Green Door*. The narrative begins in a greasy spoon café. The male cook asks two truck driver customers to tell the story about the green door. As one of them begins the story the credit sequence cuts in over the image of a woman (Chambers) driving to a fancy hotel. Later that night the same woman is abducted and taken to a club where male and female members wear masks. The two truck drivers, in evening dress, enter the club where they, too, put on masks.

Masked and tied, the woman, who is called Gloria, is taken to a green room where an older woman promises her that she is about to experience the most "exquisite moment" of her life. This woman soothes and massages Gloria, who does not resist. In the adjacent cabaret, a diverse audience is settling down for the show. A male voice announces: "Ladies and gentlemen, you are about to witness the ravishment of a woman who has been abducted . . . a woman whose initial fear has mellowed into expectation. . . . No harm will come to those being ravished. Tomorrow she will know that she has been loved as she has never been loved before. So with the knowledge that you can do nothing to stop the performance, just relax and enjoy it."

Gloria is brought on stage and slowly worked over by several women in a "lesbian" number that is clearly a warm-up for future heterosexual action. Reaction shots of the audience isolate the visual pleasure of the masked truck driver. Gloria's arousal mounts as she is placed on cushions on the floor; one of the women performs cunnilingus, others kiss her breasts, another kisses her lips.

A spotlight directs attention to a green door at the back of the stage. A black man (Johnny Keyes) in vaguely African attire—body paint, necklace, and yellow tights with a hole in the crotch, from which a semi-erect penis protrudes—comes on stage and performs cunnilingus. The straight sex that follows is shot to emphasize whole body relations and facial reactions. Body movements build to a crescendo of fast rhythms as jazz music breaks the purely synch sound, with the camera often holding tight on Keyes's and Gloria's faces while head motions suggest, but do not specify, mutual climax. As Gloria lies quivering the man withdraws. She is carried off stage.

The second stage number begins with the squeak of several trapezes lowering onto the stage. Two white men and one black, also in crotch-hole tights, are on the three trapezes. Gloria enters and fellates each in turn as audience members begin to masturbate. She sits on a lower trapeze and fellates one man while manually servicing the other two. At this point the audience's own sexual performances move momentarily to the film's foreground: one woman pulls a man down on top of her; two male transvestites engage each other; the truck driver whose story this is masturbates. A Mitchell Brothers trademark, this orgy democratically mixes a wide variety of body sizes, shapes, and sexual practices, and it reaches its climax along with the three men on trapeze.

Back on stage, a series of slow-motion money shots in extreme close-up follow one another in exaggerated heroic spurts. Gloria's face and mouth are there to welcome each. Optical printing adds stylized orange-green and red-green color effects. At the end, particles of slow-motion, optically printed ejaculate fly about the frame as if in an animated Jackson Pollack painting.

Suddenly the truck driver–narrator runs onto the stage, picks up Gloria, who does not mount a fight, and flees through the green door. Back in the greasy spoon the cook asks, "And what happened next?" The truck driver says, "I'll tell you next time," and leaves. As he drives his truck through the night there is a lap dissolve to his lovemaking in a bed with Gloria—as if this *is* what happened next and as if it will keep on happening. As in the first straight sex number on stage, there is no climactic money shot, only the prolonged continuation of sex ad infinitum.

Invoking again the analogy of the musical, we can see that *Behind the Green Door* is not unlike a Busby Berkeley backstage musical, in which the Broadway show's success resolves all narrative problems in the depression-era real world. In the classic 1930s Warner

Brothers musicals, audience and characters alike escape into the phantasmagoria of the show. In this utopian realm the decorative abundance of "gold-digging" girls compensates for the narrative's reality of depression poverty—the very poverty that drives the girls to sell their bodies in shows in the first place. The big production numbers of these shows, such as *42nd Street, The Gold Diggers of 1933,* and *Dames,* were usually performed in a big clump of extravagant spectacles, each one bigger than the last, functioning as extended climactic solutions to the narrative problems of the film simply by being successful.

In the truncated narrative of *Green Door,* working-class men seek a night out on the town in the escapist sexual utopia of the world "behind the green door." What they find there is like the stage phantasmagoria of the Berkeley production numbers. In this fantasy realm the normal rules of stagebound space and time are opened out into cinematically abstract but sexually significant patterns of symmetrical and decorative female bodies transformed, multiplied, and fetishized. *Green Door's* stage production "numbers" offer numerically reduced but analogous forms of spatially and temporally expanded, abstract variations on a single sexual theme. The difference, however, is that where Berkeley employed, often in relation to a single man, an abundance of interchangeable, stereotyped women who, in his own words, "matched like pearls" (quoted in Fischer 1989, 74), *Green Door* employs an abundance of interchangeable men—and their penises—in relation to a single woman.

As in the depression-era movie musical, the utopian energy, intensity, and abundance of the numbers in the *Green Door* stage show are such a hit with their audience that the good feelings seem to spill over. Like the plentiful ejaculate of the optically printed money shots, the wealth of good feeling "solves" the (only briefly acknowledged) narrative problems of the "exhausted" and "dreary" world of truck drivers who frequent greasy spoon cafés.

The image of Marilyn Chambers's face covered with the ejaculate of three indistinguishable, slow-motion, and garishly colored penises is not unlike that of identically coin-clad but otherwise naked "dames" from among whom Ginger Rogers stepped to sing "We're in the Money" in *Gold Diggers of 1933.* In that film this famous song, in which depression reality is expressly denied ("we never see a headline about a breadline today"), is itself interrupted by that very reality: the bank closes the show in mid-number for nonpayment of bills. But soon another show arises from the ashes of the former one and through the superior energy, intensity, and abundance of its production numbers succeeds where the earlier one failed.

Movie musicals and feature-length hard-core films are thus alike in offering escape from the problems of ordinary life. It is common for analyses of the musical genre to distinguish between musicals that separate numbers from narrative, like the early Warner Brothers movies, and those that integrate numbers and narrative, like the later Freed Unit films from MGM. It is equally common to consider the integrated musical as aesthetically more evolved.[1] Richard Dyer, however, has offered a description of the genre that is not based simply on historical evolution; rather, he poses three broad categories of movie musical, which he bases on these films' differing treatments of utopia: (1) musicals that *separate* the narrative from the number; (2) those that retain the division between narrative as problem and number as escape but work to *integrate* number into narrative through smoothing-over devices like cues for songs; and (3) those that *dissolve* the distinction between number and narrative, thus implying that the world of the narrative is already utopian (typical of relatively fewer films, usually set in the golden age of a nostalgic past, in which problems are trivial and often enter the narrative very late—for example, *The Merry Widow* or *Meet Me in St. Louis*). These categories are useful in understanding the nature of the utopian solutions enacted by the hard-core feature as well.

Separated Utopias

If the separated musical is the most obviously escapist of the utopian solutions to problems introduced in the narrative, so too is the separated pornographic feature. In the musical, the energy and abundance that are figured in the show and assured by the show's success represent the solution to problems (of poverty and dispiritedness) contained in the rest of the narrative. Yet these solutions are such obvious escapes from reality that it is difficult to take them seriously. The tendency toward nonrepresentational abstract formal patterns, as in the famous Berkeley production numbers associated with surrealist fantasy or dream, only emphasizes this escapist quality more.

Similarly, *Behind the Green Door* represents the most (misogyn-istically) extreme utopian solution to the problem raised in the movie, namely the "exhausted," "limited," "dreary," and econom-ically "manipulated" sex lives of a great many men. As the tall-tale male braggadocio of its frame story suggests, the utopian energy, abundance, intensity, and transparency of the world "behind the green door" offers an escape from the real world the men normally inhabit. In the backstage movie musical the world that is escaped into is the world of showgirls and abundant sex; the hero gets the girl through the show's success. In *Green Door* the coerced "showgirl" performs sex and the hero abducts her after the show successfully concludes, to engage her in his own private show.

If mass entertainment, in general, offers escapist images of the feeling of utopia, then the separated escapism of a film like *Green Door* transforms dreariness and scarcity into phallic and commod-ified intensity and abundance. Like the Busby Berkeley musical, this separated pornographic utopian sensibility solves the problems of the male viewer in ways consistent with a dominantly phallic, het-erosexual consumer economy. These solutions, however, necessar-ily fail to deal with a problem that, in the 1970s, was emerging but had not yet been articulated: namely, the unspecified desires of fe-males who might not wish to be consumed objects and who certainly did not wish to be ravished or raped.

In the 1933 separated backstage musical, fetishization of the woman was not unusual. Musical after musical could solve the prob-lem of depression-era dreariness—the poverty and impotence of the "forgotten man"—with the fetishized production numbers of the "gold-digging" women. If the male characters in these musicals found utopia in the achievement of sex, success, and money, the gold-diggers, it was implied, got success and money through sex. In this the separated musicals were not unlike the stag films of the same era, especially those, like *The Casting Couch*, that showed ambi-tious women and pleasure-seeking men.

By 1972, however, the separated pornographic feature's solution of explicitly hard-core images of objectified female bodies is not as successful in *its* world as Busby Berkeley's or the stag films' solutions were in theirs. Chambers's ejaculate-covered face may be the hard-core equivalent of Berkeley's coin-clad chorus, but as images of sex-ual and monetary abundance (centered in both cases on women, significantly) they do not work in the same way. While the depression-era symbolism may have "solved" the problem of scarcity and dreariness for Berkeley's audiences, in *Behind the Green Door*, as this film's treatment of "ravishment" suggests, the imagery is a less successful solution to the historically emerging problem of woman's desire and pleasure.

The 1933 musical could unproblematically pose the solution to scarcity as the male *use* of female sexual capital: their bodies. The 1972 *Behind the Green Door*, however, could not "solve" the problem of the opposed, though still unequal, male and female centers of power the same way *Deep Throat* could. Unlike *Deep Throat*, whose female pursuit of pleasure spawned a host of imitators in which women sought more and better sex (the pleasure of which was *not* located in their throats), this film did not seem to risk enough in its "play with fire"—even though technically and aesthetically it was a much better film.

Many other movies were cast in this separated mold. Often they were big-budget costume dramas—like *Captain Lust and the Pirate Women* (Beau Buchanan, 1979), *Flesh Gordon* (William Osco and Michael Benveniste, 1979), and *Sodom and Gomorrah* (Mitchell Bros., 1977)—in which utopia was situated in either the past or the future. Yet despite their big budgets and technical proficiency, these films are not the popularly memorable ones of the period. Part of the problem, I believe, is that their otherworldliness as utopian fantasies made them seem like so many film versions of *Fanny Hill* and thus not immediately relevant to the questions of modern sexuality.

One exception, however, is found in the films and videos of the Dark Brothers. Although these works, too, separate the utopian world of sexual performance from the real world, rather than seeming to escape from the problems of contemporary sexuality they self-consciously exaggerate their own misogyny and even their own sleaziness. *Let Me Tell Ya 'Bout White Chicks* (1984) and *Let Me Tell Ya 'Bout Black Chicks* (1986?) are blatantly misogynist films that reproduce in their narratives the atmosphere of the smoker—the place where men talk about sex without having to worry about what women think. The difference, of course, is that unlike the stag film, these films obviously *do* worry about what women think: their macho stance has become self-conscious. Black men in the first, white men in the second, sit around telling tall tales of their sexual escapades. These escapades are enacted in a world apart, like that "behind the green door." In *The Devil in Miss Jones Part III: The New Beginning* (1987), the world apart is a sexual version of hell itself, scene of a Dantesque voyage through a sexual inferno of exaggerated phallic power and domination.

In another of their films, *New Wave Hookers* (Gregory Dark, 1985), two working-class men similar to the truck drivers in *Green Door* fall asleep in front of home-video pornography. Their shared dream is that they are the proprietors of a "new wave hooker" agency that "hooks" female "hookers" up to new wave music that turns them into sex machines. With original music by a group called the Plugs and Sockets, the film is a music video–style musical with a big production number in which twelve women are placed on a revolving stage à la Busby Berkeley and photographed from above while four men "plug" into their various orifices. As in *Green Door*, the success of the utopian world of the show permits the resolution of problems from the world of the narrative. Nonetheless, in both films the sexual numbers are frank escapes into pornotopias offering unrealistic solutions to the sexual problems (of scarcity and exhaustion) presented in the nonfantasy section of the narrative.

Perhaps the most significant aspect of these most overtly misogynist forms of the genre is their self-conscious quality of anachronism and fantasy. Separated utopian hard core is the feature-length narrative form that most resembles the stag film. Like the stag film it invites an exclusive identification with male characters and their point of view, reproducing in its narratives a "males only" camaraderie similar to that of stags.

In a recent book entitled *Pornography: Marxism, Feminism, and the Future of Sexuality* (1986), Marxist philosopher Alan Soble argues that contemporary pornography offers compensatory fantasies designed to make up in the domain of sexuality the power that is denied men in their work and political lives. As he sees it, the contemporary increase in pornographic consumption can be accounted for by male loss of power in the wake of feminism and women's new unwillingness to accommodate their pleasures to those of men. Men who develop a dependence on pornography have, according to Soble, given up the struggle for power in reality. Soble thus characterizes male consumers of pornography as already defeated in their economic, political, and sexual lives. Recourse to pornography would, for these men, be an escape into a nostalgic past where rape, ravishment, and abuse of women was without censure.

While Soble's argument is intriguing, it is, I think, too dependent on a purely escapist notion of pornography's utopia; it lacks the subtlety of Dyer's "playing with fire" and Jameson's notion of problem solving. Still, his explanation would seem to apply closely to the escapist, *separated* instances of the genre under discussion here, films like *Behind the Green Door* and *New Wave Hookers*. As one enthusiastic male aficionado of the Dark Brothers puts it, these films make one think that "neither the sexual revolution nor the women's liberation movement had ever happened." That, precisely, is their utopian appeal for some male audiences.

The celebration of ravishment in *Behind the Green Door* is symptomatic of this separated utopianism. Although not all separated hard-core films depict rape, one is most likely to encounter in this category forms of sexual coercion ending with the female victim "lying back and enjoying it." Because the separated utopia offers a world in which female power is virtually nonexistent, rape, considered as a violent sexual crime that coerces its victims, is an impossibility. In this sense, too, separated hard core resembles the stag film: both forms portray all sexual acts as pleasurable, but the only person whose pleasure counts is the man.

A 1927 stag film entitled *Rape in a Warehouse* is typical: a woman applies for a job in a warehouse. A man makes advances and the woman does not resist, except in the titles, which ironically proclaim: "She struggles," "She fights!!!"—this in contrast to what we see: a woman giving in. Another title speaks for her: "It hurts so nice!" Although rape is invoked as a word, the film undercuts the idea of rape as coercive sex by showing the woman enjoying it, an image contrasted to the resistance she is supposed to put up. Here we have the classic dilemma of rape in a sexist society: the suspicion that the victim wants to be victimized, a suspicion that has made rape notoriously difficult to prove in courts of law. In this film, the image offers an involuntary confession of pleasure that clearly contradicts the official moral rectitude of women. Like Diderot's fable and Hesiod's myth, pleasure for the woman is damning whether she experiences it with or against her will. If it is against her will, of course, the drama of her conversion to consent is of special interest to the male viewer: it vindicates his desire to believe that what he enjoys, she enjoys. For traditionally, the crime of rape only becomes a crime on the level of mental states; rape is rape only if the victim does not consent to the sexual act performed on her or him (Ferguson 1987, 91). Traditional, male-centered pornography's fondest fantasy is to insist on this consent by repeated representations of the rape that turns into ecstasy: ravishment. At its core this fantasy would seem to be yet another means of measuring the difficult-to-measure evidence of woman's desire. The distance traversed between "no" and "yes" becomes, in this instance, the standard of measurement. The woman's pleasure vindicates the man's coercion. For all-male audiences—as with all-male juries—it was easy for this fantasy to go unchallenged. Rape was, and in many ways still is, the crime that most doubted the veracity of its victims.[2]

By the early and mid-1970s, however, the patriarchal fantasy behind the law, and behind the representation of rape in traditional pornography, was being challenged. The emphasis on sexual violence of the women's movement in general, and of Susan Brownmiller's *Against Our Will: Men, Women, and Rape* (1975) in particular, dramatically challenged the double standard that has held women responsible for the sexual crimes that victimize them. As the example of *Behind the Green Door* shows, hard-core film pornography was certainly not in the vanguard of sensitive response to this new awareness; indeed, incidents of rape did not begin to reduce dramatically in hard-core narrative until the early 1980s.[3] But perhaps more important than numbers of rapes in these films is the way rape is utilized in a given narrative. *Behind the Green Door* is close to *Rape in a Warehouse* in its blithe willingness to assume that a woman will enjoy being sexually coerced. Although *Green Door* works harder than the stag film to stage the woman's "enjoyment" of her "ravishment" and gives her a much more active role in achieving this pleasure (typically in fellatio numbers), the film's basic assumption is that the woman will learn that she wants to be ravished. A 1975 film entitled *Joy* (Mansfield) is even more insistent about this enjoyment: it begins with the rape of a high school virgin who not only "lies back and enjoys it" but yells out at her attackers as they flee that she wants "more"; she then becomes an insatiable "rapist" herself, attacking men and women all over New York.

By the early eighties several factors converged to alter the above situation. What with the continued expansion of the couples mar-

ket, an increase in serious reviews of pornography by male and female critics, the heightened acceptance of the feminist critique of
male sexual violence, and the new phenomenon of in-home videocassette consumption, these enjoyment-of-rape scenarios became
increasingly unacceptable in an industry trying to expand its view-
ership and disassociate itself from the sleaze of stag. Two early-
eighties hard-core films with representations of rape are typical of
this new ethos. In *A Very Small Case of Rape* (Ted Roter, 1981) and
Roommates (Chuck Vincent, 1982), the rapes represented do not
show women learning to enjoy their coercion; instead the rapes violate their bodies and wills. While the rapists in each film enjoy performing the rape, and while at least some viewers may enjoy watching the depiction of the act, what is emphasized is the anger,
humiliation, and pain of the female rape victims. In both cases rape
represents the unsuccessful, bad sex to which the films' other numbers respond. These films seem most typical of the new hard-core
feature. They forcefully present sex as a problem and propose to find
better sex as the solution; and rather than separate the performance
of sex from the real world of social conflict and problems, they integrate this world with that of sexual performance.

Integrated Utopias

Integrated hard-core films are thus like Dyer's integrated musicals.
Rather than separate the pornotopia of sexual abundance from the
more realistic world of a frame narrative, these films integrate sex
into this world. Like musicals, whose narratives call forth and motivate song and dance numbers, this type of hard-core film shows
sexual numbers occurring at the slightest cue. Again we can take our
key example from the career of Marilyn Chambers in yet another
film directed by the Mitchell Brothers.

The Resurrection of Eve (1976) is a more or less realistic narrative of the shy, repressed Eve's relationship with her sexually
"hip" lover and, eventually, husband. The narrative begins with a
flashback to the brutal first seduction of Eve, who is supposed to be
twelve (but is played by an actress who looks twenty). An older male
friend of her mother's teaches Eve about sex by asking her leeringly
if she knows "how they do it" in various countries. He begins with
kissing and progresses to fellatio, each time simulating the act with

Eve's Raggedy Ann doll before doing it with Eve. He reaches a noisy orgasm through fellatio at the moment that Eve's mother enters, his orgasmic scream merging with her outraged one as she beats him with her purse.

We next see Eve as an adult in the hospital, her face covered with bandages from a car accident. In disjointed flashbacks we learn of Eve's affair with Frank, a disc jockey. In their first number Eve asks him to "be gentle"; he answers, "I don't know any other way." The straight sex that follows *is* gentle and emphasizes the emotions on their faces. Happy scenes of their domestic life are then mixed with foreshadowing shock cuts to the future car accident that will land Eve in the hospital.

Frank grows irrationally jealous of Eve's innocent relationship with a black male friend, a boxer played by Johnny Keyes. During sex with Eve, Frank fantasizes Keyes's penis in her mouth instead of his own. His lovemaking grows frenzied and violent—this time he is not gentle—and afterward, when she confesses that she did not climax, he snaps, "Maybe you need some of that black stuff."

At this juncture the jealous Frank causes the accident that destroys Eve's face and necessitates its "resurrection" through plastic surgery into the cinematically better known face of Marilyn Chambers. A contrite Frank marries the resurrected Eve, who then becomes a happy housewife. But soon Frank, growing restless, introduces "group sex" and "swinging" into their sexual repertoire.

At the first swingers party Eve is a spoilsport, visibly upset at the sight of Frank penetrating another woman from behind. Later, Frank is furious: "I screwed Tom's wife and nobody screwed you. That's not the way the game is played." A dutiful Eve promises to do better next time. At the second party both get "screwed," but Eve is still unenthusiastic. Frank, though, is gratified to learn that her partner did not "measure up" to him. "See?" he says. "Our marriage is getting better already." At the third party Eve *does* get into it, but with a black man, which reawakens Frank's racism and fear of sexual inadequacy. At the fourth party Eve engages in an orgy with several others, both male and female, as Frank only watches.

At the final party, Eve meets her black friend Johnny again. They do an erotic jazz dance. An extended sexual number—the film's spontaneous "big production" number—grows out of the rhythms created by the dance. This orgy intercuts with the sexual activities of many other couples, including Frank and the woman he is with. These other couples' activities function as background to the primary activities of Eve and Johnny, who are soon "jazzing" with great abandon to musical and sexual rhythms that are enhanced by fast-paced editing. Eve finally performs the fellatio on Johnny that Frank had once imagined her doing and with Frank now watching. Then a bongo player jams to the rhythm of Eve's prolonged orgasms. Shock cuts of the car accident reflect Frank's jealous agony and comment on his past violence. After the number a humbled Frank asks Eve if they could go back to the "way it used to be." Eve says only, "It's over, Frank," and there the film ends.

In *Behind the Green Door* we saw how the separated form of the pornographic feature uses its sexual numbers in an obviously escapist way, with the world of narrative reality kept rigorously apart from the fantastic, utopian world of the numbers "behind the green door." As in the Busby Berkeley musical and the stag film, every number is an all-out showstopper, the ultimate in energy, abundance, intensity, transparency, and community. In *The Resurrection of Eve*, however, the greater integration of number and narrative gives rise to relatively more realism in both registers. Here, not every number has to be a showstopper. Some kinds of sex can be better than other kinds; some kinds, such as the abusive sex that begins the film, or rape, can even be oppressive and bad. All sexual numbers do not necessarily represent utopian alternatives (in energy, abundance, etc.) to the realities (exhaustion, scarcity, etc.) of everyday life. Nevertheless, even though conflict and contradiction exist in both registers, it is still the comparatively more utopian world of the number that carries the primary burden of resolution. When Eve and Frank argue about whether to participate in swinging parties, they do so during sex. In the excitement of the moment and to get on with the present sex, Eve says yes to Frank's demand for sex with different partners later.

This example suggests how much more of the tension between power and pleasure in sexual relations can be admitted and "played with" in the highly integrated hard-core film than in the separated form. This is not to say that the integrated feature admits anything like a feminist critique of male power and pleasure. Yet this form of the genre is more likely to address precisely those problems of gender, class, and race—and the power imbalances they represent—

that Dyer noted were banished from the classic musical.[4] In *The Resurrection of Eve*, such issues come into the bedroom *as issues*, as unresolved problems within the culture, and become part of the material of sexual performance. When the older man abuses the twelve-year-old Eve, for example, the abuse is introduced in a way that could never occur in a separated film—that is, *as a problem*. Thus it is rather like the treatment of rape in post-eighties films: both are the bad sex that better sex must make up for. Similarly, when Frank imagines Johnny giving greater satisfaction to Eve than he can, a whole range of social, sexual, and racial attitudes are integrated into the number.

Just how different this treatment of issues is in the integrated film versus the separated can be seen by comparing Eve and Johnny's number with the black man/white woman number in *Behind the Green Door*. There, in the film's first heterosexual number, Keyes, as the primitive African, stalks and then ravishes Chambers, the white woman. Yet even though the ravisher is more powerful than the ravished, in contrast to the audience who pays to see them both are socially powerless (though sexually potent) performing animals. Their powerlessness, however, is not integrated into the film as a problem in need of solution. It simply facilitates the sexual performance and cues the spectators in the club to do what the stag film so often advises: go "grab someone" and do the same.

Conversely, in Chambers and Keyes's climactic number in *The Resurrection of Eve*, power and pleasure inform each other in ways that affect the ability of the original couple—Eve and Frank—to find pleasure. What Eve finds with Johnny means that she need no longer depend on Frank for pleasure. The shy Eve who once passively begged Frank to "be gentle" has been "resurrected," through pornography's familiar narrative of female sexual initiation, into an actively sexual woman—though significantly, she is not shown to be an active woman in any other sphere. Thus Eve gains in power as she gains in pleasure, while Frank loses both. The game of swinging, originally intended to increase and maintain Frank's power *and* pleasure by extending his sphere of sexual influence, backfires. Frank was supposed to "screw Tom's wife," and another male was supposed to "screw" Eve. The game is supposed to be played in the name of everyone's sexual "freedom"; but beneath the surface lurk unavoidable contradictions, which emerge as soon as the stereotypically "less equal" and "more sexual" black male enters the game. The presence of this black interloper upsets the precarious equilibrium of power and pleasure for the "sexual revolutionary" white male.

Thus, while the *separated* form of pornographic utopian fantasy seeks escape from the sexual realities of a presumed white, male, heterosexual viewer, the *integrated* form represents a newer—and, I think, more representative—aspect of feature-length hard core: it more directly confronts, on some levels, some of the sorry realities that created the desire for pornotopia in the first place. In this way, for example, *The Resurrection of Eve* can admit such problematic realities as children's sexual abuse and racism into both narrative and number. However, it would cease to be pornography were it not to adhere to the principle that sexual pleasure still offers the best solution to all the problems afflicting the sexual realm. So even though the film admits certain problems into its representation, the primacy of sexual pleasure as a generic given ultimately precludes a nonsexual solution to the power imbalance in Eve and Frank's relationship. It would, for instance, be unthinkable within the limits of the genre for Eve to get a job in order to find the same self-confidence she attains in her sexual experiences at swingers' parties.

Even though pleasure is paramount, however, negotiation *for* power and *within* pleasure often occurs in this integrated form of the genre. This point is worth stressing. Pornography is not a monolith, either of apolitical pleasure or of unpleasurable power. Integrated pornos "play with fire" the most actively. *The Resurrection of Eve* is an extreme case, taking on the sexual abuse of children, white male sexual envy of blacks, and white male insecurity in the face of female pleasure. Other films that fall into this integrated category include *A Very Small Case of Rape* and *Roommates*, cited above for admitting rape as a real problem into their narratives; *Misty Beethoven*; and some of the best-known contemporary hardcore titles: *Deep Throat*, the incestuous family melodrama series *Taboo* (I–V) and *Taboo American Style* (I–IV), *Debbie Does Dallas* (Jim Clark, 1978), *Talk Dirty to Me* (Anthony Spinelli, 1980), the narratively unrelated *Talk Dirty to Me (One More Time)* (Anthony Spinelli, 1985), and *Classical Romance* (Richard Maller, 1984). These films suggest that within the limited realm of the bedroom men and women have some room for the negotiation of pleasure.

In integrated hard-core films negotiation often occurs between traditionally active males and passive females. Thus at the resolution of *Misty Beethoven* Misty becomes the teacher and Seymour her submissive slave in dog collar, and *Deep Throat* finds Linda making the arrangements for her happy ending with Wilbur. In *Taboo*, a familiar fantasy of oedipal desire is conceived and acted on from the perspective of the mother's transgressive desire for her son rather than from the more usual perspective of the son; and the conclusion of *The Resurrection of Eve* finds Eve telling Frank that their relationship is over. Each of these films offers a patently facile solution to the real problems of power in patriarchy, with solutions ranging from the utterly simplistic finding of a better endowed lover or the "right" number to a more subtle give-and-take of power and pleasure in films like *Misty Beethoven* or *The Resurrection of Eve*. Nevertheless, in all these films pleasure is still viewed as something to be negotiated within an acknowledged structure of power.

In their recent book *Re-Making Love: The Feminization of Sex* (1986), Barbara Ehrenreich, Elizabeth Hess, and Gloria Jacobs defend the important gains women made during the sexual revolution. Whatever one might think about the new materialism of empirical studies of sexual behavior, begun by Alfred Kinsey and ushered in definitively by Masters and Johnson's scientific "discovery" of the female orgasm in 1966, these authors suggest that in the women's liberation movement it provided important political leverage against previous theories of the propriety and naturalness of female passivity in sexual relations (p. 65). Sex no longer needed to be described, as the burgeoning crew of male sexologists, marriage manual writers, and psychoanalysts had done until now, as a "microdrama of male dominance and female passivity" (p. 69).

As Ehrenreich et al. see the situation, a whole new generation of radical feminists now had a corpus of "objective" scientific findings on which to build a feminist interpretation of sexuality. In their chapter "The Battle for Orgasm Equity: The Heterosexual Crisis of the Seventies," they argue that in the late sixties and early seventies the sexual revolution took on very different meaning for men as opposed to women. Where for men it meant more sex, for women it was beginning to mean *better* sex, a notion that ultimately entailed a redefinition of the heterosexual act itself. No longer did sex mean intercourse plus whatever preliminaries were required to achieve it.

Now, in the wake of Masters and Johnson and such widely read essays as "The Myth of the Vaginal Orgasm" (Koedt 1971), the "sex act" was no longer defined by physiological necessity; its very constitution entered a remarkable state of flux (Ehrenreich, Hess, and Jacobs 1986, 70, 74–102).

Gay liberation had a similar effect on this "heterosexual crisis." With a logic not unlike that of *Deep Throat*, gays of both sexes argued that sexual relations were not necessarily defined by the insertion of a penis into a vagina. Given the new uncertainty about the very definition of sexual relations, oral sex came to stand, as we have already seen, for a greater diversity of erogenous zones. By isolating the active organ of the mouth (which could be seen simultaneously to give and to receive) and by overlooking the comparatively passive and procreative vagina, it seemed to offer, as Ehrenreich et al. (p. 81) note, at least the possibility of making sex more reciprocal and egalitarian.

We can, of course, question the degree to which sexual relations actually did become more reciprocal and egalitarian, as well as the degree to which mere sexual materialism and fetishism—the practice of more various or more skilled sexual acts—could, in themselves, bring this change about. Nevertheless, the "diff'rent strokes" ethic was indicative of a limited redefinition of sex: as a social and political interaction in which a certain amount of negotiation and give-and-take *could* take place. It is in the integrated hard-core utopia that we most see this negotiation being acted out—if always from unequal male and female centers of power; for what these films offer, what is new in them in contrast to either the stag film or separated hard core, is quite simply a franker acknowledgment of the role of power in sexual relations than had ever been seen before. Power emerges in these films not, as anti-pornography feminists would have it, as the ultimate poison of all heterosexual relations, but as an important and inevitable component of increasingly material and fetishized forms of pleasure and of learning how to negotiate pleasure with partners.

The film *Loose Ends* (Bruce Seven, 1984), starring Rikki Blake, is a striking example of this negotiation. Like most integrated hard core it begins in medias res with a less-than-satisfying sexual performance. Heather's partner notices that she is not very excited. She explains, "I'm sick and tired of being a receptacle for somebody's come. You think your cock is an almighty gift. Well it's not!" The man leaves, and Heather is left sadly fingering a dildo which she does not use. Instead she phones an old girlfriend from college for advice.

The friend, Linda, is a swinger and at the very moment she receives the call is engaged in sex; her pleasure thus substitutes in the film for that which was previously interrupted. When the two girlfriends meet, Heather confesses that although she is "liberal," she can't have an orgasm. Her friend rectifies this situation immediately in a "lesbian" encounter that goes from slow striptease to cunnilingus to rimming. (Apparently the one thing Heather has not tried is anal eroticism.) As this encounter continues, the film cuts to another, simultaneous, encounter between people we have not yet met, an explicitly sadomasochistic ritual with a female dominatrix holding a whip over two male submissives.

The film intercuts several more times between these two prolonged simultaneous encounters, each of which grows more kinky. Linda, for example, concludes her encounter with Heather by putting a motor-driven vibrator up each of Heather's orifices. Linda then arranges for Heather to meet her friend, the dominatrix, to be initiated into "the art of bondage." A sadie-max number follows. Heather is tied and tortured through the manipulation of nipple and clitoris rings. Later she becomes the centerpiece of a more conventional orgy involving Linda, the dominatrix, and the two unnamed men. The climax occurs with a dual meat shot of Heather's anus and vagina occupied by the two men's penises, followed immediately by twin, and nearly simultaneous, money shots on each side of Heather's breasts. A final sequence shows a smug Heather at her masseuse's bragging that she has had her first orgasm. The masseuse admires and massages Heather's body, devoting special attention to the buttocks. The now assertive Heather asks for "one finger" in her "pussy" and a thumb in her "ass," and with that easily comes. Heather then returns the favor to her masseuse. The film ends here with a satisfied Heather saying, "It feels great to be a real woman—look out, world, here I come!"

In her own belated (1984) and reified "battle for orgasm equity," Heather learns the same lesson that Ehrenreich, Hess, and Jacobs say many feminists were learning in the late sixties and early seventies: that sex no longer has to be a "microdrama of male dominance and female passivity." Heather rejects both straight sex and fellatio to find her first real pleasure in anal eroticism with a female partner. Even though the film concludes with a scene with another female partner, the lesson is not that Heather's newfound sexual identity is lesbian; and though her experiments with bondage place her in the submissive role, this very submission is contrasted with the active way she seeks out "diff'rent strokes." Whether or not one agrees with her assessment that she has finally become a "real woman," it is significant, and increasingly typical of mid-eighties hard core, that although both the phallus and the money shot are construed as part of the pleasure, neither is necessary to it. The ending thus suggests that Heather is ready for further experimentation.

Although the double entendre of Heather's final proclamation— "look out, world, here I come!"—may seem a facile expression of power-in-pleasure because it elides the real power sources in that "world," it nevertheless clearly states one of the new "truths" of integrated feature-length hard core: that pleasure can be negotiated through (limited) power, that sex is no longer a "microdrama of male dominance and female passivity" but a drama of both power and pleasure.

Dissolved Utopias

The third and final hard-core mode for structuring the relations between pornotopian number and narrative is called *dissolved*. This mode is almost as escapist as Dyer's first category, but where the separated hard-core film offers escape into a pornotopia of sexual numbers whose abundance and energy stand in opposition to the scarcity and exhaustion of the real-world narrative, the dissolved film minimizes the distinctions between sexual fantasy and narrative reality. Here there is no need to escape from realities depicted in the narrative; pornotopia is already achieved. The world of the narrative is nearly as problem-free as the separated form's world of numbers "behind the green door." The two worlds simply dissolve into each other.

In the musical, this dissolved form often presents a nostalgic, idealized vision of the past: a Lubitschean imaginary kingdom or the glowing memory of turn-of-the-century St. Louis during the world's fair. Pleasure produced by musical numbers seems to arise naturally from such already pleasurable places. The narrative register offers such a rosy picture of reality that song and dance just seem to come with the territory. In feature-length pornography, however, the pleasurable place of the dissolved utopia is more often set in the present or future, offering idealized fantasies of current notions of sexual liberation.

The 1980 film *Insatiable*, directed by Godfrey Daniels and starring, once again, Marilyn Chambers, exemplifies this form. The top-selling adult video of 1980–1982, *Insatiable* has only the barest minimum of real-world narrative conflict. Chambers plays the independently wealthy high-fashion model Sandra Chase, whose only problem appears to be reconciling her variable, insatiable sexual appetites with the expectations of a kindly but old-fashioned aunt. Since this aunt does not figure prominently in the narrative but only in a series of flashbacks that intersperse colorful travelogue with Sandra's sexual escapades, the narrative problem never arises. Instead, Sandra seeks and finds pleasure in one sexual encounter after another, only occasionally expressing mild discontent—as stars must do—with the loneliness of "life at the top."

The film opens as it will end, with Sandra masturbating; in quick inserts we see glimpses of her imagined partners as the title song is sung. The next morning a friend, Flo, arrives at Sandra's estate. She sees Sandra and another woman performing cunnilingus on one another at the poolside. Later, out in her sports car, Sandra picks up a delivery boy who has run out of gas. She helps him siphon gas and then initiates fellatio. These episodes all portray Sandra as a cheerful, self-confident, and self-assertive woman who initiates sex with whomever she wants. Since she wants sex a great deal, she is not particularly selective about who her partner is. The delivery boy, for example, has no special desirability; even his penis is of ordinary length, a feature that is itself extraordinary in the genre.

The next scene offers a partial explanation for Sandra's behavior. As we see the scene in flashback, Sandra tells Flo about her first sexual experience, with the gardener of her father's estate. The number is uncommonly brutal and phallic. The gardener (Richard Pacheco) enters the poolroom where the presumably adolescent Sandra is alone. In response to some mild flirting on Sandra's part he teases, humiliates, and taunts her with her own desire to "be fucked." In a prolonged scene on the pool table, the gardener hits her with his penis on face and labia, performs cunnilingus, and has her perform fellatio. Finally he enters her, sneering that she's not worried about her father surprising them now. After more fellatio followed by a money shot, Sandra concludes her narrative: "I just loved being held down and made love to by him. I was young, but sexually I was ready for him."

In an otherwise ostentatiously cheerful narrative about the frequency and facility of sexual satisfaction in which an active, sexually liberated woman pursues her own pleasure, this number comes as something of a shock: the free, independent woman is not only insatiable but, at least in this episode, a budding masochist as well—one who describes the experience of being brutally overpowered as being "made love to." What are we to make of the film's presentation of both insatiability and masochism as desirable forms of female pleasure?

Both forms of pleasure are stereotypically female, with self-control playing no apparent role. It would be a mistake, however, therefore to conflate them with the powerless Chambers who is "ravished" in *Behind the Green Door*. For in this "dissolved" utopian fantasy, insatiability and masochism receive a most unusual inflection: both contribute to Sandra Chase's power. From a feminist perspective, it is easy, of course, to dismiss this notion of power, to see Sandra's apparent satisfaction in insatiability and masochism as the height of false consciousness and alienation from any real source of power or pleasure for women. But to do so is to foreclose the possibility of seeing women as the subjects of sexual representation, for however we, as gendered individuals with individual sexual tastes and preferences, may judge this film's sexual acts, *Insatiable* does construct its female protagonist as a subject, and not just an object, of desire. This is the major difference between the dissolved hardcore *Insatiable* and the separated hard-core *Behind the Green Door*. *Green Door* is undeniably misogynist, not because of the nature of any acts represented but because, like the stag film, it is content to represent the female body as a pure object of pleasure with no significant will or desire of its own. *Insatiable* may be judged misogynist depending on how one interprets the masochistic passivity of the pool table scene, but this film is focused, in a way the stag never was, on the new problem of pleasing the woman and of constructing her pleasure from her own point of view. There is sexual coercion in both *Green Door* and *Insatiable*, but in the latter the ravishment is all about finding the sexual number that will permit the woman the most pleasure.

This new emphasis on the woman's pleasure does not solve the problem of pornography for feminism; nor does it solve the sensitive issue of male domination in sex. Yet it does shift the problem beyond a mere judgment of the sexual numbers represented. We may still feel uneasy about a subjectivity that locates pleasure for the woman in masochism and insatiability. Indeed, the very term *masochism* is so politically charged as to have been recently expunged from the revised edition of the widely used *Diagnostic and Statistical Manual of Mental Disorders* (known as *DSM-III-R*). Traditionally, the masochist was defined as one who abandons himself or herself to a pleasure achieved through being controlled by another. Although many men enjoy acting the role of masochistic submissive and many women enjoy the role of sadistic dominator, the more typically feminine role in patriarchal culture is that of the passive submissive who exercises no will or authority in the achievement of her sexual pleasure—beyond, that is, the original contract to engage in such activity. Since precisely this traditionally submissive role of women is undergoing change in contemporary Western culture, it is not surprising that masochism, now called a "self-defeating personality disorder," has become one of the diagnostic categories described as "needing further study" (*DSM-III-R* 1987, 367).

In pornography, however, we are not talking about personality disorders. We are talking about the representation of sexual acts, the deployment of power and pleasure. And masochism, for both men and women, is the name for sexual acts in which one finds sexual pleasure in being controlled or abused by another. The next chapter will examine the phenomena of masochism and sadism more thoroughly so that we may discuss those pornographic films which explore one or the other as a primary or ultimate mode of pleasure. For the present, however, it will suffice to emphasize that the "sadomasochistic" number encountered in a film like *Insatiable*—or in *Loose Ends*, or even in *Deep Throat*—differs markedly from the classic forms of either sadistic or masochistic pornographic fantasy. The difference is that in these newer films the pursuit of one or the other form of pleasure is not presented as monomaniacal. In the industry's terminology introduced in the last chapter, the pool table scene in *Insatiable* is simply sadie-max—one kind of sexual number in the smorgasbord of numbers. Its mood and iconography do not dominate the rest of the film, nor do they dominate the fate or character of the female quest figure the way they do, say, the character of O in *The Story of O*.

Masochistic pleasure is presented in *Insatiable* as simply one of many possible forms of pleasure available to the sexually questing female subject. Unlike Misty Beethoven, Linda Lovelace, or Eve, all heroines of *integrated* hard-core films, Sandra is already in complete knowledge and control of the means to her pleasure; she does not need the familiar figure of the doctor/teacher/sexologist to show her the way to either power or pleasure because she already recognizes herself as a desiring subject.

Thus the dissolved utopianism of the film lies in part in its banishment of the ill effects of power in a pursuit of cheerful pleasure. Sandra is able to accept any kind of sexual experience as pleasure without suffering repercussions from the sexual power exercised upon her because from the start she occupies the typically male position of power. Even in the violent pool table scene with the gardener, the person who would stand to lose the most by the entrance of her father is not Sandra but the gardener himself. The fact that the father never does appear (Sandra's parents are presumed to die in an accident soon after this scene) suggests that dissolved utopias tend to banish patriarchal power from the realm of the narrative, leaving only its phallic organ, attached to the bodies of a great many anonymous men, as the object of Sandra's pleasure.

The insatiability of this pleasure needs to be understood in the context of the film's dissolved utopianism. Like the masochist, the insatiable woman is a stock figure of earlier literary male pornographic fantasy: she is the woman who is never satisfied, who cannot get enough of what she needs and so is always desperate for more. In the 1975 (separated) film *Joy* we saw the female victim of rape calling out for more as her attackers leave. At the end of *Insatiable* Sandra Chase–Marilyn Chambers also calls out for "more, more, more" even though she has already "had" a great deal. Rather than give her more, the film simply ends with the end title that is also its advertising slogan: "Marilyn Chambers is Insatiable." But as the scene leading up to this conclusion suggests, this insatiability differs from that in *Joy*, for here it is a sign not of frustration but rather of the most utopian of all possible hard-core endings. Instead of the end of desire in the satisfaction of climax, a new kind of satisfaction is offered: climax's infinite prolongation.

The "final" number occurs as follows: as at the film's beginning, Sandra masturbates to the sound of the affectionate lovemaking of her friends Flo and Roger. Glimpses of moments from all the previous numbers of the film appear, followed by a succession of anonymous men not seen in the film's narrative. In more conventional hard core, the money shots that follow would conclude the episode with a rhetorical flourish; in this film, however, the men come and go, but the end of their pleasure does not signal the end either of Sandra's pleasure or of the number. Sandra whispers, "Please don't leave me," but her prolonged desire does not seem a source of frustration; rather, as her desire continues, so does her fantasy, this time conjuring a long and lanky man (the famous John C. Holmes) with a proportionately long and lanky penis who performs cunnilingus as she apparently orgasms. Still the number continues, with fellatio and then straight sex represented in a rapid montage that seems to imitate the various rhythms of her orgasm and ends, for the man, with a money shot onto her abdomen. Yet here there is no end either, just a close-up of Sandra's face as she calls out for "more, more, more," and the end credit: "Marilyn Chambers is Insatiable."

If ever a film cried out for a sequel, it was this one. That sequel, *Insatiable II*, also ends with Chambers as Sandra again calling out for "more." But what is significant in both these films—and their endings—is that insatiability does not suggest a congruent lack of satisfaction. One needs only to consider a similar moment in the 1972 *Devil in Miss Jones* to appreciate the difference. In that film, Georgina Spelvin's perpetually unsatisfiable desire is represented at the end as a state of damnation: she is, in fact, in hell. In contrast, Marilyn Chambers's insatiability represents the continuous, unending pleasures of a utopian world in which the power imbalance between the sexes does not directly enter the represented world of the film. In this utopian world of infinite energy and abundance, a female Don Juan seduces, and is seduced by, men and women alike. Her own seductions, however, are not simply nymphomania run wild. Instead, Sandra's insatiability represents a new view of the active female pursuit of pleasure, a view congruent with contemporary sexologies' construction of female sexuality as, in Mary Jane Sherfey's (1970, 138) words, a "paradoxical state of sexual insatiation in the presence of the utmost sexual satisfaction."

Of course, such new and (comparatively) progressive images of female orgasmic potential can and will be read by traditional patriarchal viewers as nothing more than old-fashioned nymphomania: as being in excess of the phallic norm, the story of Zeus and Hera once again. In the logical terms of the genre and what it is "talking to itself" about, though, this dissolved form of the feature-length hard-core film, with its absence of the typical narrative movement from disequilibrium through climax to equilibrium, is of particular interest, because narrative dissolution seems to point to an equal dissolution of the phallic money shot as pleasure's ultimate "frenzy of the visible."

In many of the hard-core features discussed so far we have encountered the visual paradox of a genre in transit from the stag film's representation of female objects of desire displaying their "goods" to male subjects, to full-length films purporting to represent male and female subjects of desire to male and female viewing subjects. One major obstacle in this transition has been the incongruity of a filmic iconography still suited to phallic norms. I am not sure just when the change begins to occur, but sometime in the early eighties, and especially in the dissolved category of hard-core utopia (most markedly in the 1980 *Insatiable* and its 1984 sequel *Insatiable II*), the phallus falters: it no longer acts as the standard of measurement for either male or female pleasure. For no matter how many penises "come and go" in these films, no matter how long or erect they are or how powerfully they spew forth ejaculate, there is an increasing sense of disjunction between what the money shot shows and what it tries to represent, as if its visible finitude can no longer measure up to the infinitely expanding, invisible pleasure of the insatiable woman.[5]

Whether this means that the very standard of measurement for cinematic and visual pleasure is also beginning to change I will leave to the discussion of current hard core and the new hard core by women in Chapter 8. For the moment, however, let us simply examine the end of *Insatiable II* and draw some further conclusions about dissolved utopias. Chambers-Chase has invited both a man and a woman friend into her bed. This ménage à trois leads to a prolonged number in which the writhing Chambers again calls out for "more." Here, however, we are not given a money shot to signal either the man's climax or hers; instead we see Chambers at first orally engulfing his penis and then writhing with pleasure, her whole body in a kind of spasm as a male voice sings the title song. The title song, of course, seems to go on and on as well. . . .

Perhaps one would have to have seen a great many post-1972 hard-core features to appreciate the novelty of this break with the money shot. *Insatiable II* is not the first film to dispense with this convention. *A Very Small Case of Rape* contains no money shots, and *Loose Ends* breaks with the convention in some numbers, as, in fact, do a great many pre-eighties films, such as *The Resurrection of Eve* and *Behind the Green Door*. I therefore cannot suggest that only dissolved pornotopia abandons this most phallic of hard-core customs. Moreover, there are certainly examples of dissolved utopias in which money shots reign supreme, such as *Barbara Broadcast* ("Henry Paris," 1977). Nonetheless, it does seem appropriate that this break with convention occurs more easily and more frequently in this particularly utopian category of feature-length hard core, perhaps because dissolved utopias present worlds in which power and pleasure are at odds neither in the numbers *nor* in the narratives. This ideal alignment of power and pleasure for all participants would then seem to create, in the case of the female protagonist at least, a situation quite the reverse of the one encountered by Hera in Hesiod's fragment. In that story power and pleasure were distinctly opposed for both the man and the woman: the possession of one precluded the possession of the other. Zeus possessed power; Hera possessed pleasure and lost the quarrel with her husband because a blind prophet defined her as the pleasure-saturated nympho of her day. Marilyn Chambers, in contrast, is the newly defined *insatiable* woman of her day, where insatiability suggests precisely that positing the "one part" of male pleasure as the norm against which the excessive "ten" of woman is measured no longer suffices.

We have seen that in contemporary film and video pornography the quest for greater knowledge of the truth of pleasure has moved through three discernible stages of representation: (1) the exhibitionist display of normally hidden body parts—what I have called the stag film's fascination with "genital show"; (2) a more narrativized stage of "genital event" typified by the "meat shot"; and (3) the escalation of the principle of maximum visibility in a "money shot" that seems designed to answer the visual insufficiencies of meat. Each of these conventions is, of course, inadequate to the representation of heterosexual sexual *relations*. But each is even more inadequate to the representation of that which it particularly and increasingly solicits: the female side of that relation—woman's desire and woman's pleasure. In a genre that perpetually seeks to figure an involuntary frenzy of the visible sexual "thing," we might take Marilyn Chambers's call for "more, more, more" as reflecting the realization that this "more" cannot be driven by a phallic standard of measurement which sees pleasure as a countable entity. Although the decline of the money shot in some recent hard-core features hardly indicates a new utopia of hard-core awareness of the difference of women and the incommensurability of male and female desire for power and pleasure, it does perhaps suggest a spirit of restlessness and variety that finds its ultimate expression, as we shall see in Chapter 8, in the new phenomenon of women behind the camera, calling the shots for the first time in a genre that previously was produced, directed, and consumed by men only.

Conclusion

My use here of Dyer's categories of utopian separation, integration, and dissolution is obviously just one way of understanding new narrative hard core. As a method, of course, it conflicts with any attempt to construct the history of the genre and thus to trace important changes in iconography. A real history would have to come to grips with these methodological problems. I will say here only that generic change has no simple one-to-one correspondence to changes taking place in the real world. New ideas about female sexuality do not just get reflected in hard core. Rather, as Rick Altman (1987, 117) points out with regard to musicals, genres begin as simple "semantic clusters" providing certain kinds of contents, but they do not achieve true generic status until these contents begin to form a stable syntax.

In this and the last chapter we have seen how number and narrative work together to form a syntax of feature-length hard core: patterns of meaning that formulate sex as a problem and then try to solve this problem through sexual performance. But a particular syntax, as Altman points out, is never a neutral pattern of meaning. Meaning is made possible only because other meanings have been repressed—and this repressed side will often return in self-reflexive and self-destructive bursts during late moments of a genre's history.

The study of hard-core pornography as a genre, and indeed the genre itself, are so new that I am not prepared to offer anything like Altman's semantic-syntactic history for hard core. Still, the idea that a given syntax represses elements of its own meaning is suggestive in light of the traditional stag film's repression of the female subject. It seems possible to argue that the new narrative syntax showing female protagonists seeking pleasure has facilitated the return of this repressive component. Similarly suggestive is Altman's idea that a genre can undergo "semantic shifts" which take on entirely new subject matters—such as the introduction of "folk motifs" into the forties musical in response to the wartime need for nationalistic fables. In other words, although a new semantic element may be triggered by historical phenomena, it cannot enter a genre except through accommodation to already existing syntaxes—to use the musical example again, by means of backstage narratives of troop shows.

It seems possible that the new female insatiability, seen as a positive rather than a comic, grotesque, or threatening feature of female sexual performance, is undergoing a similar semantic shift, one that would have been unthinkable in the older syntax of the stag film. This positive construction found its first expression, I suggest, in the syntactically loose, but still temporally extended, dissolved utopian form, where narrative, with its linear progressive notion of a beginning leading to climax, is least in evidence. In the final chapter we will test parts of this thesis as we look at the evolution of Femme Productions. Before examining these possible semantic/syntactic changes, however, let us turn to what many consider to be the frightening dystopian side of hard-core visual pornography: violent sadomasochistic fantasies.

7

Power, Pleasure, and Perversion
Sadomasochistic Film Pornography

*The objective nature of photography confers on it a
quality of credibility absent from all other picture-
making. . . . The photographic image is the object
itself, the object freed from the conditions of time and
space that govern it.*

André Bazin,
"The Ontology of the Photographic Image"

Bazin's ontology of the photographic image has long formed the basis of a realist theory of cinema. At its most extreme this theory
states that cinema does not represent objects, it *re-presents* them.
Photography, especially motion photography, is not a conventional
iconography that simply resembles the world; it *is* the world by virtue of the automatic registration of the object from the world onto
photographic emulsions. But as any film student knows, this realist
theory of cinema is but one pole of a dialectic, the other half of
which Bazin (1967–1971, 1:16) states at the end of this same essay:
"On the other hand, of course, cinema is also a language." Film theory since Bazin has been divided over which of these two statements
carries the more weight, most recently through exploration of the
language analogy and by modifying the naive realism of the "transparent reflection" idea of reality.

The genre of pornography, however, works hard to convince us of its realism. It should come as no surprise, then, to find the Meese Commission quoting the above passage from Bazin in its effort to explain the special dangers of pornography in a chapter entitled "The Use of Performers in Commercial Pornography." To the commission, realism is the fundamental problem of any photographic pornography: with cinema, representations of sex in pornography become *re*-presentations of sex, "captured and preserved in exact, vivid detail" (Attorney General's Commission on Pornography 1986, 1:839). The filmic representation of an "actual person" engaged in sexual acts is exactly the same as if witnessed "in the flesh." Thus, the reasoning goes, film audiences bear "direct" witness to any abuse or perversion therein enacted.

An Ontological Pornography

The inherent and unprecedented realism of movies seems to lead directly, then, to an equally inherent and unprecedented obscenity. Most realist theorists of the cinema seem to come up against this "ultimate" obscenity of the medium at some point in their thinking. Stanley Cavell in *The World Viewed* (1979, 45), for example, asserts that the "ontological conditions of the cinema reveal it as inherently pornographic." And Steven Marcus, who is not a film theorist but whose attitude toward cinema could be termed realist, writes (1974, 208) that the motion picture was what the genre of pornography "was all along waiting for," since language in literary pornography had only been a "bothersome necessity."

Various forms of technological teleology typically accompany such realist theories. Like most teleologies, these can lead either to utopia or to apocalypse. Bazin, the utopian, believed that the technological evolution of cinema would ultimately result in the discovery of new and liberating truths about life. Seeing an "object freed from the conditions of time and space that govern it" would, he said, empower us. But when he came up against some of the possible "hard-core objects" of this liberation, Bazin could be seen to be grappling, much more thoughtfully than the Meese Commission, with the pornographic limits of his realist ontology. Writing about a newsreel sequence showing the execution of Communist spies by members of Chiang Kai-shek's army, he anticipates the current concerns about "snuff" films: "The obscenity of the image was of the same order as that of a pornographic film. An ontological pornography. Here death is the negative equivalent of sexual pleasure, which is sometimes called, not without reason, 'the little death'" (Bazin 1967–1971, 2:173).

Bazin is disturbed by the "obscenity" of this image and by the analogous specter of hard-core pornography. By the logic of his realist ontology, the vision of such ultimate or extreme "truths" should be admitted to view no matter how shocking, simply because they exist. But the idea of going to the cinema to watch a death spasm is obscene. Since Bazin does not want the new medium to replicate the abuses of the Roman circus, he takes refuge in art; in a fiction film, "actual sexual emotion by performers" is "contradictory to the exigencies of art" (ibid.). Real sex, like real death, is unaesthetic and therefore out of place. Yet elsewhere in his writing Bazin has celebrated documentary realism in fictional contexts, and he is honest enough here to acknowledge the inconsistency: "To grant the novel the privilege of evoking everything, and yet to deny the cinema, which is so similar, the right of showing everything, is a critical contradiction which I note without resolving" (2:174). The only way Bazin can reconcile his dilemma is through an appeal to the symbolic, nonrealist aspects of cinema acknowledged in the other, symbolic pole of his theory: the idea that "cinema is also a language" (1:16).

Two primary concerns animate these discussions of extreme and violent contents in pornography. The first centers on the possible harm done to individuals whose bodies are used to create these images. The second centers on the possible harm done to viewers. The Meese Commission and anti-pornography feminists argue that both types of harm occur: that the women used in pornography are also abused by pornography and that viewers of this abuse perpetuate it by inflicting it on others.

Both the Meese Commission and anti-pornographers cite the work of Edward Donnerstein, Neil Malamuth, and other researchers on the effects of media sex and violence as evidence of the second harm. Since these researchers themselves do not agree with this interpretation of their data, and since how one interprets the data greatly influences one's assessment of the "harms" of pornography, their claims are worth examining here. Donnerstein's book, *The Question of Pornography: Research Findings and Policy Implica-*

tions (1987), published soon after the Meese Commission report, offers a useful summary of research. It also clearly disassociates itself from the conclusions of the Meese Commission, calling the commission's recommendations "unwarranted extrapolations from the available research" (p. 172).

Donnerstein and his colleagues offer conclusions based on their own and others' investigations in an attempt to correct popular misconceptions. The first such myth is that violent pornography has increased over the years; in fact, studies show that since 1977 the depiction of sexual violence in pornography has in general decreased. Donnerstein (pp. 90, 173) notes, for example, that content studies of X-rated versus R-rated films show far more violence against women in the R-rated films, and he cites an investigation by T. S. Palys which found more "egalitarian" and "mutual" sexual depictions in X-rated than in R-rated films. He concludes (p. iv) that concern about violent pornography has been so overstated that many more troubling combinations of nonpornographic depictions of sex in conjunction with aggression have been overlooked as a consequence.

This is not to deny any reason for concern about violent pornography. In Donnerstein's own laboratory experiments, male subjects exposed to film depictions of violent rape were more likely than male subjects not exposed to sexual violence to inflict harm on test victims through electrical shocks, and then more often on female victims than male ones; moreover, exposure to nonviolent but explicit sex had no apparent effect on aggressive behavior (p. 94). Donnerstein concludes that no clear evidence exists to show that watching violent images of rape causes males to go out and commit rape themselves. (See the related discussion of the unproven correlation between violent pornography and rape in Chapter 6.)

Donnerstein is more confident in concluding that such films can change subjects' *attitudes*, as opposed to behavior, toward women. He adds, however, that attitudes in which it is assumed, for example, that rapists are not responsible for their acts or that women enjoy rape are a function less of sexually explicit representations than of the pervasive images of victimized women prevalent throughout nonpornographic media (p. 174). As with the R- versus X-rated films, sexual explicitness per se does not seem to be the cause of callous attitudes.

As we saw with the changing deployment of rape in the last chapter, it is important to understand how a particular violent number functions in a narrative and in relation to other numbers before we can speak confidently of the effect that violence has on viewers in a laboratory situation. How, for example, was the violence constructed? How was it shot? Were whole films shown to the experiment subjects, or only the rape segments? Were these films separated, integrated, or dissolved? Did the male subjects watch them on film or videocassette? Were they alone or in groups? How did the experience of being observed affect their reactions? Do the experiments themselves possibly participate in a belief in the ultimate measurability of behaviors and effects that is itself pornographic? And is it possible that the experiments encouraged, even cultivated, sadistic behavior in their male subjects? Such questions as these are enormously important if we are even to begin to talk about "effects" on viewers.

Nevertheless, Donnerstein's own opinion that viewers of violent aggression in pornography are not necessarily led to commit such aggression in life can be taken as one "scientifically" accepted statement of inconclusion about the effects of pornography. Such inconclusion points, however, to the need to expand the question of pornography to include the very nature of the cinematic apparatus and spectatorship, as well as discursive address over the empirical measurement of effects and the tabulation of contents.

As for the first concern about harm—not the harm of viewing but the harm to the person viewed—here, too, the problem cannot be separated from the medium that permits the viewing. Bazin's example indicates that the problem is not, as the Meese Commission has it, that the image of violence is the same as if it were happening before our very eyes; rather, it is that the spectacle seems both so real and yet so distant from us, both temporally and spatially. Our complicity as viewers of the act is different from what it would be if we were actually in the room with the "object"; it is connected to the fact that we are watching (whether with fascination, pleasure, horror, or dread) an act that seems real but with which we have no physical connection ourselves.

Bazin's concern thus points to a more complex and cinema-specific perversion of the usual situation of viewing something horrible, violent, or obscene. The problem he raises is one not only of contents that pervert what to Bazin was the noble realism of cinema, but of a cinematic form that is, in its very way of representing objects outside of their usual time and space, perverted. The first concern, the concern of the naive realists, involves what might be called a *perversion of cinema*—that is, a simple misuse of the natural (to Bazin, noble) realism of the medium. The second concern is more complex: it addresses *cinema as perversion* in itself, as an economic, technical, social, and symbolic system.

This chapter will explore both kinds of perversion. The emphasis, however, will be on the latter, cinema as perversion, a form that has persisted as a theme in much post-Bazinian film theory and criticism, especially in feminist film theory employing "psychoanalytic tools" of analysis.[1] In this second type, violence and abuse are understood less literally, not as real violence and aggression perpetrated on the real women depicted in films, but as perversions "implanted" in cinematic discourse itself: the sadistic, masochistic, voyeuristic, and fetishizing structures that operate throughout the whole of cinema to deny female subjectivity and to render women the exhibitionist objects of male desire and aggression; and the more general play of illusion and belief in the cinema's "imaginary signifier."

These two concerns over perversion seem to agree on one point: at the root of literal or symbolic aggression toward women is some form of dominant, even sadistic male power, whether the actual clinical perversion of sadism or the more socially normative condition of voyeurism and fetishism inscribed in cinematic discourse. Viewers in both cases can be said to learn that sadistic aggression is acceptable, even "normal." It is the adequacy of sadism as an explanation for either the perverse pleasures of dominant cinema or the marginal, quasi-legitimate pleasures of pornographic cinema that I wish to examine in what follows. I will do so through examples of especially violent and perverse pornographic texts as well as the psychoanalytic theories that have been used to explain them. Let us begin with the absolute "worst case" scenario.

The Case of *Snuff*

In 1975 rumors circulated in New York City that police had confiscated several underground films from South America containing footage of women who were killed on camera as the gruesome climax to sexual acts. Dubbed "snuff" films because the women engaged in sexual relations were "snuffed out" as they (presumably) reached their climax, the possible existence of such works gave American feminists cause for new concern about the victims of cinema's "ontological pornography."

These fears were seemingly confirmed by the release, in the spring of 1976, of a feature-length commercial film with the very title *Snuff*. As one feminist writer in the influential anti-pornography anthology *Take Back the Night* puts it,

> *Snuff* . . . marked the turning point in our consciousness about the meaning behind the countless movies and magazines devoted to the naked female body. *Snuff* forced us to stop turning the other way each time we passed an X-rated movie house. It compelled us to take a long, hard look at the pornography industry. The graphic bloodletting in *Snuff* finally made the misogyny of pornography a major feminist concern.
>
> (Beverly LaBelle in Lederer 1980, 274)

The only trouble with the revelations precipitated by *Snuff* is that the film in question, though unquestionably violent and especially, if not exclusively, so toward women, does not belong to the pornographic genre, unless the fantastic special effects of exploitation horror films are included in its definition. The "long, hard look at the pornography industry" was really a rather cursory look at a related genre of "slice and dice" butchery—"meat shots" of a very different order. How a film filled with the violence of special-effects horror came to be the "turning point" in feminist thinking about the "misogyny of pornography" is therefore of some interest to a discussion of those "extreme" works of violent, sadistic, or masochistic pornography often held to be the most reprehensible of an already censorable genre.

Snuff opens with a sensationalist bit of action involving two women on a motorcycle pursuing another woman who has made off with a cache of drugs. They capture her and put her legs in stocks, where she sits until a mysterious man to whom they all seem in thrall arrives to reprimand her. This man is a Charles Manson–style cult figure named "Satán." Satán and his female followers are preparing for an apocalyptic orgy of violence directed against the upper-class decadence of Montevideo. A film producer making an exploitation sex film is their first victim; a subplot involves the American actress who has come to play in the film. Satán and his followers will eventually attack the American actress, her husband, father-in-law, and friends while they are engaged in an afternoon of sexual debauchery.

The violent orgy of Satán's slaughter overtakes the film's soft-core orgy of sex. The decadent upper classes are presented as involved in immoral profiteering in both sex (the unmade sex film) and violence (the father-in-law deals arms to Arabs as well as Israelis). Satán proposes to purge the world of both forms of profiteering through his own ritual butchery, enacted on appropriate victims of both sexes. In the film's penultimate bloodbath the deranged cult members act out Mansonesque murders that culminate in the stabbing of the now-pregnant American actress as she lies in bed.

The violence portrayed in the film is similar to that popular among adolescent audiences in exploitation horror films of exaggerated violence against young women. In these "slasher" films, of which *The Texas Chain Saw Massacre* (Tobe Hooper, 1974) is generally regarded as a key text, sexually disturbed males stalk and kill young female victims, achieving along the way a maximum visibility of blood and internal organs. In this genre, Carol J. Clover (1987, 196) observes, "violence and sex are not concomitants but alternatives." The human "monsters" of such films rarely rape, they more often kill; but killing functions as a form of rape. The violence is frequently presented as having origins in unresolved oedipal conflicts —not surprising in a cycle of films that seems indelibly marked by Alfred Hitchcock's *Psycho*. Like pornography, the slasher film pries open the fleshy secrets of normally hidden things. As Clover (pp. 198, 205) notes, the genre's obsession with maiming and dismemberment exposes "in extraordinarily credible detail" the "'opened' body."

Snuff thus seems today to be a variant of the slasher film, though its South American setting, post-synchronized dialogue, and focus on adult rather than teen-aged victims make it atypical. Yet an epilogue tacked on to the narrative of Satàn's violence made some viewers at the time think otherwise—for in this epilogue they saw not the fantastic special effects of horror but the hard-core realism of "snuff." After the pregnant actress is stabbed, the camera pulls back to reveal a movie set with camera, crew, and director. A "script girl" admires the director's work and tells him she was turned on by the scene. He invites her to have sex; she complies until she realizes that this scene, too, is being filmed. When she tries to pull away, the director grabs the knife from the previous scene, looks directly at the camera and says, presumably to the operator, "You want to get a good scene?" and proceeds to slice off first her fingers, then her hand, and then the rest of her. The sequence culminates in the director cutting open the woman's abdomen, pulling out her inner organs, and holding them over his head in triumph while the sound track mixes heavy panting with the beat of a throbbing heart. The organs seem to convulse. The image goes black as a voice says, "Shit, we ran out of film." Another says, "Did you get it all?" "Yeah, we got it. Let's get out of here." No credits roll.

It was this coda of self-reflexive violence, arising on the very set of the exploitation horror film that precedes it, that seemed to some viewers to live up to the generic promise of the film's title. The sequence is as heavily edited and replete with "medical FX" as any other instance of mutilation in this (or any other horror) film. Nevertheless, its added signals of documentary evidence—the director's speech to and "look" at the camera, the indication of film "run out," the shocking transition from sex scene to violence—all operated to convince critics that if what they had seen before was fake violence belonging to the genre of horror, what they were seeing now was real (hard-core) violence belonging to the genre of pornography. The particular obscenity of this last sequence thus resided in a perverse displacement of pornographic hard-core sexual activities, which typically end in penetration, onto the penetrating violation of the body's very flesh.

Snuff, then, seemed an utterly sadistic perversion of the pornographic genre's original desire for visual knowledge of pleasure — the desire of the male performer and viewer to probe the wonders of the unseen world of the female body. Understood in this way, the "it" spoken by the male crew member in the film's last words ("we got it") could refer not only to the images photographed but also, in the context of hard core's perpetual quest for documentary evidence of involuntary motion, to the perverse substitute of death spasm for pleasure spasm: the replacement of orgasm's "little death" by real death. Immediately, petitions were signed and pickets posted wherever the film played. But it soon became evident that *Snuff* was not "hard core." As the *New York Times* (27 Feb. 1976) succinctly put it, "Nobody gets vérité killed"; and reviewers pointed out a similar dismemberment in the Andy Warhol–Paul Morrissey *Frankenstein* that was "much more obnoxious."

The uncredited film turned out to be the work of the American husband-and-wife filmmaking team Roberta and Michael Findlay. Even before the rash of slasher films in the mid-seventies, the Findlays had been known for their low-budget exploitation violence and horror films featuring bizarre death scenes.[2] The portion of the narrative concerning "Satán" and his victims was recycled from *Slaughter*, a film the Findlays had shot in South America in 1971 and to which they later added a sound track. The Findlays had hoped that its South American locales and post-dubbed sound would make it appear to be a foreign product. In the long run this did happen, but at the time their low-budget horror effort was deemed uncommercial and shelved. Later, amid publicity about the possible existence of "snuff" movies smuggled into the United States from South America and in the wake of the new "gross-out" slashers, producer Alan Shackleton of Monarch Releasing Corporation added the final scene of evisceration, retitled the film *Snuff*, and made a small fortune.[3]

The outcry over *Snuff* forced the New York City district attorney to investigate the circumstances of the film's making and to interview the actress who was supposedly killed in the final sequence (*New York Times*, 10 March 1976). Even after the hoax was revealed, though, the idea of snuff continued to haunt the imagination. For many, the horror shifted from the bloody content of the film to the spectacle of viewers who would pay to see what they thought was the ultimate orgasm. "Going all the way" in hard core could now encompass the possibility, already imagined by Bazin but not widely contemplated in the American popular filmic imagination, of the perverse pleasure of witnessing the involuntary spasm of death. The specter of the marquis de Sade—not just the writer of sadistic pornographic fiction, but the real man who tortured real women—began to haunt the reception of formerly ignored or indulged works of hard-core film.

The generic confusion of horror and hard core, so successfully capitalized on by *Snuff*'s distributor, continues to the present. Certainly many of the most sensational accusations made about pornography apply better to exploitation horror films than to pornography. (Some of Donnerstein's [1987, 90–91, 125–129] most convincing examples of the media's harmful effects on aggressive beavior in male viewers come from horror films.) Yet this confusion is evident not only in the comments of naive realists disturbed by the perversion *of* cinema—for instance by the misuse of a natural cinematic realism to document obscene or violent realities—but also in the more sophisticated analyses of those arguing for cinema *as perversion*—for example, that the very act of cinematic representation cultivates perverse tendencies in viewers on the level of discourse alone.

That significant parallels hold between these two illegitimate, low-budget genres with particular appeal to male viewers is undeniable. As Clover (1987, 187) notes, the slasher film can be seen "encroaching vigorously" on the pornographic—though precisely how remains to be examined. It would be a mistake, therefore, to dismiss the issues raised by *Snuff* as a mere hoax made possible by the confusion of genres and the unsophistication of naive realists unfamiliar with generic conventions. What seems particularly disturbing about such visions, in the case not merely of *Snuff* but of violent aggression within pornography proper, is the sense in which a new form of the "frenzy of the visible"—here, an involuntary spasm of pain culminating in death—becomes imaginable as a perverse substitute for the *invisible* involuntary spasm of orgasm that is so hard to see in the body of the woman. We see, then, how snuff seemed a perversely logical extension of hard-core pornography's quest to see pleasure displaced onto pain. Read in the context of pornography as opposed to horror, a flinch, a convulsion, a welt, even the flow of blood itself, would seem to offer incontrovertible proof that a woman's body, so resistant to the involuntary show of pleasure, has been touched, "moved" by some force.

The mistake that reads *Snuff*'s violent horror as pornography demonstrates the need to be very clear about what kinds of violence and what kinds of perversions do operate in contemporary hardcore commercial film pornography. To facilitate this clarity I shall introduce a range of examples of sexual violence that are located securely within cinematic pornography, in order to construct a typology of the ways sexual violence is used in that genre. First, however, we must place the discussion of sexual violence in hard-core film and video within the broad and complex realm of the conjunction of sadistic and masochistic pleasures.

S/M

It is possible—Andrea Dworkin (1987, 63) has done it—to define all sexual acts involving heterosexual penetration as real or symbolic aggression and thus as sadism. Yet even if we agree with Dworkin's point that the sex act is inherently an act of occupation and colonization by a hostile force, there is a difference between this act and sadomasochistic practices. The first is characterized as "normal" within heterosexual sexuality; the second covers a wide range of perversions characterized by the derivation of sexual pleasure from either domination or submission. The quality that marks the second group of acts as "perverse" is not necessarily the extremity of the violence enacted or endured for purposes of obtaining pleasure, but rather the way in which violence, aggression, and pain become vehicles for other things—for staging dramas of suspense, supplication, abandon, and relief that enhance or substitute for sexual acts. Thus, as Kaja Silverman (1988b, 31) notes, the distinctive feature of perverse sexuality as defined by Freud is its way of not ending in coitus, its lack of subordination to a genital goal of discharge or "end-pleasure."

S/M as represented in pornographic film and video thus forcefully raises all the Bazinian questions as to the ontological status of cinematically represented extreme "things." For the violence of what has come to be called bondage and discipline can be both real—it can really affect a body, whether to give pain, pleasure, or both—and illusory—it can be ritualized and staged by individuals who consent to play prearranged roles. Sadomasochistic sexual acts are thus problematic *as acts*: they move us by their sensationalism even more than "hard-core" genital sex acts, and there is every reason to believe that they can really affect the bodies of their participants; yet they can also be acts in the theatrical sense of shows performed for oneself or others.

The matter is further complicated by the fact that, as commonly practiced in the United States among consenting individuals—and as commonly treated by analysts and therapists—S/M is not a perversion dominated by male sadists. So whereas popular perception sees sadomasochism as the perverse abuse by male sadists of female masochists, something closer to the reverse appears to be the case in actual practice: large numbers of male or female "bottoms" are in search of male or female "tops" to dominate them in their quests for sexual abandon (Ehrenreich et al. 1986, 113–118). The predominant desire in both male and female sadomasochism is apparently to be dominated rather than to dominate, although as we shall see below, these terms are themselves complicated, for in a sense the dominated seeks indirectly to dominate as well.

For the moment, we should note that while the pleasures of sexual domination have begun to be introduced into mass-cultural representations of all sorts (in the fetish implements of bondage and discipline introduced into the sexual marketplace; in the persona of rock stars; in high fashion; and in mainstream films like *9 ½ Weeks* [Adrian Lyne, 1986], *Blue Velvet* [David Lynch, 1986], and *Something Wild* [Jonathan Demme, 1986]), in hard-core pornographic fantasy the male submissive side of this sadomasochism—the more vulnerable and feminized "bottom" of sadomasochistic practice—is little in evidence, especially as compared to more or less mainstream, and less explicitly sexual, cultural forms. One reason for this one-sidedness seems to reside in the taboos against male homosexuality that operate with special force in visual pornography segregated according to heterosexual or homosexual viewer address. In gay male pornography, where there is no heterosexual identity to maintain, male submissives predominate. In heterosexual pornography, however, these taboos actively limit the sexual acts that can be deployed to solve the problems of sexuality introduced by the films. Thus, although male submissives apparently outweigh dominators in real-life heterosexual sadomasochistic practice, the incompatibility of this role with the more traditional use of heterosexual pornography as confirmation of viewers' masculine identity inhibits its incorporation into hard-core narrative.

Sadomasochistic Pornography: Three Categories

The first category of cinematic S/M, which I call *amateur sadomasochism*, contains the most extreme examples of this subgenre:

whole films in narrative or loose vignette form given over not to a wide range of sexual numbers as in standard hard-core features but to the exclusive pursuit of domination and submission. These works are frequently shot on video rather than film and often have low production values and amateurish acting reminiscent of stag films and loops. Many of these works are available only at exclusively adult outlets rather than at the neighborhood video outlet, and some are available only through special-order catalogs aimed at specialized audiences with sexual tastes for "bondage and discipline" or "S/M." (One distributor is called "Loving S/M Productions," another is called "Bizarre.") Titles often indicate the sadomasochistic content, such as *Bondage Fantasies* (Patrick Barnes, 1975), *Bound* (1979), *Bound in Latex* (Patrick Barnes, 1981), *Journey into Pain* (1983), *Femmes de Sade* (1976), *Perverse Desires* (Caroline Joyce, 1984), and *Platinum Spanking* (1983).

The type of number emphasized in these tapes is typically a prolonged scene of "bondage and discipline" showing the binding and torture of the victim by either dominator or dominatrix. In some instances a single scene of torture occupies the entire work. Paraphernalia such as nipple and genital rings, chains, ropes, whips, and wax drippings from hot candles may be employed, the application of which frequently replaces other forms of sexual activity. Everything is focused on the highly ritualized forms of violence and domination enacted on the body of the woman.

In *Journey into Pain* (a film I have not seen in a video store but which I viewed at the Kinsey Institute), the leather-clad dominator is like a circus ringmaster, putting two women through elaborately staged tableaux that dramatize their suffering: the first woman is gagged and tied to a coffee table; a rope attached to her nipple rings is pulled hard. Another woman is tied up and her clothes are cut off; the dominator slaps her bottom until it grows red. Minimal editing emphasizes the real time and space of the enactment. The emphasis throughout is on the suffering and emotion of the victims. At one point the two women cry on each other's shoulders; at another point close-ups of their faces reveal mixtures of excitement and pain. There is no visible climax, in either the dramatic or the sexual sense of the word, only a suspenseful spectacle of prolonged suffering. At the end the man and women are back in their regular clothes, warmly hugging and happy.

A second, more frequent use of onscreen violence in hard-core pornography is that limited to a single number, the extreme end of the range of numbers typical of contemporary hard core's "diff'rent strokes for diff'rent folks" spirit. These numbers, which I will continue to call by the industry's name for them, sadie-max (see Chapter 5), occur in the course of the female protagonist's wide-ranging search for new and better sex characteristic of feature-length narrative hard core.[4] The female protagonist may enjoy and repeat these numbers, or she may sample and reject them. Practices here include a little bondage (*Three Daughters* [Candida Royalle, 1986]), a spanking and light sadie-max (*Depraved Innocent* [Jonathan Burrows, n.d.]), anal penetration (*Loose Ends* [Bruce Seven, 1984]) or lurid fantasy sequences with exaggerated paraphernalia, monsters, or beasts, such as the monster with the giant penis who invades the bedroom in the hard-core cult film *Driller* (Joyce James, 1985), a porn parody of Michael Jackson's *Thriller*. The violence in these numbers often adds drama, excitement, danger, and exoticism to otherwise standard fare, functioning perhaps as foreplay to more "normal" genital acts. Whatever form it takes, however, this violence is usually not essential, as in the films devoted entirely to sadomasochism, to the female protagonist's pleasure.

The woman who is aggressed against in these films is experimenting with different forms of pleasure; only rarely is she presented as habitually dependent on S/M alone. One movie that verges on this fixed identity, in that its heroine describes herself as a "submissive," is *Insatiable II*. In a prolonged sadomasochistic encounter with a leather-clad male dominator (Jamie Gillis), Marilyn Chambers as Sandra Chase is tied, whipped, spanked, choked, and has hot wax poured on her nipples. The long takes and minimal editing of this scene resemble the realism of the more amateurish exclusively sadomasochistic films mentioned above. Yet in every other aspect of the narrative, and in every other of the varied sexual numbers but one, she is in absolute control of her pleasure and that of others. So while the sadie-max number typically places the woman in the position of being dominated, the pleasure it offers viewers does not seem fixed on identification with this pleasure exclusively.

A third category of violence against women I call *aesthetic sadomasochism*. The works that use this form of S/M are often shot in the more expensive medium of film rather than video and self-consciously situate themselves within an elitist sadomasochistic literary tradition where rarefied sexual tastes are explored. Although these films may also focus on prolonged scenes of sadomasochistic torture to the exclusion of all other sexual numbers, they differ from amateur sadomasochism in their comparatively high production values, professional acting, literary sources, and complex psychological narratives in which characters become self-aware. The overwhelming effect of *amateur* sadomasochism is that the violence seems "real" in the Bazinian sense: it appears neither acted nor faked in editing. *Aesthetic* sadomasochism, in contrast, is violence as "art"; the hard-core "evidence" of violence remains beneath the surface. Instead of amateur sadomasochism's fixed stare at flesh that is slapped, whipped, or pierced in order to catch involuntary flinches of pain, in these films we see the whip poised over the vulnerable flesh, hear the noise of its crack, and, in a separate shot, see the reaction on a face. The effect is more Eisensteinian than Bazinian, with the reality of event elided for metaphoric effect. The moment of threat counts more here than any hard-core evidence of violence, and the confusing emotions of humiliation, degradation, and pleasure-pain are paramount.

In *The Story of Joanna* (Gerard Damiano, 1975), for example, Jason, a mysterious aristocratic man (Jamie Gillis) brings Joanna, a young woman who is attracted to him, to his château to "perform a task that I am unable to perform myself." He is dying of a mysterious disease and wants to be killed by the hand of someone who loves him. Instead of loving her back, however, he coldly humiliates and degrades her in a manner reminiscent of the degradation of O in *The Story of O*, giving her up to the use of other men and telling her she is "not a woman" but "a cock sucker." Initiated into bondage and discipline, she continues to adore her torturer. Gradually, however, she catches on to his plan to make her the instrument of his own destruction and, turning cold and inscrutable herself, finally shoots him. As in Sacher-Masoch's *Venus in Furs*, the drama is resolved through surprising shifts in roles between dominator and dominated, "hammer" and "anvil."

Another, more complex example of aesthetic sadomasochism is *The Punishment of Anne* (Radley Metzger, 1979), based on the 1956 novella by Jean de Berg. A sophisticated French writer, Jean, meets an acquaintance, Claire, at an elegant literary soirée. Jean's voice-over informs us that although he likes Claire, a lack of vulnerability in her had dampened his desire. Claire's young friend Anne, however, is all youthful vulnerability, and he is intrigued by the relationship between these two women. In a tour of a rose garden, Jean witnesses Claire's sadistic humiliation of the masochistic Anne, who is made to urinate before Jean. Claire then has the thorn of a rose prick Anne's thigh. Jean is fascinated.

Later he is invited to see Claire's photographs of Anne. They are black-and-white images of Anne being tortured. A play of glances between Claire and himself is the first hint that their own relationship is at stake as well. A final photo shows only a pubic area caressed by a hand. Jean notes that the hand appears different from the others. When he asks whether this is still Anne, Claire becomes nervous. Her own dark red fingernails are emphasized in the shot, and it seems possible that this last photo is of her, not Anne.

A series of elaborate tortures and social humiliations of Anne follow. In most of them Claire and Jean remain dressed (as Claire notes, their "roles" require it). In most, also, Claire teaches Jean the pleasures of dominating Anne and the pleasure Anne feels in being dominated: "She loves it when we put her on her knees so we can whip her. . . . She gets all set for her orgasm." A mostly mute Anne varies in her moods from abject humiliation to triumphant pleasure.

The various instances of torture culminate in a penultimate encounter in Claire's torture chamber for which Jean has already been prepared by the photos Claire showed him. In this prolonged scene with full paraphernalia, Claire with a needle and Jean with a whip keep Anne in a sustained state of writhing pleasure and suffering. But the scene ends badly: both Claire and Anne break with their established roles, and Anne determines to leave Claire.

The next morning, however, Claire arrives at Jean's apartment dressed in one of Anne's innocent schoolgirl outfits, an indication that her "role" has changed. Jean, understanding, orders her to undress. The naked Claire assumes one of Anne's vulnerable poses. Kneeling, with hands over head, she says, "I'm yours. You can do whatever you want with me." Jean pulls her onto the stairs, slaps her on the face, lays her down, and immediately thrusts himself into her. He asks, "What's my name?" she answers "Jean" and repeats over and over, "I love you, I love you," as he continues to thrust into her and she cries out in pleasure. The camera pulls back through the apartment window and the film ends on a shot of the Eiffel Tower while Claire's cries continue. There has been no hard-core evidence, in either money shots or flinches, of pleasure or pain. Aesthetic sadomasochism is not concerned with such evidence; neither the slaps nor the penetration of this last scene are (necessarily) "vérité."

What pleasures do these different forms of violence offer audiences? To simplify matters, let me try to describe only the pleasure of an exclusively male, heterosexual audience. The answer that feminists have most frequently offered is sadism, understood either in a general sense as the aggression that underlies patriarchal power or in a more specific sense as the sexual perversion that haunts masculine sexual identity and controls a quintessentially masculine desire to see, know, and control. Anti-pornography feminists see violent hard core as the most representative instance of the essential sadism embodied in patriarchy's dominant power—men who "especially love murder" and who create "concentration camp pornography" (Dworkin, quoted in Attorney General's Commission on Pornography 1986, 1:770). For these naive realists, to see a woman phallically penetrated, bound, gagged, tortured, or (as presumably in *Snuff*) murdered for male sexual pleasure is tantamount to watching a real woman present in the viewer's own space-time continuum being victimized by these outrages.

What can we say about the ontological status of this violence? The first two categories listed above, amateur sadomasochism and the isolated sadie-max number, both attempt to create in the mind of the viewer an impression of reality, a violence that is as "hard core" as "meat" and "money" are elsewhere in the genre. The violence in these films is thus quite opposite in its effect to the special-effects violence of the slasher horror film, where we know that the actor has not been slashed but the narrative asks us to believe it anyway. Here knowledge and belief converge. Ultimately we do not *know* that the violence is real, but we *think* it is. The violence of the third category, aesthetic sadomasochism, in contrast, is not real, nor does it aim at the effect of reality. Here the *effect* of violence—the slap, the whip lash, the flinch—is created through editing, acting, and sound effects; the "frenzy of the visible" is not offered as hard core.

What about the "frenzy of the visible" in the other two, less manifestly edited, less "aesthetic" categories? Is the sexual violence a

fictional depiction, or is it an enacted reality? And if it is enacted—
if, that is, the violence is really inflicted on a body that feels pain—
then how does the film invite us to respond? This is where the concern over the first kind of harm, the presumed harm to the performers who receive the violence, is complicated by our relation to
the cinematic image—for the image, like the woman's performance
of orgasm but unlike the man's, can easily fake it. To what extent is
the film or video asking the viewer to take sadistic pleasure in the
real suffering of others? Is the suffering real? If it is, is it perversely
(masochistically) enjoyed or painfully endured? In the sadie-max
number from *Insatiable*, at least some of the violence does appear
to be enacted: the wax could be faked, but the red marks in the un-
edited shots of spanking do *seem* real. And in the amateur sadomasochism of *Journey into Pain*, the poor technical quality of the
videos themselves enhances the documentary effect. Here, too, the
tugs on ropes attached to nipple and genital rings certainly seem
real. "Seem" is all we can say, however, since we have no absolute
way of telling where special effects might be at work or how things
really feel to performers.

We can, however, observe our hypothetical male viewer's reaction
to this indeterminate status of pleasure and pain. In the case of the
sadie-max violence enacted or depicted on Marilyn Chambers, he
might think of Chambers as a professional actress engaging in the
scene only for the sake of her art. If so, then he might say that whatever pain she experiences is in the service of this art. Thus he can
either applaud the sacrifice in the name of art or condemn it as humiliating, dangerous, and degrading. In this respect Chambers is
not that different from any actress who "exposes" herself to emotional and physical risk to achieve a convincing performance. Lillian
Gish, for example, famously exposed herself to both kinds of risk by
repeatedly enduring cold water and ice in the river sequence of
D. W. Griffith's *Way Down East*. She paid, so she says, with the
lifelong effects of frostbite on one hand. The extratextual anecdote
of Gish's frozen hand thus became part of the film's lore and is
now, arguably, an element of the pleasure many viewers take in
Way Down East.[5] Today we see the hand in the icy water, note the
duration of the shot, and speculate on the pain Gish must have
endured.

Conversely—and as is more likely in amateur sadomasochism—

the viewer could think that the performers are appropriately cast in the roles they play, that is, that the women are practicing submissives who enjoy their roles. Here, too, extratextual information—interviews or ads—may offer assurance that the actress really "got into her role" or that these are real submissives who enjoy "doing it" for the camera. Marilyn Chambers, for instance, has given many interviews to this effect (e.g., Turan and Zito 1974, 191–199). There is also the other kind of testimonial, as in Linda Lovelace's *Ordeal*, attesting to behind-the-scenes coercion in which the actress was forced to play the part. In this case attentive viewers who have read Lovelace-Marchiano's story can look for the bruises on her body— bruises that become evidence of that off-camera coercion. As spectators, we cannot possibly determine the truth of either statement from the films themselves. Nor can we tell, just by watching, if the actress really enjoys the kiss, the porn actress really orgasms, or Lillian Gish's fingers really hurt (in this last case, of course, Gish's whole performance resided in *not* showing the pain she must have felt, since she was supposed to be unconscious). In these cases we can only see apparent evidence of pain or pleasure; we cannot tell if, or how, it is felt.

There is in fact every reason to worry about the potential abuse of hard-core violence, since the very conventions of pornography work to enforce a realism similar to that of documentary film. In a genre that has often staked its all on visible evidence of the involuntary convulsive experience of pleasure, the ultimate perversion could be the displacement of a hard-to-see pleasure onto an easier-to-see, and apparently similarly involuntary, response to pain. But although the sight of bodily pain, especially that inflicted by torture, is a "frenzy of the visible" that dramatizes and objectifies power, this power cannot rely on pain itself to manifest the truths it solicits. As Elaine Scarry (1985, 36) has shown with regard to noncontractual scenes of political torture in real life, power relies on theatrical strategies of the display of instruments, elaborate questioning, and confessional answers achieved through torture. In the end, though, pain is known to the torturer only as proof of power.

Contractual sadomasochistic violence of the sort described in the films discussed above is different. Although the drama of power is dominant, it does not absolutely negate the other. As drama, it keeps viewers guessing about the mix of pleasure and pain and the

shifting positions of protagonist and antagonist in the scenes depicted or enacted. Although anti-pornography feminists would like
us to believe that the sexual violence of these films offers sadistic
pleasure to male viewers at the expense of violating the civil rights
of the female victims in them, one cannot say that the woman is a
victim of the torturer's power (as the political prisoner is), for the
contractual participant in the S/M scenario has willed the role he or
she will play. Even more complicated is the question of whether a
viewer who enjoys watching such a scene is a sadist and in what
sense the woman *in the film* is his victim.

To the psychoanalytic feminist film theorist, at least in one enormously influential strain of this criticism, the dominant "male gaze"
of cinema encodes male dominance and sadism into the very structure of looking. The "look" that governs cinematic narrative is
founded on voyeuristic and sadistic male desires that, at best, treat
women as exhibitionist objects, fetishizing their difference, or, at
worst, aggressively master their threat of difference through various
forms of sadistic punishment. Thus all of the normalized perversions of dominant narrative cinema are, according to Laura Mulvey,
E. Ann Kaplan, and others, defensive mechanisms—"avenues of escape" (Mulvey 1975, 13)—for phallically threatened male viewers.[6]

In this cinema as perversion view, the whole of the institution
of cinematic narrative is dominated either by sadism (Mulvey
writes, "Sadism demands a story, depends on making something
happen, forcing a change in another person, a battle of will and
strength, victory/defeat, all occurring in a linear time with a beginning and an end") or by a sadistic interpretation of fetishism, what
Mulvey calls "fetishistic scopophilia." This latter perversion is interpreted as an "erotic instinct focussed on the look alone"; it more
directly confronts and disavows the difference of woman through a
nonnarrative fetishistic "overvaluation" by which the fetishized
woman as glamorous object is possessed (p. 14). In this psychoanalytic perspective, the male fear of castration becomes the cause of
an aggressivity that is ultimately a defense against female difference.

Just how much does this thesis, that sadism lies at the root of all
patriarchy, pornography, and dominant narrative cinema, explain in
the texts we are considering? As recent feminist film critics and theorists have begun to assert, sadism—and the related perversions of
voyeurism and the fetishization of woman as object—may not be the

whole "story."[7] D. N. Rodowick (1982, 7), for example, pointed out some time ago that Mulvey's adaptation of the very term *fetishism* into the hybrid *fetishistic scopophilia* is typical of the lopsided emphasis on aggressive male mastery to the exclusion of the more "feminine" and passive pleasures of spectatorship. In other words, the male-active-voyeuristic-objectifying side of cinematic spectatorship has been stressed, at the expense of the female-passive-identifying-fetishized (instead of fetishizing) side. Even more problematic is the fact that activity and passivity have been too rigorously assigned to separate gendered spectator positions with little examination of either the active elements of the feminine position or the mutability of male and female spectators' adoption of one or the other subject position and participation in the (perverse) pleasures of both.

As Rodowick suggests, and as Gaylyn Studlar (1988) further develops in an extended challenge to Mulvey's position, the term that is most repressed in Mulvey's original statement of the perversity of narrative cinema is *masochism*. Significantly, it is a term that has also been repressed as an explanation of pleasure in pornography. There are good reasons for the repression on both sides. The recovery of masochism as a form of pleasure does not bode well for a feminist perspective whose political point of departure is the relative powerlessness of women.

Gaylyn Studlar argues, however, that many of the more passive pleasures of film viewing can be explained by masochism and that those films which do not fit the dominant Hollywood pattern of inviting viewer identification with active goal-oriented heroes determined to "make something happen" actually belong to a category she names the "masochistic aesthetic." Studlar's book, *In the Realm of Pleasure: Von Sternberg, Dietrich, and the Masochistic Aesthetic*, is impressive in its thorough reconsideration of many of the issues of masochistic pleasure that have been swept under the rug in the wake of a feminist politics of empowerment; in the final analysis, though, it may be too much of an overreaction to Mulvey, caught up as it is in the either/or oppositions that Mulvey herself posed. Thus Studlar argues that cinematic visual pleasure is not sadistic but rather masochistic, that it partakes of pre-oedipal pleasures of merger and fusion rather than oedipal issues of separation and individuation.

As Tania Modleski (1988) argues in her recent book on Hitchcock, the solution to this dilemma is not, like Studlar, to replace a political critique of phallic-sadistic dominance with a counteraesthetic that values pre-oedipal–masochistic forms of merger. It is more important, Modleski (p. 12) argues, to see how these sadistic and masochistic pleasures interrelate—for "pure" sadistic mastery is not what even Hitchcock's films are all about. Some recent feminist film criticism has thus more fruitfully shifted to a model of bisexuality, of more fluid movements on the part of both male and female spectators that "alternate," as Teresa de Lauretis (1984, 142–143) puts it, between masculine and feminine identifications. Such a model can permit us to understand previously overlooked passive-identifying-masochistic pleasures of male viewers and the active-objectifying-sadistic pleasures of female viewers—as Modleski does, for example, for *Vertigo*. Nonetheless, these analyses can be helpful, Modleski (1988, 10) warns, only if theories of spectatorial bisexuality are not considered apart from larger relations of power that devalue femininity and ultimately repress male masochism. With this warning in mind, and with the goal of delineating the bisexual appeal of sadomasochistic film pornography, I would like first to borrow some insights from a study by Carol J. Clover on slasher horror films as a way of approaching the issue.

The Female Victim-Hero

Clover's (1987) study of slasher films argues against the idea that such works simply carry on the tradition of Alfred Hitchcock's sadistic misogynist dictum, "Torture the women" (p. 206). For although these films typically invite an apparently sadistic viewer identification with knife-wielding male killers, one must take into account the narrative role of the "Final Girl": the one girl in the film who survives to defeat the killer-monster. This character's function in the film is to mediate the complex issues of bisexuality so persistently raised by the genre. While viewers may initially identify with the killer as he stalks his victims, midway through the film audience identification shifts to a Final Girl who, despite being terrorized by the killer, resourcefully fights back and survives, destroying the killer in the end—at least until the next sequel (pp. 206–209). Clover's examples range from the first *Halloween* (John Carpenter, 1978) to *Friday the Thirteenth* (Sean Cunningham, 1980) and *Nightmare on Elm Street* (Wes Craven, 1984) and to all their sequels.

Clover (p. 207) argues that the decidedly "male gaze" of the predominantly male adolescent viewer of these films does not necessarily identify "with men" and "against women," since the Final Girl is clearly an active hero (not a passively rescued heroine) even in her most extreme moments of victimization. Clover (pp. 210–212) also emphasizes the ambiguous gender of both the killer and the girl, noting his confused sexuality or impotence, borrowed from the *Psycho* model, and her androgyny, sexual inactivity, and difference from other girls; she concludes that the killer is a feminine-male, the Final Girl is a masculine-female. In the end the masculine-female prevails over the feminine-male to wield the knife and symbolically (or literally) castrate him. So even though masculine (phallic) power and potency prevail, the viewer has temporarily been put in a passive feminine position through identification with the aggressed-upon and terrified female victim-hero. A "female gaze" has been introduced into a masculine discourse, and it has been introduced to allow, within limits, the predominantly adolescent audience the pleasure of identifying with helplessness. At the climactic moment when the killer is at his "bisexual mightiest, the victim-hero at her tiniest," the "component of sadomasochism" is at its "most blatant" (p. 210).

Clover's analysis of the slasher movie, like Modleski's analysis of Hitchcock and Kaja Silverman's analysis of male subjectivity in masochism (Silverman 1988b), suggests that there is often a more complex "play" of gender roles in films and fantasies than can be accounted for by appealing either to a sadistic "male gaze" or to a pre-oedipal masochistic merger. "Abject terror" is "gendered feminine," writes Clover (p. 212), and it is a pleasure mixed with the vicarious threat of pain; for the adolescent male viewer it is a perverse visual pleasure repeated in slasher after slasher but always resolved by the female victim-hero triumphantly wielding the knife-chainsaw-phallus at the end.

Like the person who engages in sadomasochism, the viewer has made a kind of contract with the film to undergo a certain uneasy identification with a character experiencing terror or pain, at the end of which is the great pleasure of its relief. In Clover's view (p. 217), the image of the woman wielding the chainsaw or knife at movie's end is a moment of "high drag," and part of the pleasure the male viewer takes in this moment resides in the fact that a girl wields the phallus. The important points for Clover are thus the power of the female victim-hero, the extreme theatricalization ("play") of gender roles, and the pleasure of (adolescent male) viewers who temporarily submit to feminized, masochistic forms of identification so that they may emerge from them in bisexual triumph—a triumph that, to Clover, is potentially subversive of the "normal" hierarchies of male dominance and female submission.

There are problems, however, with the subversive emphasis of this analysis. I have argued elsewhere (L. Williams 1984, 88) that at the moment Clover's "female victim-hero" confronts the monster-killer and "looks" back at him, she too becomes monstrous, as much a freak as he. She becomes, in other words, not so much both male and female as *neither* male *nor* female. Bisexual identifications may thus not be quite so subversive as Clover suggests. Nevertheless, the heightened "play" of gender roles in place of the literal biological sex of male and female, the idea that the slasher "solves" oedipal problems for the sexually anxious adolescent male viewer by permitting a more fluid movement between masculine/feminine, active/passive, sadistic/masochistic, oedipal/pre-oedipal, can be helpful for understanding similar structures in violent hard-core pornography.

In hard-core film and video the hero with whom the viewer is asked to identify is only rarely the male, for male activity and pleasure, as we have seen, are generally taken for granted in hard core. Instead it is the female, in her mixed function of activity and passivity, who most interests the genre, an interest that Dennis Giles (1977, 56) attributes to the unconscious *"projective* identification with the pornographic female." In the wake of Laura Mulvey's influence, projective identification has not been adequately appreciated by film theory. Yet almost all the hard-core features we have examined share this quality, rare in the narrative feature, of the female actively seeking her pleasure. It could very well be that in sadomasochism too, she actively seeks it, though indirectly and paradoxically, through playing the role of helplessness and abandon.

This single fact of the female hero (versus heroine) deserves emphasis. Nonsadomasochistic hard-core pornography may be the only film type that at the level of its narrative does *not* regularly punish the woman for actively seeking her sexual pleasure (as opposed to simply "following her heart"). In the slasher film, sexual pleasure and heroic activity are, as we have seen, mutually exclusive. The woman in these films may be the victim of the feminine male's misplaced sexual desires, but she must be the asexual "good girl" rather than the sexual "bad girl" if she is to gain power against her assailant. And her only recourse in the struggle against her assailant is to take up the phallus herself, as weapon rather than instrument of pleasure—to join them in order to beat them, as it were.

In the various forms of sadomasochistic pornography described above, the male viewer's identification would seem typically to be with a female victim-hero. But unlike the slasher film, where the sexual "bad" women do not survive as female victim-heroes with whom male viewers identify, in sadomasochistic pornography these identificatory victim-heroes *do* survive—though they are punished for their sexual pleasures. The mere fact of punishment in both types of film shows the superiority of male sadistic pleasure over the "abject terror" that is "gendered feminine."

In sadomasochistic pornography, when the female victim cringes at the phallic power of the dominator, she gains a power over that dominator that resembles the momentary power of the slasher film's victim-hero. Yet while slasher victim-heroes do not so much defeat the power of the phallus as take over its power in drag, in sadomasochistic cinema the woman engages in a more self-conscious strategy of role-playing. For only by playing the role of "good girl"— that is, by pretending to be good and only coerced into sex—does the woman who is coerced and punished by the phallic dominator get the "bad girl"'s pleasure. She gets this pleasure *as if* against her will and thus *as if* she were still a good girl. By pretending to succumb to the authority of the male double standard that condemns and punishes women for pleasure, she defeats the system—but only part of it: here, too, she cannot defeat the power of the phallus. She gets pleasure, but she must pay obeisance to a value system that condemns her for her pleasure; the rules of the game are not her own. Unlike the slasher victim-hero, however, this woman does not deny herself pleasure. While good girl/bad girl dichotomies are kept in place in both types of film, in the sadist's game the ultimate authority is force. Yet masochism, too, also deploys force and achieves a modicum of power by turning punishment into pleasure.

In *Masochism: An Interpretation of Coldness and Cruelty* (1971), Gilles Deleuze separates masochism and sadism entirely, arguing that there is an enormous difference between a pornography that is about the pleasure and power of a sadist who exercises complete control over an unwilling victim and one that is about the pleasure (and power) of a masochist who willingly contracts with another person to be dominated in a sexually charged scenario of pleasure and pain. (This difference, of course, is typified by the pornographic works and personal lives of the two men who gave the perversions their names: Donatien Alphonse François de Sade and the lesser-known Leopold von Sacher-Masoch.)

Unfortunately, Deleuze's study of Sacher-Masoch avoids the question of both female readers and female victim-hero. For Deleuze, the subject of the sadistic scenario is the male torturer; that of the masochistic scenario, the male who is tortured. Women figure in this theory of masochism only as objects to male subjects: what the sadistic subject desires is repudiation of the mother, from whom he wishes to differentiate himself, and acceptance by the father and phallic law; what the (male) masochistic subject desires is merger and fusion with the mother and subversion of the father's phallic law. What the female masochistic subject wants and how she gets it are left unexamined.

Indeed, pleasure in (female) masochism has, for obvious reasons, been questioned as to whether it is pleasure at all. A feminist perspective dictates some distance from any sexual fantasy or practice in which women give themselves up to the power of another, even, or perhaps especially, if they do so for pleasure. Yet precisely because masochistic desire has been unthinkable in much feminist theorizing about sex and sexual fantasy (e.g., Caplan 1985), these writers have had difficulty speaking clearly about fantasies that to Dworkin smack of the "concentration camp orgasm" and thus of the total annihilation of women. What, then, *is* a feminist understanding of female masochism?

Most attempts to understand masochism begin with sadism. Psychoanalytic theories of sadism generally agree that the perversion has its genesis in the trauma of a male child's oedipal relation to his father. In identifying with the power of the father and the phallus, the child rejects the mother in himself, expels his ego, and over-invests in the superego. The unconstrained superego runs wild and seeks external victims—victims who represent the rejected ego. This punishment of the female aspect of the self then yields sadistic fantasies of the obsessive and violent punishment of women who substitute for that rejected part (Deleuze 1971, 109–110).

Psychoanalytic theories of masochism, in contrast, are much more diverse and have been the subject of considerable debate, almost always centering on one of Freud's most enigmatic essays, "A Child Is Being Beaten" ([1919] 1963). Many theorists, including Deleuze, Janine Chasseguet-Smirgel (1984), and feminists Kaja Silverman (1988b) and Parveen Adams (1988), have diverged from Freud's original assumption that masochism is simply the flip side of sadism—a deflection onto the self of a "death instinct" that in sadism is directed outward at others.[8] Deleuze (1971, 28–29), for example, argues that masochism has its genesis in the male child's alliance with the powerful oral mother of the pregenital stage. Here the child's fear is that he will lose the nurturing all-powerful figure of his initial oral gratifications. Instead of expelling his ego, he splits it into narcissistic and ideal halves; he then expels the superego, which will assume the role of his torturer. In this way the male masochist disavows adult genital pleasure and his own similarity to the father, because possession of the phallus prevents his return to an infantile sexuality and re-fusion with the oral mother (see also Studlar 1988, 15–16).

In disavowing phallic power, the male masochist suspends orgasmic gratification and conditions it with pain. This is the price he must pay for possessing a genital sexuality that is at odds with his infantile desires (Studlar 1988, 16). Exaggerated suffering is like a show put on for the benefit of the superego: it disguises the masochist's complicity in the contracted alliance with his female torturer, a contract that reverses the normal patriarchal order in which the woman is only an object. Although the woman torturer is in this psychoanalytic formulation only a player in a male fantasy, she is a player who exercises power over the man.

Deleuze, Studlar, and Silverman—in her descriptions of the preoedipal story behind masochism—help to explain the different, less phallic function of violence in sadomasochistic film scenarios. Unlike the brutal coercion of the Sadean orgy with its misogynistic crimes of incest, sodomy, and matricide, the violence of masochism is contractual. In all three types of sadomasochistic pornography de-

scribed above—amateur, sadie-max, and aesthetic—violence invariably arises out of an agreement between dominator and dominated. Although the physical violence may be extreme, its effect
hinges on careful timing, the suspense and anxiety of prolonged suffering, delayed consummations, surprise gestures of either cruelty
or tenderness (the whipping of Anne followed by the careful tending
of her wounds), frequent role-playing, and inversions of hierarchies
leading to confusion regarding who is really in power.

Sadistic pleasure and fantasy can thus be viewed as patriarchal
power run rampant: the negation of the difference of the mother and
the exaltation of the power of the father who is beyond all law (Klos-
sarski, cited in Deleuze 1971, 52). In no way does the sadistic subject—the lonely hero of the Sadean scenario—solicit the pleasure
of his victim. He (or she) solicits compliance to power, whether in
the show of pain or the show of pleasure. In this sense it is not accurate to speak of the complementarity of sadistic and masochistic
pleasures. Both sadist and masochist seek recognition in the eyes of
their sexual objects; but where the sadist seeks recognition by ne-
gating this object, the masochist seeks it through complex mas-
querades played to the superego and designed to give the *appearance* of passive submission.

What is tricky about masochism, however, is that this search for
recognition through apparent passivity is a ruse intended to disavow
what the masochist actually knows to exist but plays the game of denying: his (or her) very real sexual agency and pleasure. Psychoanalyst Robert Stoller (1979, 123–124) writes of a masochistic female
patient whose recurring erotic fantasy featured theatrical pain and
humiliation during sex, which Stoller claims functioned as a smoke
screen to convince a hypothetical (superego) audience of her lack of
complicity in the sexual relation. The patient's evident submission
to a greater power allowed her to preserve a facade of integrity and
morality in the face of orgasms that she could then claim not to have
willed. It is in this way that masochism preserves the good girl/bad
girl dichotomy we have seen to be so important in slasher films and
so much a part of traditional views of female sexuality. But it does
so as a ruse, a manipulation of appearances, so that pleasure can be
attained.

Because women have so often been presumed not to have sexual agency, to be objects and not subjects of desire, masochism has in many respects been taken as the "norm" for women under patriarchy. It has offered women a way of negotiating pleasure by submitting—though never entirely—to patriarchal law. To a certain extent, then, and certainly more for the male than for the female, masochism represents a subversion of this law, a devious act of defiance. As Deleuze (1971, 77) puts it, "the very law which forbids the satisfaction of a desire under the threat of subsequent punishment is converted into one which demands the punishment first and then orders that the satisfaction of the desire should follow upon the punishment."

Deleuze thus views masochism as a kind of plot carried out between mother and son to replace the father with the mother as the figure of power. But as Kaja Silverman (1988b) has noted of Deleuze's study and other "utopian" interpretations of male masochism's challenge to paternal law, this exaltation of the powerful preoedipal mother does not mean that mother and son are free of oedipal power. The disavowal of phallic power that the male masochist achieves is itself determined by the oedipal power in which it suspends belief. "Here, as elsewhere," Silverman (p. 55) writes, "perversion reflects what it undermines." Male masochism reflects oedipal law and subverts it at the same time. To Silverman (p. 57), an important aspect of this subversion lies in its construction of a "feminine" yet heterosexual male subject.

No equivalent subversion is available to the female masochist, who, Silverman notes, appears less perverse precisely because masochistic desires seem so culturally "natural" to the prescribed sexual passivity of female subjects. It would seem, on the surface at least, that for women masochism simply offers the "good girl" pleasures that are contingent on previous, or perhaps accompanying, punishment. Punishment thus serves a function: it absolves the supposedly desireless woman of responsibility and blame for pleasures she nevertheless enjoys.

Sadism and masochism can thus be viewed as (theoretically) separable though related perversions of the desire for recognition by an "other"; in sadism this other is the father, in masochism the preoedipal mother. Deleuze and Stoller argue that the two perversions are, in both practice and fantasy, rigorously separate. I, however, am less convinced of the divisability of these two perversions, and of the attendant strict separation of male and female sexuality along lines of activity/passivity.

Writing about the female spectator of classical narrative cinema, Mary Ann Doane (1982, 87) has argued that this viewer is given two options: "the masochism of over-identification or the narcissism entailed in becoming one's own object of desire." Doane's point is that both these options produce an untenable position for the female spectator; by placing her too close to the image, they deny her the distance so important to male mastery and pleasure. But this is to presume the operation of, on the one hand, a pure sadism (presumed to be dominant and the only tenable position for spectators) and, on the other, a pure masochism (not dominant and ultimately unpleasurable).

Doane goes on to say that the strategy many women employ when faced with the narcissistic, masochistic overidentification and closeness to the self culturally assigned to women is that of masquerade. Through the "masquerade of femininity" women "manufacture a distance from the image" that allows the further manipulation and production of images (p. 87). Although in Doane's view this masquerade is a defense against a masochistic fixed position of (over)identification with the suffering and victimized woman, I think that the masquerade is part of the very nature of a sadomasochism that has been too often understood as inalterable passivity and powerless suffering. In other words, the masquerade of femininity which Doane conceives of as a limited way out of the untenable position of the masochist—and by extension, of femininity itself—is actually an oscillation within sadomasochism which is not identical to pure passivity.

I suggest that when a female spectator of film or video looks at a woman who is the object of violence in a contractual sadomasochistic scenario, she may not identify with this woman as pure, passive victim, for it is always clear in these scenarios that the tortured woman has arranged to play the role of suffering woman, to put on a show of suffering the better to enjoy her pleasure. Identification with the suffering woman is thus not *simply* identification with pain, humiliation, and suffering—with being the object of someone else's desire or aggression. Nor is identification solely with the woman who is tortured.

As Parveen Adams (1988) argues in a recent reconsideration of female masochism, this perversion should not be defined as subordination, passivity, and femininity in opposition to a sadistic superordination, activity, and masculinity. Indeed, Adams is able to go to the very heart of the female spectator's possible "identification" with the masochistic scenario because she also goes to the heart of difficult questions concerning sexual identity in the formation of gendered subjects. She conceives of this identity as an oscillation between male and female subject positions held simultaneously, in a play of bisexuality, at the level of both object choice and identification. Thus one answer to the question of how the female spectator identifies with the masochistic scenario is, first of all, that she does not necessarily identify only and exclusively with the woman who is beaten; she may also, simultaneously, identify with the beater or with the less involved spectator who simply looks on. And even if she does identify only with the tortured woman, she might identify alternately or simultaneously with her pleasure and/or her pain.

Adams reworks the beating scenario in Freud's "A Child Is Being Beaten" to show that identification with any one of the three roles posited by this scenario—beater, beaten, or onlooker—is not dependent on a fixed masculine or feminine identity and the sexual object choice that presumably follows from this gender identification. Citing several cases of sexual fantasy on the part of female hysterics, including the much-discussed unconscious fantasy of Freud's Dora of a scene of sexual gratification *per os* (by the mouth), Adams (pp. 17–18) argues that it is in the very nature of fantasy to permit multiple identifications with the full gamut of positions within the scene imagined. It is not true, she claims, that if Dora identifies with her father in this fantasy she takes up a masculine position, or that if she identifies with Frau K. she takes up a feminine position. The reason Freud went wrong, in this case and with masochism in general, Adams argues, is that he too rigidly assumed that identification—the very process by which subjects say, "*I am like* him or her"—was linked to, and produced by, object choice—the process by which subjects say, "*I like* him or her." Dora is both subject and object of the fantasy of oral gratification; she is, as Adams puts it, both sucker and sucked. Adams also argues that the point is not whom Dora loves (the male or the female object) but rather that her bisexual identification with the various roles in the scenario is not limited by her male or female object choice.

Given this play of bisexuality at the level of object choice and identification, Adams maintains that male and female subjects experience both a mother identification and a father identification, between which they oscillate. Observing Freud's conflation of the oedipal story concerned with the law and the phallus with another story about the oscillation of the drive, Adams (p. 28) states: "He [Freud] is right in thinking that the positions of femininity, masculinity, perversion, can be defined through the subject's relation to the phallus; he is wrong in thinking that these positions can be defined in terms of the oscillatory pairs." Oscillation is movement between. Adams's lesson about the importance of oscillation, then, would seem to be that for male or female masochists there is no such thing as pure merger with the object of identification.

The woman viewer of sadomasochistic pornography may be in closer "contact" with the suffering of the female victim-hero, but she is not condemned, as Doane seems to suggest in the case of classic women's films, to lose herself in pure abandonment, pain, or pre-oedipal merger. The crucial point is not to subsume one gender-inflected form of desire or pleasure within another, but to see how they interrelate. If the figure of the mother underlies masochistic fantasy and pornography, and if the figure of the father underlies sadistic fantasy, clearly the father is still the one with ultimate power. As Tania Modleski (1988, 10) has persuasively argued, the most significant thing about masochism, and about the pre-oedipal in general, is its repression: its eventual unacceptability to patriarchy, and now, of course, to feminism as well. But it is also clear that elements of an active subjectivity are at work in masochism—that masochism is a perversion whose absolute passivity has been overestimated.

It is important to distinguish between pornographies that construct fantasies of control, power, and mastery, accompanied by defenses against losing the self in merger, and those that construct fantasies of abandoning the self to merger with a more powerful "other." But it is also important to realize that the mere presence of violence does not mean that the fantasy is essentially sadistic. Feminists must, I believe, recognize that the violence that has generated so much heated discussion in debates about pornography is enjoyed by male and female spectators alike who, for very different reasons owing to their different gendered identifications and object choices, find both power and pleasure in identifying not only with a sadist's control but also with a masochist's abandon. For all the reasons outlined thus far, it seems to me preferable to employ the term *sadomasochistic* when describing the perverse fantasies that inform these films. While still problematic, the term at least keeps in play the oscillation between active and passive and male and female subject positions, rather than fixing one pole or the other as the essence of the viewer's experience. At the same time, it does not allow us to forget, as some celebrations of masochism (e.g., Studlar or Samois) do forget, where ultimate power lies.

We still need to return, however, to the masochistic component of the pleasure offered the female viewer who identifies with the female victim-hero. Since masochism is such a "norm" for female behavior under patriarchy, it would seem that the utopian component in such pornographic fantasies—of escape from the usual constraints on power and pleasure—would be less in evidence for women than for men. As we have already seen, many feminists consider such fantasies the ultimate in false consciousness, what Andrea Dworkin calls a "concentration camp pornography" (although as Kaja Silverman [1980] has effectively shown, in an article precisely on a film about a sadomasochistic relationship in a concentration camp, even in this context identificatory positions can be extremely complex). For many others, however—sexual minorities whose distinctive pleasures lie in such fantasy, sexual adventurers who wish to explore new forms of pleasure, sexual theorists who want to understand the processes of feminine sexuality—these fantasies may offer ways of exploring pleasures once reserved only for upper-class "gentlemen." There is no controlling, in other words, the "use" to which such fantasies may be put, and it is a mistake to assume that the fantasy that triggers pleasure in one person, disgust and displeasure in another, is the same as reality itself.

Sadomasochistic fantasy for and by women does not necessarily mean the increased domination of sadists; more likely it means a further exploration of the role of power in pleasure. It is precisely this conjunction that traditional (sexually "good") women have been taught to ignore in themselves. Sadomasochistic fantasy offers one important way in which groups and individuals whose desires patriarchy has not recognized as legitimate can explore the mysterious conjunction of power and pleasure in intersubjective sexual relations.[9]

Much of the recent work on romance fiction has explored the subversive and oppositional side of a literary genre that once seemed only regressively masochistic—a kind of wallowing in powerlessness.[10] A persistent theme of this criticism has been to suggest, with varying degrees of disapproval or acceptance, that mass-market romance is in fact but another form of masochistic pornography. In "Mass Market Romance: Pornography for Women Is Different" (1983), Ann Barr Snitow argues that romance fiction has female protagonists successfully negotiate the sexual danger of situations to which they would like to submit by hiding their desires under the passivity of conventional "good girl" qualities of nurturance and virginity. The narrative eventually rewards the heroine for being "good" with the marriage proposal of the hard, inscrutable, and sometimes cruel phallic male (p. 260). Apparently the "difference" that Snitow locates in romance fiction's pornography has something to do with the play of being a good girl and, through the successful performance of that role, achieving what one really desires.

More recent work has concentrated on how female readers identify with such heroines. Tania Modleski (1982, 48–49), for instance, has argued that the narrative form of the romance novel "solves" the contradictory situation of heroines who, if they directly pursued the wealthy and powerful men they desire, would be considered "scheming little adventuresses." The "solution" is to construct a narrative that shows the naive heroine misreading her real desires: she may think she hates this cold, unfathomable male, but as every female reader knows, her hatred, fear, and suffering mingle with, and mask, desire. This self-deception thus saves her from the self-conscious duplicity exercised by many "good girls" in courtship. The pleasure of the reader, then, might derive from knowing better than the heroine where her true pleasure lies yet still sympathizing with her confusion.

The heroines of these works could best be described as unconscious masochists who fail to recognize—are "falsely conscious" about—their own desires. An interesting recent phenomenon in mass-market romance fiction for women has been the transformation of the passive victim-heroine of the late-seventies Harlequins and "bodice rippers" into a more knowingly desirous, active, sexually adventurous female *hero*. This "romance revolution," as Carol Thurston (1987) calls it, in which the latent sexual content of the early romance was translated into a much more explicit eroticism, was achieved partly as a result of reader pressure on writers. With the sexually self-conscious female hero came a great many explicit sex scenes focused not only on the woman's active sexual pleasure but on her unashamed knowledge of this pleasure as well.[11]

Of interest in this "revolution" is the process by which female readers—and not necessarily feminists—began to recognize a politically unacceptable powerlessness in the unconscious masochism of earlier romance heroines. This transformation from unconscious passivity to more conscious forms of female sexual expression, both active and passive, dramatically suggests how consumers of genres can act to change them. Also important in this transformation was a recognition that the original form of the genre held a submerged sadistic pleasure in the suffering of the hard phallic male who, although he couldn't show it, was underneath, as Modleski (1982, 45) puts it, "grovelling, grovelling, grovelling." The expression of this suffering now seems to be a necessary ingredient in the desirability of the genre's male heroes, who must give ample evidence of their feminine and masochistic "vulnerability" before they can truly be sexy and earn the woman's love (Thurston 1987, 25).

As female readers of mass-market romance came to recognize the politically unacceptable masochistic self-deceptions of the genre's heroines, they began to demand new fictions in which men would be more like women and women more like men. The result was narratives with female heroes knowingly engaged in sadomasochistic games of power and pleasure with more "vulnerable" male love objects. I would like to suggest that something akin to this more self-consciously aware mixture of active and passive roles occurs in sadomasochistic film pornography as well. To examine this possibility, let us return to some of our examples of aesthetic sadomasochism.

In *The Story of Joanna*, the aristocratic male dying of a mysterious disease at first seems cruel and sadistic to the woman he initiates into rituals of domination. Unlike the audience, she is unaware of his doomed status. As the film continues, however, we begin to glimpse Jason's suffering and Joanna's growing power until, at the end, Joanna becomes his murderer, fulfilling his desire to die at the hand of one who loves him. Jason thus begins the film as "sadist" to Joanna's "masochist," but these roles are not fixed. We soon learn of Jason's secret vulnerability, and we see Joanna's secret pleasure in humiliation. At the end their roles are reversed: Joanna has become the cold dispenser of punishment, Jason is her victim. In a "confused" middle section of the film before this reversal takes place, a remarkable scene occurs that suggests the extent to which fixed sexual identities can be upset by the play of sadomasochistic pleasures.

We see Jason, who has not been feeling well, receiving a massage from his butler. Gradually, and without Jason's asking for it, the butler's massage turns into fellatio. Jason is naked and supine; the butler, who has previously performed sexual acts with Joanna at Jason's bidding, is fully clothed and shows no sign of sexual arousal himself. Jason's only action is to place his hand on the butler's shoulder. The act is not continued to orgasm.

This male-to-male fellatio is quite exceptional in feature-length heterosexual pornography. In fact, it is the only film of this period that I have seen that breaks the taboo against males touching males. Why does it occur here? Possibly the greater bisexuality and role-playing involved in sadomasochistic scenarios permits the admission of such a scene. Up until this point in the film, Jason has been in absolute control. Nonetheless, his desire is not the sadist's desire to gain control by annihilating the woman who represents the woman in himself; rather, it is the sadomasochistic desire to use his initial control to place himself in the power of another, to be "released into abandon by another who remains in control" (Benjamin 1986, 97).[12]

For the male viewer, identification with either participant in such a scene threatens heterosexual male identity, which is perceived as mastery and control—hence the rarity of these scenes in hard-core films. Yet it is precisely this propensity to upset forms of heterosexual identity organized around phallic control—here taken to an extreme—that we need to understand in sadomasochistic pornography. *The Story of Joanna* does not subvert phallic mastery, but it does play with it within limits, as we see in the male fellatio number. Jason, however, remains the true power in the narrative, even though his power lies, perversely, in his ability to get Joanna to destroy him.

Another sadomasochistic film that can be said to test the limits of the phallic power that organizes the narrative does not, properly speaking, belong in this discussion because of its foreign origin and art house distribution. Still, it is worth mentioning briefly. Nagisa Oshima's *In the Realm of the Senses* (1976) is a Japanese film produced with French money that, though never shown uncensored in Japan, attracted considerable interest among intellectuals in France, Britain, and the United States. It concerns the *amour fou* of a wealthy Japanese merchant, Kichi, and his woman servant, Sada.

The film begins with Sada spying on Kichi having sex with his wife; it continues with Kichi aggressively demanding to be serviced by Sada and then follows the course of their obsessive relations. In the process, the balance of power shifts from Kichi's phallic demands on Sada to her demands to have him in her always. The fantasy explored by the film is the impossible one of the couple's continuous desire, arousal, and possession. Kichi is perpetually erect; Sada is perpetually aroused. In marked contrast to the regular "payoffs" of more conventional, nonsadomasochistic, hard-core pornography, *In the Realm of the Senses* never ends a sexual encounter with the climax of male orgasm. Instead it moves through a sexual *combinatoire*—voyeurism, straight sex, "lesbian" sex, orgies, various positions—to build toward a sadomasochistic apocalypse that ends in the slow strangulation of Kichi by Sada during intercourse and her final "possession" of his penis through a castration performed on his dead body.

Like the male-to-male fellatio in *The Story of Joanna* (only much more so), this post mortem castration is obviously not an act designed to reassure male viewers of their autonomous masculine power and potency. Possession here takes on a truly perverse sense of reversing the usual hierarchies of the supposedly "natural" biological and social orders: Sada the servant emasculates Kichi the master, not in revolt, but as an expression of their mutual desires carried to the limits of life itself, and with the symbolic gesture of eradicating (though fetishistically memorializing as well) the phallic symbol of difference itself. On his body Sada writes with Kichi's blood what is translated in the film's subtitles as "Sada/Kichi: two of us, together." This togetherness (the actual word is a pun on *alone* and *cut* in Japanese), taken to these fantastic extremes, subverts the separateness of male and female sexual identity.

Jason's fellatio and subsequent murder by Joanna and Kichi's strangulation in the act of intercourse and subsequent castration by Sada are both cases of the male body perversely eroticized through exploration of its weakness and vulnerability. Both of these scenes could be said to represent moments of upset hierarchy in which the usual dominance of the male sexual organ is threatened. In neither case, however, is this weakness a negation of the male subject's own desires or, ultimately, of the phallic economy of a dominant masculine desire, since paradoxically, as Peter Lehman (1987, 24) has shown with respect to Oshima's film, any film so centered on the penis as object of desire is by definition phallocentric.

Kichi certainly displays the ultimate degree of vulnerability and sexual abandon to the control of another. One might expect, then, that Sada, as her name seems to suggest, would be the "Sadean woman" torturer,[13] whose domination of Kichi stems from an imitation of male phallic power aimed at neutralizing all sexual difference. Yet as we have seen, both Sada and Kichi, like Joanna and Jason, are actors in scenarios whose sexual poles are in flux. Even though Sada ends up as the castrating woman, this castration, which ends literally in her possession of the penis, does not signify the sadist's triumph over difference. Nor does it signify the negation of the pleasure of the "other," since Kichi has conspired with Sada in all their attempts to "possess" each other. Instead, Sada's goal is to effect an impossible merger with/engulfment of her lover through mutually agreed upon strategies that cannot be reduced to fixed positions of domination or submission. This, I think, is the meaning of the final castration: it is not so much an emasculation (in the sense of what Kichi loses) as a fantastic and utterly perverse image of what the mythic sadomasochistic couple, "Sada/Kichi together," gains. And this gain does not at all subvert the power of the phallus; rather, it moves it around, manipulating its dominance between the two poles of the couple.

Similarly, the scene in which Jason is the passive recipient of his male servant's ministrations shows the extent to which male dominance can be played with. In both these films we encounter a manifestation, in hard-core, explicitly sadomasochistic terms, of the male vulnerability that in the romance revolution is so necessary to the female hero's love. We should not fool ourselves, however, into thinking that the phallus is defeated as ultimate signifier of difference on which the articulation of power and pleasure depends.

In our final example of aesthetic sadomasochism, *The Punish-*

ment of Anne, the dominated Anne seems to offer a female figure who encourages the kind of masochistic overidentification with victimization described by Doane. To the extent that a female viewer identifies *only* with Anne, this interpretation would be appropriate. But in this film about Claire and Jean's apparently sadistic punishment of the masochistic Anne we gradually learn that Anne is something of a cipher—an image manipulated by Claire to seduce Jean. At the beginning of the film Claire plays the role of Anne's dominator; the goal here, however, is to educate Jean in how she wishes him to dominate her. In other words, although Claire, with her whip, needles, and black leather outfits, seems to be the "Sadean woman," a closer look reveals her to be what Deleuze calls the sadist in the masochistic story. This sadomasochistic scenario in which Claire originally plays the role of the sadist, then, turns out to be not Anne's story, as the film's title suggests, but Claire's.

When Claire shows Jean the black-and-white photos of "the punishment of Anne," she uses these images of Anne's contorted body to fascinate Jean with the oscillation between pleasure and pain, artifice and reality, so crucial to masochistic pleasure. His voice-over reaction, which alternates between admiration of the art involved and horror at the apparent pain displayed, is quoted almost directly from Jean de Berg's novel (1966, 73–74):

The next picture, extremely fascinating in its horror, despite the somewhat romantic exaggeration, could only be the result of a trick. But it was done so well that one could easily be fooled, especially since the contortions of the victim were so convincing. . . . The next is an apparently logical conclusion. The tortured body of the girl, apparently lifeless, is stretched out. . . . Claire's skill as a photographer is apparent in her loving attention to detail.

Jean's description registers a tension between the knowledge of artifice and the contrary belief in its reality, a tension that is the essence of the masochist's dramatic exhibition of suffering in secret pursuit of pleasure. Jean's final appreciation of Claire's skill as a photographer, as well as the play of glances between them as Claire watches Jean's excitement at the images she has made, indicates her control of the scene, her power to manipulate his desire so as to please them both. But the film holds in store the revelation of the more complex and indirect route of her own desires. We get a hint of these desires when we infer that Claire includes a photo of herself—a hand masturbating a pubis—with those of Anne, and when she breaks with her role of cold, inscrutable manipulator to become momentarily embarrassed and nervous when Jean asks if this photo is of another woman. The film will teach us that this substitution of her "image" for that of Anne is her indirect route to pleasure and that her present, temporary, role as sadist is part of a larger picture of sadomasochistic manipulation of appearance and desire.

Deleuze's claim that the masochist expels "his" superego, then casts it in the role of his torturer, seems to apply here to Claire's expulsion of the torturer in herself. This part is assigned to Jean, who learns to play it to perfection. The education of one person in the sexual fantasy of another through complex role-playing cued to works of art and imagination is arguably the most distinctive feature of sadomasochistic fantasy. (This, rather than physical punishment, for example, is the most typical element of the writing of Sacher-Masoch and of the films I call aesthetic masochism.) Here, it is as if Claire's early excess of superego, her calculated creation and manipulation of the photographic images, and the even greater design that teaches Jean the proper response to the image she will present to him are all investments in a future pleasure of abandon, the gratification of which is suspended until the film's final scene. Deleuze (1971, 112) writes, "Masochism is a story that relates how the superego was destroyed and by whom, and what was the sequel to this destruction." The sequel, in this case, is the projected utopia of Claire's pleasurable "abandon to another who will remain in control" and is played out in the final scene where she takes on Anne's former role and seeks recognition from Jean, who must now dominate her rather than Anne. So while the film ends with the spectacle of female victimization by a male dominator, the sadomasochistic components of Claire's desire reveal a pleasure that is quite actively of her own making. Claire's oscillation between sadist and masochist ultimately tips toward merger and recognition rather than separation and differentiation. This strategy, moreover, is not dependent on the phallus—as actor and ultimate subject of the scenario—to achieve its goals.

Phallic acts in the usual hard-core sense of visible evidence of penetration and ejaculation are, in fact, not emphasized in this or most sadomasochistic films. Although Jean's erect penis is sometimes visible, we see it penetrating neither Anne nor Claire. Claire, for her part, is seen naked only once, at the very end. Jean and Claire's final number on the stairs reveals no genital action at all. Strictly speaking, sadomasochistic pornography, because it is structured on fantasy and is ultimately, as *The Punishment of Anne* reveals, about the desiring characters' relation to images and to shifting sexual identities rather than to organs, resists being "fixed" by a measurable hard-core "frenzy of the visible." As Deleuze (p. 30) writes, masochism is an ideal suspended in fantasy. Even Kichi's severed penis, shocking and visible as it is, is but a fantasy of the undoing of sexual differences that ultimately resist being undone. "Here, as elsewhere," Silverman (1988b, 55) reminds us of masochism in general, "perversion reflects what it undermines."

Though phallic acts are curtailed (*Anne*), though the penis itself may be challenged in its heterosexual identity (*Joanna*) or even severed (*Realm*), the phallus still functions in these works as the articulator of meaning and difference. Sadomasochistic film pornography is not a form that, even at its most aesthetic and playful, challenges male dominance. It is, however, a form that reveals a remarkable awareness of two qualities inherent in all sexual relations but frequently effaced by more typical hard-core forms: the intersubjective nature of all desire and pleasure and the inevitability of power in pleasure.

The ending of *The Punishment of Anne* illustrates these qualities well. When Claire arrives at Jean's apartment in Anne's schoolgirl clothes, he immediately recognizes her in her new role as the dominated one. He asks, "What's my name?" In answering "Jean" while being penetrated on the stairs, in abandoning herself to this other who will now remain in control, Claire recognizes him in his new dominant relation to her, a relation that she herself has fashioned. The appeal to recognition by an "other," the desire for merger, transcendence through suffering—these are the qualities shared to different degrees by all the sadomasochistic films discussed in this chapter. In each, the solution to the problem of the protagonist's desire is to yield to the more powerful other, and at some point the dominator invariably claims to recognize the dominated in his or her way of taking pleasure. It is for this pleasure that the dominated one is tortured, and it is in this torture that he or she finds, perversely—

but perhaps also more self-knowingly than in forms of unconscious masochism such as pre-"revolutionary" romance fiction—yet more pleasure.

The rise of sadomasochism in the full variety of its forms may very well indicate some partial yet important challenges to patriarchal power and pleasure in the genre of film pornography. S/M's emphasis on oscillating positions over strict sexual identities and its extension of sexual norms to include sadomasochistic play and fantasy suggest a rising regime of relative differentiations over absolute difference. Some of the apocalyptic force of much sadomasochistic pornography undoubtedly derives from these challenges to phallic laws that stand for strict dichotomization.

Historically these are the laws that have told women that sexual pleasure makes them "bad girls." It is a law that must be destroyed if women are to find power and pleasure without being overwhelmed by the phallus. Of course, this is not to say that sadomasochistic pleasure for the woman destroys this law. Like the slasher film, sadomasochistic pornography is still caught up in the cultural law that divides the "good" girls from the "bad." The slasher film kills off the sexually active "bad girls," treating them as the victim-heroines who cannot save themselves, and reserves heroic action to the sexually inactive "good girl" victim-hero. Sadomasochistic pornography, in contrast, combines the "good" and "bad" girls into one person. The passive "good girl" still needs to prove to the audience of the superego that her orgasms are not willed; but the active "bad girl" is author and director of the spectacle of coercion designed to fool the superego, and part of her pleasure lodges in the very fact that this superego knows she enjoys it. While sadomasochism does not solve the inequities of patriarchal power and authority, it does reveal some of the more devious and indirect forms of subversion/perversion. The superego and the cultural law which decides that some girls are "good" and others are "bad" have not been destroyed; their cultural authority has only been deflected, played with a bit.

This chapter has, I hope, gone part of the way toward an understanding of masochistic elements of pleasure available to male and female viewers of these sexual fantasies. Likewise, I hope it has begun to explicate what within a feminist perspective has often seemed inexplicable. It must end, however, with the feminist concern with which it began: with the specter, if not the proven reality, of a cinematic perversion of sadistic control that is total and that, in being total, does not allow even masochistic pleasure.

Although not "real" and not "really" pornography, the film *Snuff* still represents a highly problematic cinematic articulation of a sadist's desire to annihilate all forms of difference. And since real snuff *is* possible (though perhaps not provable except via extracinematic means), we cannot dismiss concern for the perversion of cinema and cinema as perversion. But we need to be clear that this concern is not so much for the perversions that might motivate it as the actual disregard for the will, subjectivity, and humanity of the victim. We must also be clear that the issue does not hinge on the possible pleasures of the person whose will is so overrun, but on the abuse of a victim.

We only confuse issues, and ultimately abet the further victimization of women, if we conflate all sadomasochistic pornography under this single hypothetical example. The "concentration camp orgasm" *is* a troubling concept, certainly if we think of it as belonging to the sadist who destroys, but perhaps even more so if we take it to include the victim. The idea of this latter pleasure is what most troubles feminism, for it represents the possibility of an absolute loss of humanity and intersubjectivity in sexual relations, the total abandonment of the self to the will of the other.

Perhaps the most unthinkable thing in the specter of snuff is not the sadism of the viewer who identifies with the torturer, but the masochism of a woman viewer identifying with her annihilated surrogate. If ever there was a politically incorrect pleasure, this is it. It is important to acknowledge that this specter, much more than that of the evil sadist, disturbs us most. My point is not that this is a politically incorrect pleasure, but that it is an impossible one. If "concentration camp orgasm" means the pure pleasure of victimization, then such pleasure cannot exist. For we have seen that without a modicum of power, without some leeway for play within assigned sexual roles, and without the possibility of some intersubjective give-and-take, there can be no pleasure for either the victim or the totally identified viewer. There can be no pleasure, in other words, without some power.

The examples of sadomasochistic film pornography examined in this chapter demonstrate that there is always some element of power at stake for the masochistic victim. These films have shown themselves to be less the limit-case of extreme violence and perversion than might have been expected, whether by the Meese Commission in its appropriation of Bazinian realism to argue the sadistic *perversion of cinema* or by the psychoanalytic feminist in her reliance on sadism to explain *cinema as perversion*. Sadomasochistic fantasy is certainly regressive to feminism in its obsessive repetition of hierarchical, nonmutual forms of power and pleasure—the very same hierarchically based notions that have traditionally prevented women from actively seeking their pleasure or that have forced them to pay for it with pain in advance. But sadomasochistic fantasy recognizes the role of power in the woman's often circuitous route to pleasure, and in that recognition it is much less the case of female "false consciousness" than it has been taken to be. It may even represent for women a new consciousness about the unavoidable role of power in sex, gender, and sexual representations and of the importance of not viewing this power as fixed.

I argued earlier that contemporary pornography, whatever else one may think about it, can be valued for posing "sex as a problem," even though its solutions, like the solutions of most genres, tend to solve those problems by re-mythicizing the entity "sex." If sex is the problem, then in hard core more, better, or different sex is the solution. Sadomasochism offers a variant of this; here "different sex" involves not only the latest techniques or paraphernalia for achieving more or better orgasms, but also a clearer confrontation with the oscillating poles of our gendered identities and the role of power in them.

8

Sequels and Re-Visions

"A Desire of One's Own"

> To close the avenues of sexual speech, at a time when
> women are only beginning to listen in on and
> participate in hitherto largely male-dominated
> conversations, and to hold conversations of our own,
> seems to us to endanger the climate of cultural
> demystification that has made these welcome
> beginnings possible.
>
> Kate Ellis, Barbara O'Dair, and
> Abby Tallmer, *Caught Looking*

> Porn was always for men. Now that women are
> finally allowed to have a sexuality, we are looking for
> stimulus. Women are saying, "Okay, now let's look at
> a film." Well, now is the time to start making films for
> women. That doesn't just mean quality and scripts.
> It means what's the sex all about.
>
> Candida Royalle, quoted in
> Annette Fuentes and Margaret Schrage,
> "Deep Inside Porn Stars"

Throughout this study we have observed hard-core film and video's attempts to make sex speak through the visual confession of bodily pleasures. We have seen that however much hard core may claim to be a material and visible thing, it is still fundamentally a discourse, a way of speaking *about* sex. In all forms of pornography the vast majority of this speaking has been by men. In twentieth-century motion picture and video pornography speech has become pervasive, insistent, and explicit. Yet despite the fact that bodies in hardcore cinema have seemed to realize the involuntary confessions of Diderot's female "indiscreet jewels," anyone who looked closely could always tell that these confessions of sex were written by men for men.

This is still generally true of most pornography. But we may be approaching a moment in the history of hard core when Diderot's fable is no longer an entirely apt emblem of the genre. For now women, too, have begun to speak of pleasure in pornography, and not through male ventriloquists. They must speak, of course, within the dominant discourse of patriarchal language and in the context of a genre that is by definition obsessed with visible proof. Quite naturally, then, this new speech by women in pornography is still tentative, having developed slowly as hard-core film and video made a larger effort to address women more directly. Moreover, this pornographic speech by women has not developed out of any altruistic spirit of democratic inclusion but rather strictly as a matter of capitalist expansion, or what Lawrence Birken (1988) calls "consuming desire." The pornographic marketplace is now almost as eager to address women as desiring consumers as it once was to package them as objects of consumption. The result has been a remarkable democratization, perhaps the most striking development of a genre whose modern history has already been one of expansion beyond the "gentlemen" of its original audience.

As long as only men were looking at hard core, the double standard that judged male and female participation in sex differently remained in force. Women who looked at film pornography prior to its greater legalization in the early 1970s were in the particularly vulnerable position of being "caught looking" at works that were distinctly not for their eyes. Beginning in about 1972, however, and especially in what I have dubbed the "integrated" and "dissolved" forms of the genre, women have entered the pornographic conversation—not just as the confessors and performers of sex, but as readers and viewers who are increasingly addressed by the films and so are less likely to feel "caught" when they are found "looking."

In order to fathom the change that has taken place, we might try to imagine Zeus and Hera's argument about pleasure in sex in a modern context. For now the stakes have altered. No longer does the gain of pleasure necessarily mean the loss of power. Now both Zeus and Hera want pleasure, and both see its exercise as a form of personal power. This is not to say that they have become magically equal. Zeus still has more economic and social power; Hera still risks pregnancy and being stuck as the primary caretaker. Nor is this to say that sexual pleasure means the same thing for each of them. To Zeus it is much more a proof of power and potency than it is for

Hera. Hera still isn't sure what sexual pleasure proves, but she desires it nonetheless. And both are now terribly worried about the new danger of AIDS, a worry that may have reduced Zeus's philandering and has encouraged them both to use condoms.

Both members of this mythic couple want pleasure—however differently they might define it—and both have learned enough from the proliferating discourses of sexuality to know that the surest way to get pleasure is also to give it. But they are a little uncertain how best to do this, and so, without consulting Teiresias (who now really is too old and blind to be of any help), they decide to rent some videotapes and settle down to watch in the privacy of their own home. The first one they rent scandalizes Hera. It shows a penis in close-up ejaculating all over a woman's face and the woman acting like the semen is a gift from the gods. Hera criticizes the film's lack of realism. Zeus is surprised at her reaction. He liked the phallic show of power; it reminded him of his thunderbolts. They rent another. Hera likes this one better; it shows a couple experimenting with a wide variety of sexual acts, livening up their relationship. Zeus takes note again; although this isn't like watching stag films with the other male gods, it has its advantages.

I suggest that the experience of this modern Zeus and Hera is typical of a great many couples who are well enough off to own VCRs. The statistics of this VCR home-porno revolution are remarkable. X-rated theaters, bookstores, peep shows, strip joints, and magazines have all suffered a decline in business; there are now only 350 X-rated theaters in the United States, half as many as a decade ago. Hard-core videocassette rentals, however, are booming. According to *Time* magazine (30 March 1987, 63), women now account for roughly "40% of the estimated 100 million rentals of X-rated tapes each year." Even if we temper this startling statistic with the knowledge that women still do most of the shopping, the conclusion is inescapable: women must be watching pornography in great numbers. A 1987 *Redbook* magazine survey of twenty-six thousand women confirms the suspicion: nearly half the women surveyed say they regularly watch pornographic films, and 85 percent say they have seen at least one such film, as opposed to 60 percent in 1974.[1]

One purpose of this chapter is to determine what difference this new female component of the home audience has made in the genre. How has the genre been revising itself under the scrutiny of female eyes? Another purpose is to determine to what extent this general revision might also extend to an actual *re-vision* of hard core by women authors. To what extent, in other words, has hard core simply cleaned up its act (much the way a man might clean up his apartment and change the sheets before he receives a female visitor), and to what extent might it be undergoing a much more thoroughgoing revolution of its form and meaning?

The added hyphen, which I borrow from Adrienne Rich's well-known essay "When We Dead Awaken: Writing as Re-Vision," suggests the revolutionary potential of "the act of looking back, of seeing again with fresh eyes, of entering an old text from a new critical direction" (1979, 35). Re-vision in this sense is undertaken by women authors as a necessary "act of survival," in order to be able to create at all. The visual aspect of this metaphor of re-vision has been particularly useful for thinking about film.[2] Although Rich herself might not approve of this further extension of the notion to include pornography, it seems to me that it is precisely within this traditionally male genre that the idea of re-vision is most compelling: "survival" here means transforming oneself from sexual object to sexual subject of representation.

Let us begin with the more obvious, and less revolutionary, of these two changes in hard core, that of simple revision: the evident fact that hard-core pornography has "cleaned up" its act for female eyes in an effort to corner the "couples" market. "Clean" must, of course, remain a relative term in a film genre that was once defined as "dirty movies." Yet it is readily apparent that films aimed at couples offer a softer, cleaner, nicer version of the stock numbers and narratives of feature-length hard core. The improved qualities include higher production values, better lighting, fewer pimples on bottoms, better-looking male performers who now take off their shoes and socks, and female performers who leave on shoes *and* expensive-looking lingerie.

More important in this new address to women, however, is the different tone that the genre sometimes manages to strike, a more genuinely adult quality in films whose adolescent smirking has always rendered the term *adult film* ironic. This is not to say that couple-oriented hard core is suddenly mature in the sense of being in tune with reality: as sexual fantasy, hard-core pornography concerns feelings and emotions that are, almost by definition, infantile and regressive. It is to say, though, that the specifically male-adolescent tone that characterized the American pornography of stags and early feature-length narratives seems, in these films for couples, to be in abeyance.

For example, in many films today, the mere fact that a naked woman appears seems in itself to be no immediate cause for snickering. Adolescent male bonding at the expense of female difference (and about which Di Lauro and Rabkin are so nostalgic in their book *Dirty Movies*) no longer seems to be the point. Rather, this appearance becomes an occasion to ask what she wants. The answer might be exceedingly simplistic, but we must remember that the stag film could not even ask the question. As we have seen, early feature-length porno narratives like *Deep Throat* asked it incessantly. There, however, the answers usually proceeded from the viewpoint of the phallus; the aura of the dirty joke (and its inevitable butt, woman) lingered. Now the question has become more earnest, and the answer—which provides the occasion for "more or better" sex—takes more seriously the different nature of the woman's own desire and pleasure and accepts the challenge of helping her to achieve them. In other words, within the realm of couples pornography, the reduction of the sexual double standard has meant that the performance of "good," satisfying sex has become a priority to all.

The 1984 Adult Film Association Award–winning "couples film of the year," *Every Woman Has a Fantasy*, by the husband-and-wife team Edwin Durell and Sandra Winters, is typical of this kind of revision. A married woman meets with her women friends once a week for talk. The talk is hardly consciousness-raising, but in this supportive, (supposedly) private and safe atmosphere the women exchange their sexual fantasies, which we then see acted out on the screen. In bed together later the wife tells her husband her friends' secrets, and *he* then fantasizes about being in bed with each of them. But fantasy is not enough. The husband, like Diderot's Sultan Mangogul and like the male voyeur spectator of most hard-core features, wants to see and hear all, while remaining invisible himself. So, à la Dustin Hoffman in *Tootsie*, he dresses as a woman and joins his wife's group. *His* fantasy then comes true when the women, discovering his maleness, make love to him in a final orgy.

I cite this popular couples film to suggest that the supposed differences of these merely revised films are perhaps not all that great. The predominant structure of male voyeurism and female confession is kept intact, and no one in the film worries at all about the betrayal of female secrets. What does differ is that voyeurism is now carried out in the interest of male research that aims to improve the sex life of the couple. Finding out what women "really want" is a high priority in these films. In this case it is presumed to justify male spying and the betrayal of female secrets. What the women want turns out to be highly varied, ranging from a TV news commentator's fantasy of taking off her clothes on the air, to a woman's desire to have her husband take pictures of her tied up, to another woman's inviting a delivery boy into her home so they can watch each other masturbate. "Money shots" are little in evidence. But the problem of the visual evidence of satisfaction, of catching the involuntary confession of pleasure, remains.

The "solution" to this problem, then, is achieved in another way, in yet another typical couples film of the mid-eighties, *The Grafenberg Spot* (Mitchell Bros., 1985). This film also emphasizes finding out what women want, and it even goes so far as to set up female doctor authority figures (as in the original G-spot sex manual)[3] who know the answer: just find the G-spot and women will have giant orgasms with oceans of ejaculate that rival those of men. All this solicitation of the difference of women's pleasure is, of course—as in other couples films—in the interest of improving the sex life of the couple. In this case the male partner has to learn, through experimentation, that G-spot ejaculation is perfectly "normal," whereas the female partner learns, through her own experimentation, how to perfect visible evidence of her pleasure. As in *Deep Throat*, however, the solicitation of difference is suspiciously in the interest of, and produced on the model of, the phallic "norm."

Sequels

A convenient way to assess what changes have occurred in these revisionist couples films is to examine mid-eighties sequels to two of the most popular hard-core films of the early seventies: *Deep Throat* and *Behind the Green Door*. These two sequels, entitled *Throat—Twelve Years After* (Gerard Damiano, 1984) and *Behind the Green*

Door—The Sequel (Mitchell Bros. and Sharon McKnight, 1986), are especially interesting not only as updates of two of the best-known early feature-length porn titles but also because they retain their original directors (though in the latter film the original directors collaborated with a woman director). Since both movies work equally hard at paying homage to, and at differentiating themselves from, their precursors—even to the point of including scenes in which the protagonists of the present films view scenes from the earlier ones—they represent highly self-conscious revisions of the earlier films.

Damiano's *Throat—Twelve Years After* is the more explicitly couples-oriented of the two, an orientation that is evident both in its focus on two couples in its narrative and in the happy ending that celebrates their continuation as couples. The film ends with the narrative's two contrasting heterosexual duos—one "swinging," the other monogamous—together in a living room watching Linda Lovelace in *Deep Throat* perform her deep-throat technique. Though suitably appreciative of her talent, and especially appreciative of the "great line" "Diff'rent strokes for diff'rent folks," the couples criticize the film's overuse of fellatio as an expression of the ultimate in sexual pleasure. One of the characters even makes an oblique reference to Linda Lovelace's apostasy from hard core, saying: "I hear she doesn't make porn films any more." Another character jokingly attributes the reason to too much deep-throat fellatio: "That's because she had it up to here" (gesture to throat). The film then ends with the four characters toasting "practice," which makes for perfect sex.

The toast to practice is also, of course, a toast to the movie that got the credit for introducing the importance of practice to a newly constituted hard-core audience that was no longer exclusively male. *Twelve Years After* thus salutes the earlier film and at the same time reworks its significance. In place of the pure technique of deep-throat fellatio taught by a male expert to a female initiate, the new film stresses no single sexual technique and no sexual hierarchy of male teacher and female initiate. It makes a point, rather, of emphasizing the give-and-take by which men and women learn to find out and to tell each other what they want in sex. And the one thing the women in this film clearly do *not* want is fellatio followed by a money shot—a point that is stressed in no fewer than two scenes when women engaged in vaginal intercourse explicitly tell their male partners nearing climax to "come" inside them.

Although the film abandons the familiar male sexologist/female initiate scenario for more equalized exchange, the essentially therapeutic value of sexual experimentation—of "diff'rent strokes for diff'rent folks"—remains. It is elaborated through the interactions and contrasts of male and female characters who know where their pleasure lies and others who seek to learn this very thing. A sexually repressed housewife, who loves her husband but is too ashamed of her sexual urges to indulge them with him, learns to do so in an afternoon affair with the meter man. That same afternoon, her repressed husband has recourse to a prostitute, who pities his constrained sex life and instructs him on how to please her. That evening, the husband and wife enthusiastically seduce each other in a number that emphasizes cunnilingus and fellatio equally but does not culminate in a money shot. Neither tells the other of their affair. Despite a certain irony in their mutual agreement that they are a self-sufficient couple, it is clear that their experiments were temporary explorations designed to improve—and uphold the ideology of—fundamental monogamy.

In contrast, a second couple, resolute swingers both, aggressively cultivate extracurricular pleasures of all sorts. We first see the woman engaged in sex with a male prostitute (she gives *him* advice), and then we see the man with a date at a swinger's club orgy, in which the kinky activities involve men as much or more than women. In the end this couple, too, enthusiastically seduce each other in an intimate and caring scene that contrasts with the impersonality of their previous activities. Again the ideology of monogamy is upheld, paradoxically through sexual adventure that extends the boundary of the monogamous relationship. Here the "diff'rent strokes" ethic serves to enhance the desire for one's mate. Finally the two couples (and unlikely friends) get together for an evening's entertainment that significantly does *not* culminate in a private orgy, but only in a sedate evening of viewing *Deep Throat* and toasting sexual "practice."

What is particularly interesting in this film's celebration of variety and knowing-what-you-want is its insistent emphasis on the role of the *image* of sexual pleasure. These images appear as visual memories, fantasies, or, as in the direct quotation of *Deep Throat*, the videotaped version of film imagery itself; and their function is to mediate more present and immediate forms of pleasure. For example, two parallel numbers use memories to mediate the represented pleasures. In one, the female prostitute who teaches the repressed husband to have a good time has just finished a fairly perfunctory straight sex encounter with him (we know it is perfunctory because she continues to chew her gum while making phony orgasmic sounds). Soon after, though, when she has come to appreciate his gentle shyness, she fondly recalls her "first time" with sex. She evokes a scene on a high school playground, where she fellates through a cyclone fence a guy who used to stare at her from behind that fence. The scene is presented in flashback and intercut with the present scene of fellatio so that both the remembered high school boy and the man in the bed orgasm simultaneously in images that provide ample evidence of ejaculation but are not, strictly speaking, money shots. At the end of this scene, the prostitute's own pleasure is signaled (with great restraint for a hard-core film) by the fact that she has finally stopped chewing her gum.

This mediation of a present image of pleasure by a remembered one is repeated in the parallel encounter of the female pleasure-seeker and the male prostitute. Again it is the female who narrates a past episode of first-time sex. But here the woman's experience was as a client of a female prostitute. The intercutting between past and present thus affords a visual contrast between the two numbers, which the participant-narrator then comments on verbally. As the male prostitute performs cunnilingus on his client, she tells him of a similar experience with a female prostitute, holding it up to the less experienced male prostitute as a model he should aspire to emulate. We see both numbers in alternation; they are quite similar up until the end, when the woman, in the present, orders the male prostitute: "Do to me what no woman can do to me, fuck me harder, come in me!" He does (presumably), but not in a way that appears to outdo the remembered "lesbian" number. Rather, the pleasure of that memory of cunnilingus is seen to enhance her pleasure in the present straight sex.

In both scenes, the remembered images of original sexual experiences inform the pleasure of the present experiences. The female prostitute's subsequent life as a giver of pleasure is consistent with her original experience in the school yard, and the woman swinger's subsequent life as an aggressive taker of pleasure is consistent with her original experience with the female prostitute whose services she purchased. In both cases also, the narrated and viewed confession of an early experience functions to educate a person of the opposite sex on the "diff'rent strokes" that may constitute an individual's pleasure.

In every way, then, Damiano's sequel to the most famous porno film of all time attempts to expand and vary the therapeutic sexual quest of the original while revising the sexual inequality of the therapist-patient relationship to show that men and women have something to teach each other. In typical integrated fashion (that is, through integration of the utopian world of sexual pleasure into the film's narrative of its characters; see Chapter 6), the problems of sex are always best solved not by adjustments in the day-to-day world of social relations—whereby women might acquire more power—but in the narrower solution of better sexual performance. A case in point occurs in the dilemma of the repressed housewife whose limited options are dramatized by the opposed advice of her mother on the one hand (who urges her to have children) and the meter man on the other (who urges her to have improved sex with him). "Better sex" is, of course, the only possible generic solution. But to have better sex, the housewife must behave in bed with the same confidence and authority that the Sandra Chase character has out of bed in the dissolved *Insatiable* films, that is, as if she were in a narrative that had already solved the usual problems that impede the play and replay of desire and satisfaction—as if she were in "pornotopia" already. Since the wife does *not* have this confidence and authority, the supposed liberation she achieves has a certain hollowness. The meter man, for example, admires the wife's housewifely virtue of baking buns (with all the predictable puns on buns). But baking buns does not give this woman power and authority in her own eyes: she can only get sexual power through *his* releasing it in her.

Thus, although the revisionism of couples films attempts to give women sexual power and authority, the route to this power and authority is still through a quite narrowly construed sexual "revolution" operating to the primary advantage of Zeus-like philandering. Yet within this ethic of the democratic pursuit of pleasure, the older, more experienced woman who knows what she wants is not, as in so many narratives of dominant or mainstream cinema, pitted against the innocence and lack of self-knowledge of the ingenue. As noted in the last chapter, pornography is perhaps one of the few popular genres in which women are not punished for knowing, pursuing, and finding their pleasure.

Most of the films with appeal to the couples market belong to the integrated category of hard-core entertainment.[4] Because this is the category most capable of admitting problems from the social world into narrative discourse for purposes of utopian resolution, it is also the category most capable of addressing the sexual problems of modern couples. *Behind the Green Door—The Sequel* (1986), however, presents, like its precursor, a separated pornotopia in which the world of narrative reality, though highly stylized and fantastic, stands in grim contrast to the sexual abundance of the world of the Green Door cabaret, where performers and audience join freely in uninhibited orgies. Even though this film's narrative contains no image of the monogamous couple, the revisions of the original film's narrative quite explicitly aim at modifying its misogyny, at making it more acceptable to women and thus to viewing couples.

As in the original film, the real-world story concerns tired workers, in this case a group of male and female flight attendants en route to San Francisco, on their way home. Even though both the flight attendants and their bizarre passengers seem obsessed by sex, the tenor of this obsession is cynical and wary. In one fragment of conversation we hear one woman telling another, "He said, 'Did I find your G-spot?' I said, 'Learn your alphabet. G comes after five minutes of F.'" A male flight attendant flirts with a female attendant, the protagonist Gloria (the name of the Marilyn Chambers character in the original film), but without success. This is the mid-eighties world of sexual conservatism—a Jamaican passenger reads a newspaper whose headline declares the reason: AIDS.

Thus, in typical separated fashion, the real-world narrative depicts a sexual scarcity that, like its precursor, will find an escapist solution in the utopian world of sexual abundance "behind the green door." But scarcity and conservatism receive a new inflection here: first, with the specter of AIDS, a new sexual problem that the utopian pornographic fantasy will attempt to "solve"; and second, with the brooding presence of a wheelchair-confined "weirdo" (presumably a disabled veteran) who lives across the courtyard from Gloria and who has set up elaborate sound and image surveillance of her apartment. This working-class man is the truck driver of the original film; his immobility and his "rear-window" view of Gloria evoke other familiar film references as well.

When Gloria returns to her apartment, she and the man in the wheelchair ride the elevator to their separate apartments on the same floor. Gloria takes a shower and enters her bedroom with a drink, where she starts *Behind the Green Door* on her VCR and begins to masturbate (as Steven Marcus [1974, xiv] puts it) "with the aid of a mechanical-electrical instrument" plugged in next to her TV. The vet observes her on a monitor and through the large picture window of her bedroom. He, too, gets a drink, puts the same tape on one of his (several) monitors, and masturbates—both to the film and to his voyeuristic view of Gloria's masturbation to the same film. The scene playing on both their monitors is the one in which Marilyn Chambers's Gloria is massaged by the woman who prepares her to be "ravished."

The escapist sexual fantasy that follows thus seems at first to belong to the vet in the wheelchair, triggered and facilitated by images from this "classic" pornographic film. But the fantasy we see is also peopled with many of the characters Gloria knows from her work on the plane, including the flight attendant who flirted with her. It can therefore be viewed as Gloria's fantasy as well—and also as a measure of the Mitchell Brothers' belated sensitivity to the misogynistic, coercive sex of their original film. Like Damiano's sequel, this one revises the original with new elements of a more "authentic" female desire, conceived as parallel to, though not necessarily congruent with, that of the male. Thus both sequels tacitly acknowledge a deficiency in the representation of female desire and pleasure in their precursors. Nevertheless, the revised solutions they offer—the repudiation of money shots or ravishment, the attempted equalization of different male and female fantasies and the images that trigger them, the presentation of women protagonists who know what they want and don't need a male expert to teach them—are still quite limited, remaining embedded in a predominantly phallic visual economy where the dominant pleasures of male voyeurism and female fetishization still rule. This inertia is particularly true in the case of the separated fantasy world "behind the green door."

This fantasy begins with the working-class man from the wheelchair—now miraculously walking and wearing a tuxedo—gaining admittance to a clandestine night club with the words (borrowed from the "Green Door" song not used in the original film) "Joe sent me." Inside, in a smoky, sleazy, yet convivial atmosphere, a wild assortment of types, including a dwarf maître d', a strongman who passes out safer-sex kits, and an obese woman, fraternize with people of more normal shape and size in a setting adorned with classical statuary. The singer-impersonator Sharon McKnight (who shares directorial credit for the film with the Mitchell Brothers) sings the title song in styles that imitate Mae West's innuendo, Lotte Lenya's malice, and Bette Davis's hauteur. The number ends with McKnight going through the door leading to the exotic dangers of promiscuous sexuality while issuing a warning to the audience: "If you're taking chances, honey, remember, stay safe." And indeed, everyone in the club does play it safe: waitresses serve latex gloves and condoms along with the champagne and wine.

The first sex number brings Gloria on stage. A group of Grecian maidens stroke her with vibrators identical to the one she used on herself in her bed. In the audience the man from the wheelchair is surprised and delighted to see her, identifying her proudly to another audience member as "my next-door neighbor." In true Mitchell Brothers style, the audience performs its own sexual warm-up right along with the performers. In the second number, three naked men wearing body paint (a variation on the yellow tights of the men in the original) are lowered down to the stage on trapezes. Gloria puts condoms on each of them before engaging in simultaneous fellatio and hand manipulation. In the midst of this—and with intercuts of the more varied (but still safer-sex) activities of the audience—a Greek statue comes to life and penetrates Gloria from behind as she continues to manipulate the men on the trapezes.

Although this complex scene builds to a dramatic crescendo, it does not climax in an equivalent of the optically printed money shots that highlighted the original film. The reasons are worth examining. Superficially, of course, there is the physical impossibility of showing a money shot with a performer who wears a condom. But in fact, an ejaculation that involves no exchange of bodily fluids does not violate any of the strictures of safer sex; it could have been shown in glorious, close-up isolation had the filmmakers wanted to end this act with a phallic climax. Instead, except for its background homage to the original movie, the film eschews the money shot altogether. The present number ends with the statue withdrawing and the three men on trapeze being hoisted back to the skies before Gloria, her partners, or anyone in the audience, male or female, has given any visible evidence of orgasm.

The visual drama of orgasm is saved entirely for the next act. The forlorn, abandoned Gloria sits on the edge of the stage listening to the moans of the still entwined audience. Suddenly a spotlight on the green door illuminates a pipe-playing satyr (complete with horns, hooves, and furry legs—and a condom already on his penis) who eagerly penetrates Gloria on a ringside table. Their straight sex, performed both on the table and standing up, is energetic and lascivious. It is intercut with the even wilder and kinkier activities of the audience: the obese woman is on her back naked with three men attending her; the dwarf maître d' has straight sex with a normal-sized woman. At no point, however, does the film claim to locate a precise moment of visible climax. Rather, it uses the cumulative effect of the simultaneous configurations of likely and unlikely bodies in the audience orgy and Gloria and the satyr's performance on stage to build to a kind of Eisensteinian accelerated (and intellectual) montage.

As if to signify the paradoxically metaphoric nature of this sequence, the ending to this third number of the film is an absurd parody of a hard-core finale. It shows the giant obese woman upside down with legs spread. A small, thin man who has been one of her attendants makes a dramatic dive from above, like a circus diver, into what purports to be her gigantic vagina. A splash is heard, and a freeze frame of the man upside down, halfway buried in the woman like some Icarus fallen into the sea, ends the entire episode.

This theatrical and patently artificial tableau offers a fantastic metaphor for the penetration of the meat shot. The next segment offers an equally fantastic rendition of the meat shot's complement, the optically printed and colored slow-motion money shot from *Behind the Green Door*—this time, however, Marilyn Chambers's face, with colored particles of ejaculate flying about it, is presented as though through a kaleidoscope, in symmetrically doubled profile. Thus one fantastic version of climax, the theatrically staged metaphor of "meat" in the cabaret, is followed by a quintessentially cinematic and equally stylized metaphor of "money," quoted from the 1972 film. Immediately after, we see that this last scene has appeared on the disabled vet's video monitor and that we are momentarily back in the real world. The scenes "behind the green door" appear to have been the vet's masturbatory fantasy-variations on the original film. In them, he has taken the place of the truck driver, the actress Missy's Gloria has taken the place of Marilyn Chambers's Gloria, the satyr has taken the place of the African, and a stylized, metaphoric celebration of meat has taken the place of a stylized celebration of money—though the display of money is still included via filmic quotation.

According to the model of the precursor film, the stage is now set for the vet's big moment, the equivalent of the truck driver's intimate offstage duet with Chambers. The difference between this version and the original film, however, is that while in the 1972 film the truck driver seems really to run off with Gloria—he appears to be in actual possession of her—in the 1986 version the vet only uses the videocassette and his voyeuristic view of her to imagine, with the aid of the earlier film, such possession.

This straight sex fantasy scene (with condom) takes place in the morning light of Gloria's bedroom. It is again accompanied, this time on Gloria's monitor, by the continuing slow-motion money shots from the original film. The flamboyantly flying ejaculate of the 1972 fantasy of sexual climax here seems a nostalgic reminder of a mythic, freewheeling past when body fluids could flow with greater abandon. The number concludes with a segue back to the close-up of Marilyn Chambers's face and mouth covered with ejaculate and finally to the real world of the vet who is still masturbating alone.

Thus far, the fantasy has clearly been the vet's. Now, in a sequence that has no parallel in the original film, it becomes Gloria's. We see her masturbating alone, with the same section of the film still playing on her monitor, as now *her* fantasy man—not the vet, but the flight attendant with whom she flirted in the opening sequence—shares similarly intimate and emotional straight sex. Since this flight attendant is also one of the men on trapeze, there is the suggestion that the previous episode "behind the green door" was a merger of Gloria's fantasy with that of the vet, both of which, after all, were mediated by the same film.

Finally, the film returns to real-world "scarcity" and "exhaustion" (Dyer 1981, 180). We see the vet the next morning waking up alone in his wheelchair. In a long shot looking into Gloria's apartment, he (and we) see Gloria also waking up in her bed; the blank television screen pulsates behind her. Naked, she goes to the window to open the blind. Looking idly out the window, her gaze finally focuses on the camera, and she registers shock and surprise. Her reaction is the classic pose of the naked woman covering her nakedness. A freeze frame of this pose ends the sequence.

What does Gloria see? It is certainly implied that she sees the vet spying on her. But since her reaction occurs at the exact moment that she looks directly into the camera whose gaze allows *us* to see her, what she sees may be the very apparatus that "shoots" her (and, by extension, us looking at her). If so, does this mean that her look back deconstructs the apparatus that sees and objectifies her? Does this make the film critical of the phallic visual economy that permits us to spy, along with the vet, on Gloria's masturbation and fantasy?

The answers to these questions may suggest the limits of this kind of revisionist hard core. Gloria's body is revealed in this coda as the unwitting exhibitionist object of a voyeurism that aligns the male subject with the desiring gaze of the cinematic apparatus. Her return look calls attention to the collusion of all of the looks at her—those of diegetic character, camera, and spectator—but it cannot overturn or retrieve her own previous masturbatory and fantasy participation in these voyeuristic structures: she has already been used, and the misogynist "classic" *Behind the Green Door* was the primary trigger to her present desires. So while Gloria's look back may expose the inequity of a visual economy that still poses the woman's body as the primary exhibitionist spectacle, it cannot undo the pleasure that has already been taken in the look at her.

There is also a more insidious and pessimistic message in this exploitation-revelation of voyeurism. This message has to do with the film's explicit mention of the problem generating a new kind of scarcity in the real world of sexual relations: AIDS. To my knowledge, no previous work of heterosexual pornography has directly mentioned the word, let alone overtly propagandized methods of prevention. (Gay male pornography has been much more responsible in this respect.) The safer-sex message of this film is illustrated in every sexual act and driven home by the mistress of ceremonies, a puppetlike doll named Wanda who functions as an Alfred Hitchcock–style host to the whole proceedings, at the beginning and end.

After the final freeze-frame on Gloria's exposed nudity, Wanda's face appears in close-up saying, "You get the message. You don't get VD or AIDS by holding hands or breathing the air—only by sharing body fluids. If you're going to have multiple sex partners, take Wanda's advice and play it safe. Good evening and good night."

The explicit and "progressive" message of this film is thus clearly a commendable one: use condoms, latex gloves, and spermicides if you want the kinds of pleasures herein depicted. This message "saves" hard-core film and video pornography from the charge of advocating promiscuous sexual practices that might be harmful to the health of its performers or consumers; moreover, it is a message that producers in the industry would do well to heed, for both the protection of their performers and the sexual education of viewers. The film's latent meaning, however, seems less sanguine about sexual relations than its overt and laudable safer-sex message, for the entire movie might well be interpreted as saying that physical relations between live human beings are actually very dangerous and best left to intangible fantasies. In reality, the film implies, the only person you need to touch is yourself.

It is significant, for example, that the main male and female protagonists, whose fantasies of sexual abundance are so enthusiastically depicted in this film, only come in contact with each other in a fantasy number framed by their mutual but separate spectatorial looks at the videotaped film *Behind the Green Door*. Here, voyeurism and fantasy safely distance the characters from actual physical contact. Hence, the masturbatory cinematic fantasy that projects the masturbator into the sexual events of the number (but without pretending that the number really happens) offers both an apotheosis and a vindication of voyeurism: the man and the woman are voyeurs whose pleasures are in watching and imagining—his even more so than hers, however, since he watches not only the film but also her watching. Considered this way, the physical incapacity of the film's wheelchair-confined voyeur could be read as a metaphor for the new incapacity of the AIDS-terrified spectator who finds in visual hard core the solution to his (and her) contradictory desire to engage in sex and yet to avoid sexual contact.

In *Behind the Green Door—The Sequel* we thus encounter a film that capitalizes on the very thing that embarrasses a great many other hard-core films: the spectator's inability to be present on the scene of the obscene. As Marc Vernet (1988–1989) has noted, the founding fact of cinematic discourse is that the various "looks" that articulate the medium—the look of the camera at the moment of filming, the look of characters in the moment of the film's diegesis, the look of spectators at the moment of projection—never coincide. Since the receiver of a look is always "in a place elsewhere" from where it was sent (p. 62), cinema is in its very structure a system of missed connections. Far from challenging the structure of cinematic articulation, Gloria's startled look back at the camera (or at the character of the vet spying on her, or at us looking at her) seems almost to celebrate a cinematic condition of absence and missed connection that is most desirable in pornography in the era of AIDS.

The darker side of the upbeat safer-sex message of this film thus resides in its recognition that we have now entered an age in which the problem of sexual relations can be defined in a way that would have been unthinkable in the stag film, that is, as the problem *of* relations per se: physical contact, connection, touch with the other. The solution to the problem of relations offered in this most prescient of hard-core films, then, is quite ambivalently hard-core. For if hard core means "sex itself," the message of this film is that instead of doing "it," we should be satisfied just watching other do it (voyeurism), which in turn means admitting "mechanical-electrical instruments," such as vibrators, or simply "electrical" instruments, such as VCRs, as fetish substitutes.

Feminine Re-Vision: "What's the Sex All About?"

The foregoing examples introduce some of the limitations of revision as simple modification—of just cleaning up the act of pornography so women will be less offended by it. A more fundamental *revision*, in Adrienne Rich's sense of seeing again with fresh eyes and from an entirely different, woman's point of view, would have to ask more questions of the genre: not only how to go about representing hard-core sex, but also, as the woman pornographer Candida Royalle puts it, determining just "what's the sex all about."

In asking this question of hard-core pornography for women, Royalle shows that she is far ahead of the simple revisionism game. The films of Femme, her predominantly female production company run with husband Per Sjostedt, have all the revisionist elements: aimed at couples, they have high production values, literate scripts, relatively good acting, handsome female *and* male performers, and abundant female fantasy. They also take time for extended "foreplay" and "afterplay." But the real importance of Femme is its serious attempt to visualize women's desire in a genre that has consistently continued to see sex, as even the films just discussed show, from the viewpoint of the phallus.

One important question for female pornographers is what to do with this phallus that has loomed so large in hard-core pornography. As we saw in the last chapter, the symbolic dominance of the phallus is not overthrown by the literal curtailment of the penis. The problem does not lie in the show of the penis itself; the elimination of the money shot does not address the root problems of power and pleasure that only *appear* to reside in this display. Genre, as we have seen, is not just a pattern of imagery, but the relation of this imagery to narrative structure. Hard-core pornography situates the iconography of sexual numbers in conjunction with certain kinds of narrative that permit the posing, and "solving," of problems of sexuality within strictly limited parameters.

If a heterosexual woman's desire is for a man, and if the man's sexual difference resides primarily in the penis, then how shall we represent woman's pleasure in pornography? Can it be represented as anything but envy of or submission to a penis that symbolizes phallic power and potency? Even in many "lesbian" numbers, the cinematic look at the woman is structured from the perspective of the phallus. Hiding the penis merely yields "soft core"; the phallus's power and dominance are still reproduced, only now in more indirect ways (see Donnerstein, Linz, and Penrod 1987, 90–91). Is it possible to represent the penis so that it is not also the phallus, that is, so that the penis is not asserted as the standard and measure of all desire? Although the elimination of the money shot noted in the revised sequels of *Deep Throat* and *Green Door* and in Chapter 6 is an apparent attempt to revise this standard, it does not constitute a thoroughgoing re-vision of sexual relations altogether.

I do not want to suggest that Femme Productions has the answers to the above questions or that these answers have successfully "revised" hard core. I do want to suggest, however, that since traditional forms of the genre have handled the question of female desire and pleasure in ways that seem to foreclose the possibility of its representation altogether, the very fact that a group of women hardcore pornographers is posing these questions makes them worthy of serious examination.

When the Goods Get Together

Luce Irigaray, in her collection of essays *This Sex Which Is Not One* (1985, 193), writes of the economy of masculine desire that is based on the exchange of women between men. Given the dominance of masculine desire, Irigaray asks, how can we account for sexual relationships between women? Routing her answer through Freud's notoriously blind (and phallic) account of femininity, she comes to the conclusion (p. 196) that female homosexuality has eluded psychoanalysis, to which the "interplay of desire among women's bodies, women's organs, women's language is inconceivable." Yet the fact that "female homosexuality does exist" is proof to Irigaray that there is another economy of desire, albeit one that so far has only been prostituted to men's fantasies. Because of this prostitution, she implies, it is out of the question for "female commodities" to "go to 'market' on their own, to enjoy their own worth among themselves, to speak to each other, to desire each other, free from the control of seller-buyer-consumer subjects." Hence Irigaray (p. 197) makes a utopian leap beyond the market altogether, imagining what would happen if female commodities *refused* to go to market, if they carried on instead "another" commerce among themselves: "Exchanges without identifiable terms, without accounts, without end . . . . Without standard or yardstick. . . . Use and exchange would be indistinguishable. . . . Pleasure without possession. . . . Utopia? Perhaps."

I would like to pursue here Irigaray's first suggestion, the one that precedes refusing to go to market and posits instead going there "on their own." The recent economic success of Femme Productions suggests that Irigaray's utopian leap beyond economics, patriarchy, and even men themselves, while important to imagine, may not be the only or best way to effect change in the reigning phallic economy. At any rate, it is worth examining what has happened within this economy when the "goods" do "get together" and go to market themselves.

In 1983 a group of well-known female porn stars got together, not to go to market, but to throw a baby shower for a fellow worker, Veronica Hart. In the process they began to talk about their common problems working in the industry. Soon they had formed a consciousness-raising support group called "Club 90," and out of that arose a collaboration with a feminist art group called Carnival Knowledge, which produced a theater piece entitled *Deep Inside Porn Stars* based on material produced at Club 90 meetings.[5] In an interview published in *Jump Cut* (Fuentes and Schrage 1987, 42), the women discussed their sense of themselves as feminists and their ambivalence about working in the porn industry. Although their ideas were vague at this point, talk focused on the lack of "realism" in hard-core films, as well as on poor-quality plots, character motivation, scripts, and acting. The group did, however, express the sense that new possibilities existed for women in pornography. This point was made most forcefully by Candida Royalle, both in the statement that is the epigraph to this chapter ("what's the sex all about") and in her observation that "we're the first generation of porn actresses to become stars." One question that apparently emerged from this consciousness-raising was what to do with the new "capital" residing in the star value of their own names.

What Royalle eventually did was form the production company Femme and enlist the Club 90 women as directors to make new pornography for women. In this unprecedented enterprise, then, we start to see the goods getting together—not to set up an alternative economy, but to reinvest the capital value of their names into a new product which they plan, create, and now have begun to distribute, marketing the product as a distinct line of "films" (actually all are shot on videotape). As the preview on the most recent of their videocassettes puts it, in the seductive voice of Royalle herself:

Finally there is Femme. Erotic film star Candida Royalle dares to bring to the screen the fantasies that women have been dreaming about all these years. Femme, conceived and produced by women, explores human desires from the exhilarating perspective of the woman who knows. . . . Discover the series: *Femme, Urban Heat, Three Daughters, Christine's Secret.* . . . Femme—it's only the beginning.

In another trailer Candida Royalle's voice informs us about her most recent project. She tells about the formation of the women's group and how its five central members, "adult's biggest stars" Gloria Leonard, Veronica Hart, Annie Sprinkle, Veronica Vera, and Royalle herself, have now produced three additional "volumes" of Femme, each tape consisting of two stories. After introducing all six segments and their stars, the trailer ends with the invitation to "come deep inside the minds of these famous women . . . as we bare our souls to you in Femme Productions' Star Directors Series."

Borrowing the time-honored rhetoric of hard core's quest for secrets, for taking viewers "deep inside," to the "wonders of the unseen world," Royalle and company have also turned this rhetoric around, posing their female selves as the different "explorers" of human desires who "know" that realm as well as the entrepreneurs. And since women are included in this address and the knowledge offered is not single but varied, more questions are generated. What is really different in this publicity, and in the films themselves, is the encouragement of more male-female conversations about sex, more give-and-take, more questioning of "what's the sex all about"—and much less answering exclusively from the perspective of the phallus.

The first two films of Femme Productions are *Femme* and *Urban Heat*, both directed by R. Lauren Neimi and produced by Royalle in 1984. Although one might have expected these films to have immediately countered the bad scripts, plots, and character motivations of the vast majority of hard-core features, the direction taken was quite the opposite. Instead of the better stories called for in the 1983 interview quoted above, these two tapes have almost no story at all. Both are a series of vignettes, six couplings per tape, each the approximate length of a stag film. Given that there is little or no dialogue (though there is a lot of unusually good original music), these single encounters are indeed quite similar in outward form to stags. It is as if discovering what the sex was all about necessitated a return to the genre's most basic form: the single number typical of the one-reel stag and a reexploration of the musical analogies so crucial to the hard-core "number."

The first number of *Urban Heat* (the uniting theme here is summer in the city) is exemplary. In a steamy disco bar with male and female flash dancers performing, a bartender and a waitress eye each other and sneak off to the basement. Their hard-core number in the basement is intercut with the dance number of a couple performing upstairs on the disco floor; at times the two numbers are superimposed. The hard-core number is executed like a dance: much of it is performed standing, with whole bodies and movements emphasized over body parts and fragmentary motions. In contrast, the upstairs, "legit" dance number grows increasingly sexual. Eventually, as the basement lovers complete their number, put back on their clothes, and go back to work, the upstairs dancers enter more deeply into the sexual nature of theirs: they take off clothes, dance naked, and are soon writhing on the floor. For quite a while, however, their movements remain stylized and the man's penis remains soft. Eventually the two sweating, naked bodies begin to touch, in fluid shifts from tongue kisses to cunnilingus to fellatio. But again, the framing is more in the whole-body, fluid style of Astaire and Rogers than the fragmented-body (separated) style of Busby Berkeley, a framing that permits the display of body lines and movements in unbroken space and time. Rhythms are developed by the intertwining of whole bodies, which perform for each other as well as the camera. The number ends on a full shot of the man on top of the woman, their arms and legs spread-eagled on the floor as the rhythm subsides and the camera pulls away.

In this number, and in many others from *Urban Heat* and *Femme*, there is a distinct shift from the confessional, voyeuristic mode of much feature-length narrative—a quality of catching bodies in the act of experiencing involuntary pleasures—to the performative mode of the jam session—a quality (akin to Astaire-Rogers) of bodies performing pleasurably for each other. Here the performers use their bodies as dancers do, acting out for their mutual benefit, and that of the audience, their responses and desires. This mode exists in some stag films—*The Nun's Story* (a.k.a. *The College Coed*), for instance, a justly famous (though traditional) stag of the early fifties with exceptionally fine production values and performances—and in other hard-core forms as well—the jam session from *Misty Beethoven* is an example in an integrated feature-length narrative. Yet this particular sense of a sustained and shared live performance is rare in these forms because the more important hard-core imperatives of providing visual evidence of "meat" and "money" have intervened, interrupting whatever mood, rhythm, or momentum the performers have established with their bodies in order to force and focus on the visual evidence of organ pleasure alone.

Not all the numbers produced by Femme have this exceptional

quality of performers performing spontaneously to and for each other. Still, more do than do not, since the filmmakers have opted to emphasize real time—that is, to establish the time, space, and duration of the performance rather than to assemble it afterward in the editing. Of course, this spatial-temporal "integrity" is meaningless if the performance itself is not good. Likewise, the judgment as to what constitutes a good performance is very much a matter of personal taste. Perhaps all that can be said for sure is that Femme productions make a consistent attempt to elicit "good" performances by providing the space, atmosphere, and mood in which they might occur and by shooting numbers in extended, long takes that can exploit these qualities to best advantage. At its best, this procedure can produce sequences like that described above; at its worst, it simply dresses up performance with foregrounded potted plants. Nevertheless, the ability to shoot numbers in long takes has been one of the few aesthetic advantages of the recent shift to video recording and away from the more expensive (and better-looking) 35 mm film.

Another number from *Urban Heat* illustrates this new importance of integral time and space, particularly in portraying a woman's desire. An attractive woman walks down the street in an industrial part of town. She passes a younger man in a T-shirt, pauses to look at him, and goes on. A moment later she enters a freight elevator and finds herself alone with the same man, who is operating the elevator. Suddenly her hand extends over his to force the elevator to a stop. They kiss. She removes her dress and then his T-shirt. He kisses her breasts and, half undressed, they begin to perform with great abandon in this space. For the first half of the number the man's penis, like that of the male dancer, remains soft.

In most of the numbers discussed in this book, male softness at this point in the proceedings would be out of place, a sign of impotence. Indeed, Stephen Ziplow's *Film Maker's Guide to Pornography* advises pornographers to employ "fluffers"—women whose job off camera is to keep the men hard for the action. In this elevator scene, however, when the emphasis is already on what whole bodies are doing in a fictional space and time with a particular mood and atmosphere, the softness of the penis simply permits the rest of the body to perform; here the dominating image is of the suddenly aroused woman's position backed up against the wall of the elevator while the man performs cunnilingus. We do not sense that the sole goal of the number is for the male organ to perform. It does perform, finally, but not as the climax or end of the action. Even when the number seems over, after a prolonged, post-passion comedown and after the elevator bell rings and the couple hurriedly dress, the final fade-out shows them beginning to rub up against each other again.

Each of these numbers offers a utopian fantasy of sex occurring in a dissolved world that neither separates the number from nor integrates it into a different register of narrative reality. Even the disco club number, which we first perceive as proceeding on two separate levels, one more fantastic and utopian than the other, works, through superimposition and similarity of performance, to dissolve the differences between the downstairs sex that is like a dance and the upstairs dance that becomes sex. Each of these numbers, too, has a particularly utopian quality simply in that they are continuously pleasurable, not divided into discrete fragments.

As we saw in Chapter 6, the dissolved form of hard core is as escapist as the separated form, but in contrast to the latter its effect is to deemphasize the separation between the real world and utopian sexual fantasy. In the dissolved musical, for example, the pleasure of the musical number seems to arise naturally out of the nostalgic, glamorous, or stylized features of the utopian place—the place where it is easy to break into song and dance without feeling ridiculous. In dissolved hard core, the important feature is not so much the stylized unreal look of the place but the fact that there people, especially women, can enact their desires without fear of punishment, guilt, or self-consciousness. In this sense, the elevator or dance floor of *Urban Heat* is like Sandra Chase's mansion and swimming pool in *Insatiable*. Though very different spaces, all are simultaneously safe and exciting places where women can be sexual without being labeled nymphomaniacs, femmes fatales, or simply bad. We have only to compare the dissolved elevator sex of *Urban Heat* to the integrated, soft-core elevator sex of *Fatal Attraction* (Adrian Lyne, 1987) to appreciate the difference.

The third Femme film, *Christine's Secret* (Candida Royalle and R. Lauren Neimi, 1984), is also dissolved narrative, about the visit of its title character to a country inn. Everyone at "Love's Inn" except Christine is happily coupling with a partner, from the husband

and wife proprietors who go at it each morning, to their daughter and the hired hand, to a honeymooning guest couple. Christine, however, masturbates alone and fantasizes fleetingly about a mysterious slender youth who seems to be waiting for her in a nearby cabin. Against the background of the proprietor couple's bed slats going "blam de blam in the morning," the newlyweds' cries of pleasure, and the daughter and hired hand's rolls in the hay, Christine's sexual desire mounts.

The simple device of keeping Christine and her young man apart, except in occasional fantasy brushes, sustains suspense throughout this seventy-two-minute film. One of these fantasies is a remarkably graceful sequence in which Christine, on a tree swing, imagines herself swinging naked with legs spread in slow motion up to the waiting arms and mouth of her young man. This cunnilingus on a swing, enhanced with optical effects of slow motion, repetition, and superimposition, is a lyrical re-vision of the acrobatic pyrotechniques of *Behind the Green Door*'s fellatio on a swing.

The reasons for Christine and her lover's separation are kept vague. A brief line of dialogue explains something about class differences. The youth himself never says a word: he simply stands by a window gazing across the distance that separates him from Christine, waiting, we find out at the end, for her to come to him. Before this happens, though, both further demonstrate their desire for the other in solitary masturbatory numbers performed near windows that frame the space between them. The man's masturbation is particularly interesting for its languid eroticization of nonphallic parts of his body—his abdomen especially. When he finally ejaculates, it is in a full shot that shows his entire body and the space into which his ejaculate falls.

The finale lives up to its buildup. At dawn, as everyone else at Love's Inn sleeps (except the proprietor couple, who have already started in on their bed slats), Christine runs barefoot across the field that has separated her from the youth's cabin. She enters and without a word they begin to make love. She pays particular attention to his abdomen, kissing the entire area that has been previously eroticized for the viewer by the look of the camera. He remains soft a long time, and this softness, like the attention to his abdomen, seems to arouse Christine all the more, for now she can watch him slowly grow hard to her touch. The scene is romantic, intense, passionate. Sweat beads form on both their bodies, a criss-cross of shadows from the window is thrown on them. He kisses her lightly all over as she stretches out on a couch near the window. Then he performs cunnilingus and lies on top of her. Later he penetrates her from the rear; she cries out and strokes her clitoris and clutches him. Finally they lie together exhausted, without speaking.

Although this film has a rudimentary narrative, *Christine's Secret* is more dissolved than integrated. Love's Inn is a summer vacation utopia where images of nature merge with those of sex. The only narrative tension is the separation between Christine and the youth. Christine's secret is more private than guilty. Her aloneness while everyone else couples is presented not as unhappiness, but as the cultivation of a desire that in the end allows a greater satisfaction than achieved by anyone else in this sexual utopia.

This cultivation and exploration of specifically female desire is especially evident in all the Femme films. The narratively integrated *Three Daughters* (Candida Royalle, 1986) exemplifies this orientation best. More the film one might have expected from women pornographers making hard core for women, this melodramatic family saga of, for hard core, almost epic length (108 minutes—a good 20 minutes longer than most hard-core films) treats the sexual lives of an entire upper-middle-class family one summer when all three daughters are at home. Every couple—daughters and boyfriends, even mom and dad—has at least one number that is motivated by and integrated into the narrative. With this extended cast of characters, the film is unparalleled in hard core.

Three Daughters is centered on the sexual awakening of Heather, the youngest, who has begun to be aroused by observing the sexual activities of her older sisters. The narrative plays out the drama of the older sisters' romances against the mounting tension of Heather's newfound desire. One sister, a concert pianist, is observed by Heather as she interrupts her piano lesson for a roll around the shag rug with her male teacher (he has advised her to play pianissimo rather than hectic and frantic). As in many Femme films, the sexual number takes its cue from the musical number: the sex that follows is in close synchronization with the rhythms of a jazz score.

Later, in bed alone, Heather reads sex manuals. She alternates reading (we hear the words in voice-over), looking at drawings of female anatomy, and investigating her own anatomy with a hand mirror. She begins to stroke herself and discovers a wetness that surprises her. We see the anatomical drawings from the book, hear her voice read about how to massage, and then see superimposed flashbacks of her sister's encounter with her teacher-lover. As with Christine's fantasy of herself on the swing, we share Heather's imagination of her own pleasure. As she begins to masturbate in earnest, the screen goes red. Heather has done something quite unusual for a woman in a hard-core film: she has become curious, watched others, investigated her own body and desire, and satisfied herself—for the moment—with the power of her own imaginings. She settles down quite happily to sleep.

Heather's sexual awakening continues as she has occasion to see another sister make love with her fiancé. Soon her desires are focused on this fiancé's friend, Paul, with whom she mildly flirts at a family engagement party. In the meantime, however, her college-age friend Susan helps her along in a "lesbian" number. In terms of the narrative, this scene explicitly serves to prepare Heather for the big heterosexual finale with Paul. Thus, like "lesbian" numbers in most heterosexual pornography, it is not presented *as* lesbian; but unlike typical hard core, here "lesbian" sex is shown to be a desirable stage of self-exploration in which one girl helps another, younger girl discover her pleasure. Significantly also, it occurs in the context of the two girls' conversation about pornography. Susan shows Heather a male porno magazine. Heather questions her: "Do you do those things? What's it like?" Susan answers that she does now but that she "practiced beforehand with girls." Heather is entirely passive as Susan begins to "practice" on her; after she has been brought to pleasure, though, she begins to explore Susan's body and pleasure herself. The scene ends in affectionate giggles.

What is different about this "lesbian" sex is not what the two women do but rather for whom the sex is intended. In the context of Heather's developing sexuality, which the film takes seriously in its soap opera way, this number has the important function of exploring Heather's desire before she encounters the more insistent probing and investigation of the penis. In this sense, the film can be seen as the narrative quest of the virgin not simply to have a desire of her own before she comes face-to-face with the symbol, and reality, of male desire but, as in the images framing the masturbation scene, to begin to visualize what this desire comprises. The utopia of *Three Daughters* thus encompasses more than just the sexual abundance of the Clayton family, in which everyone is satisfied; it also embraces the specifically feminine, maternal, and melodramatic quest for desire itself.

It is worth noting in this connection a vignette from the first Femme Productions tape, *Femme*. Entitled "Sales Pitch," it shows a beauty products saleswoman showing her wares to another woman in the second woman's home. From face makeup the saleswoman moves to body makeup, applying powder and rouge to breast and nipples, lotion to legs, until soon she is caressing the customer's body all over and the customer reciprocates. What is remarkable in this vignette, however, is that there is no further development. No man walks in on them, no further wantonness occurs, there is no shame or guilt. The saleslady, a little flushed, puts back on her clothes, and the customer says good-humoredly that all she really wants is a lipstick. The "climax" has occurred, and it had nothing to do with a male organ. We are a far cry from the scene in *Throat— Twelve Years After* in which the woman calls out to her male prostitute, contrasting sex with him to a memory of sex with a woman: "Do to me what no woman can do, fuck me harder!"

A key issue in many of the Femme films—and the answer to the question "what's the sex all about"—would therefore seem to be how to make a woman the hero-subject of the sexual narrative without, as in the sadomasochistic films, making her a victim-hero as well. A key strategy in constructing this hero-subject is to focus on dramas of female sexual awakening that offer utopian re-visions of the often furtive, hasty, and guilt-ridden ways most young women attain their sexuality. While it is not surprising that the melodramatic mode of *Three Daughters* provides the fullest context for exploration of these feelings, fuller plot and more realistic character motivation may not be what makes this hard-core soap opera work; rather, underlying this film's success is the simpler fact that "realism" functions here, in this integrated form, much as it functions in the non-integrated dissolved form—to provide better reasons and motivations for the sex. These better reasons do not necessarily need a more elaborate plot; they just need to develop the one thing that cinematic hard core, and indeed all forms of narrative film, have had great difficulty representing with any conviction: woman's desire.

Here we come to the crux of the issue of hard-core power *and* pleasure for women. The project of representing woman's desire is not simply a matter of subduing the phallus or curtailing its symbolization; rather, as Jessica Benjamin argues in "A Desire of One's Own" (1986), it is a matter of replacing the monopoly on the sexual subjectivity that this phallus stands for, its monolithic symbolization of desire. As we saw in the last chapter, this dominance is one of the reasons for female masochism, for masochism, as a way of achieving pleasure without also taking on the appearance of power, eschews the control and agency associated with phallic mastery that is so foreign to the construction of "normal" female subjectivity.

To Benjamin, masochism is an alienated and devious way of becoming a hero-subject, and the price paid for this accomplishment is victimization. Yet Benjamin also posits a deeper cause for this alienated female sexual subjectivity, and that is the construction of female identity based on an original identification with the figure of the mother, a figure rigorously de-eroticized by much Western culture. In a traditional family situation, even before the oedipal stage, the paradox for all children is that they need to be recognized as independent by the very person they once depended on. Benjamin argues that what both the boy and the girl need at this point and later is to be recognized as subjects of desire. Boys, she says, get through this phase with more bravado and less depression than girls because in reconciling dependence and independence they can turn for identification to the outside, exciting figure of the father. By recognizing himself in the subject of desire that is the father, the boy can deny the helplessness he feels (Benjamin 1986, 87).

Desire, in this context, is linked to freedom, excitement, and the outside world—not only, as some theorists have suggested, to separation from the mother. So when we speak of the woman's difficulty in "owning" desire, the problem is not that of the little girl's "missing penis" or, as Teresa de Lauretis (1984, 67) writes, of making "visible the invisible"; rather, it is "to construct the terms of another frame of reference, another measure of desire" (p. 68). Nor is the problem anatomical; it has to do, Benjamin insists, not with the missing penis but with the missing father, with the difficulty the little girl has routing her identification through a being attached to the exciting world outside. Women do not envy the penis; instead the theory of penis envy in Freudian thought fills a gap left in the theory of the girl's subjectivity. This gap is really her need to identify with a sexual agent—an agent who could just as well be the mother if the mother was also associated with the outside and articulated as a sexual subject of desire. The problem, in short, is social.

Benjamin's ideas offer an interesting challenge to the way many psychoanalytic feminists have posed the question of feminine sexuality. These theorists, following Lacan, tend to see the problem of woman's desire as located precisely in her different relation to the phallus and thus to symbolization in general. Although psychoanalytic feminists often speak of the importance of the social in the construction of gendered subjects of desire, the theory of the subject revolves so entirely around the phallus as primary signifier, and around castration as the loss that engenders desire, that history and social change often seem inconsequential beside the fixed universality of sexual polarities. In this view, then, social change cannot affect the primacy of the phallus, nor is it possible to imagine desire not being ruled by the phallus.[6]

Jessica Benjamin's interest in a "desire of one's own" is more in line with the ideas of object relations feminists, who view gender and desire as formed through identifications with objects—mothers, fathers—that exist in the social world and are therefore subject to change.[7] Although Benjamin's explanation differs from that of the object relations group in many ways, what seems most pertinent here is Benjamin's use of object relations to suggest, as Nancy Chodorow has suggested in another context, that the problems of female subjectivity and agency are not insurmountable if only we can break with traditional sex-role associations. One part of a real-world solution to the representation of desire thus concerns the social construction of mothers as sexual subjects. Since mothers actually *are* sexual subjects (though hardly ever in movies), such a solution is not beyond the pale; it means that the time-honored notion of the father as belonging exclusively to the outside world of freedom and the mother as belonging exclusively to the inside world of safety and holding needs to be changed—both in the real world and in our representations.

Pornography for women could be, and to a certain extent already is, an important arena for this change, especially if it is a pornography that can combine the holding and nurturing of motherhood with sexual representation. As noted before, pornography is one of the few areas of narrative where women are not punished or found guilty for acting on their sexual desires, even when these desires, as in the long-running *Taboo* series, are incestuous. Seen in this light, the lovemaking of mom and dad in the attic in *Three Daughters* is significant. Just as the daughter is discovering her sexual subjectivity, mom (played by veteran porn actress Gloria Leonard) is reawakening hers in anticipation of being alone with her husband again. But showing the parents rediscovering desire does not solve the immediate problem, confronted by many Femme films and addressed by Benjamin's essay as well, of how to represent woman's desire *visually*. Although plenty of female genitals are displayed in all hardcore pornography, and in *Three Daughters* we even see Heather looking at drawings and investigating her own genitals with a mirror, the answer is not simply to provide an alternative symbol, Judy Chicago–style, with which to replace the phallus. For the real issue is not the symbol at all, but rather what it stands for—and the vulva traditionally does not stand for the exciting movement to the outside, the exploratory freedom and agency, associated with sexual subjectivity. Indeed, as Teresa de Lauretis (1984, 118–124) has shown, too often it has been the place to which such agency comes.

More important than an object or symbol, then, which might function only as a fetishistic substitute for the phallus, is, as Benjamin suggests, the creation of an "intersubjective space," a space of exchange between people in which, by being with the other, one also experiences a profound sense of self. In this space the woman's interior is experienced as part of her own being, as an extension of the space between her and the other, and not as a passive object or place to be discovered (Benjamin 1986, 92).

We encounter something like this space in the most recent work of the Femme Productions "Star Directors Series," *Sensual Escape* (Gloria Leonard and Candida Royalle, 1987). A half-hour segment directed by Candida Royalle and called "The Tunnel" begins with a young woman artist and her disturbing dream about a writhing male torso that appears to beckon her into a forbidden space. We see the woman, in a spiderweb garment, move through the surreal space of the tunnel, where religious statuary lines the walls, yet she fails to discover the place where the male body beckons.

In her waking hours the woman tries to draw the image of this male body, but its face remains blank. The young woman's voice-over informs us: "My life just isn't mine . . . all I can think about is this dream. I've never been able to relate to men." We see her reject the advances of a fellow artist in a café. Similar dreams follow. In a park in winter she meets a man who, when she says she's an artist, asks to see her hands. Briefly their ungloved fingers touch. When she leaves he invites her to come see him "in the tunnel," and she runs away. At home she now draws herself into the space of the painting, and the face of the man in the park onto the male body.

In another moment—probably another dream, although this is not clear—the woman visits a space that resembles but also differs from her original dream. She walks along a railroad track that disappears into the tunnel. She seems to be looking for the phantom man. But instead of the writhing, naked (except for pelvis cloth) body of the man on the pedestal, the man from the park emerges from the tunnel's depths. Images from earlier dreams blend with this image. The man from the park begins to help her onto the pedestal, but she runs away along the length of the tunnel and out onto the tracks. Stopping suddenly, she looks back at the man and retraces her steps. This movement back into the tunnel visually merges with shots of the first dream's track forward toward the writhing male torso. Only when the two versions of herself arrive at the same goal—the man and the pedestal—does the video's first number begin. This number continues to dissolve the differences between the space and action of the dream (distinguished by the woman's spider garment) and the space and action of the present scene (whether dream or reality) with the man from the park. This emphasis on the *journey to* the number suggests the importance of the woman's own imagination and fantasy in creating the scene of her pleasure; it also suggests that her imagination and fantasy do well to make the journey on their own, beckoned by a vague figure whose own desires remain temporarily unknown.

In this utopian dream merged with reality, getting ready for sex *is* sex. Foreplay, afterplay, and all the possible measuring distinctions of stages, amounts of arousal, and degrees of intensity blur; one can no longer say that the sex takes place at a single moment or in a single event. As the woman grows more and more excited, we see an image of her body breaking through a caul-like latex barrier in an action reminiscent of the removal of the gloves that earlier had prevented the couple's hands from touching. At this juncture, this instant of breakthrough and birth, of emergence from an inside into an outside, the woman finally touches the man. (So far he has done all the touching.) The implication is that only now is she ready to be a subject of desire. Now, too, the more complex rhythms of two bodies responding to each other's touch really begin. They continue for the duration of the number, with touch occurring along the length of their bodies and never only by the penis—which, indeed, we never even see.

The space of this tunnel, the imaginary space of the seeking, imagining, image-making woman's encounter with another, offers an excellent analog to the intersubjective space that Benjamin describes as being so important to female desire and subjectivity. What the woman artist finds in her fantasy is similar to what Benjamin argues girls need to get from both their mothers *and* their fathers: identification with the agency that explores and moves toward the outside and excitement, as well as identification with inside safety and security. The tunnel is simultaneously the outer, exciting space she must explore with excitement *and* the interior space of herself. For the woman's journey to have ended in the discovery of the phallus would have been inappropriate—not because the penis should always be suppressed for woman's own desire to emerge, but because this particular representation functions as an allegory of the journey to one's own desire.

It is perhaps significant, then, that when the woman awakes from her dream, she goes to her easel and draws what she could not draw before: the man and woman with faces—in an embrace. Here we encounter a feminine re-vision of pornography's new emphasis and its address to the couple. Proof that it is re-vision, and not just revision, resides in the very foregrounding of the woman's problem concerning how to represent the embrace. "The Tunnel" thus illustrates what, according to Benjamin, women require if they are to become something other than mere receptacles for the desires of male subjects: inside safety and holding as well as outside projection and excitement. The railroad tracks traversed by the woman represent this intersubjective space.

If I understand Benjamin correctly, what is at stake here for women's sexual subjectivity is a self-discovery associated with discovering one's inside—an inside that can only be known, however, through a trajectory that also takes one to the exciting outside. The recognition of one's own sexual subjectivity and outward agency comes, then, from the desire for access to one's own interior. Citing Carol Gilligan's work on the myth of Psyche, Benjamin (1986, 96) stresses the importance for women of achieving sexual awakening in a state of benign aloneness, as a counter to the overfamiliar state of being an idealized object.

We saw in the last chapter that the sadomasochist deviously seeks recognition from the "other" of a desire that comes from within the self. For women a more direct recognition of the desire of the self begins with its very discovery, through a balance of inward holding and outward excitement. This balance is important to consider, I think, in evaluating pornography for women. Much male criticism of this subgenre is that it is too tame, not transgressive, taboo, dangerous, or exciting enough. This may be true, but perhaps only for men.

A case in point is culture critic Andrew Ross's response to Femme Productions pornography, a response that differs from my own. Ross (forthcoming) argues that Femme works play on an association of the "feminine" with tastefulness and fine art, to the detriment of sexual excitement. Citing a half-hour segment entitled "The Pick Up" (Veronica Hart, 1988), from the tape *A Taste of Ambrosia*, Ross complains that the work is overly concerned with "educating" proper viewer desires. The episode shows a man and woman in separate spaces dressing to go out. The woman does dishes, puts away children's toys, bathes, dresses, puts on excessive makeup, and dons high heels. Out on the street men eye her. The man we saw dressing picks her up. They go to a drugstore, buy a condom, and then go to an apartment where they drink and make love, using the condom. Ultimately it is revealed that they are a married couple with children: we see their photo in the room. The woman's mother is at that very moment babysitting at home. The drugstore condom was thus part of their pretense to illicit sex. As Ross puts it, it is the signifier of eroticism for the film as a whole. The film's credits then offer yet another level of tameness: the information (now on all the company's credits) that Femme "utilizes safe sex techniques except where the talent are real-life lovers."

To Ross this statement "compromises the erotic status of the fantasy," which he believes needs to be a world apart from real sexual life. Yet as I have argued with my analysis of separated, integrated, and dissolved film, various distinctions between reality and utopia are posited in hard core. Ross, then, may be quite naturally conflating hard core as a whole with what I call its separated and dissolved forms. Nonetheless, "The Pick Up" is best described as an integrated work, in which the narrative problem that the sexual number solves—married familiarity—is not introduced until the end, after it has already been "solved."

Ross's larger point, though, is that all attempts to "educate desire" by pornography, or by intellectual talk about pornography, are doomed if they aim too earnestly at correcting what is wrong, unruly, or unhealthy about sex.[8] The education of desire, he insists, is a "turnoff" inimical to the very production of pleasure that is pornography's first goal. Now, I agree that education can be a turnoff and that the "education of desire," if understood as a form of correction, is therefore potentially problematic. I also agree that Femme Productions tends to play it safe with an overemphasis on prettiness. But I would ask Ross, who is getting turned off here, men or women? For female viewers, traditionally less adventurous and exploratory for the reasons outlined above, the mixture of safety with excitement that this scenario offers may be just what is needed *for* excitement. Perhaps the education of desire is not such a bad idea for a group that traditionally has lacked, as Jessica Benjamin puts it, "a desire of one's own." Like Virginia Woolf's eminently practical argument for a woman's having "a room of one's own," the excitement of this desire is contingent on the possession of a safe, interior space that knows itself and is comfortable with itself; only when these criteria are satisfied can a guest be invited to visit. So perhaps this education of desire need not be a matter finally of someone at the top telling someone else at the bottom how to cultivate desire, but precisely a re-vision by those at (or on) the bottom of the nature of the places and positions in which sexual relations can occur.

If the new pornography for couples and women exemplified by Femme Productions seems safe, almost too legitimate for some masculine eyes, it could be that this legitimacy is needed to enable women to create for themselves the safe space in which they can engage in sex without guilt or fear. And if mothers are to be erotic and adventurous as well as nurturing and holding, then why not this image of the married mother washing the dishes and cleaning the house before she goes out on the street to seek excitement with a "john" who is really her husband? This much is clear: it is no longer for men alone to decide what is, or is not, exciting in pornography.

Conclusion

Not a Love Story . . .

In the documentary film about the hard-core pornography industry *Not a Love Story* (Bonnie Klein, 1982), various feminists who have led the fight against pornography speak emotionally about the horrors and harms invading from this industry's nether world. The sensationalist—even pornographic—presentational mode of this documentary about a stripper who discovers the error of her ways has already been cogently criticized by feminist film scholars as diverse as B. Ruby Rich (1982) and E. Ann Kaplan (1987). What interests me here, however, is an unusually thoughtful moment in a film whose moral outrage against pornography otherwise leaves little room for thoughtfulness. Writer Kate Millett sits on her floor at home surrounded by her own erotic drawings of women. Like the other women in this film, she expresses the familiar lament that pornography is not "a love story": "We got pornography, and what we needed was eroticism." The drawings seem to stand for the nonexplicit eroticism that women allegedly need in place of explicit "hard core."

This separation between eroticism and pornography is typical of the anti-pornography position and consistent with the argument of the rest of the film. The very next moment, however, Millett adds something less typical, even inconsistent: "There is some usefulness in explicitness," she says; it can help us get over "dreadful patriarchal ideas that sex is evil and that the evil in it is women." Although I disagree with the film in which she appears, I agree with Millett about this "usefulness in explicitness." As I hope my own study has shown, explicit pornography can teach us many things about power and pleasure that once seemed mystified and obscure. But explicitness alone cannot lay bare the "truth" of pornography's "dreadful patriarchal ideas." And if we limit ourselves to using the explicit sensationally, to condemn men's sex as evil, then we have not used it to our best advantage; we have not demystified sex, we have only reversed the "dreadful patriarchal ideas that sex is evil and that the evil in it is women."

Not a Love Story performs just this kind of reversal in those instances when it cites explicit pornography. For example, in a scene immediately preceding the one in which Millett appears, a woman porn photographer conducts a still photo session with a male and a female model. She is curt and callous as she directs a scene depicting a leering pirate with a long penis hovering over an innocent maiden. To emphasize the unnaturalness of the pirate and maiden's pose, we see the woman photographer manipulating the phallic props of sword, knife, and even penis while joking about the degree of erection (limit of explicitness) permitted by the magazine that employs her. The scene ends almost ludicrously with the male model trying to hold an awkward stance and asking the photographer, "Do you want me to hide the dick?"

The problem with *Not a Love Story* is that it proceeds as if suppressing the "dick" could solve all the sexual problems of patriarchal power. By showing us the penis in its attitude of threat over the passive female victim, the film uses explicitness to mock and demystify the symbolic power of the phallus. This feminist critique of explicit pornography fails, however, precisely in its attack on the literal organ of the penis. Satisfied simply to deride the organ of presumed male power itself rather than the system of oppositions by which the symbolic meaning of the penis is constructed, the critique does not even approach the discursive root of the problem of pornography and sexual representations for feminism. The explicit representation in pornography of (not just ordinary but quite spectacular) penises makes it all too easy to locate the oppressor in this organ. In attacking the penis we seem to attack the phallic authority that it symbolizes as well. But the tempting conflation of meaning between the two accedes to the impossibility of change. We would do well to remember, therefore, that the phallus is fundamentally not real and not possessed by anyone. In psychoanalytic theory, it is the illusion of the power of generation, the control of meaning, the belief in an integral unity of self that no one actually attains but everyone desires. A penis, in contrast, is an organ that men really have. Hardcore pornography is not phallic because it shows penises; it is phallic because in its exhibition of penises it presumes to know, to possess an adequate expression of the truth of "sex"—as if sex were as unitary as the phallus presumes itself to be. While the physiology of sex is not likely to change, its gendered meanings can. In attacking the penis rather than the phallus, anti-pornography feminism evades the real sources of masculine power.

Certainly the explicit can be useful for observing the difficulties that women encounter in the meanings attached to the organs of biological difference. Yet the "frenzy of the visible" in which contemporary sexual representations are caught is not inimical to women because it is explicit and visible; it is inimical to women because even its obsessive focus on the female body proves to be a narcissistic evasion of the feminine "other" deflected back to the masculine self.

Even if we were to accept the anti-pornography opposition between an explicit/bad/male pornography and a nonexplicit/good/female erotica, it is not at all clear that the censoring of one would produce the flowering of the other. As Edward Donnerstein's research shows (see Chapter 7), nonexplicit sexual representations can be more hierarchical and violent than explicit, X-rated ones; moreover, they appear to be just as effective at "teaching" callous attitudes toward sexual violence against women as explicit violent pornography.

This book has argued that the "frenzy of the visible" of cinematic hard-core pornography is *not* a self-evident truth; it is a system of representations with its own developmental history and its own historically changing gender relations. The most central feature of this history has been the increasing problematization of that seemingly natural and universal thing called sex. Sex, in the sense of a natural, biological, and visible "doing what comes naturally," is the supreme fiction of hard-core pornography; and gender, the social construction of the relations between "the sexes," is what helps constitute that fiction.

Pornography as a genre wants to be about sex. On close inspection, however, it always proves to be more about gender. The raw materials of sexual difference are dramatically at play in pornography, but they take on meaning only because consumers already have gender: they have, in effect, been engendered in discourse. Sex only *seems* to speak directly and explicitly in hard-core moving images because the rhetoric of the genre works diligently to convince us that we are witnessing the involuntary confession of so many "indiscreet jewels." Yet hard core, understood as a material, mechanical, measurable moment of truth, proves to be something of a chimera. Although phallic power tries to erect the penis as the unity symbol of plenitude, the truth is that no single organ or entity can perform such a function. This does not mean, of course, that the genre will stop trying; genre films thrive, after all, on the very persistence of the problems that they set out to solve. But it does mean that a new insistence on these problems opens up a space for challenging phallic symbolizations.

The overview presented in this book of the key moments in the history of hard-core cinema shows that even a genre looked on as the last bastion of masculine, phallic discourse has been in crisis over the changes occurring in the gendered relations between the sexes—most noticeably in the new, legal films and videos produced since the early seventies and coinciding with the challenge by the women's movement of male power and privilege. The full assessment of this challenge and its repercussions in diverse sexual discourses remains to be done. I argue only that in filmic hard-core pornography, the "self-evident" is not as self-evident as it seems: it is simply not possible to regard a represented penis per se as a literal instance of male dominance. I realize, however, that the order of this study, with its end on the recent sequels and revisions (or re-visions) by women of a male-centered hard core, may imply somewhat dubious progress. While I believe that the genre *has* progressed, in the sense of challenges to the viewpoint of the phallus, this progress is not a simple movement from one thoroughly misogynist to a less misogynist and finally to a feminist stage—or from stag film to problematizing feature-length narrative to Femme. Examples of all the films and videos discussed in this book can be found at any adult video outlet. Even stags have been resurrected as "classics," recycled onto compilation videotapes much like the nostalgic, *That's Entertainment*-style highlight films of the movie musical past.

Now that most pornography is shot and distributed directly on video, without first opening in a theater or receiving the notoriety of a work collectively witnessed by a large group, the text's temporal context is even less apparent. The tape slips onto a shelf, is rented or not, and its possible sociological or historical impact recedes into the background. This apparent timelessness, though, is only the illusion of a group of texts that the parent culture would prefer to disown; part of the challenge of reading them is to put them back into time, to note the historical demarcations in the seeming monolith, the way they are as much about change as about repetition.

To many the distinctions I have drawn between various kinds of texts will, I am sure, seem trivial compared to the overwhelming similarity of sexually performing bodies and organs. The difference, for example, between the original (1972) version of *Behind the Green Door* and its 1986 sequel may appear insignificant to someone unused to seeing sex on a screen. As separated forms of pornotopia, in which sexual utopia is divorced from the real world of its narrative, both represent the most escapist and misogynist form of the genre. Yet even though separation is the most escapist of the three feature-length hard-core film types, and thus the least responsive to women's demands to be regarded as subjects, the differences between the two *Green Door* versions suggest new approaches to the ever evolving problems of power and pleasure between the sexes.

A much more detailed textual, historical, and sociological inquiry will be needed before we can say with any security what changes have taken place in a genre that produces close to two thousand films and tapes annually and that accounts for about 9 percent of all videotape rentals.[1] Certainly we need more information about audiences, especially with regard to class, race, and ethnicity, before we can suggest what uses the genre performs within different groups. Pornography by women may prove only a brief phase in the history of hard core; Femme Productions attempts, for example, could fail in the long run, being too "arty" for most men and still too "hard core" for most women. My argument is simply that hard core has changed, that it is a genre more like other genres than unlike them, and that although it is still very patriarchal, it is not a patriarchal monolith.

Let us return to Beverley Brown's definition of pornography quoted in Chapter 1: "a coincidence of sexual phantasy, genre and culture in an erotic organization of visibility." We are now in a better position to consider the significance of these coinciding elements. Most important of all, perhaps, is the very fact of coincidence itself, that pornography is not one thing, but sexual fantasy, genre, culture, and erotic visibility all operating together. And if fantasy, coming from the deepest regions of the psyche, is most resistant to change, then genre and culture are most capable of change.

As a theory committed to change, Marxism, as well as the culture criticism to which it has contributed, has offered the most "progressive" approach to this analysis. Moving beyond the earlier Marxist critique of mass culture as false consciousness, recent Marxist culture criticism attempts to see how social rupture and change can be inscribed in a generic form. In this respect pornotopia is not unlike other utopias: it, too, undertakes to solve problems that the texts tacitly acknowledge.[2] By emphasizing the similarity between the familiar movie musical and contemporary hard core, I have tried to isolate the phenomenon of utopian problem solving as accomplished through body performance—of utopian "numbers" that represent solutions to narrative problems. This extended analogy to the musical has allowed us to assess qualities of body performance that, although inherent to hard core, are often overlooked because sex, in contrast to song and dance, appears so natural and unperformed. I have therefore emphasized the reverse of the truism that dance in the musical is really about sex by suggesting the ways in which sexual numbers are like dance; in showing how sexual performances are choreographed, placed in a scene, and deployed within a narrative context, I have tried to get beyond the "fact" of sex to its rhetorical function in texts.

Much less utopian and less committed to change is the psychoanalytic component of this study, encapsulated in the "sexual phantasy" portion of Brown's definition. In many ways, sexual fantasy, though itself an escape from reality, functions as the limit to change and progress in the genre, just as psychoanalysis often functions as a theoretical limit to change in the human psyche. Despite the many reservations that can be leveled against it, psychoanalytic theory has proved an unavoidable partial explanation of the desires that drive sexual fantasy and pornography.

The question, of course, is just how far to take an explanatory system that is frequently blind to the subjectivity of women, a dilemma that my discussion of fetishism elucidates. While the explanatory power of fetishism with regard to male fantasies of the female body is undeniable, the sticking point in the understanding of these perversions—the reason they have had to be engaged from a feminist perspective rather than simply adopted unquestioned—rests on the undeniable fact that the theory itself is constructed from the perspective of a phallus that perceives the female anatomy as "lacking." Nevertheless, fetishism continues to have explanatory power in pornography because it points to the remarkably substitutive nature of desire: the fact that anything and everything can come to stand in for the original object of desire.

To the degree that pornography has been articulated from an exclusively male point of view, it is not surprising that the hard-core fetish par excellence has been the "money shot." But we have also seen that this particular "erotic organization of visibility" cannot satisfy the genre's increasing curiosity to see and know the woman's pleasure. The single viewpoint of the phallus thus tends to frustrate the increasingly polymorphous desires of the genre to see and know all pleasure. Even the money shot, perhaps the most dramatic conjunction of fetishism and phallicism in the whole of hard-core cinema, proves ambiguous, expressing a crisis of representation in a genre that must now include something its tradition of the involuntary "frenzy of the visible" was ill equipped to represent: visual evidence of female pleasure. The money shot can thus be regarded as a perverse substitute for more direct representations of genital pleasure, just as cinematic deployments of voyeurism can be regarded as a perverse substitute for more direct connections with sexual objects. Given the increased institutionalization of both perversions in the mass media generally, it has seemed appropriate to speak of them in the context of Foucault's notion of the historical "implantation of perversions."

Throughout this book I have tried to remain nonjudgmental, to avoid the trap of condemning the perversions of pornography *as* perversions, of censuring the sexuality of the "other," whether that other be voyeur or fetishist, masochist or sadist, man or woman. At the same time, however, my feminist perspective has dictated some criticism of the ways in which pornography has ridden roughshod over the sexuality and sexual subjectivity of women. It has not always been easy to keep both of these sometimes conflicting goals in view.

Psychoanalytic theory has been useful in this regard, because there desire is seen as animating all human life regardless of gender. Although desire takes different forms in men and women, in heterosexuals and homosexuals, and in masochists, sadists, and fetishists, its foundation in indirection, its quality of swerving away from deferred lost objects, has meant that some form of perversion, some form of deflection from mythical "original" objects onto substitute ones, is absolutely necessary to all sexual representation, whether in film or fantasy. Eroticism, understood not as Kate Millett's gentle or vague soft-core alternative to hard-core explicitness but as the investment of desire in nonexplicit objects, is itself infused with just such a quality of substitution and displacement.

For if we accept the most basic psychoanalytic premise that original objects are lost, whether owing to the entrance into the symbolic, as Lacan has it, or simply because the mother or breast must eventually be given up by the child, then we must likewise agree that the whole of infantile and adult sexuality—including the genital sexuality usually considered the "normal" route for sexual instincts—is perverted, or swerved away, from its original object. Of course, psychoanalysis as a theory and practice does not always succeed in maintaining this nonjudgmental definition of perversion, especially in its views on sexual difference. Nevertheless, the basic concept of a continuum of perversions which underlies human sexuality—of a desire-driven sexual economy capable of choosing quite diverse objects—along with Michel Foucault's notion of the intensified deployment of sexuality in the modern age, has helped to show that pornography is not a special aberration and that its appeal cannot easily be curtailed by condemnation or censorship.

A serious question remains, however, and that is how we should regard the specific "implantation of perversions" that this massively popular cinematic hard-core pornography represents. Although I have tried to avoid either condemnation or advocacy of what is clearly a diverse phenomenon, total success may in the end be impossible. Foucault, we will recall, was quite pessimistic about the net increase in repressive control over bodies and pleasures represented by the increasing deployment of discourses of sexuality. I began this book in general agreement with this pessimism; but as I persisted in exploring specifically pornographic discourses of sexuality from a feminist perspective, and as I probed the sexual politics of works usually viewed as inimical to women, I began to see that the more discourses of sexuality there are, the more the hierarchies governing such oppositions as male/female, sadist/masochist, active/passive, and subject/object tend to break down.

As long as sexual pleasure is viewed as having a proper function and an end—whether that end be reproduction, love, control over another, or even orgasm considered as a climactic goal-driven release—it tends to reside within the relatively parsimonious masculine economy of production. But when sexual pleasure begins to cultivate (already inherent) qualities of perversion; when it dispenses with strictly biological and social functions and becomes an end in itself; when it ceases to rely on release, discharge, or spending for fulfillment; when a desiring subject can take up one object and then another without investing absolute value in that object; and finally, when this subject sees its object more as exchange value in an endless play of substitution than as use value for possession—then we are in the realm of what must now be described as a more feminine economy of consumption, an economy best represented by that image which Steven Marcus (1974, xiv) found so disturbing: the orgasmic woman masturbating "with the aid of a mechanical-electrical instrument."

The nineteenth-century pornography that Marcus wrote about was marked by a productivist economy of control and ownership. Desire in this economy was predominantly masculine; women were its objects but not its subjects. The twentieth-century pornography of the moving image that this book deals with can be seen shifting from the productivist mentality of work, rigid gender differences, and need for control and toward a consumerist mentality of unending pleasures, shifting gender relations, and a desire for self-abandon. While this mentality may be more caught up in the "implantation of perversions," it nevertheless is more democratic in its inclusion of women. Women's desires are now addressed as different from men's, but not so different as to belong outside the economy of desire altogether. So while Foucault's pessimism is not unfounded—we, and women more than men, are more securely in the grip of sexual ideologies than ever before—the new diversity of sexualities and the spread of perversions, of "diff'rent strokes for diff'rent folks," bring with them greater sexual citizenship for women, the potential for breaking down hierarchical oppositions, and a general movement toward a degendered libido.

Two brief examples from the foregoing pages should suffice. We have seen the "lesbian" number function in a variety of ways in heterosexual pornography, but rarely as a problem-solving big-production number. More typically it is the titillating warm-up to more heterogenital pleasures. As a consequence, feminists and lesbians have quite naturally viewed these numbers as oriented predominantly toward male visual pleasure and as inauthentic for lesbian viewers. However, two contradictory factors converge to call this absolute assertion of inauthenticity into question. First, as recent research into mainstream cinematic representations of lesbians suggests, lesbian audiences are capable of finding pleasure in films and genres that might otherwise seem to deny their felt identities as lesbian.[3] Second, precisely because these numbers do not threaten the dominant masculine heterosexual appeal of the genre, they have proliferated as islands of nonphallic sexuality in hard-core film and so invited all the variations common to generic repetition. In a similar way, sadie-max numbers and sadomasochism in general work to abolish clear distinctions between male and female, to promote a greater bisexual sensibility, and to strip sexual pleasure of the traces of an older ideology of purposeful, productive function. Even though the "lesbian" number and S/M are circumscribed within a genre that has been geared to male heterosexual pleasure, then, both manage to chip away at the rigid separation between the sexes and at the hierarchic dichotomies of active/passive, sadist/masochist, male/female.

Does this mean that the "implantation of perversions" is a good thing, or that the compulsion to speak about sex represents a net increase in sexual freedom? Perhaps, but only in very limited ways. The proliferation of pornographic discourses of sexuality, as well as of differences among these discourses, suggests that although we are caught up in and by these discourses, within this situation the differences that can be expressed have increased. Polymorphous perversity does not "win out" over strict male-defined heterosexual normality; instead the two are in tension. The rise of pornographies of all sorts, however, does suggest that the nineteenth-century gentleman's "secret museum" no longer characterizes the form or function of pornography today. For better *and* for worse, our "speaking of sex" is now much more diverse.

Pornography Is the Theory . . .

If writing this book has taught me one thing, it is that the familiar slogan of anti-pornography feminism, "pornography is the theory, rape is the practice," is a woefully inadequate explanation of the causes of sexual violence against women. Ironically, however, pornography may in fact be much more like a theory than Robin Morgan realized when she coined this phrase. For theory is defined as a supposition, resting on speculation, that attempts to explain something—the point of view of the person who develops the supposition being inherent in the word itself, which stems from the Greek words *theōria*, a looking at, viewing, speculation, contemplation; *theōrein*, to look at; and *theōros*, spectator.

Until very recently pornography of the gentleman's "secret museum" variety was inevitably a male speculation on the difference of female desire and pleasure. With pornography's modern proliferation as one among many discourses of sexuality, however, the points of view from which this speculative looking at sex has been undertaken have expanded. Just as there are now many pornographies for many "diff'rent folks," and not only for the gentlemen, there are many theories of desire and pleasure. Although these pornographies have not expanded with democratic inclusiveness, they have expanded enough to include female observer-theorists who add their own speculations about the pleasures of sex.

In a sense, then, the first half of the feminist anti-pornography dictum, "pornography is the theory," has proved unexpectedly true: cinematic hard core can be read as a theoretical speculation on and analysis of the mythically concrete pleasures it purports to display so directly and naturally. Indeed, it is precisely in film and video that this visual aspect of looking at and speculating about pleasure in sex, as Luce Irigaray has already argued with respect to the "speculum" of Western philosophical tradition, encounters its limits. Visual hard-core pornographic speculation about sexual pleasure demonstrates more convincingly than any abstract theoretical statement of the nature of power and pleasure that resistance is built into the very structure of the power and knowledge that speak.

Contemporary pornography's speculation about sexual pleasure —what Sade once called "philosophy in the bedroom"—does not generate rape, however, for the simple reason that feminists have done such a good job of showing that rape is not pleasurable for the person who is raped. Rather, pornography's speculation about pleasure would seem, first and foremost, to generate only more, and different, pornography. In short, pornography, by formulating sexual pleasure as a problem, with solutions involving the need for further sex and further speculation about that sex, begets pornography. Perhaps the real question for the future of pornography, then, is the one asked by Jessica Benjamin: how can desire be worked through to achieve intersubjectivity *and* recognition, separation *and* merger?

Although Benjamin's notion of intersubjectivity is both utopian and essentialist, some qualified form of both seems necessary if we are to speak of differences that have not yet been spoken. Discourse is a way of speaking about something which constructs what that something is. This examination of the hard-core quest for the involuntary, confessional "frenzy of the visible" has revealed hard core to be nothing more than ways of speaking about and constructing the speculative "truths" of sex. Perhaps the true measure of the feminist re-vision of pornography would be if it were to produce a pornographic "speculation" about the still relatively unproblematized pleasures of men. When hard core begins to probe the nature and quality of male pleasure with the same scrutiny that it devotes to female pleasure, when erection, penetration, and ejaculation are no longer primary, self-evident measures of male pleasure, then a realm of female pornotopia may be at hand.

That particular re-vision of hard core still seems a long way off. For the present our goals must be more modest. Perhaps now that pornography has entered the home and begun to adapt itself to women's space—and now that some women venture with more assurance out of the home and into the world of masculine event and action—we may hope that pornography will increasingly be found, for both women and men, in the context of a mixture of safety and excitement, and that sound together with image will (mutually) communicate dialogues of pleasure in which what men feel and think is no longer taken as given. If this is possible, then feminist re-vision might revise obscenity itself. For obscenity is simply the notion that some things—particularly the dirty confessions of female difference—must remain off the scene of representation. If those "sexual things" are no longer dirty, if sexual desire and pleasure are no more unseemly in women than in men, then perhaps pornography will serve women's fantasies as much as it has served men's.

Kate Millett is wrong. We do not need eroticism *instead* of pornography. The very notion of erotica as "good," clean, nonexplicit representations of sexual pleasure in opposition to dirty, explicit pornographic ones is false. The erotic and the pornographic interact in hard core. The one emphasizes desire, the other satisfaction. Depending on who is looking, both can appear dirty, perverse, or too explicit. But Millett *is* right in asserting that explicitness helps us to see how things are. I hope that this book has demonstrated something of how things have been and now are in the limit-texts of hard-core film and video pornography. We need to see pornography in all its naked explicitness if we are to speak frankly about sexual power and pleasure and if we are to demystify sex; but we need also to recognize that gender, sexual fantasy, and sexual desire derive fundamentally from mystifications—infantile misrecognitions of what Kaja Silverman (1988a, 1) eloquently calls "lost objects and mistaken subjects." Hard core is not the enemy. Neither are fantasies, which by definition are based on unruly desires rather than politically correct needs. The one speaks to us plainly about bodies and organs; the other describes the often circuitous roles these bodies and organs can play in satisfying our desires. Pornography speculates about both.

Two stories, neither one pornography exactly, have proved useful in this study as parables of the pornographic enterprise. The first, Diderot's fable "The Indiscreet Jewels," is invoked obliquely by Foucault in volume one of his *History of Sexuality.* In contrast to Foucault's use of the fable to invoke the general compulsion to confess sexual truths, I have used it to symbolize special solicitation of the truth of the *female* body. My point has been that although cinema, and later video, seem to enable direct knowledge of pleasure, their confessional magic is like that produced by the sultan's magic ring given him by his genie—nothing more than a male fiction about loose-lipped women. But as with many of the foregoing readings of hard-core films, it is possible to read this fable against the grain of its own apparent ideology. Jane Gallop (1988b), for example, argues that Diderot's fable is also a criticism of the dream of the perfect knowledge of pleasure. Noting that the *indiscret* of the work's French title could mean not only "indiscreet" but also "indiscrete"—that is, not countable or separable into parts—Gallop detects the fable's self-conscious criticism of its own fantasy: "If the jewels are 'indiscrete' they are not countable, and are the derision of the mathematical fantasy" (p. 76).

Gallop sees the sultan's insecurity about this knowledge as tied up with his insecurity about the love of his mistress Mirzoza, who forbids him to turn the ring on her. Emphasizing the "well-matched battle" of this couple, she argues that the "entire baroque path of the novel is but a deferral of [the sultan's] confrontation with the voice of the loved woman's desire" (pp. 76–77). I agree with Gallop about the insecurity of the sultan, which by extension is the insecurity of all pornographic knowledge of the sexual "other" that relies on the staging and inducing of involuntary confessions. I doubt, however, both the "well-matched" nature of their battle (since the sultan abuses his magic to turn the ring on Mirzoza after she forbids it) and the "happy ending" of the confession of her desire for him (since the confession is not freely given). This romantic conflict between Mangogul and Mirzoza over the confession of jewels is reminiscent of couples porn in which the pleasure of the couple is paramount, the desire of the woman solicited, but the "truth" of that desire too circumscribed by a larger patriarchal world.

In contrast to this fable, we might return to another that I have invoked here as emblematic of hard-core pornography. This one, which also arises in the context of a larger, ongoing battle for power between the sexes, is the argument in Hesiod between Zeus and Hera over who has the most pleasure in sex. The dispute, we will recall, was settled by Teiresias, who, because he was once a woman, could presumably confess the quantitative secret of women's pleasure: "of ten parts a man enjoys one only; but a woman's sense enjoys all ten in full." For this pronouncement Hera blinds him while Zeus rewards him with the "seer's power."

In this story, too, we recognize a pornographic compulsion to measure and quantify "discrete" pleasures which, when the mathematical reasoning is examined, proves at least as contradictory as Diderot's. For while the myth seems to construct the number ten as a totality and fullness of pleasure that the man and the woman might share (say, in a five-five split), it immediately contradicts this idea of fullness in the assumption that the only proper (discreet) quantity is the one part of male pleasure; everything else, whether nine or ten, is the excess of the other.

The argument between Zeus and Hera thus recalls a classic stag film in which the seemingly respectable woman turns out to have naughty (indiscreet and indiscrete) desires. But as with Diderot's fable, this Hesiodic emblem of pornography is now readable by a latter-day Hera against the grain of its apparent meaning to reveal how questions of pleasure are always, ultimately, questions of power; she knows, moreover, the importance of continuing the argument on both fronts so that the analysis of pleasure includes an awareness of power. In this reading, Hera's blinding of Teiresias is not a result of anger at being found out in her pleasure; rather, it is poetic justice: he is punished for his metaphysical blindness to women's pleasure, for a woefully inadequate vision of/speculation about the secrets of the other.

We have seen that hard-core pornography is a speculation about pleasure that begins, as does Teiresias, from a phallic perspective, journeys to the unseen world of the sexual other, and returns to tell the story. An ideal of bisexuality drives the quest for the knowledge of the pleasure of the other: that one sex can journey to the unknown other and return, satiated with knowledge and pleasure, to the security of the "self." While most pornography belies this ideal—like Teiresias, it can only speak from its phallic point of origin—it does speculate that such a journey is possible. Of course it is not, since there is no such thing as a discrete sexed identity who can journey from fixed self to fixed other, and since these identities themselves are constructed in fluid relations to fictional "others" who exist only in our relation to them. But the impossibility of pornographic knowledge does not prevent the fantasy from flourishing; indeed, it may even encourage it. If the sexual other is ultimately unknowable, then all the more reason to desire this knowledge, especially now that what was once the "other" has begun to make the journey herself. A pornographic speculation about pleasure that begins in the "other place" of a heterosexual feminine desire and pleasure, that constructs meaning in opposition to the unknowable mystery of masculine desire and pleasure, and that journeys to the male other would now seem possible. It remains for women to decide whether to undertake such a journey.

Epilogue

On/scenities

"Speaking Sex" in the Nineties": The Elusive "Hard Core"

There was a point in the much-publicized sex scandals of the Clinton administration when it looked as if the Paula Jones sexual harassment lawsuit might involve testimony invoking the shape, color, size, or some other distinctive characteristic, of the presidential penis. Even as I write, it looks as if semen stains on a dress might become evidence in the special prosecutor's case against the president. The unprecedented degree of prurient interest generated in the escapades of our president has meant that watching politics in the late nineties has begun to be like watching pornography in the early seventies. Indeed, the very public discussions taking place about some very private presidential parts almost seem on a par with that moment back in 1972 when the film *Deep Throat* became a household word.[1] The main difference is that today, it seems almost politically necessary to talk about sex and to take a prurient interest in our president.

"Prurient interest" is a term familiar to lawyers involved in prosecuting or defending charges of obscenity. It is the first of the three prongs of the landmark 1973 Supreme Court *Miller v. California* decision used to define obscenity. According to this definition, a work is considered obscene if "the average person, applying contemporary community standards" would find that the work, taken as a whole, appeals to *prurient interest*, second if it depicts or describes sexual conduct in a *patently offensive* way, and third if it lacks "*serious literary, artistic, political or scientific value* (emphasis mine)." If all three of these prongs are in place a work may, according to prevailing community standards, be judged obscene (Downs, 17).

Many commentators have used the example of prurient interest in the presidential penis as a sign of the greater obscenity of our times.[2] Instead of seeing that politics have reached a new, obscene low, I am inclined, however, to see how sexual representation has achieved a new high—a new pervasiveness on/scene. Consider the extent to which the term "prevailing community standards" now openly countenances an interest in sexual details. The peculiar effect of the many ways in which the nation demonstrates its interest in sex has been further to unhinge the Miller Test's very concept of an unassimilable "hard core" of obscenity to be kept permanently out of sight. When an organ as important as the presidential penis becomes the subject of reportage from tabloids to *Nightline* to the *The New York Times*, when it becomes the subject of partisan national debates, its very presence on the scene of public discourse can no longer be considered *"patently offensive."* Nor can it be said to be without *"serious . . . political"* value.

In writing the 1973 decision that originally defined obscenity through what has come to be called "the Miller Test," Justice Warren Burger attempted to assert the concept of a non-socially redeemable prurience, a "hard core" of mere "sex for sex's sake," defined as explicit or graphic representations that went "substantially beyond customary limits of candor" and which were obviously "obscene." Burger even offered up some "plain examples" of these obscene depictions: "patently offensive representations or descriptions of ultimate sexual acts, normal or perverted, actual or simulated" (Downs, 17). However, as the not-so-plain nature of these examples suggests, the Miller Test, designed to reassure the public that the law could define, and thus keep off/scene the ob/scene, has in actual practice meant that unprecedentedly wide varieties of sexual representations have found their way onto the public scene of representation. The very vagueness of the definitions of the three prongs of the test, coupled with the undeniably growing importance of sexuality as an overt force in contemporary society—not to mention presidential politics—have combined to bring on/scene precisely what the test was designed to keep off: ever more explicit representations of sex.

I don't mean by the foregoing to condone what Judge Susan Wright Webber, in dismissing the Paula Jones sexual harassment lawsuit, has called the "boorish and offensive" behavior of the president.[3] Rather, I mean to note the subtle process by which what was once deemed obscenity, in the literal sense of deserving to be kept out of public sight, has gained admittance to the increasingly "prurient" scene of public representation. The term that I use to describe this paradoxical state of affairs is "on/scenity." On/scenity is the gesture by which a culture brings on to the public scene the very organs, acts, "bodies and pleasures" that have heretofore been designated ob—off—scene, that is, as needing to be kept out of view, locked up in what Walter Kendrick has named the Secret Museum.[4]

This is not to say that sexually explicit representations, like the presidential penis, are placed before our eyes and ears without controversy or scandal. It is to say, however, that we are no longer able to claim, as convincingly as we once did, that sex is a private matter. Yet neither have we attained the "end of obscenity" optimistically predicted in the late sixties by Charles Rembar (1969). Rather, we have undergone an increasing politicization of represented sexualities in a context of proliferating sexual discourses, and an intensified "speaking sex."

The term on/scenity marks both the controversy and scandal of sexual representation *and* the fact that its details have become unprecedentedly available to the public at large.[5] On/scenity is the flashpoint where conventions of public and private, lustful and lascivious, prurient and ordinary collide, public discussion is produced and old-fashioned obscenity—the kind that really was locked up and kept hidden off/scene in private museums—is no longer possible.

Consider the public familiarity with the following pornographic scenarios. In one episode the President drops his pants in a hotel room in Arkansas, in another he corners a woman just outside the Oval Office and presses her hand against his penis. In yet another, the media eagerly await details of how he might have stained a particular blue dress. Of course, it is not entirely consistent with the genre that in two of the above cases he encounters sexual rejection and—to the credit of the woman's movement—has learned to take 'no' for an answer. As conventional heterosexual hard core pornography—rather than a new level of on/scenity in presidential politics—these episodes may lack a little luster. But our interest in them, our compulsion to speak about the explicit details of organs and body fluids is entirely pornographic.[6]

Foucault, it seems, was right. The modern age has been caught up in an unprecedented compulsion to confess the sexual, to "speak" sex (Foucault 1978, 77). To follow Foucault's insight about the modern incitement to sexuality, as opposed to the liberation or sublimation of a "repressed" sexuality, is to see the above example of presidential on/scenities as part of a "discursive explosion" rather than a sudden liberation from, or transgression of, "old-fashioned" sexual taboos. If telling all, showing all, seeing all, has become a national preoccupation, it is because an apparatus of power and knowledge has been at work to organize the confession of increasingly explicit details of sexual life. The new explicitness that I call on/scenity is not to be regarded, then, as the repressive hypothesis might regard it, as a new "honesty" or "truth" about matters sexual. It is not automatically to the good that we are compelled to speak about sex. Certainly it may not be good for the presidency. But we all know that to repress sexual speech is to repress those sexual minorities who have spoken by it and who take advantage of "reverse discourse" to fight repression. The less sex is spoken the more monolithic that speech is likely to be and the more that speech will tend to repress sexual minorities. It it thus strategically preferable to be on the side of more, rather than less, sexual speech.

Consider just some of the ways in which the speaking of sex has become commonplace: in a 1998 surprise hit movie adolescents roar at a joke in which ejaculate is mistaken for hair gel. At the same time, presidential lawyers and pundits ponder the seriousness of the evidence of a "semen stained garment." This is also a time when women have embraced pornography proper in unprecedented numbers. In Chapter 8 of *Hard Core* I discussed some of the effects of the VCR revolution's ability to provide a "safe" education of desire for women, who have continued to rent hard core videos in great numbers. In a new book Jane Juffer has shown just how extensive this move towards the feminine domestication of pornography has been, citing "women's literary erotica, masturbation discourse, adult cable programming, couples' video porn, cybersex, sex toys for women, lingerie catalogues and sexual self-help books" (ms 5)—all of which have tended to "tame" sex by bringing it into the domain of traditional female space. This on/scene move into the home is certainly not without controversy, but the overall trajectory has been, as Juffer eloquently puts it, "from the profane to the mundane." (Juffer 1). While many sex radicals might disparage the tame nature of these sexual representations, Juffer is right to point out that this integration of previously ob/scene works into

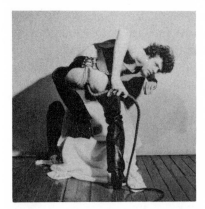

Robert Mapplethorpe, *Self Portrait 1978*
(*above*)

Annie Sprinkle giving public viewings
of her cervix (*right*)

women's everyday lives represents a remarkable change in what
Foucault calls the "uses of pleasure."

In tandem with the move of a tamer pornography into the home,
we might also consider the move of somewhat wilder pornographic
content into the venues of high art. At the beginning of the decade,
Robert Mapplethorpe's "The Perfect Moment" exhibit was canceled
at the Corcoran Gallery in Washington D.C. for alleged obscene
content but it re-opened at the Contemporary Arts Center in Cin-
cinnati (and then closed and opened again after a trial that acquit-
ted its director of "pandering obscenity"). Some of its photographs
depicted sadomasochistic homosexual practices once confined to
specialized, underground circulation but now exhibited as high art
on gallery walls. In a parallel move, also in 1990, porn star and
pornographer Annie Sprinkle ceased performing in porn films and
"live sex" shows and began inserting a speculum into her vagina at
the Cleveland Performance Art Festival.[7] Although most defenses
of these works necessarily claimed they were examples of "high"
erotic art rather than "low" pornography, the most interesting aspect of these on/scenities was the blur between them.

Art historian Lynda Nead has noted the tendency of erotic art to
legitimize the representation of the sexual "through the assertion of
form which holds off the collapse into the pornographic" (Nead

1993, 147). Erotic art thus takes the viewer to the frontier of legitimate culture, allowing the viewer to be aroused but containing that
arousal within the "purified, contemplative mode of high culture"
(147). Debates about whether the above sorts of representations
constituted a "collapse into the pornographic" were rampant. Those
who argued that such works were erotic rather than pornographic
were saying, in effect, that as viewers they could withstand the
temptation of the pornographic appeal to the body. As Nead puts
it: "What better way to demonstrate your cultural disinterestedness
and superiority than to come into contact with the erotic and to be
—practically—unmoved?" (147) Yet, as Nead also argues, the polar-
ization and careful line-drawing between erotic art and pornography, which became the flashpoint of debates about these and many
other controversial works, may be much less relevant than the common fact that both works do seek to move us; in one form of reception our job is to maintain composure; in the other it is to be
moved. The second half of this essay will take up the question of
the different ways pornographies seek to move us. For the time being, however, it is worth noting a new and in many ways productive
instability between visual forms of the erotic and the pornographic.
Even though the "hard core" kernel of clearly recognizable obscenity was rapidly disappearing, these high-end "art" venues were being
prosecuted more vigorously than ordinary low-end porno. Certainly
many more viewers saw Mapplethorpe's photographs and Annie
Sprinkle's performances because of the controversy surrounding
them than would have ever seen low-end porn.[8]

Indeed, the very public debates about the possible obscenity of
these images and performances became themselves examples of
on/scenity when, for example, Senator Jesse Helms made his own
exhibit of Mapplethorpe's photographs on the very floor of the U.S.
Senate. Arguing in 1989 against further funding from the NEA for
artists whose work might be deemed obscene under the Supreme
Court's *Miller* definition, Helms waved copies of NEA–funded photographer Robert Mapplethorpe in the air and cried:

Look at the pictures! Look at the pictures! Don't believe the *Washington
Post!* Don't believe *The New York Times!* . . . I'm going to ask that all the
pages, all the ladies, and maybe all the staff leave the Chamber so that senators can see exactly what they're voting on (de Grazia 637).

The exhortation to look at the dirty pictures represents a paradoxical bringing on/scene that violates the very ob/scenity Helms seeks
to enforce. Helms' anachronistic attempt to reproduce something
of the atmosphere of the nineteenth-century Secret Museum
where the mostly male club of senators could contemplate the "obscenity" of sexual representations—with the interesting twist, of
course, that now it is homoerotic images they are contemplating—is
self-defeating if the goal is to ban from view such pictures.[9] This
contradictory gesture—of bringing *on* what the exhibitor defines as
obscenity in order to keep it off—seems to me the very quintessence of on/scenity.

On yet another front, in the realm of sex education and health,
on/scenity has resulted from the increasing need to specify sexual
functions, whether they have to do with the effects of Viagra on
masculine tumescence or the need for condoms in protection from
AIDS. Even the firing of American Surgeon General Joycelyn Elders for suggesting that masturbation might be an activity worth
teaching about in the schools, while often taken as yet another example of American puritanism, seems to me most noteworthy for its
indication that we now live in an era in which the explicit discussion
of sexuality is emphatically on/scene for surgeon generals to discuss.
Elders, in fact, was not fired for *discussing* masturbation—no one
found the reporter's fateful question about masturbation out of line
at a public press conference—but for saying that *children* should be
discussing it.[10] Elders was thus ironically caught in the trap of having
to pronounce upon a politically untenable sexually on/scene subject.[11]

In the academy, some of us have been more fortunate than Dr.
Elders in managing to discuss explicit sex and keep our jobs. Formerly ob/scene sexual subjects have increasingly become a part
of the curriculum over the last five years, with new majors ranging
from Sexuality and Society, to Gay, Lesbian, Bisexual and Transgender Studies, Queer Studies and courses all over the map of contemporary debates about sexualities. While conservative critic Roger
Kimball has raised a supercilious eyebrow at the supposed choice to
learn how to "use dildos" rather than to read Kant (invoking the
same bogus theory-versus-practice dichotomy invoked in the case of
Elders), the curriculum is rapidly becoming entrenched.[12]

In this atmosphere even academic courses on pornography as
a genre have flourished.[13] For example, my U.C. Santa Barbara col-

league Constance Penley has boldly pioneered large undergraduate courses under the genre rubric of film studies. My own teaching of pornography began, in contrast, as an attempt to address the scapegoating of pornography by anti-porn feminists like Catherine MacKinnon,[14] and has evolved into a much more direct engagement with the history of the genre.

The fact that pornographies are now so much more firmly on/scene does not mean, however, that they, or their academic study, are still not vulnerable to censorship. Indeed, censorship has increasingly become a matter of scapegoating the more "deviant" of the sexual representations that come on/scene.[15] Recall, for example, the Miller Test term, prurient interest—the first prong of the definition of obscenity. Legal terms like "prurient interest" and "patently offensive" may seem annoyingly vague but if we consider what happens when these terms are clarified, we can see how this very imprecision has actually been their value. In 1985 the Supreme Court attempted to clarify Miller's sense of prurient interest, saying that it is that which "incites lasciviousness or lust." What then was lasciviousness and lust? Justice Burger decided that *lust* referred to "normal" while *lascivious* referred to abnormal sexual responses (Downs 19–20)[16] Thus prurience was "clarified" as containing both abnormal and normal sexual response. The "normal"—merely lusty—part of this response was, in effect, admitted on/scene, while a lasciviousness considered abnormal was proscribed. Where a "pure lust" for "sex's sake" had once been the very definition of obscenity, now sex itself had become such an important motive force, so entwined with aspects of human desire and endeavor as to be difficult to isolate as obscenity. But what the court was desperately trying to hold on to was an obscene "hard core" that could now be distinguished from normal lust.

Thus, the Miller Test's lack of specificity has been its value in establishing freedom of speech in sexual expression (see Vance 1990). Whenever prosecutors or judges were pressed to provide some "plain examples" of what constitutes obscenity, it was most often, as was the case with Jesse Helms, the more easily scapegoated practices of sexual minorities that would be cited. Burger's redefinition of "prurient interest" as opposed to the Miller Test itself, thus opened the door to a possibility that obscenity is not limited to explicit sexual acts (typically but not exclusively male and female genitals in coitus), but actually leans toward more "deviant" sexualities—those sexual acts and fantasies that "prevailing community standards" do not want to admit to be arousing. In the intervening years *these* perverse sexual acts have been targeted as the most important obscenities. We may note, for example, as both Carol Vance (1990) and Judith Butler (1990b) have done, the wording of Jesse Helms' NEA bill forbidding the spending of Federal funds in the arts if the works funded "promote, disseminate or produce obscene materials, including but not limited to depictions of sadomasochism, homoeroticism, the exploitation of children, or individuals engaged in sex acts" (Vance, 51).

Helms' amendment to censor NEA funding of "obscene" art was ultimately superseded by legislation that asserted that no grant of assistance would be made to any work that offends "general standards of decency and respect for the diverse beliefs and values of the American public" (de Grazia 681). The law clarifies that "obscenity"—as still defined by the Miller Test—is not protected speech and shall not be funded. It is this law that the Supreme Court upheld in a June 25, 1998 ruling. This fallback to the Miller definition of obscenity is a clear rejection of Helms' more specified "laundry list" of scapegoatable deviancies. However the introduction of the new term "decency," which it is now the function of the NEA, not the courts, to enforce, tends to suggest that decent sex is normal sex, especially in the wake of both Burger and Helms' iteration of lists of deviant acts. Indeed, the difference between the 1973 Miller Test and the 1989 Helms Bill, now modified by the word decency, is striking. Today, in legal as well as popular consciousness, some variant of perverse sexuality, typically sadomasochism or homosexuality, is well on its way to becoming the implied definition of obscenity.[17] To become more visible and on/scene is thus not necessarily to gain acceptance and normality. It is also to become more vulnerable to attack.

Jesse Helms says, in effect, look at how disgusting these deviant sexual acts and fantasies are. Yet in pointing the finger to condemn, we have seen that he brings the representation on/scene just as surely as any pornographer. He assumes that audiences will share his disgust. The risk he runs is that they, and perhaps some senators, won't. Prosecutors in obscenity cases report jury members can sometimes be unexpectedly aroused, especially if permitted to see offending works in their entirety. Once jurors have so responded it becomes understandably harder for them to declare a work obscene (Downs 21). Obviously, the more that sexual representations of all sorts are on scene, the more they contribute to the recognition, by jurors and casual viewers alike, that it is possible to be turned on by quite a few different things. The experience of arousal itself then becomes an important element in the contemporary experience of on/scenity. Yet arousal is the one thing about which both critics and theorists of pornography have had the least to say.

Indeed, the seemingly simple fact of hard core pornography's "direct" appeal to the body has led many of its critics to assume a certain obviousness to porno as if its understanding could be reduced to the reality effect of the sexy bodies, and sex acts, depicted on the screen.[18] But how obvious *is* the visceral spectatorial response to moving-image pornography? Critics have spent so much time and energy attempting to draw the line between a "properly" sublimated and distanced erotic art and a supposedly improper, raw and immediate pornography that they have ignored some equally important questions about the nature of the reception of moving-image pornography over its near one-hundred-year history.

On Being Moved by Moving-Image Pornography

Visual culture critic David Freedberg has argued for the need to examine erotic response in high *and* low images and against the obsessive need to disentangle sexual response from the erotic. Pointing to the contortions art historians have undergone in order to avoid mentioning sexual response to the pudenda of countless images of Venus or the frequently fondled genitals of the Christ child, Freedberg argues for the importance of admitting more basic and raw human responses to such images (Freedberg 1989, xx, 13, 17). How, then, shall we begin to talk about the rawer, less sublimated, responses of viewers to moving-image pornography? We might begin by confronting our vulnerability to moving-images in general.[19] Writing about the physical experience of watching movies, film theorist Vivian Sobchack notes a need for film theorists to

come to grips with the *carnal foundations of cinematic intelligibility*, with the fact that to understand movies, to comprehend them, we first must *make sense* of them. . . . Despite the relatively recent academic fetishiza-

tion of 'the body,' theorists still don't quite know what to do with their unruly responsive flesh and sensorium—particularly insofar as these pose an
intolerable question to prevalent understandings of the cinema grounded
on lack, absence, illusionism, and the geometrical assumption that the film
image is two-dimensional ("What My Fingers Knew" ms. 6).

Arguing for a phenomenological account of the ways human beings are "moved" and "touched" by moving images, Sobchack positions the lived, spectating body as a carnal "third term" that mediates
vision and language, experience and image to "make sense" of film.
What is particularly useful in her approach is the focus on a sensation most appropriate to, but missing from, discussions of pornography: the sense of touch. Writing about Jane Campion's *The Piano*,
Sobchack asserts that her reaction to the moment Baines touches
Ada's flesh through a hole in her black woolen stocking, gives rise in
her to an "immediate tactile shock" (14). Yet it is not as if Sobchack
feels she literally touches Ada. Rather, as she puts it, this shock
"opens me to the general erotic mattering of flesh and I am diffusely—ambivalently—Baines's body, Ada's body, what I have elsewhere called the 'film's body,' and my 'own' body" (14). Her fingers,
then, are in the touching, and in the touched.

Here, I think, is a key but unexplored meaning of the word, "attraction," importantly introduced by historians of early cinema in
recent years to describe the basic, sensuous appeal of all moving
pictures.[20] The perception of a moving image of an object (or body)
that is not literally there to be touched, gives rise to an attraction towards—a solicitation by—the mediated object or body. This solicitation is an attraction not just of the eyes, but of the flesh. Indeed, our
entire sensorium is activated in a synaesthetic manner with one
bodily sense translating into another. Sight, in Sobchack's example,
commutes to touch. We do not touch the flesh that appears on the
screen but our senses "make sense" of the vision of touch in our
own flesh. It is in this sense that we can say we are "touched," or
"moved" by the virtual bodies on the screen.

Sobchack's phenomenological approach to cinema asks us to consider ways in which the literal and figurative senses make sense together. We do not literally taste the food in *Tampopo*, or touch the
flesh in *The Piano*, but we have a generalized sensual experience
that cannot be reduced to sight.

My intentionality streams toward the world on screen, marking itself not merely in my conscious attention, but always also in my bodily tension, the arrangement of my material being. However, insofar as I cannot literally touch, smell, taste the figure on the screen that solicits my sensual desire, my body's intentional arc will reverse its direction to find reciprocity in an accessible, realizable literal object: *my own lived-body*. Thus, on the re-bound—and without a reflective thought—I will reflexively touch myself touching, smell myself smelling, taste myself tasting, and, in sum, feel my own sensuality (26).

Here is a model of visual pleasure that includes the visceral, a model that does not limit itself to the disembodied eye—one in which all the senses of a body, "on the rebound" from an attraction toward a moving image are implicated. It is a model that certainly "fits" the diffuse, yet powerful encounter with one's own flesh en-tailed by watching moving-image pornography. And it is a model that could prove more useful than that of a disembodied and dis-tanced "male gaze" so frequently employed to describe the visual "phallic mastery" of objectified bodies on the screen.

Gaze theory in film studies has often seemed to be too much about the eye and not enough about the body.[21] Yet it may not be accurate to portray the psychoanalytic description of film spectator-ship as an entirely disembodied model of vision. More recent theo-rists have deployed both Freud and Lacan to stress the imbalance of the models of phallic mastery and voyeurism, which once reigned supreme in feminist film theory and criticism to emphasize the more vulnerable, "introjective" and "reactive" aspects of film view-ing.[22] The most relevant of these discussions for our purposes is Carol Clover's insistence on the importance of the underappreci-ated "reactive" gaze in horror cinema. This gaze posits a vulnerable, soft receptive flesh—the physical carnality of the eye itself—into which the visual horrors of horror films are received as the flip side to the more familiar, "projective" and "assaultive" gaze of phallic mastery. Clover's point about horror spectatorship (and my point about pornographic spectatorship) is that this latter, "introjective" and "reactive" gaze is what the genre is more importantly about. The so-called "phallic mastery" of distanced voyeurism is more of-ten than not a fantasy to which spectatorship may aspire, but the feminine position of what Clover calls "taking it in the eye" is closer to the visual and visceral reality of the vulnerable and impression-able spectatorial body (202).

A "Carnal Density" of Vision

Clover and Sobchack emphasize the ways viewers reincorporate a gaze that begins as an outward projection *from* their physical bodies and which returns *to* the body—for Sobchack self-reflexively and without special recourse to gender; for Clover masochistically as feminized pleasure-pain for male viewers. Both theorists impor-tantly reconnect the organs of the eyes to the flesh. Indeed, Clover is quick to remind us of the many ways the "eye of horror" *is* vul-nerable flesh (202–211). Both thus apply to the study of moving im-ages—one phenomenologically, the other psychoanalytically—what historian of visual culture Jonathan Crary has usefully termed the "carnal density" of modern vision (149). Crary argues that a new "carnal density" of modern vision began, throughout the nineteenth century, to displace an older, Cartesian, "camera obscura" model marked by the disembodied, mastering eye so familiar to seventies film theory. Crary maintains that the body, which had a neutral or invisible status in the classical Cartesian "camera obscura" model of vision, began to acquire a new "thickness" and density in newly de-centered nineteenth-century ways of seeing.[23] Thus, instead of trac-ing a straight line of development from the classical camera obscura of Durer to the camera obscura of photography, stereoscopy and film, Crary asserts that the body grows more vulnerable to visual sensation as the camera obscura ceases to be the dominant model of vision.[24]

Our thinking about the visual and visceral pleasures of moving-image pornography can benefit from Sobchack, Clover, and Crary's approaches to the "carnal density" of modern vision. For each of them, in their own way, posits a model of spectatorship vulnerable to and implicated in the images he or she sees. Placed in conjunc-tion with the different social situations in which pornography has been viewed, this model can permit us to begin to think of a plural-ity of differently disciplined viewers solicited by, and attracted to, a wide variety of pornographic images. With this concept of a visual attraction extending and "projecting" out from the viewer towards the moving images on the screen but then "rebounding" reactively

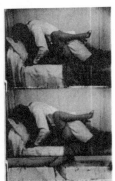

A Country Stud Horse, a man peers into a mutoscope
A Country Stud Horse, the woman in the mutoscope strips
A Country Stud Horse, the man cranks the machine and himself
A Country Stud Horse, the man and the woman have sex

and introjectively back into the viewer, where phantasmatic work is then performed on the images, let us begin to consider the nearly one-hundred-year history of the social viewing situations of moving-image pornography.

Ob/scenity: The Stag Era:

The first, and longest, stage of the history of American moving-image pornography is the era of the stag film, extending, as I note in Chapter 3, from the origin of moving pictures through the late 1960s. I discuss some typical stag texts in that chapter. Here I would first like to speculate a little further about the material conditions of the reception afforded these episodic, crude, often humorous short films. Consider a film from the 1920s, called *A Country Stud Horse*. Like many examples of early cinema it is obsessed with the machinery of vision. A man peers into a mutoscope—a popular hand-cranked peephole viewing machine from the turn-of-the-century using photographed flip cards—to see a woman stripping and wiggling in erotic poses. As he gets aroused he begins to "crank" himself along with the machine. Eventually a woman picks him up, he leaves the mutoscope, and they have sex.[25]

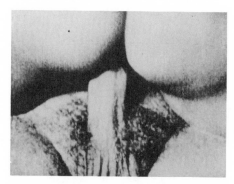

Slow Fire Dentist, a typical meat shot

What characterizes this film, and the thousands of others produced and distributed in this way, is a brief attempt at narrative, followed by the close-up exhibition of bodies engaged in actual sex acts which always culminate in close-up scrutiny of penetration—what the pornographic genre would later come to call "meat shots". Both male and female bodies sexually perform, but the stag film is consistently more interested in exhibiting the female body, given the exclusively male and the putatively heterosexual nature of the stag audience. Men gathered in smokers, bachelor parties, brothels, and fraternal organizations, to see films that could not be seen anywhere else. Because women were almost never the viewers of these films, there is a kind of misogynist "purity" to this unique source of sexual education, and sexual fantasy, for many generations of American men.

While *A Country Stud Horse*'s representation of the solitary man at the mutoscope does not duplicate the experience of the stag audience, his masturbation before the machine, and his later consummation of sex with a woman who picks him up beside this machine, squarely indicates that some form of sexual gratification is an anticipated result of watching these works. Stag films seem to assume, unlike later, feature-length porno, that viewer "attraction" to these bodies will ultimately "rebound," in Sobchack's terms, back toward the self because there is no present woman to touch. The vicarious satisfaction of viewers who identify with sexual protagonists seems less important than the more immediate attractions and satisfactions of physically excited viewers. Pleasure, here, cannot be reduced to the reality-effect of the body of the absent woman who engages in stripping and sex. Rather, pleasure needs to be understood, as Claudia Springer has put it, as a "pleasure of the interface" between viewer, technology of vision, and object viewed (Springer 1991, 306). In stag films that interface is the film screen before whose black and white, silent, mechanically moving, projected bodies, sat a group of horny, vocal, curious, misogynist boys and men, not "gazing"—in the sense of omnipotent mastery, but "looking"—in the sense of vulnerable fascination.[26]

To best understand the nature of the pleasures taken in this form of pornographic spectatorship we need to imagine a viewing situation that includes the audible whir of a projector (in the stag party in the home, fraternal hall, or brothel there would most likely not be a projection booth to filter out this sound), the "embarrassment of silence"—no piano, no sound track—which verbal jokes and embarrassed laughter would probably have attempted to fill, and frequent breaks between short films for smoking and drinking. We need to imagine, also, films with only rudimentary narratives with female performers who often offer a "direct" erotic solicitation of the audience. And finally we need to imagine a group of men and boys intensely embarrassed and aroused by the attractions of these moving images, "making sense" of what they see, but also relating to what they hear in the comments of their peers, diffusely "extending" and "projecting" towards the non-present "film's body" and, "introjecting" "on the rebound" from the unpossessibility of that body, encountering their own phantasmatic reception and their own "carnal density" in the dark room that is both public and private.

In this era, bodily responses to moving-image pornography were both powerfully solicited and entirely contained within the walls of a male-only "Secret Museum."[27] But this "museum," while unquestionably all male, is certainly not a picture of a mastering "male gaze" but of an impressionable, fascinated, and vulnerable "male look." We do not know if these men and boys masturbated in the dark or if, in the intensity of arousal, they sometimes turned to one another, or, as some of the films themselves suggest they do, they turned to whatever "loose women" were about or if their pleasure consisted in simply feeling horny together. What we do know is that these men were in a very special, private space, the place where a blatant, physically moving, obscenity was permitted among men only, a place free from the scrutiny or disapproval of those not sharing a frankly visual and visceral pursuit of sexual pleasure. The walls of this museum were relatively high in the 1920s for moving image pornography if not for literature, but in the late sixties they came tumbling down, producing a very different discipline of reception.

On/Scenity: The "Classical" Era of Theatrically Exhibited Porno

Although something like "stag" viewing situations certainly persist in private parties and in some arcades (described below), the era of the secret museum and the exclusive men's club has been dying a slow death in the West since the late sixties. As we have seen, this does not mean that formerly obscene images now circulate with absolute freedom, but it does mean that they have increasingly become part of the contemporary scene. As these images came on/scene the kind of unsublimated, direct appeal to the viewer's sensorium that marked the privacy of the secret museum was curtailed.

By the early seventies it had become much more common for moving pornographic images to be viewed in public theaters by audiences that were comparatively heterogeneous mixes of race, class, and gender. Moving-image pornography thus dramatically arrived on/scene in what I would now, with some qualification, call the "Classical" Era of Theatrically Exhibited Porno. This is that relatively brief period in the seventies and early eighties, depicted with some affection in the 1997 film *Boogie Nights,* and described in Chapters 4–6 of the preceding pages, when hard-core spectatorship seemed to approximate that of the so-called "classical" narrative cinema. While I argued in these chapters that hard-core film in this period was more like mainstream "classical" Hollywood cinema than it was unlike it, it is possible, as Peter Lehman has pointed out, to overemphasize a period that, unlike the "classical" cinema, has actually been quite brief.[28] Nevertheless, from the point of view of spectatorial discipline, this comparatively public, mixed-company viewing situation presumed a much greater suppression of visceral response than that of the gregarious, but much more private secret museum.

I have argued that hard-core film of this period settles on two contradictory gestures: On the one hand it begins to offer a smorgasbord of diverse sexual acts; the typical heterosexual hard core film of this period contrives, like *Deep Throat,* to integrate a wide

Deep Throat (Gerard Damiano, 1972),
Linda Lovelace has her throat examined

Deep Throat (Gerard Damiano, 1972),
Linda Lovelace performs her speciality

variety of numbers into its narrative: fellatio, so-called "lesbian" sex, oral, anal, s/m, etc. On the other hand it usually tries to subsume all of this diversity under the ultimate sign of phallic pleasure in the money shot. Rather than being the spontaneous and natural outcome of desire, the achievement of sexual pleasure becomes a special problem, a conscious goal that both men and women characters in the films discipline themselves to perform. This discipline is very different from that evidenced by the stag film, which was satisfied simply to show unclothed females and proof of genital action but not concerned to show visible proof of male orgasm.

Gay male pornography emerges on/scene as a popular genre in public theaters at the same time and in some of the same spirit of on/scenity as straight porno. But because it was exhibited in the context of emerging gay subcultures rather than in general theaters, it was somewhat more tentatively on/scene. On the one hand, its exhibition in public theaters in gay communities partly continued the underground, semi-illicit tradition of the stag film in the sense of appealing to a more specialized, single gender audience rather than a general adult public. On the other hand, it cautiously extended itself into a more public sphere. Though formally quite different from stag films—as feature length films with sound and color—they also persisted in what might be called the "unproblematic," relatively unnarrativized celebration of sex found in the stag film. No one seemed to be working very hard to solve sexual problems. The

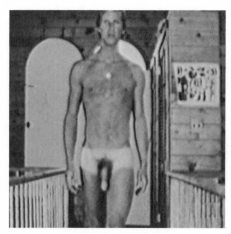

Boys in the Sand (Wakefield Pool, 1972).
The first gay porno star, Casey Donovan.

classic early example, as well-known in its milieu as *Deep Throat* was, is *Boys in the Sand* (Wakefield Pool, 1972). In it, three dialogue-less vignettes set on Fire Island show a different male figure fantasizing a dream lover and then enjoying the ensuing sex.[29]

Gay and straight are the two main types of porn films to emerge in great numbers, in this period. Both were and still are phallic, both are obsessed with visualizing penetration followed by ejaculation, but gay pornography was aimed narrowly at gay male viewers while straight porno was trying, somewhat awkwardly, to please a mixed-gender heterosexual audience.

How, then, to characterize the more "classical" cinematic regime of visual pleasure typified by feature length porno? It was once a cliché of this era's theatrical pornography to think of its prime audience as a brigade of lonely, "dirty" old men sitting far apart from one another in the theater with raincoats in their laps. Yet this picture of the porn spectator as akin to a stereotype of a solitary voyeur ignores the revolutionary gender, class, and racial mix of the heterosexual pornographic audience in contrast to the homogeneity of the private club stag audiences. It also ignores the unprecedented community-building function of theatrically-exhibited gay porn. Indeed, the whole point of both gay and straight theatrical pornographic exhibitions on/scene in the seventies was that they were *not* furtive and lonely, but highly public "comings out," for gays and straights, of audience members as sexually *interested* viewers.

What does seem to characterize the pornographic spectatorship of this period, as opposed to the earlier stag era, is that the public expressions of sexual interest manifested in going to see hard core films in quasi-legitimate theaters depended upon the relative suppression of precisely the kind of overt carnal response openly solicited by stag films. It is as if the price of manifesting public sexual interest in pornography was the suppression of overt individual sexual responses that were at least possible in the private party atmosphere of the stag film and often solicited by the films themselves. Viewers in these dark yet public spaces encountered a more muted and diffuse, less directly participatory, viewing experience. This is not to say that the "classical" era of feature-length porno exhibited in theaters did not sexually arouse viewers, nor that masturbation never occurs in porno theaters (witness, for example, the sad fate of Paul Reubens, aka Pee Wee Herman).[30] However, it is to say that this arousal was not as insistently invited by the films themselves, nor as much an implicit part of "the show" as it had been in the space of the stag film exhibition.

Not only did the more public viewing situations militate against masturbation and other overt manifestations of arousal, but the films themselves constructed their arrangement of sexual acts into a climactic satisfaction meant to stand as a visual experience alone. It was the conceit of these narratives—if not always the actual practice of their viewers—that the film itself would be so absorbing and satisfying as not to lead the viewer "on the rebound" back to his or her own body. Indeed, the greater and greater spectacularizations of the multitudinous money shots of this era's pornography seemed determined to prove that the film's visual climaxes were sufficient unto themselves. It was as if viewers who might be aroused by the moving images depicted in the film could simply keep watching and ultimately transfer their own immediate arousal onto a more sublimated, vicarious plane.

Although most viewers were probably not nearly as absorbed by these narratives as the films presumed them to be, it is worth noting that no other moving-image pornography, even the sexual virtual realities we will examine below, presumes as high a degree of "escape" from the viewer's own body as these most "classical" of pornographic films seemed to presume. Of course, once these films ceased to be exhibited in the public space of the legitimate theater and were recycled on video into the privacy of the home, they could be put to new, and probably more logical, uses. Yet a hard-core moving-image form that once looked (to me at least) like the teleology of all visual sexual representation is now beginning to look more like a short blip in an otherwise fairly consistent history of more "interactive" engagements between bodies of spectators and machineries or networks of vision—whether the whirring projectors of the stag party, the remote controls of VCRs, or the "mouse" of interactive games.

Electronic On/scenities:

With the VCR revolution and interactive computer games of the eighties and nineties, moving-image pornography traveled from the big film screen to the small video and cable box and from the public theater to the private home. Big scale, (relatively) big budget narrative on/scenity had fueled the dream that hard-core pornography might become like other narrative films, only with sex. Despite the success of some of the better directors in suggesting what this kind of narrative cinema with sex might be like, this was not the direction hard-core pornography was to take in its life on/scene.[31]

Instead the VCR (and now multimedia) revolution intervened. According to a 1996 study by *U.S. News and World Report* it was in this electronic era that pornography attained an unprecedented pervasiveness in American society, becoming an eight-billion-dollar business.[32] As in so many previous new visual technologies, pornography drove first the VCR and then the interactive game revolutions. At first, hard-core films were simply re-released on video. Soon, however, porno for home use on the VCR became so popular that producers of new pornography realized that they could cut costs by shooting directly on video and skip theatrical release altogether. As porno theaters began to die out and high-quantity video production became the rule, budgets plummeted. Whole features began to be shot in two or three days, production quality sank. Yet customers continued to rent videos without regard to how cheaply, or expensively, they were made.

With the comparative lack of production value, however, came two major compensations: a much wider variety of pornographies for every conceivable taste and orientation; and a much greater "interaction" with the medium as viewers gained control of the pause, fast-forward and reverse switches of their remote controls. You could rent or buy a tape and watch it at home, alone, with friends or with sexual partners. You could select tapes from among an almost bewildering variety of sexual predilections, far beyond the simple homo/hetero binary of the previous era, and with the remote control you could choose to watch and re-watch your favorite scenes, integrating them into your own masturbatory fantasies or as a catalyst for sex with partners.[33] The private viewing situation made possible a revival of both the vociferous interactivity and frank masturbatory uses of the stag film but with the important difference that even in these more private spaces there was no guarantee, as there had been in the stag era, that women would be excluded. Indeed, there was nothing very secret about this particular museum since anyone with a VCR could now enter it, alone or with friends.

While theatrical pornography had often tried to fit a variety of different kinds of sexual numbers into its repertoire of sexual predilections—though always within the purview of its still predominantly male (hetero or homosexual) audiences—the new direct-to-video porn tended to aim at both more diverse and more specialized audiences, so many, in fact, that I can't possibly do justice to all of the varieties of moving-image pornography that have emerged since the early eighties.[34]

These include the sadomasochistic porn and the couples porn discussed in chapters seven and eight. A partial list of other varieties includes what my colleague Constance Penley calls upscale yuppie porn, a type of porn that seems to carry on the "big" budget theatrical tradition of the seventies with a special emphasis on glamour and set design.[35] Gonzo porn exists in defiant contrast to the upscale market, with intentionally sleazy effects and old-fashioned adolescent

Upscale yuppie porn: *Shock: the Sequel to Latex* (Michael Ninn, 1996)

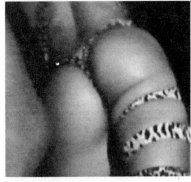

Gonzo fetish porn: *Buttman Goes to Rio* (John Stagliano, 1991)

Amateur porn

Bondage and discipline: *Learning the Ropes: vol. 3, Male Submission*

Porn performance art: *The Sluts and Goddesses Video Workshop* (Maria Beatty, Annie Sprinkle, 1992).

Instructional videos: *Nina Hartley's Guide to Anal Sex* (Nina Hartley, 1996)

New gay porn:
Honorable Discharge
(Jerry Douglas, 1993)

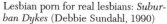

Lesbian porn for real lesbians: *Subur-ban Dykes* (Debbie Sundahl, 1990)

Bi-sexual porn: *Bi and Beyond: The Ultimate Sexual Union* (Paul Normand, 1986)

objectification of women's anatomies.[36] Even more downscale is amateur porn in which (presumably) ordinary folks originally exchange video-taped sexual performance.[37] Fetish porn can be elegantly upscale or resolutely down, but its emphasis is usually on leather and accessories. Bondage and discipline, which often displaces the display of genital sex onto elaborate scenarios of punishment is another popular subgenre. A wide range of "how-to" instructional videos offer various forms of sex education.[38] Porn performance art combines sex education with postmodern performance.[39] New forms of gay porn emerge in the wake of the need for AIDS education.[40] Lesbian porn for "real" lesbians also emerges, as opposed to the pseudo-lesbian numbers that were a staple of the classical era and that still continue in many contemporary video forms.[41] Finally, since the mid-eighties a category of bisexual porn in which homo, hetero and sadomasochistic pleasures freely mix has become popular.[42]

There are many more categories of video pornography—specializing in fat women, enemas, hetero and homosexual spanking films, transvestitism and transgender, and specific racial and ethnic categories of performers—but these example suffice to make the point: today, if you have seen one porn video you *haven't* seen them all. Contemporary video pornographies have something for every conceivable sexual predilection. Yet it would be a mistake to assume that these pornographies arise simply to cater to already-constituted, strictly compartmentalized, sexual orientations. More significantly, with the proliferation of categories, there is also an accompanying fluidity of appeal, a cross-fertilizing of eroticized polymorphous perversions. To me the most striking feature of these recent video pornographies is the extent to which unitary categories of identity begin to cross and blur. "Bi" porn, for example is often a freewheeling mix of hetero, gay, lesbian, s/m and even some amateur categories. When hermaphroditic bodies, real or constructed, begin to have sex with one another, as they do in the sequel to *Bi and Beyond*, it becomes difficult to describe the pleasures of sexual performance in any predictable binary terms.[43]

What can we say about the carnal pleasures of viewing these diverse forms of hard-core pornography at home on the TV with a remote control device in hand? It is tempting to see such interaction with electronic images as the quintessence of what Jean Baudrillard has called the postmodern "ecstasy of communication" in which simulacra replace the real and the human body becomes "superfluous" (Baudrillard 18). In pornography, however, the human body is never superfluous. In the case of this particular instance and the manual manipulation of remote control buttons it even seems that the spectatorial body has returned to some features of an older visual regime—that of manually operated, ocular parlor toys—thaumatropes, stereoscopes, flip books, even simple photo albums. Many of these were located in the private home and all represent a precinematic, "secret museum" that existed prior to the stag era proper (Williams 1995). Although pushing the button to pause on an image, repeat a sequence or fast-forward over boring narrative is not precisely the same thing as looking through a mutoscope, a flip book, or a thaumatrope (to cite only moving-image examples of manually operated optical toys once put to pornographic use), both viewing experiences engage the viewer's manual ability to establish the length and repetition of relatively discrete "views." Although any home viewing of a video, remote control in hand, gives a viewer the freedom to isolate and replay certain scenes, the pornographic "instant replay" has the added dimension of eroticizing the act of manual control in a potential context of privacy that is ideally suited to masturbation. Lisa Palac, for example, writes of "replaying certain close-ups over and over" in her first masturbatory experience with video pornography, noting that she spent "more time fingering the fast-forward button than anything else . . . I scanned for cute guys with long hair, punk, butchy women, plots with lots of psychological tension, come shots where he doesn't pull out and, most of all, genuine female orgasms' (Palac 145,).

In this restless scanning a person of any gender—no longer only the Secret Museum's elite gentleman—is able to complete, so to speak, the erotic implications of the trajectory of the outward intending, projective look that "rebounds" and "introjects" through the eyes back towards his or her own body. And as Palac notes, this completion takes place through the eroticized "fingering" of the remote button which itself becomes eroticized. Thus socially attuned arousal and satisfaction that was necessarily sublimated in public theater exhibition—where heterosexual viewers at least pretended not to be too physically interested in the larger audience group—is here quite possible. We might say that electronic interactivity takes place in a private space that in some ways resembles the private, removed nature of the stag party but it is not necessarily as furtive and "secret" nor as homogeneous, as the stag party proper.

There also exists a more public variant of the electronic viewing experience described above. This experience takes place in arcades frequently attached to adult bookstores and sex shops selling both magazines, tapes and a wide variety of sex toys. In small booths equipped with benches facing video monitors (and occasional film projectors) customers can choose to watch snippets from a selection of eight to twelve videos by feeding tokens into a slot. The videos range from conventional heterosexual porno to more specialized tastes, including s/m, gay, and bisexual. While arcades for viewing pornography have existed since the late sixties and have been described by Scott MacDonald in his classic essay, "Confessions of a Feminist Porn Watcher," (MacDonald, 1983), they have taken on a more pronounced homoerotic function as a meeting place for gay men even though the most common pornos shown are heterosexual. According to John Champagne, the predominance of heterosexual videos acts as a kind of "institutional denial" of the homoerotic function of the space of the arcade where elaborate flirting between male customers and a considerable amount of solitary and paired sexual activity in the booths takes place despite official prohibitions. Champagne also notes that since many of the video machines automatically channel-surf from video to video so that patrons can preview all the available selections before inserting their tokens, there is a certain "fluidity of boundaries between 'heterosexual' and 'homosexual' pleasures" (Champagne, 1997, 86–87). It is interesting that these arcades, many of which require inexpensive membership to enter, reproduce some aspects of the stag film—a "private" space of a party predominantly, if not exclusively, for men—while reproducing other aspects of home-video freedom to channel-surf among selections.

In order to pursue what is distinct about the spectatorial body's engagement with the home experience of electronic porno I would like to examine a more extreme case of interactivity in the pornographic computer games recently available on CD-Rom.[44] These games represent a radical extension of the power to stop, start, change tapes and repeat actions made possible by the remote control in home video (or arcade) viewing. Through these "interactions," the viewer gains a greater involvement in, and control over, the sexual scenarios of an erotic cyberspace. There are many forms of this cyber pornography, ranging from the most visionary plans for a total immersion "teledildonics" (Rheingold, 1990), to the existing relatively low-tech, written-word interactions between two live human beings taking place on the Internet today. I will limit my discussion here, however, to the existing interactions with moving images in the pornographic games now available on CD-ROM for playing on home, and office, computers.[45]

What is the spectatorial experience of viewing, and "interacting," with sexual objects in a virtual cyberspace? Virtual reality has come to mean any illusionistic reproduction that simulates, rather than represents, reality. All images, both analog and digital, can, in some way, be considered forms of virtual reality. However, virtual reality appears to offer something that these other representations and simulations do not: the illusion of being in, and interacting with, the world and the bodies "placed" in "cyberspace." In hard core terms, this can mean "having" sex with someone who isn't "there." Although all moving-image pornography might be referred to in this fashion, it is the paradoxical nature of a cyberspace "there" that seems to offer an escape from the presence and immediacy of the human body that needs to be examined in virtual porn.

Electronic computer games that "place" players in the virtual world depicted on their screens have somewhat misleadingly been marketed as the latest advance in graphic realism. In fact, compared to film, or even video, they are still rather crude imitations. Motion is not very smooth, voices and lips are often slightly out of synch, effects are not actually very "real." Yet rather than fault their makers for a lack of realism when measured against 70mm film with digital sound, I would suggest that this very lack of photographic realism may at this point be part of the uncanny fascination of these fast-selling games. Just as we now realize that the first moviegoers did not really think Lumière's train was actually "there" in the theater, but nevertheless marveled at the uncanny realism of the black and white, silent moving images—in effect, at the simulation of movement itself (Gunning, 1995)—so I would argue that today's "interactive" sensation seekers do not really think they are actually immersed in the virtual worlds depicted. Their pleasure seems to lie elsewhere.

Virtual porn on CD-ROM comes in many forms, some more interactive, some more hard-core, than others.[46] The producers of these games like to call them "interactive erotica" in order to avoid contamination with the maligned genre of pornography, but to the extent that most games recycle or at least imitate graphic sex scenes from hard-core films and videos, they are unquestionably hard-core pornography.[47]

Typically the player navigates a virtual space to achieve some kind of interaction with sexually performing bodies, most frequently women. The space depicted is often crudely schematic, even somewhat cartoonish; sometimes it is meant to be a futuristic outer space environment, sometimes it just looks like a vaguely dystopian future (the influence of both William Gibson and Ridley Scott is strong here).

In *The Dream Machine*, one of the least innovative, and least interactive, of the games I played, "I" am greeted by a hostess and then wander around a cold institutional-looking space until I happen across a hospital room where I see a nurse attending to a patient. They have sex while I watch. But after the encounter is over—signaled by the convention of the money shot which is scrupulously observed in this recycled 80s porn—the hostess asks me what I think about the sex I have seen. If I choose an option that is critical, she is too; if I approve, she does too. If at any point during a sexual encounter I get bored, I can click on a lavender "dream machine" logo and, in a digital refinement of the fast forward switch of the video remote control, the recycled porn video

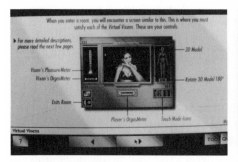

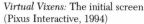

Virtual Vixens: The initial screen
(Pixus Interactive, 1994)

Virtual Vixens: "My" hand strokes Eve
(Pixus Interactive, 1994)

will leap ahead to the money shot. "Interactivity" is thus limited, in
this rather impoverished sexual fantasy, to even less control over the
representations than that afforded by video and to a short quiz at
the end of each number.[48]

A much more innovative game, judged more successfully interactive by some critics, is *Virtual Vixens.*[49] Though it is not new (1994)
it is one of the few games I can say I have "mastered," so I would
like to use it to ponder the interactive phenomenon. In it, I fly low
over a Martian-looking environment, land and descend, still in my
space suit, to an underground control room where my charge, according to the rules, is to save a male friend who is being held cap-
tive by the evil Crystal for having failed to sexually satisfy her. To
accomplish this rescue I must bring each of three "virtual vixens" to
orgasm before my iconic self in the game ejaculates. With each success, I can move on to the next woman. If I can do all this I will be
rewarded by a fourth, "real" woman who will invite me to remove
my glove and have "real" sex (representationally no different from
the rest). If I fail to satisfy a vixen she will verbally chew me out.

I begin the game by exploring an underground cavern where the
doors leading to each of the vixens can be accessed with an ID card.
I explore this virtual space through an exclusively subjective point of
view (I see the corridors, and doors, hear my footsteps, but until I
reach my hands or penis out toward one of the vixens, "I" do not
see "me"). When I enter a room I encounter a screen with a vixen
facing me. To the left of her image is her vertical Pleasure Meter
and horizontal OrgasMeter. Below her is my OrgasMeter. To the
lower right are the icons for my hand (which I can choose to be
open for caressing, or closed for removing clothes) and for my penis

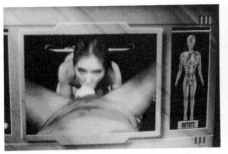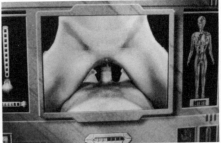

Virtual Vixens: Fellatio (Pixus Interactive, 1994)   *Virtual Vixens:* Penetration (Pixus Interactive, 1994)

(which can be in a horizontal or vertical position). If I click on the hand and then on the 3-D model above of the Vixen's face I get the result seen in this image, except that hand and vixen move. The object of the game is to caress, remove clothes and penetrate the vixen in ways that will get us both hot, but my mounting Orgasmeter must never get higher than hers.

Upon our first encounter, the first woman, Eve, comes to life and, somewhat plaintively, says, "My name is Eve. Funny name. I know I'm not a real woman. I'm just a pleasure matrix, a piece of ass in a software package." She then goes on to complain, not unlike Linda Lovelace in *Deep Throat*, that although the sex she experiences is pleasant, she never seems to get any real satisfaction. "For once I want a man to concentrate on me. I want to come. . . . I want you to be the one trembling with desire. I want to feel that I'm trembling in the light. I want to come for you. The question is, are you man enough to do it?"

Well, I wasn't "man" enough to make her come using my own resources, but eventually, along with the help of some "real" men more adept at computer games than I, I learned to begin stroking her face until Eve's pleasure meter got to the top. Then I could proceed to the next stage, removing clothes, stroking breasts, crotch and finally bringing my penis into play in both fellatio and penetration. But this is where it gets tricky, since now "I" tend to get hotter faster than she does. Eventually I needed to look at a "cheat sheet" to learn that once my Orgasmeter reaches seven it will keep mounting. The trick is to "bail out" (shift sexual activities to a new part of the body) before I reach seven. With this information, and a considerable amount of time, I could eventually satisfy the quirks of each woman.

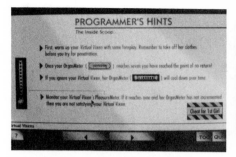

Virtual Vixens: A Cheat-sheet of "Programmer's Hints" (Pixus Interactive, 1994)

Virtual Vixens: The money shot—I win (Pixus Interactive, 1994)

If I don't bail out soon enough I will come and lose this round of the game—though just how badly I am expected to feel about this failure may depend upon my ego investment as a cyberspace Don Juan. My orgasm is rendered by the screen turning completely white followed by a severe verbal chastisement on the part of the VV. On the other hand, if I succeed in making her come I get to see an interactive, computer generated version of that sturdiest of hard core conventions: a virtual money shot.

How does this example of virtual, interactive, porn differ from previous moving-image pornography? Obviously the game prides itself on teaching a degree of male "sensitivity" to female pleasure. In this it is consciously revising both the stag film, which was indifferent to women's orgasms, and the classical *Deep Throat* model of heterosexual porno which simply assumed the woman's invisible pleasure could be measured by the man's visible ejaculation. That male orgasm emphatically does not equal female orgasm appears to be a major lesson of this particular game. The male player is clearly "taught" that lesson, by losing the game when he comes prematurely.

In the three different stages of pornographic spectatorship I have chronicled—the ob/scene stag film, the on/scene era of "classical" features, and the many diverse contemporary video pornographies produced for home viewing—we have observed an increased attention to the details of sexual function and an increased awareness, once the "men's only" club ended, that male pleasure is non-synonymous with female pleasure. *Virtual Vixens* extends that lesson and makes the technical mastery of a non-synchronous female pleasure its goal. In doing so, however, the game puts a premium on literally and figuratively "scoring" on the woman.

As a feminist historian of porn I find it just a little depressing to see the extent to which, for all its exalted "interaction," this pornography consists primarily of men doing things to women and women, for all their verbal aggressiveness, having things done to them. The man "plays" upon the virtual bodies of the women. Though the game is ostensibly about these women's demands for pleasure, the vixens cannot initiate sexual action themselves. There is a strange poignancy about a pornographic woman who knows she is "just a piece of ass in a software package," yet who asserts a desire for pleasure nonetheless.

Since an awareness of the preprogrammed quality of the activity is built into the game, and even into the personae of the vixens, the player can be presumed, on some level, to know that he is playing as much with himself—or with another man's idea of what he would like to play with—as he is with any real "other." In this sense, the game can be seen to be more masturbatory than previous moving-image pornography: playing the game presumes playing with oneself through the intermediary of a pre-programmed "other." At the same time, however, the concentration and manual engagement required by the game itself would seem to interfere with the more intense levels of sexual fantasy likely to accompany such masturbation, always bringing the player back to the mundane reality of manipulating those two, non-commensurate, pleasure meters. Nor, of course, does the man's pleasure meter necessarily correspond to what is felt in the body of the player, although the conceit of the game is that it does. Finally, as my own participation in the game attests, even though the game is designed for a male subject to play with a female object, in an era of on/scenity, there is really no limit to who will play the game.

In what precise sense can the manipulation of virtual hand and penis in cyberspace and the actual manipulation of hand, and whatever else, in actual space be called interactive? With what precisely does the player interact? Indeed, if true interactivity is to be defined as communication with the difference and unpredictability of an "other" (as opposed to interacting with the sameness of oneself), the interaction with this female "piece of ass in a software package" would seem to be the height of solipsism.[50] Where a real sex partner might surprise you, the woman on the screen has no independent agency. The paradox of these interactive games would seem to be that the greater the *simulation* of the agency of the "other," the more the *real* sense of an other is missing. The visual and visceral pleasures solicited by the game seem not to be aiming for an extreme reality effect (as in, "this is real! I am there playing with her!") but rather for an uncanny sense of dispersal (as in the more divided and distracted "'I' am here playing with myself" *and* "'I' am also there playing with the vixen!"). In this sense "interactivity" could be defined not as an exchange or communication between self and other but rather as the mobility of a "self" interacting with two vying impressions of reality each of which is slightly lessened in effect through the interference of the other.

The spectatorial experience of interactive hard core thus tends to be that of a body felt to be in two places at once: the actual viewing and feeling body, located in the physical world before the computer screen, and the virtual body which, with varying degrees of believability, interacts with simulated, symbolic space, objects, and persons that are not literally there. Some commentators have described the pleasures of virtual reality as a freedom *from* the spectator's own body as if in "entering" virtual reality, one abandoned one's "meat" (Springer, 306). I think, however, that the lesson of interactive hard core suggests that one's "meat" is never abandoned. It might be more useful to characterize what some critics call a fantasy of disembodiment (Pryor and Scott, 173) instead as a new kind of mobility, a blurring of the boundaries between here and there that in no way escapes the body. In this mobility, pleasure consists in a body that is uncannily both *here* (where I sit before the screen perhaps masturbating while manipulating the mouse) *and there* (where, in the case of this game, my virtual hand or penis—oddly no mouth— "touches" "a piece of ass in a software package").

Where all previous forms of moving-image pornography have demonstrated different degrees of extending the viewing body towards a virtual body on screen, leading to correspondingly different degrees of encounter with the viewing body, in Sobchack's terms "on the rebound," here it seems possible to say that, instead of a temporal sequence of extending and intending towards the virtual and then rebounding back upon the material body, there is a sustained simultaneous dividedness of attention and blurring of the distinction between the virtual bodies on screen—one of which is now presumed to be "my" own—and my own "carnal density" here where I sit before the screen.

I would add, however, that while this busy pleasure of being simultaneously here and there may be exacerbated in interactive hard core, giving the porn spectator something to do in both places, it does not represent a radical departure from previous visual and visceral pleasures—think, for example of the man cranking both the machine and himself in the stag film, *A Country Stud Horse*. Rather, this prolonged here and thereness allows us to recognize the extent to which the mind-body separation presumed by most models of vision may never have operated in pornographic viewing (and perhaps have never operated in non-sexual forms of visual pleasure as well).[51]

I would therefore not argue for a radical break between "cyberporn" and all previous forms of moving-image pornography. The more significant break in the social conditions of pornographic viewing occurs in the differences between the ob/scene and the on/scene, between private men's club consumption of ob/scenities in the stag era and the public, less restrictive consumption of on/scenities in the classical theatrical era. For it was this shift from restricted, private viewings addressed to exclusive clubs of men to a "general public" of sexually interested adults that made possible the later proliferation of on/scenities in the electronic age. The subsequent move back to more private viewing venues—the home equipped with VCR and computer; the booth of the arcade—is thus not a return to the true exclusivity and homogeneity of the era of the ob/scene, even if it is a return to more private viewing situations.

Indeed, the greater "interactivity" and "carnal density" of all contemporary forms of porn spectatorship may only seem radically new in contrast to the anomaly of the "classical" era. For they may simply be an extension of what hard-core viewing has always offered: a place for "interacting" with non-present, virtual sexual objects. Where they differ is simply in the combination of enhanced control and phantasmatic bodily dispersal within that "interaction."

What should we say, however, about the fact that in this pornography the identity of the person experiencing the carnal density of vision is male, the "piece of ass in a hardware package" is female, and the iconography that represents her orgasm is still the "money shot"? The diverse video pornographies described in the preceding pages are open to a wide range of different sexual subjectivities—straight men, straight women, gays, lesbians, bisexuals, fetishists, dominants and submissives, yuppie heterosexuals, egalitarian couples, etc.—and to the communication between those subjectivities. In contrast, as we have seen, even the most innovative of the hardcore interactive CD-ROMs regress to the binarism of male subject, female object typical of the stag film. Like the stag film, but without the excuse of the homogeneous "Secret Museum," these "interactive" on/scenities have not begun to take full advantage—the way text-based cyberspace on the Internet takes advantage—of the potential for sexual play.

However, there is nothing in the technology per se to prevent such play and there may be quite a bit to encourage it. Once these programmers, or their more savvy, and one hopes more diverse, successors begin to imagine the erotic potential of getting beyond the obvious binaries, interactive hard core could get as interesting as thinking about it now is. The possibilities are great. Imagine being cast in the role of a female-to-male transsexual whose task is to rescue an old boyfriend from a female dominatrix with a foot fetish. What do "you" do when you discover the old boyfriend doesn't want to be rescued?

Perhaps the most important lesson to draw from this survey of the history of American moving-image pornographic spectatorship is that it is not monolithic; like any genre, it has a history. Since much of this history was played out in the absence of women spectators it is not surprising that women often find much to deplore in it. As a feminist I find the crude stag films' endless fascination with uncovering the secrets of the female body dull and objectifying; as a film scholar I find their primitivism fascinating. Also as a feminist, I admire the female empowerment of the newer couples' pornography as well as the woman-centered adventurousness and play of lesbian pornography. As a porn consumer who seeks to stimulate my sensorium, I find that what moves me the most is the one form that has probably never considered my response: gay male porn. Finally as a woman who is hopelessly inept at navigating the maze of cyberspace, I wonder why I have to do all this work, peering at a relatively little screen, rather than just watch interesting sex in the most sensuous form available (which is still 35 mm film).

I don't presume to understand these responses but they do teach me that contemporary pornography is no simple matter of appealing to the obvious and established sexual identities of viewers. At least some of the fun of porno is watching sexual play that is different from what we might actually do. Rather than assume that each sexual predilection simply has its own kind of representative porno, it seems more apt to assume that pornographies are becoming part of the process by which spectators discipline themselves to enjoy different varieties of visual and visceral pleasure—pleasures that are both produced in the imagination *and* felt in the body.

We have seen that looking at the hard-core image of sex acts is not the same as looking at naked bodies "in the flesh." Yet we have also seen that there is a need to account for visual pleasures that occur "in the flesh," especially when these visceral pleasures might diverge considerably from what we might "do" in the flesh. It would seem that the different stages of the history of moving-image pornography have produced different degrees and kinds of "carnal density" in the bodies of viewers. If pornography matters as a cultural form, we cannot simply dismiss the history of these responses as a matter of mindless, gratuitous, masturbatory sex, nor can we continue to elide the body of the viewer by making sweeping generalizations about the phallic mastery of a disembodied "male gaze." Now that so many different kinds of pornography are so emphatically on/ scene, now that the academic study of pornography is itself on/ scene, it is time to consider the quality and kind of its visual—and visceral—pleasures.

Notes

Chapter 1

1. Foucault's three published volumes on the history of sexuality became, perhaps inevitably, much more than a history of sexuality alone. In two and three (1985, 1986), Foucault began to employ sexuality as a means of examining a culture's entire notion of self. Thus, whereas *The History of Sexuality: An Introduction* offers a broad overview of the new importance of sexuality in the modern age and the inseparability of the ideas of sexual liberation and repression, volume two, *The Use of Pleasure*, modifies this original project by tracing the "origins" of modern notions of sexuality and self back to the Greeks. Volume three, *The Care of the Self*, then moves to the Roman era and the transformation of the Greek use of pleasure. Foucault's death in 1984 means that we will never have the projected six volumes of this study or return to the modern period. Classicists, of course, have been quick to criticize the details of the historical examination (Foucault was a nonspecialist in Greek and Latin). My interest here, however, is not with the details of his knowledge of the ancients but with the general argument of the enormous contrast between the use of pleasure in our era and that of the Greeks. Recent work on the social construction of sexuality that has taken its cue from Foucault includes Weeks 1981, 1985; Ariès and Bejin 1985, an anthology with essays ranging from topics such as homosexuality in ancient Rome to prostitution, sex, and society in a fifteenth-century French town. Recently, Arnold Davidson (1987) has argued that the experience of sexuality and the concept of perversion emerged simultaneously, the latter as the deviation that threatened sexual norms. Davidson follows Foucault in arguing for the emergence of a psychic, as opposed to anatomic, conception of sexuality in the mid-nineteenth century.

2. Other feminist theorists who have challenged Foucault on this ques-

tion of the power differential between men and women include Teresa de Lauretis (1984, 1987), Meaghan Morris (1979), Sandra Bartky (forthcoming), and Isaac Balbus (1986).

3. Some of the models for this work on mass-produced genres for women include Modleski 1984; Radway 1984; Doane 1987; and, in a slightly different way, Clover 1987.

4. I do not know the origin of this conventional wisdom. Ellen Willis (1983, 463) refers to it in the paraphrase "What turns me on is erotic; what turns you on is pornographic." Maurice Charney (1981, 1) quotes, without a specific citation, Robbe-Grillet's more elegant formulation: "La pornographie, c'est l'érotisme des autres."

5. See, for example, Carol Thurston 1987; Califia 1981; Samois 1982; and my discussion of the work of Femme Productions in Chapter 8 below.

6. The terms *machines of the visible* and *frenzy of the visible* are from Comolli 1980, 121, 122. See Chapter 2, note 2, below.

7. "Relative autonomy" or "semi-autonomy" refers to the much-discussed question within Marxist interpretations of culture of the degree to which the ideology of cultural productions is ultimately determined by, and reflective of, the real conditions of existence. Marxist philosopher Louis Althusser (1971, 155) has argued that what is represented in ideology is not the real relations that govern the existence of individuals but the "imaginary relation of those individuals to the real relations in which they live." While the term *imaginary* is understood as the fictive misrecognition of the self in language, Althusser's point is that this imaginary, being the basis of all subjectivity, seems natural and true. By so understanding the individual's relation to ideology, one can see that the ideas or representations that constitute ideology are not mystifications foisted on the members of a society by a ruling class or group but arise out of each subject's relation to real conditions of existence, which are constructed in discourse. Ideology thus becomes an inescapable condition: we are all *in it*. Since there is no catapulting ourselves outside of ideology, but only the "interpellating," of subjects in discourse, it would seem more valuable to study pornography from the perspective of the subjects it constructs than as the regrettable false consciousness of (patriarchal) ideology. One of the challenges of this book's study of hard core will be to see how male and female genders are "interpellated" by its discourse.

8. There have been numerous responses to this commission, from the civil libertarian collection of essays *United States of America vs. Sex: How the Meese Commission Lied About Pornography* (Nobile and Nadler 1986) to the ACLU's *Polluting the Censorship Debate: A Summary and Critique of the Final Report of the Attorney General's Commission on Pornography* (1986). See also Carole Vance's excellent reporting on the commission in

"The Meese Commission on the Road" (1986). (Vance is currently working on a book-length ethnographic study of the commission.) My own review of the final report (L. Williams 1986c) concentrates on some of the ideas I will develop below. More recently, Susan Stewart has published a fascinating study of the commission's report, considered as pornography itself: "The Marquis de Meese" (1988); Stewart shows how the commission's public discourse shares the same quantitative logic as pornography and is caught in the same predicament of typology and enumeration. In a similar vein, Clive Bloom (1988) has argued the failure of the commission's bureaucratic machinery of scientific measurement to advance the cause of morality. Although the last two articles both call for greater specificity in understanding pornography, they sometimes fall victim to the rhetorical ploy (not unfamiliar to the Meese Commission itself) of assimilating their particular objects of study, whether bachelor machines or Meese Commissioners, to a monolithic entity the very diversity of which is never examined.

9. Justice Potter Stewart's exact words are worth quoting: "I have reached the conclusion . . . that under the First and Fourteenth Amendments criminal laws in this area are constitutionally limited to hard-core pornography. I shall not today attempt further to define the kinds of material I understand to be embraced within that shorthand description; and perhaps I could never succeed in intelligently doing so. But I know it when I see it, and the motion picture involved in this case is not that" (*Jacoblellis v. Ohio*, 378 U.S. 184, 197 [1964]).

10. In fact, as Edward Donnerstein and his colleagues have indicated (1987, 89), quite the opposite is the case. Numerous studies indicate that representations of violence increased up until 1977 but have decreased since then. See the further discussion of these "questions of violence" in Chapters 6 and 7.

11. Actually, many organizations have the central goal of suppressing pornography. Some call themselves simply Women Against Pornography. Another group is called Women Against Violence in Pornography and the Media. Still another is called Women Against Violence Against Women. Some of the key publications responsible for formulating this anti-pornography position include Barry 1978; Griffin 1981; Lederer (1980); MacKinnon 1987; Dworkin 1979, 1987; Daly 1984; and Steinem 1986a. The documentary film *Not a Love Story* (Bonnie Klein, 1982) has also been influential.

12. I shall have more to say about domination and submission in Chapter 7. For the time being, it is important to note how much this question has been obfuscated by anti-pornography feminists who are unwilling to recognize the consensual nature of the sexual acts depicted or the presence

of female dominators in the works that are so often held up as evidence of patriarchal domination. See, for example, Duggan, Hunter, and Vance in Burstyn 1985, 139. See also Ehrenreich, Hess, and Jacobs (1986, 128) on the apparent popularity in sexual practice, if not also in sexual representation, of the position of the dominated (the masochist or "bottom") over the dominating (sadist or "top").

13. Works representing this "position" include Snitow, Stansell, and Thompson 1983; Vance 1984, and the anthology in which that essay is contained, *Pleasure and Danger*; Burstyn 1985; Carter 1978; Stimpson and Person 1980; *Signs: Journal of Women in Culture and Society* 10, no. 1 (1984); Ehrenreich, Hess, and Jacobs 1986; Valverde 1985; Kaplan 1987; K. Ellis et al. 1986; and Russ 1985.

14. FACT was initially formed to combat the MacKinnon/Dworkin ordinances. After the defeat of the ordinances, however, it was continued to combat all state efforts to control, suppress, or determine the expression of women's sexuality.

15. This was the problem, for example, with Ann Snitow's (1983) ground-breaking essay, first published in 1979, "Mass Market Romance: Pornography for Women Is Different." Snitow's insight that mass-market romance is a kind of soft-core pornography for women, portraying sex as more of a social drama than a physical event, was undeniably important; however, it assumed rather than demonstrated a knowledge of the normal "pornography for men" from which women's pornography differed. Problematic is the assumption that sex-as-event is self-evidently meaningful. I believe we need to understand more of this male pornography before we venture to say how women's may differ.

16. These two genres also have important parallels that are mutually illuminating. See Clover 1987; and my discussion of women and monsters in horror films, L. Williams 1984b.

17. In a later essay on pornography Kuhn is more willing to consider pornography "proper," but she still argues that pornography is inimical to all sexual liberation—without, however, specifying its various forms and uses ("Lawless Seeing," in Kuhn 1985). Moreover, while she does not advocate censorship and, in an approach consistent with her earlier essay, argues that pornography is not a "special case," her arm's-length approach to the genre, together with her beginning premise (p. 20) that "if anything in our culture is unfathomable it is masculinity itself," ultimately limits her ability to "fathom" the genre.

18. These are features that critics of the form as diverse as Beverley Brown (1981), Alan Soble (1986), Richard Dyer (1985), and Stephen Ziplow (1977) could agree on.

Chapter 2

1. Foucault discusses these modern mechanisms of surveillance in, for example, *Discipline and Punish* (1979).

2. Materialist historian Jean-Louis Comolli (1980, 122–123) writes that the second half of the nineteenth century, which ends in the "birth" of cinema, "lives in a sort of frenzy of the visible . . . of the social multiplication of images: ever wider distribution of illustrated papers, waves of prints, caricatures, etc. . . . of a geographical extension of the field of the visible and the representable. . . . The whole world becomes visible at the same time that it becomes appropriatable."

3. I have already written about this relation between body and optical machine in an article on Muybridge and Méliès (L. Williams 1986a). Here I expand and, I hope, improve on some of those ideas by exploring the pornographic elements of this relation.

4. Di Lauro and Rabkin (1976, 43) state that it is impossible to determine the exact date of the earliest stag film, but they suggest, following Ado Kyrou and Lo Duca, that the earliest titles were probably French. Lo Duca (1958, vol. 1) cites a 1907 French film titled *Le voyeur* as one of the earliest stag films, but it is not clear how he dates it.

5. Muybridge's "place" as a pioneer of film history has aroused some controversy over the years. In one of the earliest American histories of motion pictures, *A Million and One Nights*, Terry Ramsaye (1926, 35–41) denied that Muybridge made any substantial contribution to the invention of cinema, giving credit for most of the achievements to his assistant in the horse motion studies, John D. Issacs. But beginning in 1955 with the Dover reprints of Muybridge's *The Human Figure in Motion* (1955a) and *Animals in Motion* (1955b), then with Gordon Hendricks's *Origins of the American Film* (1972), and finally with Dover's publication of *Muybridge's Complete Human and Animal Locomotion* (1979), enthusiasm for his work grew enormously. Earlier neglect was (perhaps overenthusiastically) countered by Kevin MacDonnell's *Eadweard Muybridge: The Man Who Invented the Motion Picture* (1972). The best recent discussion of Muybridge's place in photographic and film history is found in Richard Bartlett Haas's biography of the photographer (1976).

6. Supposedly Stanford made a wager of twenty-five thousand dollars. Since Stanford was evidently not a betting man, though, this wager was more likely another part of the publicity generated by the event. See Haas 1976, 46.

7. Laura Mulvey's use of Freud and Lacan in this article to argue that the body of the woman on the screen represents "lack" to a phallic male

viewer has been enormously influential in feminist psychoanalytic film theory and criticism. Extended explanations of Mulvey's ideas and their importance to feminist film criticism can be found in Kaplan 1983; and Kuhn 1982. I shall take up this question of fetishism at greater length in Chapter 4. For now, however, let me note only that Mulvey's argument that dominant cinema fetishizes women because of the threat posed by their apparent "castration," which in turn requires a disavowal of this "lack," is not easily demonstrated by visual pornographic texts. Indeed, these texts have often proved difficult to align with the prevailing theory. John Ellis (1980, 103), for example, goes to some lengths to rescue Mulvey's notion that the naked woman's genitals so obsessively investigated by hard-core pornography represent "lack" and displeasure, arguing that the fetishistic regime is upheld through the very fetishization of woman's sexual pleasure. Paul Willemen (1980), however, in an insightful reply to Ellis, argues that pornography cannot simply be aligned with dominant narrative cinema, that it implements a different order of "looks" and a different narrative regime that are not typical of classical cinematic narrative and are, in fact, more like musicals in the regular suspension of narrative. Claire Pajaczkowska (1981, 85), in a reply to both Willemen and Ellis, and along different lines again, maintains that the idea that women's naked bodies must invoke castration anxiety in spectators is a "misappropriation of a metapsychology" that conflates the instance of the visual with the instance of paternal threat. I tend to agree with Pajaczkowska. Mulvey herself (1981, 1985) has amended and modified her earlier positions. My discussion of these issues will attempt to skirt the particulars of the Freudian and Lacanian problematic, for in my view this problematic has now become part of the problem itself, especially in discussing works where sexual organs are both literal *and* metaphoric. The theory that constructs the female either as anatomical "lack" or, with respect to the phallus, as lacking "lack" in comparison to the masculine subject's more complete entrance into the symbolic begins, in its reliance on so exclusively masculine an assumption of subjectivity, to block the difficult, though not foreclosed, discovery of power and pleasure for the female subject and spectator.

8. I have argued this myself in "Film Body" (L. Williams 1986a). Now I would suggest that mastery may never be so certain; the cinematic work of fetishization differs considerably from the actual perversion of fetishism. See Chapter 4.

9. Albert Londe took many of the photographs of Charcot's hysterics with an apparatus derived from Muybridge's; Londe is mentioned briefly in Etienne Jules Marey's *La photographie du mouvement* (1892, 81–82).

10. Historians cite an interesting phenomenon related to the exhibition of this film: when shown in the small, personal viewing machine of the Ki-

netoscope, this close-up kiss aroused no uproar; but when magnified by projection onto a large screen at the next stage of "machines of the visible," the details of this to us tame and rather comic bit of puckering and smooching between a middle-aged couple caused great indignation (see Mast 1986, 25). Robert C. Toll (1982, 184) cites a Chicago critic who wrote of the same film: "Magnified to gargantuan proportions, it is absolutely disgusting. . . . Such things call for police intervention."

11. This fragment from Hesiod (1977, 169) settles the argument to Hera's disadvantage when Teiresias explains that the man has one part pleasure and the woman "ten in full." For this disclosure Hera blinds Teiresias, but Zeus gives him the "seer's power." The myth is a fitting exemplar of the quantitative means designed by men to measure the "truth" of women's pleasure against the phallic standard. For further discussion, see Chapters 6 and 8 and the Conclusion.

12. This does not include hard-core films and videos such as those that begin to be made in the early seventies, which address themselves to women as well as men. See Chapters 4 and 5.

13. Biddy Martin (1982, 17) writes, for example: "Men will no longer speak for mankind. Should women, by implication, no longer . . . speak as women?" The answer, Denise Riley (1988) argues, may very well be both no and yes: no because the category of women has no absolute ontological foundation or continuity; yes because feminism requires it. Riley's point is that the history of feminism has been just as much a struggle against overzealous identifications as it has been the assumption of the identification "women." Feminism is the site, then, of the systematic fighting out of this instability (p. 4).

Chapter 3

1. Di Lauro and Rabkin's is the best of these studies. Others include Knight and Alpert 1967; Gordon 1980; Duca 1958; and Kyrou 1964.

2. The very earliest primitive films were, of course, content to offer relatively discrete units of spectacular show, frequently centered on the moving body: a dance, a knockout, a grimacing face, a kiss, a sneeze, etc. In the stag films discussed in this chapter, otherwise accomplished, nonprimitive productions seem to regress to the kind of prenarrative show evident in these early films. André Gaudrault (1987) uses the term *monstration* to describe this theatrical mode of showing as opposed to narrative's scriptural mode of telling. The term is not intended to imply primitivism; rather, Gaudrault argues that all cinema deploys both monstration and narration and that cinematic monstration has a theatrical mode that is parallel to scriptural narration. Nevertheless, the notion of direct show contained

in the term seems an appropriate description of the more basic unit of "show" operating at these hard-core moments in the stag film.

3. *Correction Please* is a scholarly pamphlet distributed along with Burch's film of the same name; it has no publication information. Both film and pamphlet, along with Burch's (1978–1979) essay on the primitive cinema of Edwin S. Porter, offer an appreciation of primitive cinema from the perspective of its spectators rather than as stages of evolution toward more perfect forms of realist illusion. Burch's work is suggestive and original, although some of it—such as the idea that primitive cinema is like a child's conception of space, or that the phylogeny of cinema may be grounded in human ontogeny—seems tenuous at best. What I find useful in Burch is his ability to explain, through analogy to primitive cinema, how the male spectator of stags, having gotten *part way* into the picture, was content to stay there so long.

4. Other examples of primitivism occur in instances of frequent temporal overlap, that is, seeing an action over again when the film cuts to a different point of view, as from a building's exterior to its interior. The most famous example is the original version of Porter's *Life of an American Fireman* (1904). Film historians Charles Musser (1979) and André Gaudrault (1983) cite such films to conclude that early filmmakers tended to consider each shot as an autonomous unit in which spatial continuity takes precedence over temporal continuity. Noël Burch (1977–1978, 104) infers from this precedence of space that the "feeling of being seated in a theater had . . . priority over . . . being carried away by an imaginary time-flow." This certainly seems to be true for the stag spectator.

5. Judith Mayne notes this resistance in her forthcoming book *The Woman at the Keyhole*. *A Subject for the Rogues Gallery* is currently circulating as part of the American Federation of Arts "Before Hollywood" program—though the print shown here is without the coda of facial relaxation contained in the Library of Congress print I screened.

6. The term *suture* is derived from Lacanian psychoanalysis. Applied to film it has come to describe the process by which cinematic discourse, through the linking of shots, also links viewers—metaphorically "suturing" or "sewing" them—into the shifting points of view of different characters. In general, however, suture describes the initial fragmentation and disunity created by the "cuts" of cinematic articulation and the way those cuts are sutured, or covered over, by devices such as eye-line matches and shot/reverse shot to produce the illusion of unity in the viewing subject. See, for example, Kaja Silverman's chapter on suture in *The Subject of Semiotics* (1983).

7. Neither this film nor any like it is mentioned in Di Lauro and Rabkin (1976), Knight and Alpert (1967), or the "golden oldies"–style compilation videotapes now available for rental.

8. The phrase "weaving a narrative" is Tom Gunning's (1981), referring to D. W. Griffith's interweaving of one location or action with another to develop a narrative film style in keeping with bourgeois written and theatrical narrative traditions.

9. The term is described in Ziplow (1977, 34); it is also called a "come shot." Ziplow uses the two terms interchangeably. I use *money shot* throughout this book for its added connotation of reification and fetishization. See Chapter 4.

10. The term *homosocial* refers to the social forms of relation obtaining "between men." It is a much more general and pervasive force uniting men than the more specific *homosexual*; see Sedgwick 1985.

11. Koch confines her study largely to the social context of brothel screenings in major European metropolises.

12. Compared to American stag films of roughly the same period, these male-to-male sexual relations between the telegraph boy and the husband are highly unusual in the midst of otherwise heterosexual couplings. I have not seen enough French stag films to say if this is typical.

13. Emile Benveniste (1971, 206) makes a useful distinction between discourse (*discours*), which is always from someone and addressed to another, and story (*histoire*), which disguises its discursive origin and destination and presents itself as if coming from nowhere and addressed to no one. The primitive stag film is of interest in this context for its relatively unusual deployment of discourse at the moment of hard-core "action."

14. This lack of professionalism includes reactions on the part of women performers that run the gamut from boredom to surprise to disgust.

15. The "Horse" of this title appears to be a misprint of *House*, since a house and not a horse figures in the narrative.

16. See Chapter 2, note 7.

17. The case in which this ruling occurred bore the amusing title *U.S. vs. Married Love* and, like Comstock's failure to prosecute Margaret Sanger, was another instance of an oppositional woman's voice resisting the dominant discourse of men. The author of *Married Love*, Marie Stopes, argued that husbands often exercised their conjugal rights inopportunely. As Judge Woolsey himself notes, "It pleads with seriousness, and . . . eloquence, for a better understanding by husbands of the physical and emotional side of the sex life of their wives" (Kendrick 1987, 191).

18. Films in which women have sexual relations with animals, such as *Beauty and the Boxer* (British?, 1952) and *Mexican Dog* (Mexico, ca. 1930s), qualify here, as do narratives that depict rape (*An English Tragedy*, ca. 1920–1926; cited in Di Lauro and Rabkin 1976). Nevertheless, some humorous films pose the joke, or the humiliation of being "taken," as being on the man. In *The Goat* (USA, ca. 1920–1926), for example, a dreamy,

bespectacled man steals the clothes of three woman who go swimming at a beach and then bargains to return them for sexual favors. They agree that he can choose one of them, but the act must be performed through a knot-hole in a fence and he must pay fifty dollars. The three women substitute a goat for the woman he has chosen, and he proceeds to penetrate it, assuring them afterward that it was "the best girl I ever had in all my life!" Sometime later the women turn up on the beach, one with a pillow under her clothes pretending to be pregnant. She demands and gets more money from the man, but then removes her pillow and throws it at the man. All three women raise their dresses and flash their bottoms at him in ridicule. Yet another film, *The Pick-up* (USA, ca. 1923), shows a woman hitchhiker getting a ride from a man, but when he insists on sexual favors, she chooses to walk. The next day he picks her up again, and "twenty miles from town she still said no." Finally, when fifty miles from town, she agrees to give favors for the ride. When he asks her why she finally agreed, she answers, "I'll be damned if I'll walk fifty, just to keep you . . . from getting a dose of CLAP!!" Even in the misogynist stag film, the joke is sometimes on the man.

Chapter 4

This chapter is an expanded version of articles written for the *Quarterly Review of Film Studies* (forthcoming) and for the anthology *For Adult Users Only: The Case of Violent Pornography* (forthcoming). I wish to thank the editors, Susan Gubar and Joan Hoff-Wilson of *For Adult Users Only*, and Beverle Houston of *QRFS*, for their helpful advice. To Beverle Houston, who worked on the manuscript while struggling against cancer, my thank you is unfortunately too late.

1. In any case, *Deep Throat* was the first well-known film to show a penis "in action."

2. Two recent works, both touching on fetishism, have provided me with historical insights into the concept: Mitchell 1986; and Simpson 1982.

3. In her now-classic essay, Rubin (1979, 176) argues that the exchange of women is neither a definition of culture, as Lévi-Strauss says, nor a system in and of itself. A kinship system is an "imposition of social ends upon a part of the natural world. It is therefore 'production'. . . . a transformation of objects (in this case people) to and by a subjective purpose." Rubin's point is that the subordination of women should be seen as a product of the relationships by which sex and gender are organized. It is not a systematic given of all cultural arrangements but, rather, a product of them.

4. See Chapter 6 for a discussion of the waning of the money shot. It

is also possible that new (though rarely overtly acknowledged) AIDS awareness may revive reliance on this figure, since the visual spectacle of ejaculation can substitute for the now more dangerous risk of exposure to body fluids.

Chapter 5

1. Sound has been much slower to be analyzed by film theorists, partly because sound arrived late to film, long after the cinematic image had been firmly ensconced as the central element of cinematic signification, and partly because sound has traditionally played only a supportive role as anchor to the image. Other theorists who have written about sound include Stephen Heath (1981) and Michel Chion (1982).

2. Stephen Heath (1981, 189) writes that a "whole gamut of pants and cries" function to "deal with the immense and catastrophic problem . . . of the visibility or not of pleasure, to provide a *vocal image* to guarantee the accomplishment of pleasure."

3. It is remarkable how much fine work on the movie musical film scholarship has produced in the last five years, work that has considerably aided me in my effort to understand the functions of number and narrative in the hard-core feature. A precursor of much of this work is the anthology of essays edited by Rick Altman, *Genre: The Musical* (1981), followed by Jane Feuer's *The Hollywood Musical* (1982), and then by Altman's own *The American Film Musical* (1987). Most recently Gerald Mast's *Can't Help Singin'* (1987) has added to the riches.

4. There is, of course, a hard-core "version" of this musical entitled *Very Dirty Dancing*.

5. No fewer than two popular cycles of films are based on variations of incest themes: *Taboo* (I–IV) and *Taboo American Style*, Parts 1–4. The latter film series is a continuing soap opera–style family melodrama, complete with a millionaire matriarch played by Gloria Leonard, that advertises itself as "Beyond Dallas." The first installment, *Taboo American Style, Part 1: The Ruthless Beginning*, was chosen by the X-Rated Critics Organization as Most Erotic Film of 1985 (Rimmer 1986, 427).

Chapter 6

1. John Mueller (1984), for example, makes this judgment. On separation and integration, see also Morden 1981; and Delameter forthcoming.

2. For excellent discussions of the legal history of rape and the dependence on often unverifiable evidence of victims' mental states, see Ferguson 1987; and Estrich 1987.

3. An unpublished statistical analysis of thirty-two top-selling pornographic features from 1972 to 1985 by Steven Prince and associates (1987) at the Annenberg School of Communications, University of Pennsylvania, indicates that incidents of rape in films decreased from 33 percent of the sexual acts performed in 1976–1979 to only 7 percent in 1980–1985. Edward Donnerstein et al. (1987, 89) cite studies of other forms of pornography which confirm that after a high point in depictions of sexual violence in 1977 a marked decrease has occurred. The ACLU's (1986, 41–42) study of the Meese Commission's report notes that the commission eliminated from the final version a full report of its finding "that only 0.6% of the imagery was of 'force, violence, or weapons.'" For an intelligent discussion of the difficulty of assessing how violent images in adult magazines influence rape rates, see also Scott and Schwalm 1988.

4. More recent musicals, such as *Dirty Dancing* (Emile Ardoline, 1987), *Hairspray* (John Waters, 1987), and *Absolute Beginners* (Julien Temple, 1986), now make a point of bringing this formerly excluded material into their texts.

5. This disjunction is quite evident even in those films that continue to observe the rule. In the recent hard-core feature *Careful, He May Be Watching* (Henry Pachinko, 1987), Seka plays the wife of an airline pilot who moonlights, unbeknownst to her husband, as a porno actress. On the set of her latest movie, while engaged in hard-core action, her male co-star ignores the director's shouted advice to pull out. Chastised by the director after the scene is over, he insists that he couldn't, "it felt too good." Although the scene is not reshot, the rest of the film's hard-core action misses no chance to show the money shot—an excellent example of the genre acknowledging the inadequacy of its conventions even as it observes them.

Chapter 7

1. See, for example, the discussion of this tradition in Chapter 2, note 7; and in Chapter 4.

2. The Findlays are referred to in the journal *Re/Search: Incredibly Strange Films* 10 (1986) as the "most notorious filmmakers in the annals of sexploitation filmmaking." Bizarre death scenes were their trademark. Titles from the sixties include the "Flesh Trilogy": *The Touch of Her Flesh*, *The Curse of Her Flesh*, and *The Kiss of Her Flesh*; in *A Thousand Pleasures* a man is suffocated by a woman's breast; in *Shriek of the Mutilated* a mortally wounded woman revenges herself on her husband by throwing a plugged-in toaster into the bathtub where he sits. (I have not seen these films, but some would seem to be precursors of the more recent female revenge films such as *I Spit on Your Grave*.) Michael Findlay himself met

a grisly death: shortly after the release of *Snuff*, he was accidentally decapitated by a helicopter (*Re/Search* 10:193).

3. Ibid.

4. This term is not given in Ziplow; I take it from another "inside the industry"–style report, Rotsler 1973, 187.

5. Gish writes of the making of this scene in her autobiography, *The Movies, Mr. Griffith, and Me* (1969). She explains proudly (p. 233) that it was her idea to trail her hand in the water: "I was always having bright ideas and suffering for them."

6. One of the most developed and insightful examples of this psychoanalytic approach is found in Doane 1987.

7. Kaja Silverman (1980) was the first feminist film theorist to begin the psychoanalytic investigation of the masochist subject and film.

8. See also Reik 1962; and Bersani 1986.

9. See, for example, Samois 1982; Califia 1982; and Rubin 1984.

10. See especially Modleski 1984; Radway 1984; and Thurston 1987.

11. Thurston (1987, 142) notes that the romance *Corbin's Fancy* (1985) contains eleven episodes of intercourse, five of cunnilingus, and four of fellatio, taking place over 270 pages.

12. Benjamin (1986, 93) ultimately describes the pleasure of abandonment as a desire for recognition that leaves us "encapsulated in our subjective bubble, having fantasies about one another." The point I wish to emphasize is not the success or failure of recognition, since ultimately all desire falls short of the "real" recognition Benjamin posits, but the appeal of sadomasochistic solutions to the problem of recognition.

13. See Carter 1978 for a discussion of this woman in Sadean pornography.

Chapter 8

1. Rubenstein and Tavris 1987, 214. This information is from *Redbook*'s "special survey" of over twenty-six thousand readers' sex lives. The researchers both hold doctorates in social psychology. The serious limitations of such surveys are worth noting. First, since those who respond are readers of a particular magazine, their answers reflect certain attitudes. In this case, because the readers of *Redbook* might be characterized as more staid and less sexually adventurous than the readers of, say, *Cosmopolitan* or *Playgirl*, the real significance of the study for our purposes could translate to not "what do women today think about pornography?" but "what do even these women think about pornography?" Even though the women likely to respond to a survey about the "secrets of intimacy" are probably the more sexually interested of the magazine's readers, the "results" must

be something less than scientific. It does seem safe to say, however, that many more married, conventional women are watching pornography than a decade ago. The reason, as the survey authors suggest, is the ability to watch in the privacy of the home. They quote one twenty-six-year-old woman: "My husband and I have had many exciting years of masturbation, oral sex, and intercourse while watching pornographic movies. I feel we have become much closer as a result of our sexual openness" (Rubenstein and Tavris 1987, 214). This statement is revealing of a new attitude of women toward pornography; not surprisingly, it is an attitude that the films themselves frequently expressed.

2. See, for example, Doane, Mellencamp, and Williams, *Re-Vision: Essays in Feminist Film Criticism* (1983).

3. My intention is not to conflate Ladas, Whipple, and Perry's 1982 sex manual with the film; nor is it to mock the relative ease of achieving orgasm or pornotopia in both. I do note, however, that although the sex manual and couples porn are both striving to teach women the new scientific or pornographic knowledge about the "wonders of the unseen world" (with the "G-spot" representing something of a return to a "new and improved" vaginal orgasm), the model for the mapping of that world is still predominantly male pleasure.

4. These different kinds of pornotopia are derived, as we saw in Chapter 6, from Richard Dyer's categories of utopian good feeling in the movie musical. The dissolved utopia contrasts directly with the separated utopia, in which sexual abundance and so forth exist entirely outside the realm of narrative or story.

5. I have not seen this theater piece. According to Royalle, it began as a stage reenactment of the support group meetings, but with the women dressed as porn stars are expected to dress. Each woman took a turn under the spotlight performing as her persona. As the performance continued, the woman gradually changed clothes and role, ending in jeans and sweatshirt. It was while this show was running that Lauren Neimi and Royalle began Femme Productions. Although the production company did not grow directly out of the performance group, many Club 90 members directed in Femme's later "Star Directors Series."

6. Psychoanalytic feminists rarely insist on the limits to change within the theory. The theory itself is based on the role of the symbolic in the construction of gender positions, which can, in theory, change. In practice, however, the symbolic defined by this theory depends so heavily on the phallus for articulation of differences that there often seems little chance for change. See, for example, Silverman 1983, 1988b; Doane 1987; and de Lauretis 1984. For an excellent, and also appreciative, criticism of this

position from the (more practical) perspective of a feminist historian, see Joan Scott 1986.

7. Examples of the feminist use of object relations theory include Chodorow 1978; Abel 1981; and Gardiner 1981, 1989.

8. The phrase "educate desire" is taken from Dyer 1985, 27.

Conclusion

1. The Meese Commission (Attorney General's Commission on Pornography 1986, 1388–1390), for example, cites the Video Software Dealer's Association annual survey figure for 1984 of 13 percent and its estimate for 1986 of 9 percent.

2. See, for example, Jameson 1979; Dyer 1981; and Soble 1986, all Marxist approaches that diverge from the older "Frankfurt School" culture criticism, which emphasized the manipulation of consumers and fostering of false consciousness by mass-produced genres.

3. See, for example, the discrepancy between my own heterosexist negative reading of *Personal Best* (1986b) and the more positive reactions of lesbian viewers cited in Strayer 1984 and Ellsworth 1986.

Epilogue

1. I am thinking, of course, of the secret whistle-blower on the Watergate coverup, the "Deep Throat" informer who brought down the Nixon administration. In both cases an allusion to oral sex has had profound repercussions for presidential politics

2. David Remnick, for example, writes: "The highest realm of American public life now appears to summon no cultural echoes more elevated than the moist intersection of *Seven Days in May* and *Deep Throat*. One clicks on CNN or MSNBC, one clicks on the Netscape icon to cruise from the Drudge Report to the *Washington Post* Web site and back again, all with the furtive thrill of a raincoated joe ducking into the last remaining peepshows on Times Square. This surely is the first time in the history of the republic when the news columns may soon feature sentences freighted equally with the words 'President Clinton' and 'semen-stained garment'" (*New Yorker*, Feb. 2, 1998, 32).

3. These were the words with which the judge described Clinton's alleged behavior, even as she dismissed the charge of harassment (*Newsweek* April 13, 1998, 28.

4. The first OED definition of obscene is "offensive to the senses." This definition is significantly listed as "now somewhat archaic." Other meanings are "impure, indecent, lewd." In Latin the accepted meaning of the

term is more simply "off stage" or that which should be kept "out of public view." The term on/scene plays with the sense in which the ob (or off) scene is increasingly being brought on.

5. I have coined this term in two previous articles, both of which have been substantially reformulated here (Williams, 1993 a, b).

6. In this case, prosecutor Kenneth Starr's investigation will have delivered even more on/scene prurient interest than the equally hardworking Meese Commissioners of the previous decade. Both investigators have produced powerfully on/scene pornographic texts.

7. See Williams (1993 b) and Straayer (1993) for extended discussions of Annie Sprinkle's art and porn.

8. Consider, too, the controversy over Madonna's music video, "Justify Your Love," which, banned from MTV as too explicitly sexual, was then able to cross over to the more respectable end of the television audience at *Nightline* where it was shown in the context of the investigation of the controversy.

9. Helms also held up the photos at a campaign barbecue in Burlington, North Carolina (De Grazia 637).

10. As Laura Kipnis notes, it was the conjunction of masturbation and education that did Elders in (178).

11. In retrospect, Clinton and his handlers might have wished he had learned more about masturbation himself!

12. Kimball is quoted in a *New York Times* story detailing the "2d Revolution" of the study of sex, a revolution spearheaded this time—as opposed to the age of Kinsey—by humanists (Sunday, Dec. 28, 1997 Y 1 and 11).

13. See, for example, an extended discussion of the pedagogies of pornography in *Jump Cut* 40 (1996).

14. An article by Catherine MacKinnon in *Ms* magazine, entitled "Turning Rape into Pornography" called my attention to the need to engage in the pedagogy of porn. In this article MacKinnon argues that Serbian rapes of Muslim and Croatian women in Bosnia were both caused by and instances of pornography. With very flimsy evidence of the extent of the filming of rapes, and even flimsier evidence of its dissemination as pornography, MacKinnon turned the filming of some rapes (deemed equivalent to pornography) into a primary cause of ethnic cleansing. The real culprit, she argued, was not the Serbian rapists, but the supposed "saturation" of the former Yugoslavia with hard-core pornography. All of these arguments are specious and can be answered, as Erika Munk has answered them in a recent article (Munk 5). These are the kinds of hysterical arguments that can only fly if you don't know much about visual pornography. If its history, its conventions, its different uses among very different kinds of viewers are not known it is easy to scapegoat pornography as the cause

of all harm and all deviance. Thus the study of moving image pornography is the best antidote to the widespread belief among anti-pornography feminists that pornography is pure misogynist violence against women.

15. I discuss this issue at greater length in Williams (1993).

16. I discuss this case and its repercussions in "Second Thoughts on *Hard Core*" (Williams, 1993).

17. Burger's original ordering of obscene depictions included at the top heterosexual genital acts and then mentioned various "perversions." In contrast, Helms places the "perverts" at the top and "individuals [presumably heterosexual] engaged in sex acts" at the bottom, almost as an afterthought. Although the final NEA legislation does not specify what constitutes indecency, the entire controversy of NEA–funded artists centers around "deviant" depictions.

18. The fact that all moving-image pornography is based, at least initially, on an indexical, photographed moving-image of real bodies engaged in actual sexual acts has led many commentators to think that its visual pleasures are a function of the genre's extreme realism. Fredric Jameson's (1990) statement, for example, that "pornographic films are . . . only the potentiation of films in general, which ask us to stare at the world as though it were a naked body" (Jameson 1) is a typical example of the assumption that pornographic spectatorship achieves a kind of transparency; see also Stanley Cavell (1979) and Andre Bazin (1967, 1971).

19. Some years ago I attempted to map what I called the cinematic "low body genres" of melodrama, horror and pornography most frequently dismissed by cultural criticism as excessive, mindless and gratuitous. In each genre the offensive "excess" seemed to be located not only in the spectacle of ecstatic bodies convulsed by sexual pleasure, fear or pathos, but in the presumption that viewers mindlessly imitated the displays of the bodies on the screen. Whether this mimicry is exact, that is, whether the spectator at the porn film actually comes, whether those at the horror film actually scream or whether the spectator at the melodrama actually dissolves in tears, the success of these highly manipulative "genres" seemed to lie in their ability to produce these responses in viewers (Williams 1991). If pornography succeeds in producing its desired response, however, it is dismissed by culture critics in a way that the horror film or the melodrama is not. Where weeping triggered by melodrama and terror triggered by horror have attained a certain begrudging acceptance within western culture as either purgative or cathartic, sexual arousal and satisfaction triggered by pornography has never received any kind of cultural sanction. (Compare, for example, Aristotle's defense of the value of the effects of "pity" and "fear" in tragedy to his silence about sexual arousal elicited by vase painting. Or consider the way the debate about the effects

of pornography have been given over to social scientists who purport to be able to measure harmful "effects" without considering the larger context of the visual culture in which such works exist).

20. See Tom Gunning (1991;1995).

21. For an extended discussion of the limitations of gaze theory and for a selection of new ways to approach the question of an embodied vision see the selection of essays in *Viewing Positions* (Williams 1997).

22. In psychoanalytic film theory the most influential articulation of the male gaze is Laura Mulvey (1975) and E. Ann Kaplan (1983). More recently, however, Kaja Silverman (1988) pointed out the significance of Christian Metz's dual processes of projection—looking outward, like a "searchlight" in a process that duplicates the look of the camera—and introjection, receiving the image in a process that duplicates the receptivity of the screen (Metz 50–51; Silverman 23). Carol Clover elaborates on this insight as described above.

23. Crary locates this "modernization" of vision early in the nineteenth century in scientific discourses and "philosophical toys"—thaumatropes, phenakistoscopes, stereoscopes, etc.—which construct the body of the observer as a multivalent surface of inscription for newly corporealized sensations (93).

24. Crary introduces the term carnal density in opposition to the previously reigning Cartesian-influenced models of vision that posited a disembodied, centered, unitary human subjectivity capable of knowing the objective truths of the world. The body of this "decorporealized" observer was not implicated in vision's knowledge of the world; it registered, from a singular, centered, dematerialized point of view inside the camera obscura, a stable material reality "out there." In the wake of the breakdown of such idealist and decorporealized models of vision, and with the rise of materially new techniques of observation, Crary argues that a new relation of viewer to viewed arose.

25. The title of this film seems unrelated to its content and may, in fact, be a misprint of stud house instead of horse. I discuss this intriguing film at greater length in Williams (1995).

26. Following Kaja Silverman's distinction between the gaze and the look in her essay on Fassbinder and Lacan (1989), Clover describes the gaze as a "transcendental ideal—omniscient, omnipotent—which the look can never achieve but to which it ceaselessly aspires" (209–210). These especially vulnerable, fascinated stag viewers are a very long way from the gaze.

27. Kendrick informs us that when excavations on the city of Pompeii were made in the nineteenth century, it came as quite a shock that this city had freely decorated its public and private walls with frescoes and statues

of explicitly sexual topics, including images and statues depicting sexual intercourse. In ancient Pompeii images that we would today call hard-core pornography were emphatically on/scene. However, as Kendrick has pointed out, when these same frescoes and statues were unearthed by nineteenth-century modern men, they were immediately judged ob/scene and placed in a "Secret Museum" visited only by certain elite "gentlemen." Women, children and the poor were excluded (Kendrick 1987, 6).

28. In an excellent critique of *Hard Core,* film scholar Peter Lehman has pointed out that I have overemphasized the ways in which this "classical" era of porno resembles the "classical" era of Hollywood. In addition to the fact that this era in porno has actually proven to be a quite brief aberration, Lehman argues that even in its heyday it may never have had quite the dominance and stability of the classical Hollywood cinema as defined by Bordwell, Staiger and Thompson in their "classic" book on the subject. I think Lehman is correct to argue that there has been much less stability in the porno feature than I suggested in my book. Indeed, the new era of electronic on/scenities that I describe in the epilogue is an attempt to update and revise my original periodization. Furthermore, I agree that the very concept of the classical can often provide a very questionable norm against which far too many deviations are measured (see Williams 1998). For that reason I have placed the term classical in quotation marks. I am not willing to give up, however, the notion that this "classical" era of porno was more like mainstream cinema in its viewer disciplines than any other stage of moving-image pornography.

29. Like all pornography, *Boys in the Sand* is interested in showing us sex acts up close, in documenting sexual functioning. But in contrast to the hard-working quest for, or training of, pleasure apparent in the contemporaneous heterosexual pornos, gay porno of the same period is frankly more celebratory and more committed to expressing escapist sexual fantasy. Gay hard core could in fact be characterized as consistently less concerned with narrative, less concerned with embedding its characters in a realistic world, less concerned with imitating "legitimate" narrative film.

30. Reubens, host of a popular television show for children, was arrested in a porno theater for exposing himself. The theater appears to have been frequented by predominantly gay men.

31. See, for example, the later films of Gerard Damiano, all the hard-core films of Radley Metzgar (a.k.a. Henri Paris), Joe Sarno, John Leslie, and any film starring the great porn actress Georgina Spelvin.

32. This figure, which exceeds the total box office receipts of Hollywood, is a little misleading since it not only includes hard-core video, cable and computer porn, but non-electronic pornography such as live sex acts, sexual devices, and sex magazines. Nevertheless, the sheer volume of video

pornography is staggering compared to the figures for the "classic era" of the pornographic feature. In 1978, at the height of the classical era of porn, perhaps a hundred features were made at a typical cost of $350,000 in today's dollars. In contrast, in 1995 eight thousand new hard core videos were released, a few high-end productions but many costing just a few thousand dollars (Schlosser 43).

33. In fact, many of the sequels of the ground-breaking classics of theatrical porno are frankly recycled scenes from the originals. See *Hard Core* (229–264).

34. I am indebted to Constance Penley for many of the terms (for example, "upscale yuppie porn") in this list which derive from a presentation we made together at the Telluride Film Festival on the history of moving-image pornography.

35. These videos, like Andrew Blake's *Hidden Obsession* (1993) or Michael Ninn's *Sex* and *Latex* are still shot on film and, as my colleague Susie Bright has noted, spend a big portion of their budgets on hairdos (1994).

36. Though produced in sound and color, they often self-consciously assert, as in John Stagliano's Buttman series, a shoot-from-the-hip style reminiscent of the "primitive" home movie.

37. Of course once amateurs are commodified via exchange value it becomes difficult to see the difference between amateurs and professionals. This blurring of difference seems to be one important feature of this type of porno.

38. See, for example, the videos produced by the Sinclair Institute, such as *Ordinary Couples, Extraordinary Sex* or *Becoming Orgasmic*. See also the "how-to" videos produced by porn star Nina Hartley (*Nina Hartley's Guide to Better Cunnilingus*; *Nina Hartley's Guide to Better Fellatio*, etc.)

39. See, for example, Maria Beatty and Annie Sprinkle's *Sluts and Goddesses Video Workshop: How to Be a Sex Goddess in 101 Easy Steps* (1992), a tape devoted to the celebration of female sexual performance of every variety and in which Annie performs the longest orgasm ever captured on film or tape and teaches us that money shots are not the sole province of male sexual performers. See Williams and Straayer (1993).

40. While older forms of gay porno had no truck with political and social questions of gay identity, some of the newer titles, like *Honorable Discharge* (1993)—a video about gays in the military—insist on safe sex and affirm gay out identity.

41. *Suburban Dykes* (Debbi Sundahl, 1990) is the now-classic example of a story in which two tame suburban dykes invite a "big bad butch" to show them the way to their pleasure. See Williams (1993).

42. This category has been popular since the mid-eighties and is usually recognized by the word bi in the title: *Bi-Night, Bi-Dacious, Bi-Mistake,*

etc. In these videos women engage in sex with men and women and men engage in sex acts with men and women. The interesting quality of these videos seems to be their lack of fixed appeal, their ability to offer up het-ero, homo, sadomasochistic pleasures all at once and seemingly without contradiction. One way these videos attempt to break down familiar taboos against male-to-male sex is by placing men in narrative situations where a dominating woman orders them to have sex. In *Bisexual Fantasies* (1986) a woman P.E. teacher catches two high school boys peeping into the girls' shower. She then punishes them by forcing the boys to strip and perform oral and then anal sex, eventually joining them in the three-way numbers common to this subgenre. It is typical in this subgenre for women to ver-bally describe their pleasure at watching men have sex with one another. For more about this subgenre see Williams 1993.

43. See my discussion of this subgenre in "Pornographies On/scene" (Williams 1992, 258–261).

44. In 1994 more than forty percent of multimedia sales, despite lim-ited distribution and almost no advertising, was in interactive porno (*Elec-tronic Games*, 79).

45. It is beyond the scope of this essay to tackle the full extent of cyber-sex play now available with computers. I will not discuss, for example, those games in which individuals first flirt with, then "have" virtual sex with, one another by typing descriptions of the acts they perform in various sex-chat "rooms" nor will I discuss the latest form of live sexual interaction made possible by telecommunication conferencing software using cameras and computers. Both of the above games are marked by mediated two-way interactions between real persons. I am interested, however, in the "games" that involve a viewer and visual software rather than an actual "other" person at the other end of the line.

46. Since I didn't have a computer equipped with CD-ROM when re-searching this form of pornography, I sometimes had to rely on the good-will of friends much more versed in computers and electronic games than I. My experience is thus unfortunately limited to five or six games out of the hundreds now available. In addition to the games mentioned in the fol-lowing analysis, I also played *Tokyo Night Life Interactive* which combines a Japanese film noir scenario of an unexplained murder with the porno-graphic genre of frequent hard-core sex. The game begins with a scene in a movie theater: a woman sees a man exit her apartment with a wound on his arm; inside her apartment she discovers her lover dead. Now the game shifts to your point of view: "you" move next door to her, explore Tokyo nightlife, the apartment, and the sexual activities of your next door neigh-bor, eventually you become sexually intimate. Sexual interactivity amounts to little more than 1) watching one's hand extend into the screen to caress her; 2) the option of clicking on a magnifying glass icon during objectively

represented sex scenes affording a closer view. However, the game is interesting for its noir narrative overlay: clues indicate that the murderer of the woman's first lover can be none other than "me." "I" learn this too late, however, after the woman has taken her revenge by pushing me down the stairs of our apartment building: a scar on my arm matches the wound of the escaping man from the beginning. But who is the person who learns this? Like William Holden in *Sunset Boulevard* "I" am already dead. The allusions to classical cinema are indicated by having the film run within a movie theater frame with animated seats in front of it.

47. Soft core forms of these games flourish as well. Typically they cast the player in the role of a (male) photographer posing (female) models. For example, *The Penthouse Interactive Virtual Photo Shoot* has you first pose the models in provocative poses then brings on Bob Guccione to criticize your work.

48. *Seymour Butts*—about a lazy L.A. type who, in an effort to be more successful in his pursuit of a particular woman, enlists the help of the "guys" playing the game to get his act together—is equally impoverished in its illusion of interactivity. If, for example, Seymour is helping a friend make a porno movie I, the player, can help him out by reminding him to bring the dildo his friend wants. The entire game is perceived through Seymour's eyes. When he has sex, I simply watch. Interactivity is not carried out in the sex, only in the process of getting to it.

49. Pixis Interactive is the company that makes this game. They also produce *Neurodancer* which casts the player in the role of a lonely computer hacker in a Gibsonesque future dystopia who can only buy the sexual services (in cyberspace) of three Neurodancers if he can obtain enough phone credits. This premise demands that the player search for junction boxes from which he can steal credits. By thus illegally interfacing with so-called VideoFone boxes, the player then pages the dancer of his choice who appears in the HoloTube on your screen. A Touch and Feel User Interface (TFUI) allows "your" hand to caress the woman's body. Of course it's not really your hand and of course you don't really feel anything when "you" touch her, but since your clicks of the mouse control what kinds of touching occurs you are meant to feel in control.

50. Jean Baudrillard writes, for example, that in the interface with the computer, the sexual or cognitive "Other" is never really aimed at; the screen itself, rather, is targeted as the point of the interface" (Baudrillard, 5–6). Baudrillard, however, is not interested in specifying the bodily component of this connection. While it is true that interactivity does not, in this case, equal intersubjectivity, it does not seem impossible for interactivity to promote intersubjectivity in situations in which each subject has agency.

51. Jonathan Crary argues that it may have been a mistake to have assumed in the first place that the "classical," camera obscura model of vision—in which the, centered, disembodied eye of the viewer is separate from, and unimplicated in, the "objects" viewed—is the reigning model of spectatorship in modern forms of media. To Crary this centered and unified viewing consciousness, situated before a window frame or screen, absorbed but not perceptibly moved by what "he" sees, may never have had quite the dominance it has been assumed to have. Interactive hard core presents a model of vision that may thus actually be quite typical of modern and postmodern ways of seeing. In these ways of seeing the body is assaulted, seduced and implicated by simulations that appeal to the visionary capacity of the body to produce, as Jonathan Crary has put it, sensations divorced from referents, to see vision's own subjective perceptions. See especially chapters three and four of *Techniques of the Observer*

Works Cited

Abel, Elizabeth. 1981. "Editor's Introduction." *Writing and Sexual Difference* (special issue). *Critical Inquiry* 8:173–178.

Adams, Parveen. 1988. "Per Os(cillation.)" *Camera Obscura: A Journal of Feminism and Film Theory* 17:7–29.

Althusser, Louis. 1971. "Ideology and Ideological State Apparatuses (Notes Towards an Investigation)." In *Lenin and Philosophy and Other Essays*, translated by Ben Brewster, 122–173. London: New Left Books.

Altman, Rick. 1980. "Moving Lips: Cinema as Ventriloquism." *Cinema/ Sound* (special issue). *Yale French Studies* 60:67–79.

———. 1981. "The American Film Musical: Paradigmatic Structure and Mediatory Function." In *Genre: The Musical—A Reader*, edited by Rick Altman, 197–207. London: Routledge & Kegan Paul.

———. 1987. *The American Film Musical*. Bloomington: Indiana University Press.

American Civil Liberties Union. 1986. *Polluting the Censorship Debate: A Summary and Critique of the Final Report of the Attorney General's Commission on Pornography*. Washington, D.C.

Ariès, Philippe, and André Bejin. 1985. *Western Sexuality: Practice and Precept in Past and Present Times*. Translated by Anthony Forster. Oxford: Blackwell.

Attorney General's Commission on Pornography. 1986. *Final Report*. 2 vols. Washington, D.C.

Balbus, Isaac D. 1986. "Disciplining Women: Michel Foucault and the Power of Feminist Discourse." *Praxis International* 5, no. 4: 466–483.

Barbach, Lonnie. 1984. *Pleasures: Women Write Erotica*. Garden City, N.Y.: Doubleday.

———. 1986. *Erotic Interludes: Tales Told by Women*. New York: Harper & Row.

Barry, Kathleen. 1978. *Female Sexual Slavery*. Englewood Cliffs, N.J.: Prentice-Hall.

Barthes, Roland. 1975. *The Pleasure of the Text*. Translated by Richard Miller. New York: Hill & Wang.

Bartky, Sandra. Forthcoming. "Feminism and Foucault." In *Feminism and Foucault: Reflections on Resistance*, edited by Irene Diamond and Lee Quinby. Boston: Northeastern University Press.

Baudry, Jean Louis. 1986a. "The Apparatus: Metapsychological Approaches to the Impression of Realism in the Cinema." In *Narrative, Apparatus, Ideology: A Film Theory Reader*, edited by Phillip Rosen, 299–318. New York: Columbia University Press.

———. 1986b. "Ideological Effects of the Basic Cinematographic Apparatus." In *Narrative, Apparatus, Ideology*, 287–298. *See* Baudry 1986a.

Bazin, André. 1967–1971. *What Is Cinema?* Translated by Hugh Gray. 2 vols. Berkeley and Los Angeles: University of California Press.

Bell, Laurie, ed. 1987. *Good Girls/Bad Girls: Feminists and Sex Trade Workers Face to Face*. Toronto: Seal Press.

Benjamin, Jessica. 1983. "Master and Slave: The Fantasy of Erotic Domination." In *Powers of Desire: The Politics of Sexuality*, edited by Ann Snitow, Christine Stansell, and Sharon Thompson, 280–299. New York: Monthly Review Press.

———. 1986. "A Desire of One's Own: Psychoanalytic Feminism and Intersubjective Space." In *Feminist Studies/Critical Studies*, edited by Teresa de Lauretis, 78–101. Bloomington: Indiana University Press.

Benveniste, Emile. 1971. *Problems in General Linguistics*. Translated by Mary Elizabeth Meek. Coral Gables, Fla.: University of Miami Press.

Berger, John. 1977. *Ways of Seeing*. New York: Penguin Books.

Bersani, Leo. 1986. *The Freudian Body*. New York: Columbia University Press.

Betterton, Rosemary, ed. 1987. *Looking On: Images of Femininity in the Visual Arts and Media*. London: Routledge & Kegan Paul.

Birken, Lawrence. 1988. *Consuming Desire: Sexual Science and the Emergence of a Culture of Abundance, 1871–1914*. Ithaca, N.Y.: Cornell University Press.

Bloom, Clive. 1988. "Grinding with the Bachelors: Pornography in a Machine Age." In *Perspectives on Pornography: Sexuality in Film and Literature*, edited by Gary Day and Clive Bloom, 9–25. New York: St. Martin's Press.

Bonitzer, Pascal. 1976. *Le regard et la voix*. Paris: Union Générale d'Editions.

Bordwell, David, Janet Staiger, and Kristin Thompson. 1985. *The Classical Hollywood Cinema: Film Style and Mode of Production to 1960*. New York: Columbia University Press.

Braudy, Leo. 1977. *The World in a Frame: What We See in Films*. Garden City, N.Y.: Anchor Press.

Brown, Beverley. 1981. "A Feminist Interest in Pornography—Some Modest Proposals." *m/f* 5/6:5–18.

Brownmiller, Susan. *Against Our Will: Men, Women and Rape*. New York: Simon and Schuster.

Bunch, Charlotte. 1980. "Lesbianism and Erotica in Pornographic America." In *Take Back the Night: Women on Pornography*, edited by Laura Lederer, 91–94. New York: Morrow.

Burch, Noël. N.d. *Correction Please—or How We Got into Pictures*. (Pamphlet accompanying film of same name.)

———. 1978–1979. "Porter, or Ambivalence." *Screen* 19, no. 4: 91–105.

Burstyn, Varda, ed. 1985. *Women Against Censorship*. Vancouver: Douglas & MacIntyre.

Califia, Pat. 1982. "Feminism and Sadomasochism." *Co-Evolution Quarterly* 33 (Spring): 33–40.

Callahan, Jean. 1982. "Women and Pornography: Combat in the Video Zone." *American Film* 7 (March): 62–63.

Caplan, Paula. 1985. *The Myth of Women's Masochism*. New York: Dutton.

Carter, Angela. 1978. *The Sadeian Woman and the Ideology of Pornography*. New York: Pantheon Books.

Cavell, Stanley. 1979. *The World Viewed*. Cambridge, Mass.: Harvard University Press.

Charney, Maurice. 1981. *Sexual Fiction*. London: Methuen.

Chasseguet-Smirgel, Janine. 1984. *Creativity and Perversion*. London: Free Association Books.

Chion, Michel. 1982. *La voix au cinéma*. Paris: Editions de l'Etoile.

Chodorow, Nancy. 1978. *The Reproduction of Mothering*. Berkeley and Los Angeles: University of California Press.

Clover, Carol J. 1987. "Her Body, Himself: Gender in the Slasher Film." *Representations* 20 (Fall): 187–228.

Comolli, Jean-Louis. 1980. "Machines of the Visible." In *The Cinematic Apparatus*, edited by Teresa de Lauretis and Stephen Heath, 121–142. New York: St. Martin's Press.

Cook, Pam. 1978. "Duplicity in *Mildred Pierce*." In *Women in Film Noir*, edited by E. Ann Kaplan. London: British Film Institute.

Daly, Mary. 1984. *Pure Lust: Elemental Feminist Philosophy*. Boston: Beacon Press.

Davidson, Arnold. 1987. "Sex and the Emergence of Sexuality." *Critical Inquiry* 14:16–48.

Day, Gary, and Clive Bloom, eds. *Perspectives on Pornography: Sexuality in Film and Literature*. New York: St. Martin's Press.

de Berg, Jean. 1966. *The Image*. Translated by Patsy Southgate. New York: Grove Press.

Debord, Guy. 1967. *La société du spectacle*. Paris: Buchet/Chastel.

Delacoste, Frederique, and Priscilla Alexander. 1987. *Sex Work: Writings by Women in the Sex Industry*. Pittsburgh: Cleis Press.

Delameter, Jerome. Forthcoming. "Ritual, Realism, and Abstraction: Performance in the Musical." In *Making Visible the Invisible: An Anthology of Original Essays on Film Acting*, edited by Carole Zucker. Metuchen, N.J.: Scarecrow.

de Lauretis, Teresa. 1984. *Alice Doesn't: Feminism, Semiotics, Cinema*. Bloomington: Indiana University Press.

———. 1987. *Technologies of Gender: Essays on Theory, Film, and Fiction*. Bloomington: Indiana University Press.

Deleuze, Gilles. 1971. *Masochism: An Interpretation of Coldness and Cruelty*. Translated by Jean McNeil. New York: Braziller.

Diderot, Denis. [1875] 1966. *Oeuvres complètes de Diderot*. Edited by J. Assezat. Vol. 4. Paris: Kraus.

Di Lauro, Al, and Gerald Rabkin. 1976. *Dirty Movies: An Illustrated History of the Stag Film, 1915–1970*. New York: Chelsea House.

Doane, Mary Ann. 1980. "The Voice in the Cinema: The Articulation of Body and Space." *Cinema/Sound* (special issue). *Yale French Studies* 60:33–50.

———. 1982. "Film and the Masquerade: Theorising the Female Spectator." *Screen* 23, nos. 3–4: 74–87.

———. 1987. *The Desire to Desire: The Woman's Film of the 1940's*. Bloomington: Indiana University Press.

———. 1989. "Masquerade Reconsidered: Further Thoughts on the Female Spectator." *Discourse* 11, no. 1: 42–54.

Doane, Mary Ann, Patricia Mellencamp, and Linda Williams, eds. 1984. *Re-Vision: Essays in Feminist Film Criticism*. American Film Institute Monograph Series, vol. 3. Frederick, Md.: University Publications of America.

Donnerstein, Edward, Daniel Linz, and Steven Penrod. 1987. *The Question of Pornography: Research Findings and Policy Implications*. New York: Free Press.

DSM-III-R. 1987. *Diagnostic and Statistical Manual of Mental Disorders*. 3d rev. ed. Washington, D.C.: American Psychiatric Association.

Duca, Lo. 1958. *L'érotisme au cinéma*. 3 vols. Paris: Pauvert.

Dworkin, Andrea. 1979. *Pornography: Men Possessing Women*. New York: Perigee Books.

———. 1987. *Intercourse*. New York: Free Press.

Dyer, Richard. 1981. "Entertainment and Utopia." In *Genre: The Musical—A Reader*, edited by Rick Altman, 175–189. London: Routledge & Kegan Paul.

———. 1984. *Gays and Film*. New York: Zoetrope.

———. 1985. "Male Gay Porn: Coming to Terms." *Jump Cut: A Review of Contemporary Media* 30 (March): 27–29.

Echols, Alice. 1983. "Feminism, Moralism, and Pornography." In *Powers of Desire: The Politics of Sexuality*, edited by Ann Snitow, Christine Stansell, and Sharon Thompson, 439–459. New York: Monthly Review Press.

Ehrenreich, Barbara, Elizabeth Hess, and Gloria Jacobs. 1986. *Re-Making Love: The Feminization of Sex*. New York: Anchor Books.

Ellis, John. 1980. "Photography/Pornography/Art/Pornography." *Screen* 21, no. 1: 81–108.

Ellis, Kate, Nan D. Hunter, Beth Jaker, Barbara O'Dair, and Abby Tallmer. 1986. *Caught Looking: Feminism, Pornography, and Censorship*. New York: Caught Looking.

Ellis, Richard. 1988. "Disseminating Desire: Grove Press and 'The End[s] of Obscenity.'" In *Perspectives on Pornography: Sexuality in Film and Literature*, edited by Gary Day and Clive Bloom, 26–43. New York: St. Martin's Press.

Ellsworth, Elizabeth. 1986. "Illicit Pleasures: Feminist Spectators and *Personal Best*." *Wide Angle* 8, no. 2: 45–56.

Estrich, Susan. 1987. *Real Rape*. Cambridge, Mass.: Harvard University Press.

Ferguson, Frances. 1987. "Rape and the Rise of the Novel." *Representations* 20 (Fall): 88–111.

Feuer, Jane. 1982. *The Hollywood Musical*. Bloomington: Indiana University Press.

Fischer, Lucy. 1989. *Shot/Countershot: Film Tradition and Women's Cinema*. Princeton: Princeton University Press.

Foucault, Michel. 1978. *The History of Sexuality*. Vol. 1: *An Introduction*. Translated by Robert Hurley. New York: Pantheon Books. (Translation of *La volonté de savoir*, 1976.)

———. 1979. *Discipline and Punish: The Birth of the Prison*. Translated by Alan Sheridan. New York: Vintage Books. (Translation of *Surveiller et punir*, 1975.)

———. 1985. *The Use of Pleasure*. Vol. 2 of *The History of Sexuality*. Translated by Robert Hurley. New York: Pantheon Books. (Translation of *L'usage des plaisirs*, 1984.)

———. 1986. *The Care of the Self*. Vol. 3 of *The History of Sexuality*. Translated by Robert Hurley. New York: Pantheon Books. (Translation of *Le souci de soi*, 1984.)

Freud, Sigmund. [1905] 1953–1966. *Three Essays on the Theory of Sexuality*. Vol. 7 of *The Standard Edition of the Complete Psychological Works of Sigmund Freud*. Translated by James Strachey. London: Hogarth.

———. [1919] 1963. "'A Child Is Being Beaten': A Contribution to the Study of the Origin of Sexual Perversions." In *Sexuality and the Psychology of Love*, edited by Phillip Rieff, 107–132. New York: Collier.

———. [1924] 1953–1966. "The Economic Problem of Masochism." In *Standard Edition* 19:159–170. *See* Freud [1905] 1953–1966.

———. [1927] 1963. "Fetishism." In *Sexuality and the Psychology of Love*, 214–219. *See* Freud [1919] 1963.

———. [1931] 1963. "Female Sexuality." In *Sexuality and the Psychology of Love*, 194–211. *See* Freud [1919] 1963.

Friday, Nancy. 1973. *My Secret Garden: Women's Sexual Fantasies*. New York: Pocket Books.

Fuentes, Annette, and Margaret Schrage. 1987. "Deep Inside Porn Stars." *Jump Cut: A Review of Contemporary Media* 32 (April): 29–35.

Gallop, Jane. 1984. "Beyond the *Jouissance* Principle." *Representations* 7 (Summer): 110–115.

———. 1988a. "The Perverse Body." In *Thinking Through the Body*, 100–118. *See* Gallop 1988b. (Originally published as "Feminist Criticism and the Pleasure of the Text." *North Dakota Quarterly* 54, no. 2 [1986].)

———. 1988b. *Thinking Through the Body*. New York: Columbia University Press.

Gardiner, Judith Kegan. 1981. "On Female Identity and Writing by Women." *Critical Inquiry* 8:347–361.

———. 1989. *Rhys, Stead, Lessing, and the Politics of Empathy*. Bloomington: Indiana University Press.

Gaudrault, André. 1983. "Temporality and Narrativity in Early Cinema." In *Film Before Griffith*, edited by John L. Fell, 311–329. Berkeley and Los Angeles: University of California Press.

———. 1987. "Narration and Monstration in the Cinema." *Journal of Film and Video* 39, no. 2: 29–35.

Gay, Peter. 1984. *The Bourgeois Experience: Victoria to Freud.* Vol. 1: *Education of the Senses.* New York: Oxford University Press.

Giles, Dennis. 1975. "Angel on Fire: Three Texts of Desire." *Velvet Light Trap* 16:41–45.

————. 1977. "Pornographic Space: The Other Place." In *The 1977 Film Studies Annual: Part 2,* 52–65. Pleasantville, N.Y.: Redgrave.

Gish, Lillian. 1969. *The Movies, Mr. Griffith, and Me.* New York: Avon Books.

Goldbarth, Albert. 1976. *Comings Back: A Sequence of Poems by Albert Goldbarth.* New York: Doubleday.

Gordon, George. 1980. *Erotic Communications: Studies in Sex, Sin, and Censorship.* New York: Hastings House.

Griffin, Susan. 1981. *Pornography and Silence: Culture's Revenge Against Nature.* New York: Harper & Row.

Gubar, Susan. 1987. "Representing Pornography: Feminism, Criticism, and Depictions of Female Violation." *Critical Inquiry* 13:712–741.

Gubar, Susan, and Joan Hoff-Wilson. Forthcoming. *For Adult Users Only: The Case of Violent Pornography.* Bloomington: Indiana University Press.

Gunning, Tom. 1981. "Weaving a Narrative." *Quarterly Review of Film Studies* 6:11–25.

Haas, Richard Bartlett. 1976. *Muybridge: Man in Motion.* Berkeley and Los Angeles: University of California Press.

Hansen, Miriam. 1986. "Pleasure, Ambivalence, Identification: Valentino and Female Spectatorship." *Cinema Journal* 25, no. 4: 6–32.

Haug, F. W. 1986. *Critique of Commodity Aesthetics: Appearance, Sexuality, and Advertising in Capitalist Society.* Translated by Robert Bock. Minneapolis: University of Minnesota Press.

Heath, Stephen. 1981. *Questions of Cinema.* Bloomington: Indiana University Press.

————. 1982. *The Sexual Fix.* London: Macmillan.

Hendricks, Gordon. 1972. *Origins of the American Film.* New York: Arno Press.

Hesiod. 1977. *Hesiod: The Homeric Hymns and Homerica.* Translated by Hugh G. Evelyn-White. Cambridge, Mass.: Harvard University Press.

Hite, Shere. 1976. *The Hite Report: A Nationwide Study of Female Sexuality.* New York: Dell.

Hyde, H. Montgomery. 1964. *A History of Pornography.* London: Heinemann.

Irigaray, Luce. 1985. *This Sex Which Is Not One.* Translated by Catherine Porter and Carolyn Burke. Ithaca, N.Y.: Cornell University Press.

———. 1986. *Speculum of the Other Woman*. Translated by Gillian C. Gill. Ithaca, N.Y.: Cornell University Press.

James, David. N.d. "On Pornography." Unpublished paper.

———. Forthcoming. "Hardcore: Cultural Resistance in the Postmodern." *Film Quarterly*.

Jameson, Fredric. 1979. "Reification and Utopia in Mass Culture." *Social Text* 1:130–148.

———. 1981. *The Political Unconscious: Narrative as a Socially Symbolic Act*. Ithaca, N.Y.: Cornell University Press.

Kaplan, E. Ann. 1983. *Women and Film: Both Sides of the Camera*. New York: Methuen.

———. 1987. "Pornography and/as Representation." *Enclitic* 9:8–19.

Kappeler, Susanne. 1986. *The Pornography of Representation*. Minneapolis: University of Minnesota Press.

Kendrick, Walter. 1987. *The Secret Museum: Pornography in Modern Culture*. New York: Viking Press.

Kleinhans, Chuck, and Julia Lesage. 1985. "The Politics of Sexual Representation." *Jump Cut: A Review of Contemporary Media* 30 (March): 26–27.

Knight, Arthur, and Hollis Alpert. 1967. "The Stag Film." *Playboy*, November, 154–158, 170–189.

Koch, Gertrud. Forthcoming. "On Pornography." *Jump Cut: A Review of Contemporary Media*.

Koedt, Anne. 1971. "The Myth of the Vaginal Orgasm." In *Voices from Women's Liberation*, edited by Leslie Tanner, 33–46. New York: New American Library/Mentor Books.

Kuhn, Annette. 1982. *Women's Pictures: Feminism and Cinema*. London: Routledge & Kegan Paul.

———. 1985. *The Power of the Image: Essays on Representation and Sexuality*. London: Routledge & Kegan Paul.

Kyrou, Ado. 1964. "D'un certain cinéma clandestin." *Positif: Revue de cinéma* 61–63 (June–August): 205–223.

Ladas, Alice Kahn, Beverly Whipple, and John D. Perry. 1982. *The G Spot and Other Recent Discoveries About Human Sexuality*. New York: Holt, Rinehart & Winston.

Laplanche, Jean. 1976. *Life and Death in Psychoanalysis*. Translated by Jeffrey Mehlman. Baltimore: Johns Hopkins University Press.

Lardeau, Yanne. 1978. "Le sexe froid (du porno au delà)." *Cahiers du Cinéma* 289 (June 1978): 49–61.

Lederer, Laura, ed. 1980. *Take Back the Night: Women on Pornography*. New York: Morrow.

Lehman, Peter. 1987. "Oshima: The Avant-Garde Artist Without an Avant-Garde Style." *Wide Angle* 9, no. 2: 18–31.

Lovelace, Linda, and Mike McGrady. 1980. *Ordeal*. New York: Berkeley.

McArthur, Colin. 1972. *Underworld USA*. New York: Viking Press.

MacDonald, Scott. 1983. "Confessions of a Feminist Porn Watcher." *Film Quarterly* 36, no. 3: 10–17.

MacDonnell, Kevin. 1972. *Eadweard Muybridge: The Man Who Invented the Motion Picture*. Boston: Little, Brown.

MacKinnon, Catherine. 1987. *Feminism Unmodified: Discourses on Life and Law*. Cambridge, Mass.: Harvard University Press.

Marcus, Steven. 1974. *The Other Victorians: A Study of Sexuality and Pornography in Mid-Nineteenth Century England*. New York: New American Library.

Marcuse, Herbert. 1964. *One Dimensional Man*. Boston: Beacon Hill Press.

Marey, Etienne Jules. 1892. *La photographie du mouvement*. Paris: Carré.

Martin, Biddy. 1982. "Feminism, Criticism, and Foucault." *New German Critique* 27:3–30.

Marx, Karl. [1867] 1906. *Capital*. Vol. 1. Translated by Samuel Moore and Edward Aveling. New York: Modern Library.

Mast, Gerald. 1986. *A Short History of the Movies*. New York: Macmillan.

———. 1987. *Can't Help Singin': The American Musical on Stage and Screen*. Woodstock, N.Y.: Overlook Press.

Mayne, Judith. 1986. "Uncovering the Female Body." In *Before Hollywood: Turn-of-the Century Film from American Archives*, edited by Jay Leyda and Charles Musser, 63–67. New York: American Federation of the Arts.

———. Forthcoming. "The Primitive Narrator." In *The Woman at the Keyhole*.

Metz, Christian. 1977. *The Imaginary Signifier: Psychoanalysis and the Cinema*. Translated by Annwyl Williams, Ben Brewster, and Alfred Guzzetti. Bloomington: Indiana University Press.

Michelson, Peter. 1971. *The Aesthetics of Pornography*. New York: Herder & Herder.

Mitchell, W. T. J. 1986. *Iconology: Image, Text, Ideology*. Chicago: University of Chicago Press.

Modleski, Tania. 1982. *Loving with a Vengeance: Mass-produced Fantasies for Women*. New York: Methuen.

———. 1988. *The Women Who Knew Too Much: Hitchcock and Feminist Theory*. New York: Methuen.

Morden, Ethan. 1981. *The Hollywood Musical*. New York: St. Martin's Press.

Morgan, Robin. 1980. "Theory and Practice: Pornography and Rape." In *Take Back the Night: Women on Pornography*, edited by Laura Lederer. New York: Morrow.

Morris, Meaghan. 1979. *Michel Foucault: Power, Truth, Strategy*. Sydney, Austral.: Feral Publications.

Mueller, John. 1984. "Fred Astaire and the Integrated Musical." *Cinema Journal* 24 (Fall): 28–40.

Mulvey, Laura. 1975. "Visual Pleasure and Narrative Cinema." *Screen* 16, no. 3: 6–18.

———. 1981. "Afterthoughts on 'Visual Pleasure and Narrative Cinema' Inspired by 'Duel in the Sun' (King Vidor, 1946)." *Framework* 15–17 (Summer): 12–15.

———. 1985. "Changes." *Discourse: Berkeley Journal for Theoretical Studies in Media and Culture* 7 (Spring): 11–29.

Musser, Charles. 1979. "The Early Cinema of Edwin Porter." *Cinema Journal* 19 (Fall): 1–38.

Muybridge, Eadweard. 1883. *Descriptive Zoopraxography; or, the Science of Animal Locomotion Made Popular*. Chicago: Lakeside Press.

———. 1955a. *The Human Figure in Motion*. New York: Dover.

———. 1955b. *Animals in Motion*. New York: Dover.

———. 1979. *Muybridge's Complete Human and Animal Locomotion*. 3 vols. Introduction by Anita Ventura Mozley. New York: Dover.

Neale, Stephen. 1980. *Genre*. London: British Film Institute.

Nobile, Phillip, and Eric Nadler. 1986. *United States of America vs. Sex: How the Meese Commission Lied About Pornography*. New York: Minotaur Press.

Pajaczkowska, Claire. 1981. "The Heterosexual Presumption." *Screen* 22, no. 1: 79–94.

Prince, Stephen. 1987. "Power, Pleasure, and Pain in Pornographic Feature Films." Paper delivered at the annual International Communication Association conference.

———. 1988. "The Pornographic Image and the Practice of Film Theory." *Cinema Journal* 27 (Winter): 27–39.

Radway, Janice. 1984. *Reading the Romance: Women, Patriarchy, and Popular Literature*. Chapel Hill: University of North Carolina Press.

Ramsaye, Terry. 1926. *A Million and One Nights: A History of the Motion Picture*. New York: Simon & Schuster.

Reik, Theodor. 1962. *Masochism in Sex and Society*. Translated by Margaret Beigel and Gertrud Kurth. New York: Grove Press.

Rembar, Charles. 1969. *The End of Obscenity: The Trials of 'Lady Chatterly,' 'Tropic of Cancer' and 'Fanny Hill.'* New York: Random House.

Rich, Adrienne. 1979. *On Lies, Secrets, and Silence: Selected Prose, 1966–1978*. New York: Norton.

Rich, B. Ruby. 1982. "Anti-Porn: Soft Issue, Hard World." *Village Voice*, July 20, 1, 16–18, 30. (Reprinted in *Films for Women*, edited by Charlotte Brunsdon. London: British Film Institute, 1986.)

————. 1986. "Feminism and Sexuality in the 1980's." *Feminist Studies* 12 (Fall): 525–561.

Riley, Denise. 1988. *Am I That Name? Feminism and the Category of "Women" in History.* Minneapolis: University of Minnesota Press.

Rimmer, Robert. 1986. *The X-rated Videotape Guide.* New York: Harmony Books.

Rodowick, D. N. 1982. "The Difficulty of Difference." *Wide Angle* 5, no. 1: 4–15.

Ross, Andrew. Forthcoming. *No Respect: Intellectuals and Popular Culture.* London: Routledge & Kegan Paul.

Rotsler, William. 1973. *Contemporary Erotic Cinema.* New York: Penthouse/Ballantine.

Rubenstein, Carin, and Carol Tavris. 1987. "Survey Results." *Redbook*, September, 147–149, 214–215.

Rubin, Gayle. 1979. "The Traffic in Women." In *Towards an Anthropology of Women*, edited by Rayna Reiter, 157–210. New York: Monthly Review Press.

————. 1984. "Thinking Sex: Notes for a Radical Theory of the Politics of Sexuality." In *Pleasure and Danger: Exploring Female Sexuality*, edited by Carole S. Vance, 267–319. London: Routledge & Kegan Paul.

Russ, Joanna. 1985. *Magic Mommas, Trembling Sisters, Puritans, and Perverts.* New York: Crossings Press.

Ryan, Michael. 1988. "The Politics of Film: Discourse, Psychoanalysis, Ideology." In *Marxism and the Interpretation of Culture*, edited by Cary Nelson and Lawrence Grossberg, 477–486. Urbana: University of Illinois Press.

Salt, Barry. 1978. "Film Form 1900–1906." *Sight and Sound* 47, no. 3: 149–153.

Samois, ed. 1982. *Coming to Power: Writings and Graphics on Lesbian S/M.* Palo Alto, Calif.: Alyson.

Scarry, Elaine. 1985. *The Body in Pain: The Making and Unmaking of the World.* New York: Oxford University Press.

Schatz, Thomas. 1981. *Hollywood Genres: Formulas, Filmmaking, and the Studio System.* New York: Random House.

Scott, Joan. 1986. "Gender: A Useful Category of Historical Analysis." *American Historical Review* (December): 1053–1075.

Scott, Joseph E., and Loretta A. Schwalm. 1988. "Rape Rates and the Circulation Rates of Adult Magazines." *Journal of Sex Research* 24:241–250.

Sedgwick, Eve Kosofsky. 1985. *Between Men: English Literature and Male Homosocial Desire.* New York: Columbia University Press.

Sherfey, Mary Jane. 1970. "A Theory on Female Sexuality." In *Sisterhood*

Is Powerful: An Anthology of Writings from the Women's Liberation Movement, edited by Robin Morgan. New York: Random House.

Silverman, Kaja. 1980. "Masochism and Subjectivity." *Framework* 12: 2–9.

———. 1983. *The Subject of Semiotics*. New York: Oxford University Press.

———. 1984. "*Histoire d'O*: The Construction of a Female Subject." In *Pleasure and Danger: Exploring Female Sexuality*, edited by Carole S. Vance, 320–349. London: Routledge & Kegan Paul.

———. 1985. "Lost Objects and Mistaken Subjects: Film Theory's Structuring Lack." *Wide Angle* 7, nos. 1–2: 14–29.

———. 1988a. *The Acoustic Mirror: The Female Voice in Psychoanalysis and Cinema*. Bloomington: Indiana University Press.

———. 1988b. "Masochism and Male Subjectivity." *Camera Obscura: A Journal of Feminism and Film Theory* 17:31–66.

Simpson, David. 1982. *Fetishism and Imagination: Dickens, Melville, Conrad*. Baltimore: Johns Hopkins University Press.

Smith, Richard, ed. 1973. *Getting into "Deep Throat."* Chicago: Playboy Press.

Snitow, Ann Barr. 1983. "Mass Market Romance: Pornography for Women Is Different." In *Powers of Desire: The Politics of Sexuality*, edited by Ann Snitow, Christine Stansell, and Sharon Thompson, 245–263. New York: Monthly Review Press.

Snitow, Ann, Christine Stansell, and Sharon Thompson, eds. 1983. *Powers of Desire: The Politics of Sexuality*. New York: Monthly Review Press.

Soble, Alan. 1986. *Pornography: Marxism, Feminism, and the Future of Sexuality*. New Haven, Conn.: Yale University Press.

Sontag, Susan. 1969. "The Pornographic Imagination." In *Styles of Radical Will*, 35–73. New York: Dell.

Spivak, Gayatri Chakravorty. 1981. "French Feminism in an International Frame." *Yale French Studies* 62:154–184.

Stam, Robert. 1987. "Bakhtin, Eroticism, and the Cinema: Strategies for the Critique and Trans-Valuation of Pornography." *CineAction!* 10: 13–20.

Steinem, Gloria. 1986a. "Erotica vs. Pornography." In *Outrageous Acts and Everyday Rebellions*, 247–260. New York: New American Library.

———. 1986b. "The Real Linda Lovelace." In *Outrageous Acts and Everyday Rebellions*, 274–285. *See* Steinem 1986a.

Steiner, George. 1974. "Night Words." In *The Case Against Pornography*, edited by David Holbrook, 226–232. LaSalle, Ill.: Library Press.

Stewart, Susan. 1988. "The Marquis de Meese." *Critical Inquiry* 15 (Autumn): 162–192.

Stimpson, Catherine, and Ethel Spector Person, eds. 1980. *Women: Sex and Sexuality*. Chicago: University of Chicago Press.

Stoller, Robert. 1979. *Sexual Excitement: The Dynamics of Erotic Life*. New York: Pantheon Books.

Strayer, Chris. 1984. "*Personal Best*: Lesbian/Feminist Audience." *Jump Cut: A Review of Contemporary Media* 29 (February): 40–44.

Studlar, Gaylyn. 1985. "Masochism and the Perverse Pleasures of the Cinema." In *Movies and Methods*, edited by Bill Nichols, 2:602–621. Berkeley and Los Angeles: University of California Press.

———. 1988. *In the Realm of Pleasure: Von Sternberg, Dietrich, and the Masochistic Aesthetic*. Urbana: University of Illinois Press.

Thurston, Carol. 1987. *The Romance Revolution: Erotic Novels for Women and the Quest for a New Sexual Identity*. Urbana: University of Illinois Press.

Toll, Robert C. 1982. *The Entertainment Machine: American Show Business in the Twentieth Century*. New York: Oxford University Press.

Turan, Kenneth, and Stephen F. Zito. 1974. *Sinema: American Pornographic Films and the People Who Make Them*. New York: Praeger.

Valverde, Mariana. 1985. *Sex, Power, and Pleasure*. Toronto: Women's Press.

Vance, Carole S. 1984. "Pleasure and Danger: Toward a Politics of Sexuality." In *Pleasure and Danger: Exploring Female Sexuality*, edited by Carole S. Vance, 1–27. London: Routledge & Kegan Paul.

———. 1986. "The Meese Commission on the Road." *The Nation*, August 2–9, 1, 76–82.

Vernet, Marc. 1989. "The Look at the Camera." *Cinema Journal* 28, no. 2 (Winter): 48–63.

Watney, Simon. 1987. *Policing Desire: Pornography, AIDS, and the Media*. Minneapolis: University of Minnesota Press.

Waugh, Tom. 1985. "Men's Pornography: Gay Versus Straight." *Jump Cut: A Journal of Contemporary Media* 30:30–36.

———. 1987. "Hard to Imagine: Gay Erotic Cinema in the Postwar Era." *CineAction!* 10 (October): 65–72.

Weeks, Jeffrey. 1981. *Sex, Politics, and Society: The Regulation of Sexuality Since 1800*. London: Longman.

———. 1985. *Sexuality and Its Discontents: Meanings, Myths, and Modern Sexualities*. London: Routledge & Kegan Paul.

Willemen, Paul. 1980. "Letter to John." *Screen* 21, no. 2: 53–66.

Williams, Alan. 1980. "Is Sound Recording Like a Language?" *Cinema/Sound* (special issue). *Yale French Studies* 60:51–66.

———. 1981. "The Musical Film and Recorded Popular Music." In *Genre: The Musical—A Reader*, edited by Rick Altman, 147–158. London: Routledge & Kegan Paul.

Williams, Linda. 1983. "When the Woman Looks." In *Re-Vision: Essays in Feminist Film Criticism*, edited by Mary Ann Doane, Patricia Mellencamp, and Linda Williams. American Film Institute Monograph Series, 3:83–99. Frederick, Md.: University Publications of America.

———. 1984. "'Something Else Besides a Mother': *Stella Dallas* and the Maternal Melodrama." *Cinema Journal* 24, no. 1: 2–27.

———. 1986a. "Film Body: An Implantation of Perversions." In *Narrative, Apparatus, Ideology: A Film Theory Reader*, edited by Phillip Rosen, 507–534. New York: Columbia University Press. (Originally published in *Cine-Tracts* 12 [Winter 1981].)

———. 1986b. "*Personal Best*: Women in Love." In *Films for Women*, edited by Charlotte Brunsdon, 146–154. London: British Film Institute. (Originally published in *Jump Cut: A Review of Contemporary Media* 27 [July 1982].)

———. 1986c. "Sexual Politics: Strange Bedfellows." *In These Times*, October 29–November 4, 18–20.

Willis, Ellen. 1983. "Feminism, Moralism, and Pornography." In *Powers of Desire: The Politics of Sexuality*, edited by Ann Snitow, Christine Stansell, and Sharon Thompson, 460–467. New York: Monthly Review Press.

Ziplow, Stephen. 1977. *The Film Maker's Guide to Pornography*. New York: Drake.

Supplementary Bibliography

The following bibliography includes works cited in the new preface and epilogue of *Hard Core* as well as a more general selection the the important new work published since the first edition.

Adams, Parveen. "Of Female Bondage." 1989. *Between Feminism and Psychoanalysis*, Teresa Brennan, ed. London: Routledge.

Baudrillard, Jean. 1988. *Xerox and Infinity*. Trans. Agitac. Paris: Touchepas.

————. 1988. *The Ecstasy of Communication*. New York: Semiotext (e).

Bright, Susie. 1997. *The Sexual State of the Union*. New York: Simon and Schuster.

————. 1992. *Susie Bright's Sexual Reality: A Virtual Sex World Reader.* Pittsburgh: Cleis Press.

Butler, Judith. 1990a. *Gender Trouble: Feminism and the Subversion of Identity.* New York: Routledge.

————. 1990b. "The Force of Fantasy: Feminism, Mapplethorpe, and Discursive Excess." *Differences: A Journal of Feminist Cultural Studies.* Vol. 2.

Carr, Cindy. 1990. "War on Art: The Sexual Politics of Censorship." *Village Voice,* June 5, 1990.

Case, Sue-Ellen. 1989. "Toward a Butch-Femme Aesthetic." In *Making a Spectacle: Feminist Essays on Contemporary Women's Theater*, Lynda Hart, ed. Ann Arbor: University of Michigan Press, 282–299.

Cavell, Stanley. 1979. *The World Viewed*. Cambridge, Mass: Harvard University Press.

Champagne, John. 1997. "'Stop Reading Films!': Film Studies, Close Analysis, and Gay Pornography." *Cinema Journal* 36, 4 (Summer 1997): 76–97.

Clover, Carol J. 1992. *Men, Women and Chain Saws: Gender in the Modern Horror Film*. Princeton: Princeton University Press.

Conway, Mary T. 1997. "Spectatorship in Lesbian Porn: The Woman's Woman's Film." *Wide Angle* 19:3 (July): 91–113.

Crary, Jonathan. 1992. *Techniques of the Observer*. Cambridge, Mass: MIT Press.

Curry, Ramona. 1996. "Stepping across Broadway." *Jump Cut* 40: 114–118. de Grazia, Edward. 1992. *Girls Lean Back Everywhere: The Law of Obscenity and the Assault on Genius*. New York: Random House.

Dennis, Kelly. 1995. "Playing with Herself: Feminine Sexuality and Aesthetic Indifference." In *Solitary Pleasure: The Historical, Lilterary, and Artistic Discourses of Autoeroticism*. Paula Bennett and Vernon A. Rosario II, eds. New York: Routledge.

———. 1991. "Leave it to Beaver: The Object of Pornography." *Strategies: A Journal of Theory, Culture and Politics*. 6: 122–167.

Dollimore, Jonathan. 1990. "The Cultural Politics of Perversion: Augustine, Shakespeare, Freud, Foucault." *Genders* 8: 1–16.

Downs, Donald Alexander. 1989. *The New Politics of Pornography*. Chicago: University of Chicago Press.

Dworkin, Andrea. 1979. *Pornography: Men Possessing Women*. New York: Putnam.

Dyer, Richard. 1985. "Gay Male Porn: Coming to Terms." *Jump Cut: A Review of Contemporary Media* 30: 27–29.

Eberwein, Robert. 1977. "'One Finger on the Pause Button': Sex Instruction Videos." *Jump Cut* 41: 36–41.

Faludi, Susan. 1995. "The Money Shot." *The New Yorker* (Oct. 30):64–87.

Foucault, Michel. 1978. *The History of Sexuality, Vol. 1: An Introduction*. Translated by Robert Hurley. New York: Pantheon Books. (Translation of *La Volonte de savoir*, 1976.)

Freedberg, David. 1989. *The Power of Images: Studies in the History and Theory of Response*. Chicago: The University of Chicago Press.

Fung, Richard. 1991. "Looking for My Penis: The Eroticized Asian in Gay Video Porn." In *How Do I Look? Queer Film and Video*. Bad Object-choices, ed. Seattle: Bay Press.

Gunning, Tom. 1997. "The Aesthetics of Astonishment." In *Viewing Positions: Ways of Seeing Films*. Linda Williams, ed. New Brunswick: Rutgers University Press.

Jackson, Jr., Earl. 1995. *Strategies of Deviance: Studies in Gay Male Representation*. Bloomington: Indiana University Press.

Jameson, Fredric. 1990. *Signatures of the Visible*. New York: Routledge.

———. "Postmodernism, or The Cultural Logic of Late Capitalism." 1984. *New Left Review* 147 (July/Aug): 53–92.

Johnson, Eithne, and Eric Schaefer. 1993. "Soft Core/Hard Gore: *Snuff* as a Crisis in Meaning." *Journal of Film and Video* 45:2–3 (Summer-Fall): 40–59.

Johnson, Eithne. 1993. "Excess and Ecstasy: Constructing Female Pleasure in Porn Movies." *The Velvet Light Trap*. No. 32 (Fall) 30–46.

Juffer, Jane. 1998. *At Home with Pornography: Women, Sex, and Everyday Life*. New York: New York University Press.

Kendrick, Walter. 1987. *The Secret Museum: Pornography in Modern Culture*. Berkeley: University of California Press, 1997 (1987).

Kiessling, Christine. 1993. "Sex in the Subjunctive: Virtual Reality and Sex Toys." *Threshholds: Viewing Culture* Vol. 7. Spring. 40–46.

Kimmel, Michael, ed. 1990. *Men Confront Pornography*. New York: Crown.

Kipnis, Laura. 1996. *Bound and Gagged: Pornography and the Politics of Fantasy in America*. New York: Grove Press.

Kleinhans, Chuck. 1996. "Teaching Sexual Images: Some Pragmatics." *Jump Cut* 40: 119–122.

Lehman, Peter. "Revelations about Pornography." *Film Criticism* (1995), 3–16.

MacKinnon, Catherine. 1993. "Turning Rape into Pornography." *Ms.* (July–Aug):24–30.

———. 1993. *Only Words*. Cambridge: Harvard University Press.

Marks, Laura. 1996. "Straight Women, Gay Porn, and the Scene of Erotic Looking." *Jump Cut* 40: 127–136.

Mercer, Kobena. 1987. "Imaging the Back Man's Sex." In *Photography/Politics: Two*. Pat Holland, Jo Spence, and Simon Watney, eds. London: Comedia/Methuen. 61–69.

———. 1991. "Skin Head Sex Thing: Racial Difference and the Homoerotic Imaginary." In *How Do I Look? Queer Film and Video*. Bad Object-choices, ed. Seattle: Bay Press. 169–222.

Merk, Mandy. 1993. *Perversions: Deviant Readings*. New York: Routledge.

Munk, Erika. 1994. "What's Wrong with this Picture?" *Women's Review of Books*. (July–August): 5–6.

Nagle, Jill, ed. 1997. *Whores and Other Feminists*. New York: Routledge.

Nead, Lynda. 1992. *The Female Nude: Art, Obscenity and Sexuality*. London and New York: Routledge.

———.' 1993. "'Above the Pulp-line': The Cultural Significance of Erotic Art." In *Dirty Looks: Women, Pornography, Power*. Pamela Church Gibson and Roma Gibson, eds. London: British Film Institute.

Palac, Lisa. 1994. "How Dirty Pictures Changed My Life." *Playboy* 41.5 (May): 80–82, 145–146.

Pally, Marcia. 1994. *Sex and Sensibility: Reflections on Forbidden Mirrors and the Will to Censor*. New York: Ecco.

Patton, Cindy. 1988. "The Cum Shot: Three Takes on Lesbian and Gay Sexuality." *Out/look* (Fall) 72–77.

Pendleton, David. 1991. "Obscene Allegories: Narrative, Representation, Pornography." *Discourse* 15.1 (Fall 1992)154–168.

Penley, Constance. 1992. "Feminism, Psychoanalysis, and the Study of Popular Culture." In *Cultural Studies*. Lawrence Grossberg, Cary Nelson and Paula Treichler, eds. New York: Routledge.

———. 1996. "From NASA to the 700 Club (with a Detour through Hollywood): Cultural Studies in the Public Sphere." In Cary Nelson and Dilip Parameshwar Gaonkar, eds. *Disciplinarity and Dissent in Cultural Studies*. New York: Routledge. 235–250.

———. 1997. "Crackers and Whackers: The White Trashing of Porn." In *White Trash: Race and Class in America*. Matt Wray and Annalee Newitz, eds. New York: Routledge, 89–112.

Pryor, Sally and Jill Scott. 1993. "Virtual Reality: Beyond Cartesian Space." In *Future Visions: New Technologies of the Screen*. Phillip Hayward and Tana Wollen, eds. London: British Film Institute.

Reich, June. 1992. "Genderfuck: The Law of the Dildo." *Discourse* 15.1 (Fall):112–127.

Rheingold, Howard. 1990. "Reach out and Touch Someone." *Mondo 200*. no. 2. Berkeley, CA: Fun City Megamedia. 52–54.

Schlosser, Eric. 1997. "The Business of Pornography." *U.S. News and World Report*. (Feb. 10): 43–52.

Silverman, Kaja. 1992. *Male Subjectivity at the Margins*. New York: Routledge.

———. 1996. *The Threshold of the Visible World*. New York: Routledge.

Sobchack, Vivian. Forthcoming. *Carnal Thoughts: Bodies, Texts, Scenes and Screens*. Berkeley: University of California Press.

———. 1990. "Toward a Phenomenology of Cinematic and Electronic Presence: The Scene of the Screen." *Post Script*. Vol. 10, n. 1 (Fall): 50–59.

Slade, Joseph W. 1993. "Bernard Natan: France's Legendary Pornographer." *Journal of Film and Video* 45:2–3 (Summer–Fall): 72–90.

———. 1997. "Pornography in the Late Nineties." *Wide Angle* 19:3 (July) 1–12.

———. 1997. "Flesh Need Not be Mute: The Pornographic Videos of John Leslie." *Wide Angle* 19:3 (July): 114–148.

Smith, Todd, D. 1994. "Gay Male Pornography and the East: Re-Orienting the Orient." *History of Photography* 18 (Spring): 13–21.

Springer, Claudia. 1991. "The Pleasure of the Interface." *Screen* 32:3. 303–323.

Smith, Cherry. 1990. "The Pleasure Threshold: Looking at Lesbian Pornography on Film." *Feminist Review*. No. 34. 152–159.

Straayer, Chris. 1996. *Deviant Eyes, Deviant Bodies: Sexual Re-orientation in Film and Video*. New York: Columbia University Press.

Strossen, Nadine. 1995. *Defending Pornography: Free Speech, Sex, and the Fight for Women's Rights*. New York: Scribner.

Tisdale, Sallie. 1995. *Talk Dirty to Me*. New York: Doubleday.

Tucker, Scott. 1990. "Gender, Fucking, and Utopia." *Social Text 27* (Vol. 9, no. 2):3–34.

Ullman, Sharon. 1997. *Sex Seen: The Emergence of Modern Sexuality in America*. Berkeley: University of California Press.

Vance, Carol. 1990. "Misunderstanding Obscenity." *Art in America*. (February):49–55.

Waugh, Tom. 1996. *Hard to Imagine: Gay Male Eroticism in Photography and Film from their Beginnings to Stonewall*. New York: Columbia University Press.

———. 1992. "Homoerotic Representation in the Stag Film, 1920–1940: Imagining an Audience." *Wide Angle* 14,2 (April):5–19.

———. 1985. "Men's Pornography: Gay vs. Straight." *Jump Cut*. N. 30 (Spring): 30–36.

Williams, Linda. 1998. "Melodrama Revised." In *Refiguring American Film Genres*. Nick Browne, ed. Berkeley: University of California Press. 42–88.

———, ed. 1997. *Viewing Positions: Ways of Seeing Film*. New Brunswick: Rutgers University Press.

———. 1995. "Corporealized Observers: Visual Pornographies and the 'Carnal Density of Vision.'" In *Fugitive Images: From Photography to Video*. Patrice Petro, ed. Bloomington, Indiana: Indiana University Press.

———. 1993. "Second Thoughts on Hard Core: American Obscenity Law and the Scapegoating of Deviance." In *Dirty Looks: Women, Pornography, Power*. Pamela Church Gibson, Roma Gibson, eds. London: British Film Institute.

———. "Pornographies on/scene, or 'diff'rent strokes for diff'rent folks'." 1992. In *Sex Exposed: Sexuality and the Pornography Debate*. Lynne Segal and Mary McIntosh, eds. London: Virago.

———. "Film Bodies: Gender, Genre and Excess." 1991. *Film Quarterly* 44 No.4 (Summer):2–13.

———. 1989. *Hard Core: Power, Pleasure and the "Frenzy of the Visible."* Berkeley: University of California Press.

Index

Compositor: Wilsted & Taylor
        Text: 11/13 Caledonia
     Display: Caledonia